1 MONTH OF
FREE
READING

at

www.ForgottenBooks.com

By purchasing this book you are eligible for one month membership to ForgottenBooks.com, giving you unlimited access to our entire collection of over 1,000,000 titles via our web site and mobile apps.

To claim your free month visit: www.forgottenbooks.com/free193259

ISBN 978-0-428-50338-3
PIBN 10193259

THE QUARTERLY

OF THE

TEXAS STATE HISTORICAL

ASSOCIATION

VOLUME XIII

JULY, 1909, TO APRIL, 1910

AUSTIN, TEXAS
PUBLISHED BY THE ASSOCIATION
1910

The Texas State Historical Association.

Organized March 2, 1897.

———

PRESIDENT,

A. W. TERRELL.

VICE-PRESIDENTS:

BEAUREGARD BRYAN,   MILTON J. BLIEM,

R. L. BATTS,   LUTHER W. CLARK.

RECORDING SECRETARY AND LIBRARIAN,

GEORGE P. GARRISON.

CORRESPONDING SECRETARY AND TREASURER,

CHARLES W. RAMSDELL.

EXECUTIVE COUNCIL:

DORA FOWLER ARTHUR,   GEORGE P. GARRISON,

W. J. BATTLE,   DAVID F. HOUSTON,

R. L. BATTS,   S. H. MOORE,

MILTON J. BLIEM,   CHARLES W. RAMSDELL,

HERBERT E. BOLTON,   BRIDE NEILL TAYLOR,

S. P. BROOKS,   A. W. TERRELL,

BEAUREGARD BRYAN,   JOHN C. TOWNES,

LUTHER W. CLARK,   E. W. WINKLER,

Z. T. FULMORE,   DUDLEY G. WOOTEN.

CONTENTS

NUMBER 1; JULY, 1909.

THE NAVY OF THE REPUBLIC OF TEXAS, III............ .Alex. Dienst.... 1
JOURNAL OF J. C. CLOPPER, 1828...................... . ..   44
NOTES AND FRAGMENTS....... 81

NUMBER 2; OCTOBER, 1909.

THE NAVY OF THE REPUBLIC OF TEXAS....... ... ...Alex. Dienst.... 85
THE CLOPPER CORRESPONDENCE, 1834-1838.. 128
JAMES H. C. MILLER AND EDWARD GRITTEN . ..   .Eugene C. Barker ... 145
NOTES AND FRAGMENTS....... 153

NUMBER 3; JANUARY, 1910.

RECOGNITION OF THE REPUBLIC OF TEXAS BY THE UNITED STATES.... ......
....Ethel Zivley Rather.... 155

NUMBER 4; APRIL, 1910.

STEPHEN F. AUSTIN AND THE INDEPENDENCE OF TEXAS........ .. ..
.... Eugene C. Barker.... 257
REMINISCENCES OF THE TEXAS REVOLUTION.... . . ..Andrew A. Boyle.... 285
THE BEXAR AND DAWSON PRISONERS.... ... ...Edited by E. W. Winkler.... 292
NOTES AND FRAGMENTS.. 325
BOOK NOTES...:.......................... 328
AFFAIRS OF THE ASSOCIATION.............. 329

FELLOWS AND LIFE MEMBERS

OF THE

ASSOCIATION

The constitution of the Association provides that "Members who show, by published work, special aptitude for historical investigation may become Fellows. Thirteen Fellows shall be elected by the Association when first organized, and the body thus created may thereafter elect additional Fellows on the nomination of the Executive Council. The number of Fellows shall never exceed fifty."

The present list of Fellows is as follows:

BARKER, DR. EUGENE C.
BATTS, JUDGE R. L.
BOLTON, PROF. HERBERT EUGENE
CASIS, PROF. LILIA M.
CLARK, PROF. ROBERT CARLTON
COOPER, PRESIDENT O. H.
COX, DR. I. J.
ESTILL, PROF. H. F.
FULMORE, JUDGE Z. T.
GAINES, JUDGE R. R.
GARRISON, PROF. GEORGE P.
GRAY, MR. A. C.
HATCHER, MRS. MATTIE AUSTIN
HOUSTON, PRESIDENT D. F.
KLEBERG, JUDGE RUDOLPH, JR.

LOOSCAN, MRS. ADELE B.
MCCALEB, DR. W. F.
MILLER, DR. E. T.
PENNYBACKER, MRS. PERCY V.
RAMSDELL, MR. CHAS. W.
RATHER, DR. ETHEL ZIVLEY
SHEPARD, JUDGE SETH
SMITH, PROF. W. ROY
TERRELL, JUDGE A. W.
TOWNES, PROF. JOHN C.
WILLIAMS, JUDGE O. W.
WINKLER, MR. ERNEST WM.
WOOTEN, HON. DUDLEY G.
WORLEY, MR. J. L.

The constitution provides also that "Such benefactors of the Association as shall pay into its treasury at any one time the sum of thirty dollars, or shall present to the Association an equivalent in books, MSS., or other acceptable matter, shall be classed as Life Members."

The Life Members at present are.

AUTRY, MR. JAMES L.
AYER, MR. EDWARD EVERETT
BAKER, MR. R. H.
BRACKENRIDGE, HON. GEO. W.
BUNDY, MR. Z. T.
COCHRANE, MR. SAM P.
COURCHESNE, MR. A.
CRANE, MR. R. C.
DAVIDSON, MR. W. S.
DEALEY, MR. GEORGE B.
DILWORTH, MR. THOS. G.
DONALDSON, MRS. NANA
  SMITHWICK
GILBERT, MR. JOHN N.
HANRICK, MR. R. A.
KENEDY, MR. JNO. G.

KIRBY, MR. JNO. H.
MCFADDEN, MR. W. P. H.
MINOR, MR. F. D.
MOODY, MR. W. L.
MOREHEAD, MR. C. R.
NEALE, MR. WM. J.
RICE, HON. W. M.
SCHMIDT, MR. JOHN
SEVIER, MRS. CLARA D.
SUMPTER, MR. JESSE
WALKER, MR. J. A.
WASHER, MR. NAT M.
WEBB, MR. MACK
WILLACY, HON. JOHN G.
WILLIAMS, JUDGE O. W.

THE QUARTERLY

TEXAS STATE HISTORICAL ASSOCIATION

Vol. XIII.   JULY, 1909.   No. 1.

*The publication committee and the editors disclaim responsibility for views
expressed by contribitors to* THE QUARTERLY.

THE NAVY OF THE REPUBLIC OF TEXAS.

III.

THE SECOND NAVY OF TEXAS.

IX.   MEASURES TO PROCURE A SECOND NAVY.

The vessels of the first navy were lost through captures, wrecks, and other misfortunes. But Texas, possessing as she did such an extensive sea-board, could not expect to be regarded as a nation unless she had a navy strong enough to protect her coast and harbors. Emigrants would hesitate to risk their all in a voyage to a country not prepared to protect them if attacked *en route.* Trading vessels would be slow to bring those commodities to her shores which would be necessary for the comfort of the people. Exportation would likewise be dangerous. Shipowners would dread capture and loss of their vessels, with possible imprisonment in a Mexican dungeon. Excessive insurance would raise the price of all commodities to the point where the bare necessities of life would become luxuries. But, with proper protection, immigration would soon fill up the land; and the increased imports and exports, as the country became settled, would bring a revenue in the way of customs duties that would eventually pay for the maintenance of a navy. These considerations alone would justify the expenditure of a considerable sum by Texas; and when, in addition, it is remembered that Mexico had in no wise relinquished her intention of reconquering Texas, and would sooner or later attack her by land and by sea, the reader can understand why it was necessary for Texas to secure and maintain at any cost a navy strong enough to make Mexico fear and respect her, and to impress foreign nations with the stability of her government.

All this had been clearly perceived since the first session of the first congress of the Republic. On October 26, 1836, the Committee on Naval Affairs recommended "the immediate building or purchase" of one twenty-four gun sloop, a ten gun steam vessel, and two schooners of eleven guns each. The total cost of the four vessels was to be $135,000.[1] An act was passed in conformity with these resolutions, authorizing the President to appoint an agent to proceed immediately to the United States, to purchase, or contract for and superintend the building of, the desired vessels. It was approved by President Houston November 18, 1836. This increase in the navy was planned while Texas was still in possession of several war vessels; but long before any of the vessels of the new navy reached the Texan shores, the last of the old navy, excepting the *Potomac,* had disappeared. Owing to the youth of the Republic, and the uncertainty of her future, sufficient money could not be borrowed to carry out the act; and it therefore remained ineffective.

The second congress found it imperative to act. The *Independence* had been captured by the Mexicans, and the *Invincible* wrecked, leaving the *Brutus* and the *Potomac* sole defenders of six hundred miles of coast. William M. Shepherd, acting secretary of the navy, in his report of September 30, 1837,[2] begs earnestly for the expenditure of a few thousand dollars to prevent Mexico's gaining supremacy of the Gulf. Some two weeks later the *Brutus* was wrecked, and the Committee on Naval Affairs thereupon framed the following resolutions, and submitted them to the Senate for action:[3]

[1]*House Journal,* 1st Tex. Cong., 1st Sess., 97-98; Gammel, *Laws of Texas,* I, 1090; Gouge, *Fiscal History of Texas,* 54.
[2]*House Journal,* 2nd Tex. Cong., 1st and 2d Sessions, 166-172.
[3]Archives of the Department of State, file No. 764.

Resolved that the Senate and the house of representatives of the Republic of Texas in congress assembled proceed to Elect by joint ballot an agent whose duty it shall be to repair immediately to Baltimore or some other seaport town of the United States of the north for the purpose of buying or building arming and equipping for the public service of the Republic of Texas one corvette of 18.24 medium, 2-10 Gun Briggs mounting medium 18 pounders—and two substantial schooners . . . provided the cost of said vessels shall not exceed $250,000 which said amount is hereby appropriated out of any unappropriated money now in, or that hereafter may be in the treasury. . . .

The resolution was amended to authorize the purchase of a five hundred ton ship mounting eighteen guns, two three hundred ton brigs of twelve guns each, and three schooners of one hundred and thirty tons, mounting five or seven guns each; to appropriate two hundred and eighty thousand dollars for the purpose; to instruct the secretary of the treasury to furnish said agent with a draft for the above appropriated sum on Messrs. Gilmer and Burnley, the "commissioners to negotiate a five million loan";[1] and to pledge solemnly the public faith for the payment of this amount. It became a law with the President's approval on November 4, 1837.[2]

To carry out the provisions of this act, President Houston appointed Peter W. Grayson agent. Grayson had represented Texas as commissioner to the United States in 1836, when the country was seeking recognition, and his appointment for the present task was considered a wise one. At about this time, however, he became candidate for the presidency of Texas, and during the campaign committed suicide in a fit of despondency at Bean's Station, Tennessee. John A. Wharton was anxious to succeed him, but President Houston appointed Samuel M. Williams.[3] Williams at

---

[1]Gammel, *Laws of Texas*, IX, 1355-1356.

[2]*Ibid.*, I, 1355-1356; Gouge, *Fiscal History of Texas*, 70.

[3]Report of Secretary of Navy in *House Journal*, 3d Tex. Cong., 1st Sess., 15-20. The following amusing reason is given for the president's refusal to appoint John A. Wharton. He had previously appointed William H. Wharton minister to the United States to secure the recognition of Texan independence. It is related that Wharton was not pleased with the appointment, and remarked that the president was sending him into honorable exile to get him out of some one else's way. Houston did not hear of this until some months later, when John A. Wharton applied for the agency.

once executed his bond, and departed for Baltimore, to enter actively into the labors of procuring a navy for Texas.

In order to meet immediate needs, an effort was made to buy the steam ship Pulaski; and Congress authorized her purchase at an agreed price;[1] but the transaction failed through the refusal of the owners to deliver her at Galveston, on the ground that our ports were declared by the enemy to be under blockade, and that the blockade was reported to be effective. Before any agreement could be arrived at she was destroyed. The *Potomac,* therefore, was the only vessel that was in the service of Texas during 1838. And for a long time it remained doubtful whether or not the government would become the owner of this vessel. The secretary of the navy at a critical hour had bought it on his own responsibility from Captain L. M. Hitchcock for eight thousand dollars and had almost completed its conversion into a brig of war, when all further work on it was suspended because congress had made no provision for its purchase. This, however, was due to a want of funds, and not to a belief in congress that the vessel was not needed. The secretary of the navy in his report of October 30, 1838, put the matter before the president, and urged him to find some means for completing the transaction.[2] The *Potomac* seems to have been finally acquired by the government, though no record of the transfer can be found. The secretary of the navy two years later says:[3]

In consequence of the leaky condition of the brig Potomac, formerly the receiving ship, she has had everything removed from her; placed securely in the yard, and her crew transferred to the Wharton. It has since been discovered, and prevented as far as it was deemed necessary, to keep her from sinking. This vessel is new and has been for a long while, perfectly useless to the Gov-

Meeting William H. Wharton after his return from the United States, the president could not refrain from delivering a home thrust. "I did not appoint John A. Wharton naval commissioner," he said, "because I did not wish to drive any more of the Wharton family into exile."—Linn, *Reminiscences of Fifty Years in Texas,* 273.

[1]Gammel, *Laws of Texas,* I, 1392.

[2]*House Journal,* 3d Tex. Cong., 18; Yoakum, II, 242.

[3]Report of November 4, 1840, in *House Journal,* 5th Tex. Cong., 1st Sess., Appendix, 185-196.

ernment for any purpose whatever, and, as an application has been made by the Commander of the station to transfer her to the pilot of Galveston, with a view of making a light boat of her, upon such terms as he believes would be beneficial to the public interest, I advise this measure, believing it will not interfere with the best interests of the navy, and that it will be of great advantage to our growing commerce.

Not another word we can find concerning her, except in the Tennison Papers, in the original order of A. C. Hinton commanding the naval station at Galveston, and addressed to William A. Tennison, midshipman, on board the *Potomac* at Galveston, ordering him to report to Lieutenant William S. Williamson on board the brig of war *Brazos,* for duty.[1] This is the only time the brig of war *Brazos* is mentioned officially or otherwise. Where she came from, or what became of her, no existing documents relate. Under another name, she may have played some part in Texas history. That there was such a vessel in the navy in 1842, there is no question, as the document mentioning it is original and genuine.

For the sake of economy, the president ordered the secretary of the navy to disband the officers and men of the navy until vessels could be procured for them. Only enough were retained to man the *Potomac* and the naval station at Galveston.[2] This act, while a hardship on the officers and men, was proper under the circumstances, and proved quite a saving to the government; as it was some time before the men were needed.

Fate was very kind to Texas at this time, when she had no navy and was seemingly at the mercy of her enemy. The French government, having certain claims against Mexico, which Mexico declined to satisfy, assembled a considerable naval force at Vera Cruz and declared the Mexican ports blockaded. Shortly after the inauguration of the new president of Texas, M. B. Lamar, on December 9, 1838, Texas was gratified with the intelligence of the capture of Vera Cruz. The blockade of the French having failed to bring the government to terms, Admiral Baudin despatched a messenger to General Rincón, the Mexican commandant, informing him that he was about to attack the castle of San Juan

---

[1] Hinton to Tennison, an undated autograph letter signed.

[2] Report of Secretary of Navy, October 30, 1838, in *House Journal*, 3d Tex. Cong., 1st Sess., 15-16.

d'Ulloa. This fortress, situated on an island in the harbor of Vera Cruz, was defended by one hundred and sixty pieces of artillery and some five thousand men. The bombardment commenced about two o'clock, in the afternoon of the 27th of November, and was so well directed that in four hours, after a loss of six hundred men in killed and wounded, the Mexicans capitulated and marched out of the castle, and the French took possession. The Mexican government thereupon despatched Santa Anna with five thousand men to drive the French out of the place. In attempting this, he lost his leg, and many of his troops were killed and wounded. On March 9, 1839, a treaty was made between Mexico and France,. which was shortly afterwards ratified, and the French forces left the territory of the Republic.[1]

On his way home Admiral Baudin, with a part of the fleet, visited Texas. He was given a grand welcome to Galveston and to Texas. The mayor and aldermen of Galveston delivered the keys of the city to him, and Admiral Baudin, in a written response, declared that he was glad to have contributed by his work in Mexico to such a cause as the independence of the Texian nation. He said

. . . . I hope it will prove, too, beneficial to the several nations, who, either as friends or as foes, have to deal with Mexico. Nothing could be more gratifying to my feelings than to be considered as one of you, gentlemen, whose industry and energy I do so much admire. Be assured that I would vastly prefer being the humblest member of a well regulated and thriving community, like yours, than to moving in the sphere of wealth and power in a corrupt and decaying society. With the highest regard and respect, I have the honor to be, Gentlemen,

Your affectionate and devoted Serv't, CHARLES BAUDIN.[2]

To understand fully the gratitude of the people we must remember that, but for the opportune interference of the French, the whole coast of Texas would have been at the mercy of any fleet, however small, that Mexico might have sent against it. Can it be wondered at that Galveston and all Texas felt that France had helped to fight the battles of the Republic?

[1]Yoakum, II, 242, 253, 255.
[2]Baudin to Mayor and Aldermen of Galveston, May 13, 1839, in an unidentified newspaper clipping.

While Texas was thus enjoying a respite through the involuntary assistance of France, Mr. Williams, in Baltimore, was doing all in his power to obtain proper vessels for the navy. Owing to the fact that the loan was not effected with which to purchase the fleet, he was much discouraged. On October 9, 1838, he wrote from Philadelphia,[1] that the only prospect at that time was to buy the steam packet *Charleston,* which had been built eighteen months before at a cost of $117,000. She could be had for $120,000, payable in five years with ten per cent interest, and could be so altered as to make her an available naval ship. On November 3, 1848, General Hamilton, who was the regularly appointed consul for the Republic of Texas, in Charleston, addressed a lengthy communication to the secretary of the navy,[2] in regard to the purchase of this vessel. He said that while in England he had had the good fortune to induce his friend James Holford, Esq., of London, to advance the money necessary for her purchase and outfit; but Hamilton said:

As Mr. Holford is not a citizen, the title had to be taken for the boat in my name, and so it will continue until she gets out to Texas, and a regular transfer is made of her to your Government. . . . As Mr. Holford has acted with the utmost liberality and confidence, I trust your Government will have passed, in *secret session* forthwith, a resolution confirming Messrs. Burnley and Williams' contract with me, as the agent of this gentleman.[3]

Agreeable to this request, an act was passed sanctioning the contract for the *Charleston,* afterwards known as the *Zavala,* for the price of $120,000.[4] This vessel was, therefore, the first one of the new navy. Its final cost, as later altered and equipped, was much beyond the original contract price. But in this, as in other matters, the financial records of the navy are so tangled and obscure as to render details impossible. It would be alike tedious and unprofitable to attempt to unravel them. Indeed, the secre-

[1] *House Journal*, 5th Tex. Cong., 1st Sess., Appendix, 212.
[2] *Ibid.*, 214-216.
[3] Hamilton to Secretary of Navy, November 3, 1838, in *House Journal*, 5th Tex. Cong., 1st Sess., Appendix, 214-216.
[4] Gouge, *Fiscal History of Texas*, 93.

tary of the navy, in 1840, confessed the task too heavy for himself.[1]

Soon after the *Zavala* had been arranged for, Mr. Williams was successful in concluding a contract, on November 13, 1838, with Frederick Dawson, of Baltimore, for one ship, two brigs, and three schooners to be fully armed, furnished with provisions and munitions, and delivered in the port of Galveston.[2]   For this it was agreed that,

> the bonds of the Government of Texas, made and executed by the Commissioners for the Loan, shall be executed and signed and deposited in the Bank of the United States of Pennsylvania, or the Girard Bank at Philadelphia, . . . for five hundred and sixty thousand dollars, there to remain . . . as security . . . for the space of twelve calendar months, which bonds are to bear . . . a rate of interest of ten per cent per annum, . . . which bonds can be redeemed at the end of twelve months, by the payment of the two hundred and eighty thousand dollars, and the ten per cent which shall have accrued . . . in Gold or Silver. . . . If the Government of Texas shall prefer to instruct the Loan Commissioners to issue, or shall itself issue sterling bonds for the sum of five hundred and twenty thousand dollars at any time prior to the first day of February next, he will receive them in full liquidation, and payment of the debt hereby contracted, and in lieu of the bonds heretofore mentioned.

On receiving the intelligence that the navy had been contracted for, the Texas government, on January 26, passed an act which declared that, whereas the agent of the Republic had made a contract for the purchase of one ship of eighteen guns, two brigs of twelve guns each, and three schooners of six guns each, and,

> whereas it has become indispensably necessary, in order to prepare and keep in service the said vessels, as well for the protection of

---

[1]Secretary of the Navy, Report of November 4, 1840, in *House Journal*, 5th Tex. Cong., 1st Sess., Appendix, 187; see also Gouge, *Fiscal History of Texas*, 93, 94, 198-199, 206, 305.

[2]For the contract with Dawson see *House Journal*, 5th Tex. Cong., 1st Sess., Appendix, 202-204.   See also Yoakum, II, 243; Gouge, *Fiscal History of Texas*, 94; and Report of Special Committee to the Senate, January 22, 1854.   Dawson turned his interest over to S. Chott and Whitney; these two gentlemen, in a lengthy letter addressed to the government of Texas, October 9, 1851, complained bitterly of the effort made to scale the bonds, and their arguments seem unanswerable.   See Gouge, *Fiscal History of Texas*, 198-199.

the coasts and harbors of Texas, as for the protection of the commerce thereof, that an appropriation be made of the sum required for that object. Wherefore, be it enacted, . . . That the sum of two hundred and fifty thousand dollars, in the promissory notes of the Government be, and the sum is hereby appropriated for the naval service for the year 1839. . . .[1]

The navy thus contracted for, including the *Zavala,* and the appropriation just mentioned, cost the Texan government more than $800,000.[2]

Mr. Williams, having now accomplished the task he had been entrusted with, returned to Texas. That his services were appreciated by his countrymen, we note in a resolution offered in congress[3] tendering him a resolution of thanks "for the energy which he has rendered in procuring a navy." It will be recalled that while he was connected with the firm of McKinney and Williams he had been largely instrumental in securing the first navy of Texas. His talent lay in his ability to finance such matters, and later in life we see him the first banker of Texas. He knew nothing of naval construction, and the republic now needed a man at Baltimore to see that the contract was carried out according to specifications. A man in every respect qualified for this important service was found in John G. Tod, who had resigned a commission in the United States navy to connect himself with the young republic.[4] Before entering upon this work, he had, at the request of

[1]Gammel, *Laws of Texas,* II, 129-130. Gouge, *Fiscal History of Texas,* 93, and Bancroft, II, 317, say that this appropriation of $250,000 was made to pay for the ships contracted for; they are of course, mistaken, as the language of the act is clear.

[2]Secretary of the navy, Report of November 8, 1839, cited in Yoakum, II, 272; Bancroft, II, 351.

[3]*Senate Journal,* 3d Tex. Cong., 1st Sess., 72. The resolution was dated December 14, 1838.

[4]John G. Tod was born in Kentucky. Leaving Lexington when seventeen years of age, he proceeded down the Mississippi on a flatboat to New Orleans, and enlisted in the Mexican Navy as a midshipman, under Admiral Mina. Two years later, through the influence of Henry Clay, he was appointed a midshipman in the United States navy, and transferred to that service in which he rose to more important grades.—C. W. Raines, *Year Book of Texas,* 1901, p. 402.

Mr. Tod entered the Texas navy in 1837, and, as the following letter (copied from a facsimile of the original) indicates, apparently had some difficulty in convincing the secretary of the navy of his merits:

the secretary of the navy, drawn up a report upon the establishment of a navy yard, and in April, 1838, had been vested with powers to examine into and report on all matters connected with the naval interests. On June 10, 1838, he was ordered to the United States by President Houston upon that mission. He fitted out the steamer *Charleston* and returned with her to Galveston, in March, 1839, where her name and flag were changed, and she was commissioned as the *Zavala*.[1] In accordance with the Dawson contract, on June 27, 1839, the schooner *San Jacinto* was delivered; on August 7, the schooner *San Antonio;* on August 31, the schooner *San Bernard;* and, on October 18, the brig *Colorado*.[2] A corvette and a brig were yet wanting to complete the contract, but they were confidently expected by the end of the year.[3] They

Houston, May 25, 1837.
Hon. W. G. Hill.

Sir,—I take the liberty of laying the enclosed letters before you as a further introduction to your friendly enfluence in my behalf.

They will show you how I stand in civil life with men of eminance in the United States—who are not likely to confer their friendship or esteem upon any man except for his individual worth as a gentleman; more especially, when the difference of *rank* betwen us as public men is taken into consideration.

The Hon. James Harlan is from Kentucky and has known me from my earliest years. Commodores Barron and Bolton are at the head of the Navy. Maj. Graham is a distinguished officer of the U. S. Army. The first clause of his letter will inform you how I stand with my acquaintances in the U. S. Navy.

I regret that the present state of affairs should make it necessary for me (to succeed in my object) to trouble you and other gentlemen upon a subject that the Hon. Secretary of the Navy alone appears to view in rather an indifferent light. If I obtain my commission, it will be my pride to do my duty in every situation that my country places me. My greatest honor to prove myself worthy of the interest shown by my friends. My glory in defending the rights and advancing the liberties of our common country.

Very respectfully,
I have the honor to be, Sir, your ob. Servt,
JNO. G. TOD

[1] As an instance of the carelessness of the historians of Texas it may be mentioned that Yoakum (II, 271), Morphis (419), and Brown (II, 128), each represents the *Charleston* and the *Zavala* as two separate vessels. That such an error should have been made by Yoakum, who used the documents, is strange; Morphis and Brown, no doubt, followed Yoakum's statement without consulting the sources.

[2] In 1840 the name of the *Colorado* was changed to the *Archer*.

[3] Secretary of the navy, Report of November 8, 1839; Yoakum, II, 271.

were in fact delivered, one in January, and the other in April, 1840. The following account appeared in a current newspaper:[1]

Texian Navy.—The following list of vessels constitute the present naval force of Texas. As there are a number of officers of that service who were officers of our navy, these details may be interesting to many of the readers of the *Chronicle.*

Steamer Zavalla—An efficient and well appointed vessel.

Sloop Trinity—600 tons, carries 20 24 pounders, medium guns.

Brigs ⎰ Colorado ⎱ 400 tons, carries each 16 18 pounder
⎱ Galveston ⎰ medium guns.

Schooners ⎰ San Jacinto ⎱ 170 tons, each carrying 7 12 pounders, and 1 long eighteen, on a pivot.
⎱ San Bernard ⎰
⎰ San Antone ⎱

Brig Potomac—Receiving vessel.

These vessels, with the exception of the steamer and receiving vessel, were built, equipped, and provisioned under the immediate superintendence of John G. Tod, Esq., Texan Naval Agent of the United States, a gentleman well and favorably known in this country, having at an early period in his life held an honorable place in our navy.

The secretary of the navy in his report[2] of 1840 said :

. . . Mr. Dawson has delivered the brig and the sloop-of-war then due; and everything else appertaining to this contract has been complied with in the most generous and liberal manner. The brig and sloop-of-war, like all the other vessels, have been constructed on a much more commodious scale than the contract required, and have been furnished in a more suitable manner than that for which the contractors were obligated. The brig, which was the last vessel received on the contract, was delivered at Galveston with the naval equipments belonging to her, and the other vessels, on the 25th April, 1840,[3]—the ship on the 5th January previous. . . .

This officer[4] is entitled to great credit for the management and system shown in his operations. His attention to the complicated duties entrusted to him in the United States, as well as his conduct in direct connection with this Department, has always been faithful and laborious, and meets my cordial approbation.

[1]An unidentified newspaper clipping, containing matter copied from an issue of the *Army and Navy Chronicle* of date not indicated.

[2]In *House Journal*, 5th Tex. Cong., 1st Sess., Appendix, 185-196.

[3]These two vessels were the *Austin* and the *Wharton*. The latter had formerly been the *Dolphin.*

[4]Captain John G. Tod.

Captain Tod wrote a very appreciative letter of thanks to Dawson,[1] which received a suitable reply.   Captain Tod said in part:

The last vessel included in the contract entered into by yourself on one part, and the Republic of Texas of the other part, having received from me the certificate approving of the same, I feel it a duty as well as a pleasure to express to you the satisfaction I have in testifying to the very creditable and liberal manner in which the contract has been fulfilled on your part.
I will not indulge in any useless expressions of my opinion of these vessels, they speak for themselves, and many persons of acknowledged judgment in naval architecture, have pronounced them equal to any that have ever sailed from this port, in beauty of model, strength and duribility of materials and finished specimens of workmanship. . . .

John G. Tod,
Naval Agent of Texas to the U. S.

On the return of Captain Tod to Galveston, June 3, 1840, he was invited to partake of a public dinner tendered him by the citizens of Galveston at the Tremont House.   The committee on invitation were M. B. Menard, P. J. Menard, James Love, Levi Jones, and Thomas F. McKinney.   From this he excused himself on the plea of pressing business, but thanked them for their appreciation of his services, declaring that,

The greatest happiness a public servant has in this life, is the satisfaction of feeling that he has been faithful and conscientious in the discharge of such duties as may have been entrusted to him. If this pleasure can be enhanced, it is by the assurance that his humble efforts in behalf of his country's interest meet the approbation of his fellow citizens.[2]

Captain Tod's last letter as naval agent, among other matters, highly compliments "H. H. Williams, our consul in Baltimore, to whom was entrusted the purchase of our supplies under my direction," and acknowledges at the same time his indebtedness to Commodores Barron and Warrington, of the United States navy, and to Francis Grice, naval constructor of the Norfolk dock-

[1] Tod to Dawson, March 19, 1840, in *House Journal*, 5th Tex. Cong., 1st Sess., Appendix, 199.
[2] Tod to Galveston Gentlemen, June 4, 1840, in Tennison's Journal.

yards, "for much useful information imparted to me by these gentlemen."[1]

On June 24, 1840, Captain Tod was placed in command of the naval station at Galveston.

X. EARLY TROUBLES OF THE NEW NAVY.

By the end of April, 1840, the make-up of the second navy was completed. It consisted of the *Potomac, Zavala, Austin, Wharton, Archer, San Bernard, San Jacinto,* and *San Antonio.* The *Zavala,* formerly the *Charleston,* was named for Lorenzo de Zavala; the *Austin,* for Stephen F. Austin; the *Wharton,* formerly the *Dolphin,* for the Wharton brothers,—William H. and John A.;—and the *Archer,* formerly the *Colorado,* for Dr. Branch T. Archer. Besides these vessels references are found to the *Trinity,*[2] the *Galveston,*[3] the *Houston,*[4] the *Merchant,*[5] the *Texas,*[6] the *Asp,*[7] and the *Brazos.* The first two were apparently a part of the Dawson contract, and doubtless became incorporated in the fleet under changed names; the *Houston* seems to have been a Yucatán auxiliary, temporarily acting with the Texans; and the *Merchant* was the private property of E. W. Moore. Of the other vessels mentioned nothing further is known.

This brings us to the *personnel* of the new navy, and we will now introduce the officers, renewing old acquaintances and forming new ones. The man that stands out pre-eminently for his individuality, as well as high position in the navy, is Commodore Edwin Ward Moore. Born in June, 1810, at Alexandria, Virginia, where he received his education, he entered the United States navy as a midshipman, at the age of fourteen, and remained in the

[1]*House Journal,* 5th Tex. Cong., 1st Sess., Appendix, 198.

[2]An unidentified newspaper clipping, with matter copied from an issue of the *Army and Navy Chronicle* of date not indicated.

[3]*Ibid.*

[4]Jones, *Republic of Texas,* 194.

[5]Moore, *To the People of Texas,* 86.

[6]Journal of Midshipman James L. Mabry in *Galveston News,* January 9, 16, 23, 1893. This Journal, together with the Ledger and Ration Book of the Texas Navy are the property of Mrs. R. W. Shaw, of Galveston, daughter of Captain James G. Hurd, formerly first lieutenant of the *Brutus,* and granddaughter of Captain Norman Hurd, purser in the Texas navy.

[7]*Ibid.*

service for nearly fifteen years.[1] In a letter written in 1904, George F. Fuller, one of his midshipmen in the Texas navy, speaks of him as about 5 feet 8 inches in height, of fair complexion, blue eyes, light brown hair, and stocky build. He was genial, pleasant, and universally liked; a thorough seaman and a splendid officer.[2] In 1839 the prospect of an adventurous and active career in the Texas navy caused him to resign his commission as lieutenant on the United States sloop *Boston*,[3] and offer his services to Texas. He was appointed post-captain and was generally addressed by the title of Commodore, both by the public and by the secretary of the navy in his official communications. He had command of the entire Texas navy from the beginning of his service. Strange, however, as it may seem, no commission was issued to him, or the officers under him, until three years after they had entered the Texan service. In a letter to the secretary of war and marine July 5, 1842, he complained of this in the following terms:

I beg leave also to call the attention of the Department to the fact that *not an officer in the Navy has a commission,* a circumstance unprecedented in the annals of history, that a Government should have for three years, their vessels of war on the high seas, visiting foreign ports, and capturing the enemy's vessels, without a commission even in the possession of the commander of the Navy.[4]

This letter seems to have had the effect that Commodore Moore desired, for two weeks later he received his commission, as did also the officers serving under him. These commissions were confirmed by the senate on July 20, 1842. Commodore Moore's commission entitled him, "Post Captain Commanding," and was antedated April 21, 1839, some time before his resignation from the United States navy.

The first difficulty encountered by the new navy was to obtain sufficient sailors and marines to man the ships.[5] For this purpose

[1]Till July 16, 1839. *Cong. Globe,* 33d Cong., 1st Sess., Appendix, 1084; Moore, *To the People of Texas,* 10.

[2]Fuller to Dienst, October 27, 1904, in Dienst Col. Docs.

[3]Thrall, 592.

[4]Moore to Hockley, in Moore's *To the People of Texas,* 79.

[5]In regard to the proceedings of the United States government against Moore himself on the charge of illegal recruiting activity in New York Harbor in the winter of 1839-40, see Deposition of Hunter. December 30, 1839; Forsyth to Dunlap, January 15, 1840; Dunlap to Forsyth, January 16, 1840—all in Annual Report American Historical Association for 1907, Volume II.—EDITOR QUARTERLY.

the *San Antonio* was, in November, 1839, at New Orleans, on recruiting service.[1]   At the same time the secretary of the navy ordered the *Zavala* to New Orleans for refitting.   Captain A. C. Hinton of the *Zavala* was instructed not to allow his expenditure to exceed $9000, including $3200 for the enlistment of sailors and marines.[2]   He went, however, considerably beyond the modest limit set by the department, incurred a severe reprimand therefor from the secretary, and was ordered to return to Galveston.   The reproof administered to him was in part as follows:

You appear to have forgotten the very first principle of naval discipline, to wit: that *the first duty of an officer, as well as a seaman, consists in obeying orders.*   If you have so far transcended yours, as to purchase *anything* for which you can not show definite orders, be assured that you will be held responsible; and you furthermore are strictly forbidden from incurring, under any pretext whatever, any liabilities against the Government for repairs. . . . You will . . . return as soon as possible to Galveston, and report immediately to this Department.[3]

In reporting the matter to President Lamar the secretary used a different tone.   He said that, though Hinton had exceeeded his allowance by nearly twelve thousand dollars, yet

on the return of the Zavala to Galveston, her natural efficiency was found to be very much increased, and I have no hesitation in saying, that the unauthorized repairs were essentially needed, and they would have been suggested by the proper authority, except for the consciousness of inability to pay for them.[4]

The President considered the breach of discipline as serious enough to warrant the withdrawal of Hinton's commission.   Hinton appealed to congress, and a joint resolution was passed,[5] ordering the secretary of the navy to organize a court-martial for the trial of Hinton, and declaring that in future no officer should be deprived of his commission except by sentence of such a court.

[1]Moore to Hinton, *House Journal*, 5th Tex. Cong., 1st Sess., Appendix, 223-224.

[2]*House Journal*, 5th Tex. Cong., 1st Sess., Appendix, 221-222.

[3]Cooke to Hinton, December 21, 1839, in *House Journal*, 5th Tex. Cong., 1st Sess., Appendix, 238-239.

[4]Secretary of the navy, Report of November 4, 1840, *House Journal*, 5th Tex. Cong., 1st Sess., Appendix, 185-196.

[5]Gammel, *Laws of Texas*, II, 609.

The verdict of the court-martial was favorable to Hinton, and congress passed another joint resolution acquitting him "of any act of misconduct reflecting upon him as an officer or gentleman whilst a commander in the Navy of this Republic."[1]

The *Zavala,* on her return to Galveston, had brought a considerable number of men to complete the equipment of the other vessels. For a while it seemed as if this act, and all the cost of provisioning and officering the new navy were to be in vain. The lawmakers of Texas, in the mood of retrenching and economizing, were about to sacrifice an outlay of one million dollars, in order to save a few thousands. Without warning, or ascribing any cause for its action, congress passed a law which was approved on February 5, 1840, requiring the president to retire from the service temporarily all the fleet except such schooners as were needed for revenue purposes, and to retain only a sufficient number of officers and men to carry out the provisions of the act. Section 4, however, provided that, "should Mexico make any hostile demonstrations upon the Gulf, the President may order any number of vessels into active service, that he may deem necessary for the public security."[2]

That the President was not in sympathy with this act can be clearly seen in reading his message of November, 1840. He probably acquiesced in it with the intention of availing himself of the discretionary power conferred by Section 4. At any rate, he did not execute the act, and concerning his reasons for not doing so, spoke as follows:[3]

The act of the last session of congress providing for the laying up in ordinary the principal portion of the naval forces of the country, has not been carried into effect. Before the necessary preparations could be made for doing so, circumstances transpired, which in the opinion of the executive, involved potentially the contingency contemplated in the fourth section of that act, and induced him to defer the withdrawal of our gallant flag from the gulf. It was confidently asserted in the papers of the United States, and as confidently believed here, that the Mexican govern-

---

[1]The resolution was approved January 29, 1842. It does not appear in Gammel's *Laws,* but the enrolled copy of the original may be found in the Records of the State Department (Texas).

[2]Gammel, *Laws of Texas,* II, 364.

[3]See *House Journal,* 5th Tex. Cong., 1st Sess., 20-22.

ment had made a contract in Europe for the purchase of several vessels of war, and that she had actually procured an armed steam ship from a commercial house in England, with a view of making a descent upon the coast of Texas, and of cutting off our commerce with foreign nations; and during the prevalence of that opinion, the executive would have been violating the evident intention and spirit of the act of congress, instead of carrying it into effect, had he caused the seamen already in the service to be disbanded, and the vessels to be laid up in ordinary. Other events, also, occurred about the same time, and conspired with these considerations to dissuade me from dismantling a navy which had been equipped at a great expense, and which was manned and officered in a style of gallantry and efficiency inferior to none other of similar magnitude. Yucatan and Tabasco, lately forming a part of the confederate states of Mexico, wearied of the oppressions that followed the overthrow of the federal system in that republic, seceded from the central government, and uniting together pronounced their determination to be free. Similarity of circumstances and design naturally creates a sympathy of feeling, and would prompt this government to regard with peculiar interest the efforts of the citizens of the southern provinces to do precisely what we had so recently accomplished. But considerations of a higher character suggested the propriety of making a demonstration of our naval power on the coast of the new republic. It was expected to ascertain from the authorities established there in what relation this government should regard them, and whether their secession from Mexico would terminate their belligerent condition towards Texas. . . . It was considered advisable to communicate to the authorities our friendly dispositions, and to convey them with such a palpable exhibition of our power as would render them efficacious and permanent; and I am gratified to remark that these professions were readily and kindly received, and cordially reciprocated by the new government.

Under these various circumstances, I have considered it my duty to keep the Navy at sea for a short period. But I was constrained by a sense of justice and regard to the sacred faith of the country to abstain from making captures of Mexican property, while our accredited agents were engaged in Mexico in a negotiation for peace with that Government. The naval equipments of a country, and especially of this country, are essentially different to the facility of organization from the military power. Competent officers and soldiers to constitute an army, may at any time be selected from the body of the population, but seamen and efficient naval officers are not to be found among a rural people, they belong to the element on which they serve, and are nurtured only on the ocean waves. To have disbanded the accomplished and gallant officers who have embarked in our naval service, at the moment when we had reason to believe our enemy was preparing a naval armament for our coast, would, in the opinion of the executive, have not only been indiscreet and impolitic, but would, as he believes, have been contrary to the true intention and meaning of congress, as expressed in the act of the last session. It is true it might have saved us some expenditure, but it is equally true, that it might have involved the country in great disaster, and an irreparable loss of reputation.

The information afforded by this message is sufficient warrant for its lengthy quotation. We see that the navy was not laid up in ordinary,[1] and that the officers and men were not disbanded. On the contrary, soon after the new fleet was ready for service it was permitted to have a trial.

XI.   CRUISE OF THE TEXAN FLEET, 1840-1841.

In June the Texas fleet sailed for Mexico. For this movement quite a number of different causes have been alleged. According to President Lamar, the object of the expedition was to impress Yucatán with the strength of Texas, and thus establish diplomatic relations with this revolting state.   According to Commodore Moore, it was the proclamation of the Mexican president, declaring Texan ports in a state of blockade.   And, according to the secretary of the navy, it was because of a threatened invasion of Texas by Mexico, and the termination of the diplomatic mission of the agent of Texas, Mr. Treat.   While it is peculiar to see these officials disagreeing as to the chief motive for such an expedition, it is most likely that all the causes they mention contributed to the movement   For some seven months the naval establishment had been getting ready for such an expedition; and, while the act of congress had paralyzed the movement for a short time, it was only momentarily checked.   With the consent and encouragement of President Lamar, the outfitting continued.   The most formid-

---

[1] Eugene C. Barker, in *University of Texas Record*, V, 155, says: "Six months after Lamar assumed the reins of government the delivery of these naval vessels began, but the financial straits of the young republic made it necessary to place them temporarily in ordinary. For this needful act of economy he was blamed." That the vessels were not placed in ordinary this message shows; although, of course, the act approved by Lamar implied that it would be done.

able fleet Texas ever possessed left Galveston harbor on June 24, 1840, with Commodore E. W. Moore in command.

The fleet consisted of the *Austin,* carrying twenty guns, the flag-ship of Commodore Moore; the steamship *Zavala,* carrying eight guns; and the schooners, *San Bernard, San Jacinto,* and *San Antonio,* each carrying five guns.[1] The Brig *Wharton* commanded by George Wheelwright, the *Archer* commanded by J. Clark, and the *Potomac* were left at Galveston. This was done, partly for the reason that they were not in condition to sail with the squadron, and partly because they were needed to protect Galveston in case Mexican vessels threatened the city or the coast.[2]

---

[1]The lists of officers of the various ships follow: the *Austin,* E. P. Kennedy, first lieutenant; D. H. Crisp, second lieutenant; J. H. Baker, third lieutenant; William Seegar, fourth lieutenant; C. Cummings, acting master; J. B. Gardiner, surgeon; Norman Hurd, purser; T. W. Sweet, lieutenant of marines; C. A. Christman, C. Leay, C. B. Snow, George F. Fuller, M. H. Dearborne, L. E. Bennett, J. C. Bronough, E. A. Wezman, W. W. McFarlane, R. H. Clements, midshipmen; John W. Brown, boatswain; John Salter, gunner; William Smith, carpenter; C. Cremer, sailmaker: the *Zavala,* J. T. K. Lothrop, captain; George Henderson, first lieutenant; W. C. Brashear, second lieutenant; Daniel Lloyd, master; T. P. Anderson, surgeon; W. T. Maury, purser; J. W. C. Parker, captain of marines; G. Beatty, chief engineer; R. Bache, captain's clerk; C. Betts, C. C. Cox, J. E. Barrow, H. (S). Garlick, J. A. Hartman, midshipmen; James Crout, boatswain; T. Howard, gunner; Joseph Auld, carpenter: the *San Bernard,* W. S. Williamson, lieutenant commanding; George W. Estes, first lieutenant; W. A. Tennison, second lieutenant (Ben C. Stuart, in *Galveston News,* October 8, 1899, has G. C. Bunner, second lieutenant, and W. A. Tennison, as acting master); Charles B. Snow, R. M. Clarke, surgeons; J. F. Stephens, purser; W. H. Brewster, captain's clerk; C. B. Underhill, John P. Stoneall, J. B. F. Bernard, L. H. Smith, midshipmen; George Brown, boatswain: the *San Jacinto,* W. R. Postell, lieutenant commanding; J. O. Shaughnessey, first lieutenant; A. G. Gray, second lieutenant; William Oliver, acting master; Fletcher Dorey, surgeon; Robert Oliver, purser; J. J. Tucker, captain's clerk; C. S. Arcamble, A. Walker, J. O. Parker, midshipmen: the *San Antonio,* Alex Moore, lieutenant commanding; Thomas Wood, Junior, first lieutenant; A. J. Lewis, second lieutenant; A. A. Waite, acting master; James W. Moore, purser; Hugh A. Goldborough, captain's clerk; James H. Wheeler, E. F. Wells, L. M. Minor, midshipmen; Hugh Schofield, boatswain.

The muster rolls here given are from the Tennison Papers (folio 352, pp. 1-3). They are the only complete rolls I have been able to secure. Yet Tennison's rolls cannot be depended upon as absolutely accurate. For other lists see Ben C. Stuart in *Galveston News,* October 8, 1899.

Alex Moore and James W. Moore, mentioned above, were a cousin and a brother of Commodore E. W. Moore. See Moore, *To the People of Texas,* 70-72, 110.

[2]The ships and officers mentioned in Brown's *History of Texas,* II, 198, footnote (copied in full without credit being given from *Texas Almanac,* 1860, pp. 165-166), have nothing whatever to do with this squadron, though, to the general reader, it would appear from the language used that they

The itinerary and incidents of this cruise can be most briefly and clearly given by citing extracts of the report of Commodore E. W. Moore to the secretary of the navy:[1]

TEXAS SLOOP-OF-WAR AUSTIN,

At Sea, August 28th, 1840.

Latitude 25° 21′ N.: Longitude 96° 29′ W.

Sir: . . . 22d July . . . I order[ed] the Zavala to make the best of her way to the Arcos[2] Islands, touching at Sisal, under English colors, and to leave a letter for Gen. Anaya from Gen. Canales.[3] On the 26th July, the weather still very light, in cousequence of which, and my unexpected detention off the S. W. Pass, I thought it best to send a vessel off Point Mariandrea with the letters No. 1 and 2 for Richard Packenham, Esq.,[4] her Britannic Majesty's Minister to Mexico; and that I might, in conformity of my orders of 20th June, endeavor to ascertain the feelings of the authorities of the State of Yucatan towards our Government,[5] and be off the Brazos de Santiago as near the time mentioned in the same orders as possible, I sent the schooner San Jacinto with the letters, and availing myself of the usual trade winds, proceeded with the San Bernard in company to Sisal, off which place I arrived on the 31st July, and, on making signal for a boat, wearing American colors, was boarded by an officer, and learned that the Zavala had passed six days before; he informed me that an order had been received that day from Merida (the Capitol,) by the captain of the Port, who had sent him out, that, if any Texian vessel appeared off the port, to offer her every facility,—upon which I hoisted our proper colors. . . . as soon as he left, filled away for Campeachy, where I was informed Gen. Anaya was. Arrived off Campeachy on the 2d August, and, while standing in under our own colors, we were met about eight miles from

---

belonged to the Texas navy in 1840. Thrall, 306, note, says that the *Dolphin (Wharton)* sailed. There is, however, abundant evidence to the contrary.

[1]Moore to Cooke, *House Journal*, 5th Tex. Cong., 1st Sess., Appendix, 232-237. Moore's orders dated June 20, 1840, were sealed, and were to be opened at sea. On or about this date, the schooners *San Jacinto, San Antonio,* and *San Bernard,* sailed "for the west." The *Zavala* and the *Austin* were to have gone to sea on the 23d, but were detained by unfavorable weather. They sailed on June 27, 1840. See *Telegraph and Texas Register*, July 1, 1840.

[2]Arcas.

[3]Anaya and Canales were both leaders of the Mexican Federalists.

[4]Pakenham assisted Treat in presenting his proposition, and acted as mediator.—Bancroft, *History of Texas*, II, 340.

[5]This goes to show that president Lamar was correct in his statement of the object of the expedition.

the land by a schooner of war, having on board Gen. Anaya and suite, who came on board.

On being informed by the General that he had not received the letter sent by the Zavala, and being no longer in doubt as to the disposition of the authorities, from their trusting a vessel of war, mounting *five* guns, along-side of this vessel and the San Bernard, and, knowing that the letter was of importance, as it had been written by Gen. Canales, after frequent interviews with his Excellency the President, I sent the San Bernard back to Sisal, with Gen. Anaya's secretary on board for it, and anchored. Gen. Anaya remained on board until after dark, and showed me letters from Galveston written sixteen or eighteen days before I left there . . . the next day . . . I had an interview with the Governor elect, Don Santiago Mendez. . . . He was anxious that the most friendly relations should be established at an early period, and assured me that the ports of the State of Yucatan were open to any Texian vessel. . . .

I left orders for the San Bernard to remain at Campeachy on her return from Sisal, until the 13th inst. . . .

On the 6th instant I received a letter from Gen. Anaya, . . . and the next day sailed for Point Mariandrea. On arriving off the Arcos[1] Islands on the 10th, I found the Zavala, . . .

I . . . the next day . . . sailed for Campeachy . . . where I arrived and anchored on the 13th inst., . . .

The naval force of the State of Yucatan consists of *one* small brig and *two* schooners. . . .

On the 14th the San Bernard arrived from Sisal, and the next morning we got under way; and the following morning, by 7 o'clock, were off the Arcos Islands; sent the San Barnard in to put Lieut. A. J. Lewis on board the Zavala, he having broken his leg some days previous by falling from the trunk of the schooner while giving an order and looking aloft, . . . and pushed on to meet the San Jacinto.

Arrived off point Mariandrea on the 18th; on the 19th, fell in with the San Bernard, and on the 20th, with the San Jacinto, when I was informed by Lieut. Postell that he had arrived off the point on the 1st inst. . . . I have since met with . . . Her Britannic Majesty's brig Penguin, on her way from Vera Cruz to Tampico, and I was informed by her that it had been reported at Vera Cruz that there was a pirate off that part of the coast, and the brig was looking out for her. The officer appeared much pleased with the bold manner in which Lieut. Postell stood down for him, and I take this occasion to state to the Department that

[1]Arcas.

he is *much* the most efficient officer I have under my command.

. . .

On the 23d, not having fallen in with either the San Antonio or brig Wharton[1] which vessels I had ordered to meet me off Point Mariandrea, . . . I determined to stand down off Vera Cruz, under American colors, and board the first vessel that came out, in hopes of hearing whether Mr. Treat had left Mexico or not, and at the same time have a look at their shipping. That afternoon I was within three miles of the castle of Juan de Ulloa; stood off all night, and the next day, in the afternoon, an English brig came out; the wind being light, did not get near her until the next morning, when she sent her boat alongside with a letter from Mr. Treat, enclosing *one* to his Excellency the President, and *two* to the Hon. A. S. Lipscomb, Secretary of State.

The brig was Her Majesty's brig Penguin, and I learned from the officer who came on board from her, that the Centralists had no vessel of war at Vera Cruz; that the sloop-of-war *Iguala* was expected soon from France, that they were about purchasing a French ship there, lying in the harbor, and that the steamer Agyle was in the employment of the Mexican Government. . . .

. . . I thought it best to leave the San Bernard . . . under the orders of which the enclosed is a copy; and in order that the letters which I had in my possession from the City of Mexico might reach their destination as early as possible, I made sail immediately, the San Jacinto in Company, for Galveston; and by the time we get in the latitude of the Brazos de Santiago, I will have finished my letters, when I will send the schooner on with them, and proceed myself to the Brazos, off which place I will not remain more than four days, (unless I meet additional orders from the Department,) when I will return with all dispatch off Point Mariandrea.

My not having fallen in with the San Antonio or brig Wharton has placed me in a disagreeable situation, as, from the force of circumstances, I can only appear off the Brazos with this vessel, when I am required by my orders, to appear off that place with the whole squadron; besides I am behind the time named, in consequence of waiting off Point Mariandrea, in the hope of meeting the San Antonio, at all events, as there was a probability of the Wharton not getting to sea.

. . . C. S. Nash, ordinary seaman, died on board this vessel on the 4th inst, while at Campeachy; his disease was dropsy, and

---

[1]The *Wharton*, by order of the secretary of the navy, was partly dismantled and placed in ordinary. This is the reason she did not at this time reach the squadron. See Secretary of the Navy, Report of November 4, 1840, in *House Journal*, 5th Tex. Cong., Appendix, 185-196.

he was transferred from the San Bernard on the 28th June, in order that he might be more comfortable. The San Jacinto also lost one man, who had been sick some time and was very old.

The Zavala has fully realized my expectations as a sea steamer. She left New-Orleans not quite *two-thirds* filled with coal, having about 1700 barrels on board; and she can carry 2700 barrels. The coal was of the most inferior kind, the blacksmith on board this vessel not being able to get a *welding heat on iron* with some of it we got from here. Filled with good Pittsburgh coal, a good head of steam can be kept up on her for thirty-five days; and, in the event of active operations on this coast, it will be necessary for her to have two thousand barrels of good Pittsburgh coal as soon as it can reach here, say about the 25th Sept., or 1st Oct., at which time she may be found at the Arcos Islands, the latitude of which is 20° 12' N., and the latitude[1] 91° 57' W. She adds greatly to the efficiency of our force, particularly on the coast of Mexico, where there is for so great a portion of the time very little wind, unless it is blowing a gale, which seldom lasts long.

. . .

I am, very respectfully,   Your obedient servent,
       [Signed]   E. W. MOORE,
                             Captain Commanding.
To the Hon. Louis P. Cooke,
       Secretary of the Navy, Austin, Texas.

The following excerpts are taken from the diary of one of the midshipmen, and tell many events not mentioned by Commodore Moore in his despatch.[2] At the beginning of September Commodore Moore was at the mouth of the Rio del Norte.

September 19, 1840: . . . stood in chase of strange ship who hoisted Spanish colors, bearing two points on our lee bow. At 5:30 strange ship tacked and stood for us. Beat to quarters and spoke her. She proved the Spanish corvette Gueriro,[3] mounting 22 guns.

October 4, 1840: From 4 to 6, gales with passing clouds. At 5 made a vessel with a signal of distress, lying on the reef at the north end of the island (Labos[4]). Sent life boat on shore to inquire if any of the inhabitants could pilot a boat out to her. At 6 the boat returned, unable to obtain any information or assistance.

---

[1]Longitude.

[2]Diary of midshipman James L. Mabry, in *Galveston News,* January 16 and 23, and February 13, 1893.

[3]Guerrero.

[4]Lobos.

. . . Sent life boat on shore to build a fire as a beacon to the vessel in distress. At 9, manned, provisioned and sent life boat and second cutter to the relief of the distressed vessel lying on the Banquilla reef. The second cutter returned, not being able to proceed against a heavy head sea. . . .

October, 6 1840: . . . at 3.30 the life-boat and second cutter returned, bringing the remainder of the crew, passengers and baggage.[1] . . .

October 17, 1840: At 1,50 standing in for Tampico bar. . . .

October 18, 1840: . . . at 3.30 a sail hove in sight, standing for anchorage. At 4 she came to anchor a short distance ahead of us. She proved [to be] the English brig of war Racer. . . .

October 21, 1840: At 2 the second cutter was fired at 3 times from the shore and very narrowly escaped destruction, the balls striking very close to her. We directed a gun at the fort and fired it, but the distance was so great that it did not carry. . . .

October 23, 1840: At 2,30, Jas. Garrett, second gunner, died of the scurvy. . . .

October 21,[2] 1840: . . . S. O. Sawyer fell from the fore top gallant yard overboard and was lost. . . .

November 4, 1840: At 1 sent first cutter with 228 gallons of water, 1 bag of coffee, two bags of flour and ten boxes of vermicelli to the schooner San Jacinto, and the launch with two anchors and chain. The schooner was ashore, where she had been driven in a norther, having parted one of her anchors. At 6, sent the launch with the men to the San Jacinto. At 7, sent the first cutter to the San Jacinto with 217 gallons of water. The captain left the ship. At 7,30 the captain returned.[3] At 10, the first cutter returned. . . .

November 21. 1840: . . . at 3 the city of Tabasco hove in sight. at 3.30 came to with larboard anchor. . . .

November 23, 1840: . . . at 11.30 General Anaya visited the ship. . . .

December 6 1840: The federal brig-of-war fired a salute of twenty-one guns. At 9,40 she . . . hoisted the Texian ensign at the fore and fired a salute of seventeen guns. At 10 we answered it.

December 11, 1840: . . . At 10 the Zavala came alongside of us and made fast to us.

December 13, 1840: At 6 called all hands to up anchor. Got under way and backed down the river with the Zavala. . . .

---

[1]The wrecked vessel was the Mexican brig, *Segunda Fauna.*

[2]Either this entry is out of place in the original diary, or it was meant for October 24.

[3]See p. 33, below.

December 15, 1840: At 11,30 boarded and took in tow the Mexican schooner Florentine. . . . At 2,30 boarded the Mexican schooner Elizabeth and brought her to under our stern.

December 16, 1840: At 8.30 got under way and cast off the two schooners, giving them permission to proceed up the river. At 5.30 came to anchor off the town of Frenterrea.[1]

December 17, 1840: During the night, James Duffries, ordinary seaman, died of fever. . . .

December 22, 1840: at 3 p. m. Samuel Edgerton, commodore's steward, died of yellow fever. . . .

December 25, 1840: Sent for Dr. Clarke of the San Bernard to visit the sick.

In copying the log of the *Austin,* Midshipman Mabry had no occasion to describe the terrible experience of the *Zavala* in the storm of September 23. The following, from the Tennison Papers,[2] in brief language gives a vivid idea of the perils of the sailor:

23d September, . . . we went to Arcos where we expected to meet the Commodo[re] and obtain a supply of provisions from him—but unfortunately he was not there, and after waiting a week on half allowance we went to Laguna de Terminas to obtain provision. We got enough provisions there by giving draft on the Consul in New Orleans (fund being all gone) and we came here to get fuel enough to carry us to Galveston. We arrived off the bar of this river too late on the night of the 3d October to com in, and towards Morning we had a sever gale, and sea from North east, a little the worst many of us had even seen—how the old Zavala stood it bravely, and after losing our rudder, best anchor and cable, the main mast throwing the guns and about 400 eighteen pound shot, and all our grape and cannister overboard, cutting the salloon, ward room, steerage and berth deck for fuel, we came in here all well and hearty on the 7th October. The Hull of the Vessel and engines being not at all hurt.

The last notice of the *San Antonio* that has been found, respecting this cruise, is a line in the Tennison Papers: "The *San Antonio* arrived in port[3] Dec. 9, 1840, with the rems[4] of Mr. Treat, agent from Texas to Mexico."[5]

[1]Frontera.

[2]Tennison's Journals, folio 350, p. 1. For a more detailed description of the *Zavala* in the storm, see THE QUARTERLY, VI, 123.

[3]Galveston.

[4]Remains.

[5]Tennison's Journal, folio 352, p. 3.

Relative to the doings of the fleet for the next few- months the information is very meager, but a contemporary newspaper gives the following items:[1]

Last from the Fleet.

By the San Bernard, T. A. Taylor commanding, which came into Galveston a few days since, we are in possession of the last intelligence from the fleet. A private letter has been shown us, dated on board the Zavalla, San Juan Baptista River, Tobasco, Dec. 23d, from which we learn that this steam ship is in complete repair, and ready for service; that the whole fleet will not probably come in before March or April. Commodore Moore, on board the flag ship Austin, was in the harbor at Tobasco with the Zavala, but, in a few days, would proceed to sea, on another cruise.

The schooner San Jacinto went ashore in a heavy gale, a short time before the sailing of the San Bernard. At the time, she was anchored off the Arcas Islands, but having imprudently ventured to sea with but one anchor, she was driven by the gale high upon land, a perfect wreck. No lives were lost, and we believe her guns were saved.

It is rumored (on what authority we have not learned,) that the Federal authorities[2] in consideration of the services rendered by Com. Moore in reducing a small town on the coast, contributed $25,000 towards the expenses of the navy during the expedition.

Gen. Anaya is in command at Tobasco, and his forces are constantly augmented by the voluntary enlistment of the citizens. The most amicable relations exist between them and our naval forces.

Tennison states that, at the time of the departure of the *San Barnard* from Tobasco, it was the intention of the *Zavala,* with the *Austin* in tow, to proceed to Laguna for a sufficient supply of fuel, and thence to Galveston. The *Austin,* leaving the *Zavala* after crossing the bar, was to proceed to the Arcos Islands, and thence to Galveston. Under date of February 10, 1841, Tennison further states that the *Austin,* on the cruise referred to above, boarded a small schooner, bound for Vera Cruz, having on board the Federal General Lemus, prisoner of the Centralists. By orders of Commodore Moore he was released, and was landed at Campeachy. Soon afterwards he was placed in a responsible posi-

[1]*Telegraph and Texas Register,* January 13, 1841.
[2]That is, the Mexican Federal authorities.

tion by the new government of Yucatán. On March 18, according to Tennison, the *San Bernard* returned to Galveston. She had touched at Vera Cruz, where her appearance was by no means welcome to the natives. Eight boats, with about seventy men each, had prepared to attack this single schooner manned by a crew of only twenty. The timely interference, however, of the British sloop *Comus* prevented trouble. On this trip the *San Bernard* had lost her foremast, and was forced to stop at the Arcos Islands for repairs. The *Zavala* was at Laguna on March 1, since her supplies of fuel and provisions had not arrived from New Orleans.[1] The following extract gives a glimpse of her at some later time:[2]

The steamship Zavala arrived yesterday in five days from Yucatan. She had on board $8460 in specie, having received ten thousand dollars in payment of services rendered by our Navy in the taking of Tobasco, the balance being expended in the payment of debts contracted there.

At Yucatan everything was quiet. No standing army to make subordinate the civil authorities to the military, as in many parts of Mexico. All kinds of religious worship was tolerated there.

Arista has joined Canales; but had no designs against Texas. He seems determined to overthrow the existing government.

We are assured by a passenger on board the Zavala that the Navy could, if permitted to make captures, not only defray its own expenses, but support the government.[3]

Under date of July 3, 1841, Tennison states that on that day the *San Bernard* arrived, presumably at Galveston, with Judge Webb on board. He says that Mexico had refused to treat with or to receive Webb as an agent to procure the acknowledgment of the independence of Texas.[4]

[1]Tennison's Journal, folio 354, p. 1; folio 372, pp. 1-2.

[2]*Austin City Gazette*, April 21, 1841, quoting from the *Galveston Morning Herald*. No copy of the latter paper is known to the writer, and no mention of it is made in bibliographies of Texas or Louisiana newspapers.

[3]The reader will recall Lamar's statement that the officers of the Texas navy were not expected to make captures while the Texas agent was in Mexico negotiating for the recognition of Texan independence, because Lamar considered that such a policy would be dishonorable. Mexico, in this instance, seems to have outwitted Texas in diplomacy. She kept the Texas agents in Mexico in suspense as to her final decision until her vessels arrived from abroad, no doubt having been informed by the Texas agents, that, as a means of getting their proposals considered, Texas war vessels were under instructions not to molest Mexican commerce until their agency terminated.

[4]Tennison's Journal, folio 372, p. 3.

Of the Tabasco affair, Commodore Moore has the following to say:[1]

. . . went up the river Tabasco, captured that place . . . levied a contribution of $25,000 with which supplies were obtained from New Orleans to enable the squadron to keep at sea upwards of ten months . . . and there by kept the Mexican Navy from appearing off the coast of Texas to enforce the blockade. . . . We remained in quiet possession of the town of Tobasco for twenty-one days and had no shot fired at us as we were leaving. During this cruise one Mexican schooner was captured within five miles of Vera Cruz, sent to Galveston, condemned and sold for seven thousand dollars.

An item of interest in connection with the capture of Tabasco is given by Midshipman C. C. Cox in his reminiscences:[2]

But we had no fight. The enemy evacuated the town before we reached it—and after one night's stay we again dropped down the River—but a good many bags of silver were taken on Board our vessel at Tobasco and a portion at least of the same was distributed among the officers and men of the fleet as prize money. I think eight dollars was the share I got.

April, 1841, saw the return of the Texan vessels to Galveston, and the Yucatán expedition of 1840-1841 was closed. This expedition is in history frequently confounded with later expeditions to Yucatán.[3] Historians also allude to an alliance between Yucatán and Texas in 1840, but this alliance was not consummated in fact until 1841. The taking of Tabasco was the result of an impromptu arrangement between Moore and the officials of Yucatán; the official alliance between Yucatán and Texas, concluded in 1841, was one entered into by the civil authorities of both countries, the conditions of which were specified in a document entrusted to commissioners. In this respect it differed from the arrangements of 1840, which were made verbal and consequently could be easily broken at the caprice of either party, or upon

[1]Moore, Reply to the Pamphlet by Commodores Buchanan, Dupont, and Magruder, etc., 19.

[2]THE QUARTERLY, VI, 124. He is in error as regards "one night's stay." His illness at the time explains the error.

[3]Brown, II, 198; Thrall, A Pictorial History of Texas, 306. Thrall states, "They were placed in the service of the revolutionary government of Yucatan," and "sailed 24th of June, 1840." See also University of Texas Record, V, 155, and Moore's To the People of Texas, 36.

explicit directions to the commodore commanding the Texas fleet disapproving of his actions.

Soon after Commodore Moore's return to Texas he was again sent to sea for the purpose of surveying the coast of Texas. Increasing maritime interests rendered this survey very necessary. He briefly describes this labor in a publication directed to the United States naval officials:[1]

From May to November, 1841, the vessels were overhauled and the coast of Texas surveyed by Captain Moore, with the aid of schooners of the Texas Navy; a chart for the entire coast was made by him and published in New York by E. and G. W. Blunt, and in England by the admiralty. It is the only correct chart now in use by navigators . . . one of the officers whose name is attached to the published remonstrance to the honorable house of representatives has been in service on the gulf since it was published in 1842; he has doubtless had occasion to use it, and I can with confidence call on him to attest its accuracy.

The following item concerning the survey is from the *Telegraph and Texas Register:*[2]

The schooner of War, San Antonio, left Galveston on the 4th inst. for the Sabine Pass, having Com. E. W. Moore and several officers on board, for the purpose of commencing the survey of the coast. Col. G. W. Hockley, was a passenger on board. We are glad to find this important work commenced. The officers of our Navy can not at this season be employed to better advantage than in this survey.

They were actively engaged in the discharge of these labors until their recall in October by President Lamar on account of the alliance entered into between Yucatán and Texas, which we shall consider in the next chapter.

XII.   ALLIANCE BETWEEN TEXAS AND YUCATAN.

The idea of forming an offensive and defensive alliance on the part of Texas and Yucatán against Mexico, was, no doubt, discussed between the Texas commanders and Yucatán officials, while the Texas navy was in Yucatán; and doubt-

---

[1] Moore, *Reply to the Pamphlet by Commodores Buchanan, Dupont, and Magruder*, etc., 19.

[2] July 14, 1841.

less, on the return of the officers from their cruise, the
sentiments expressed by these officials, were imparted to
President Lamar.   According to Senator Sam Houston,[1] the
first overtures looking to an alliance were made by President
Lamar.   Houston says:

It was in the month of July of that year[2] that the Texas navy
was subsidized to Yucatan, an integral part of the Republic of
Mexico.   The then President of Texas, Mr. Lamar, made a communication to the Governor of Yucatan, proposing to confederate
with him to render aid, and to receive reciprocal aid from him.
In conformity to the invitation originating with the President of
Texas, a Minister arrived from the Government of Yucatan, then
in a revolutionary state against Mexico, with proposals to obtain
the navy of Texas, for the purpose of conducting a war against
the central Government of Mexico.   On the 17th of September, I
think, the proposition was submitted by Mr. Badraza,[3] and accepted through the Secretary of State by the President of Texas.
By the 18th the matter was consummated, and directions given
to the navy of Texas immediately to sail, and co-operate in the
defense of Yucatan against Mexico; or, in other words to aid and
assist in the rebellion.   This was done without any authority or
sanction of the Congress or Senate of the Republic of Texas.   It
was a mere act of grace or will on the part of the President.

Col. Peraza arrived at Austin on September 11.   On the 16th
he addressed to Samuel A. Roberts, Secretary of State, a lengthy
communication,[4] the main points of which were that Lamar had
written the government of Yucatán that he was willing to co-
operate against the common enemy; that Yucatán was threatened
by an invasion from Mexico which its navy was not strong enough
to resist; that the case was too urgent for Yucatán to wait for the
assembling of its congress.   Peraza then proceeds, "I will therefore merely say to the Honorable Secretary of State that I am
fully authorized by my Government to contribute to the removal
of any pecuniary obstacles which might perhaps for the moment
embarrass that of Texas in putting her vessels in action"; and he

---

[1]*Cong. Globe*, 33d Cong., 1st Sess., Appendix, 1081; Moore, *To the People
of Texas*, 27-29; Rejón, secretary of state of Yucatán, states that Lamar
did make overtures July 20, 1841.

[2]1841.

[3]Col. Martin F. Peraza.

[4]Anonymous translation in Moore's *To the People of Texas*, 15-17.

goes on to say that Yucatán would pay for the purpose of getting the squadron of three war vessels to sea eight thousand dollars in advance and eight thousand dollars per month, so long as the government should deem it necessary for the squadron to remain in active service. Any prize made and any revenue of the Mexican government confiscated by Yucatán and Texas was to be divided equally between them after first paying the costs of the enterprise. On the next day Col. Peraza received a communication[1] from the Secretary of State of Texas, in which he says:

When therefore you tell us that you have reason to apprehend that the same despotism which for a time waged so savage and relentless a war against us, is preparing to attack the newly established liberties of your country, we can not hesitate to cooperate with you in preparing to repel the premeditated attack by sending such a portion of our Naval force to sea as may be deemed adequate to the service required of it.

That this Government may derive incidental advantages from sending its Navy to sea, . . . is not denied; but that these advantages will afford a just equivalent for the heavy expenses of keeping our Navy at sea, and for the shock such a ste[2] may give to our nation's credit abroad; and the loss we may thereby suffer; the undersigned apprehends, it is equally unnecessary for him to deny. The President therefore in accepting the pecuniary aid offered by Yucatan, on the terms proposed in your communication, towards the support of the Navy so long as it continues to cooperate with that of Yucatan, only discharges a duty towards this Government which a rigid and economical expenditure of the public money demands. . . . The undersigned has been instructed, taking your propositions as a basis, to state specifically the terms upon which the President will feel authorized to afford the Government of Yucatan the aid which she demands.

The stipulations following are four in number, and the same as given in Peraza's letter except the second, which reads: "All captures made by Texan vessels shall be taken into Texas ports for adjudication, and all captures taken by Yucatan vessels shall be taken into Yucatan ports for the like purpose." On the same day, September 17, 1841, Col. Peraza accepted the Texas propositions. In a letter to the secretary of state he says,[3] being

---

[1]Roberts to Peraza, in Moore's *To the People of Texas*, 17-19.
[2]Step.
[3]Peraza to Roberts, in Moore's *To the People of Texas*, 19-20.

conformable to the spirit of my instructions, they are sanctioned on my part in the name of my government, which is pledged to their most punctual and religious observance." In reply to this acceptance by Yucatán, the Secretary of State addressed a letter to Col. Peraza[1] in which he says in part:

the President has this day given orders, in conformity with the stipulations and agreements which have been mutually made between the two governments, for three or more vessels to proceed with as little delay as possible to the port of Sisal, when it is expected the Government of Yucatan will furnish the Commander of the Squadron with such information as will enable him to operate to the advantage of Yucatan. . . . It is hoped the action of Commodore Moore, who will personally command the squardon, will be such as to give entire satisfaction to the government of Yucatan. His orders have been made in strict conformity with the agreement which has been entered into between the two governments.[2]

On the same day, September 18, 1841, Commodore Moore received orders from the department of war and marine in conformity with the treaty entered into by Texas and Yucatán; and he was informed that the eight thousand dollars he would receive at New Orleans was all that he would be advanced for the provisioning of the vessels and recruiting of the men for the service. Another clause in the letter is here given in full, as Commodore Moore claimed that at a later time in his service to Texas he complied with the order it contained, and was for so doing outlawed, declared a pirate, and dishonored by the Texan executive, Sam Houston:

The Department can not conclude these orders, without reiterating that the eight thousand dollars placed in the hands of yourself, and such other advances as Col. Peraza, in behalf of the Government of Yucatan, may think proper to make you upon the contract existing between his and this government, are the only funds you can rely upon for fitting out and supporting the squadron under your command: and if these are insufficient to enable

[1]Roberts to Peraza, September 18, 1841, in Moore's *To the People of Texas*, 20-21.

[2]Those desiring to go more fully into a study of the alliance may consult Rivera, *Historia de Jalapa*, III, 400-401, 514-515; Banqueiro, *Ensayo de Yucatán*, 42-45; *Niles' Register*, LXI, 66, 131, 196.

you to go to sea under these orders, you will not attempt it, but remain in port, without accepting or using any portion of the pecuniary contribution which the government of Yucatan has agreed to advance.[1]

On Friday, October 8, 1841, Lieutenant Lewis left Galveston[2] with the above dispatches and secret orders for Commodore Moore, to be opened after the completion of the provisioning. Commodore Moore was still surveying the coast, being on board the *San Antonio,* and accompanied by the *San Bernard,* commanded by Lieutenant Crisp. Lieutenant Lewis reached Moore on the 13th, and on receipt of the documents Moore sailed at once for Galveston. The money for the cruise and outfitting was deposited by the commissioner in the custom-house in Galveston. Within two months all preparations had been made; and, on December 13, 1841, the vessels under Commodore Moore sailed for Yucatán. Outside of Galveston Bar Commodore Moore opened his secret orders, and found that he was instructed to sail direct for Sisal, in the State of Yucatán,[3] and to co-operate with the sea and land forces of Yucatán in checking any hostile act of Mexico. He was also instructed to capture Mexican towns, and to levy contributions; and, for the purpose of compelling payment, he was authorized to destroy public works and edifices, and to seize public property, "taking care, however, to adhere to the principle that private property is always to be respected, and never to be violated except when unavoidable in the execution of duty." These acts it was hoped, would cause the central government no little annoyance, and would "strike a terror among the inhabitants, which may be very useful to us should it again be thought advisable to enter into negotiations for peace." For carrying out these instructions of the secretary of the navy, the Texas navy has been criticised by historians. Yet the same methods were used in the Civil War twenty years later by both North and South.

The first official communication received from Commodore Moore was dated January 31, 1842, from the Texas sloop-of-war

[1]Archer to Moore September 18, 1841, in Moore's *To the People of Texas*, 12-13. Endorsed by Moore as having been received October 13, 1841.

[2]Tennison's Journal, folio 372, p. 4.

[3]Moore, *To the People of Texas*, 13-15.

Austin at anchor off Sisal.[1] Accompanying his own letter are copies of letters exchanged between him and the officials of Yucatán, which illustrate the embarrassing situation in which he was placed on his arrival. They also show the estimation in which the Texas navy was held by the government of Yucatán, which was on the point of reuniting with Mexico, and was negotiating the terms with the commissioner, Quintana Roo, under the impression that Texas would not be able to comply with her engagements. But, encouraged by the arrival of the Texan fleet, it insisted on justice from Mexico; and the refusal led to a war, which for the time diverted the energies of Mexico from Texas to Yucatán.[2] Among other things the letter says:

Dec. 13, . . . I opened the "Secret Orders" received 1st October, in the presence of Lt. A. G. Gray, Purser N. Hurd, and Doct. Wm. Richardson. . . . I arrived and anchored off Sisal on the 6th inst,[3] the schooners San Antonio and San Bernard in company, having met the former on the 4th, and the latter on the 5th, . . . exchanged salutes with the Castle, and on the next day proceeded to the city of Merida, Lt. Com'g. Seeger in company with me.

The Yucatán political situation is next portrayed, and Moore then says:

The San Antonio takes this letter to Galveston and proceeds immediately to New Orleans for provisions, and when she joins me I will be enabled to keep at sea until the 1st May, without calling on the government for *one* dollar. If it be the wish of His Excellency the President to coerce Mexico to acknowledge our Independence, I can at once blockade all the ports of entry, viz.: Vera Cruz, Tampico, and the Brazos de Santiago; and if I had the steamer Zavala to co-operate with the Squadron, I could levy contributions on several of their towns to a greater amount than the entire *cost* of the Navy—without the Zavala little else can be effected but to pick up any vessel that they hazard out. . . . The vessels building in New York when I left Galveston, for the Mexican Navy, I will use my utmost to intercept, and if they have contraband of War on board, I will send them to Galveston—this course being strictly in accordance with International law. . . .

[1]Moore to the Secretary of the Navy, in Moore's *To the People of Texas*, 21-36. The date of the letter as printed is 1841, which is clearly incorrect.
[2]Moore, *To the People of Texas*, 21.
[3]January, 1842.

I leave to-day for Campeche and Vera Cruz; off the latter place I will cruize some time.

Commodore Moore was also instrumental in saving the cargo of the American schooner *Sylph* of New Orleans, which had been wrecked on the Alacranes, and he rescued the crew and sent them with the cargo to New Orleans in the *San Antonio*. He makes the assertion that the *Austin* was full of rotten wood and that the agent of Texas in supervising the construction of the vessels was grossly at fault. This reference was to J. G. Tod, and seems to be the beginning of the estrangement which in later years was emphasized by President Jones's nomination of Tod to take the place of Commodore Moore, who had been deprived of his position (illegally, Moore says) as commodore, by President Houston. While Commodore Moore was detained at Mérida, uncertain of his success in negotiating with the Yucatán officials, rumors of danger threatening him reached Lieutenant Alfred Gray, commanding the ship *Austin*. As Gray could not communicate with Moore, he considered it his duty to detain as hostages, until the commodore's safe return, the commissioners from the national government of Mexico and from Yucatán, who were taken from the American barque *Louisa* on their way to Vera Cruz.[1] Lieutenants A. Irvine Lewis and Cummings secured the commissioners and they were held until Moore was communicated with. As soon as possible he informed Gray that he was in no danger and directed him to release them. Moore said that under similar circumstances he would have done as Gray did; but suitable expressions of regret were addressed to the commissioners. In Commodore Moore's next report to the secretary of war and the navy, he makes mention of the capture of the Mexican schooner *Progreso*. By this vessel he sent to Galveston a letter in which he says:[2]

I have this day taken as a prize the Mexican Schooner Progreso.
I was off Vera Cruz yesterday and *saw* one of the vessels built in New York for the Mexican Navy, and learn to-day that she has been in three or four days, and the other one is hourly expected.

[1]Moore, *To the People of Texas*, 30-33; Tennison's Journal, folio 376, p. 1. These commissioners had been appointed to consider the reunion of Yucatán to the Mexican Federation.

[2]Moore to the Secretary of War and Navy, February 6, 1842, in Moore's *To the People of Texas*, 36.

A Lieutenant of Artillery (Mexican Army) was passenger in the schooner Progreso. . . . I intend keeping him, as I will all other officers of the government who fall into my hands, until I can hear something definite of the Santa Fé expedition.

The following is a contemporary account of the capture of the *Progreso:*[1]

Feby 22d 1842

Lut Wm. A Tennison of our Navy arrived on Saturday in charge of the Mexican Schooner Progresso captured by the sloop of war Austin in sight of Vera Cruz . . . on the 6th. She is ladened principally with Flour and Sugar. . . . When the Progresso left the schooner of war San Barnard was in chase of another Mexican vessel, which was stated to have on board a large amount of specie. . . . The San Barnard was to the windward of her and between her and the shore, and so certain was Com. Moore of the prize that we would not think it worth while to join in the chase. . . .

A general officer was captured on the Progresso when he saw the Texan flag run up he tore off his epaulettes thrust them in his pockets, but it was no use he was caught in the act. . . . Sat-Anz[2] has purchased an old English steam ship carrying 4 guns of an English system, and if he has any spirit—with her and the New York Brig may offer Com. Moore a fight—nothing would be more welcomb to the Tars.

On February 25, when the *Austin* was again at anchor off Sisal, Commodore Moore learned from a pilot that the Mexican ship expected from New York was lost on the Florida reef on her way out, and the other Mexican vessels would not give him battle. The schooner *San Antonio* left Sisal on February 1, for Galveston with a letter from the governor of Yucatán to the president of Texas; and she was expected by Commodore Moore to meet him at the Arcas Islands on her return about March 1, 1842. From the Areas Islands Moore intended to go to Laguna, at which place he was to overhaul the rigging and paint the ships. On March 8, Commodore Moore writes from Campeachy:[3]

---

[1]Tennison's Journal, folio 376, pp. 2-3; copied from the *Galveston Civilian*, February 22, 1842. See also *Telegraph and Texas Register*, February 23, 1842.

[2]Santa Anna.

[3]Moore to Lemus, in Moore's *To the People of Texas*, 41-42.

I arrived here on the afternoon of the 6th inst., from the Arcas Islands, where I waited two days for the San Antonio without meeting her; on my arrival here her delay was accounted for by the sad intelligence of the mutiny on board of her at New-Orleans (to which place she went for provisions,) and of the murder of one of the most promising officers, Lieut. Fuller, whom I have ever known. I expect to meet Capt. Seeger at Laguna, for which place I leave to-night, and I will mete out to the rascals the *uttermost penalties* of the law.[1]

Moore sailed that night, and two days later he received the following official note,[2] recalling him to Texas:

DEPARTMENT OF WAR AND NAVY,
15th December, 1841.

Commodore *E. W. Moore,*
　　　Commanding Texas Navy.
　　Sir.—I am directed by His Excellency the President to order that the squadron under your command return forthwith to the port of Galveston, and there await further orders. . . .

Geo. W. Hockley.

In reference to this note Moore says:[3]

No. 16 . . . was received outside Laguna Bar on the 10th March, per Schooner of War San Antonio, and was written, as will be seen by reference to the date *two* days after the inauguration of President Houston. It was the first communication that I had received since sailing, and although a peremptory order, I was compelled to disobey it. It will be seen by the subsequent letter from the Department (20) that the course adopted by me was approved by the President.

The letter referred to by Moore as approving of his disobedience to this order reads as follows:[4]

DEPARTMENT OF WAR AND NAVY,
April 14, 1842.

Com. *E. W. Moore,*
　　　Commanding Squadron.
　　Sir: Your dispatches by Capt. Crisp were handed into the De-

---

[1]See also *Telegraph and Texas Register,* February 23, 1842.

[2]Hockley to Moore, December 15, 1841, in Moore's *To the People of Texas,* 43.

[3]*Ibid.*

[4]Hockley to Moore, April 14, 1842, in Moore's *To the People of Texas,* 50-51.

partment yesterday. . . . Your proceedings personally, and of Courts Martials, specially, are approved, and the latter confirmed.

Concerning the order for the recall of the navy, Houston in his speech before the Senate of the United States, July 15, 1854, said:[1]

The new President[2] was inaugurated on the 12th of December following;[3] and we find by the records, that on the 15th of that month the navy was recalled forthwith, and ordered to the port of Galveston. The orders ought to have reached the navy in ten or twelve days. A pilot boat was dispatched to carry the orders to Commodore Moore, the commander; but that vessel, owing to peculiar influences at Galveston, or some other circumstances, was not permitted to reach Campeachy until the 10th of March following. On the first of May, I think it was, the fleet returned. . . .

In this connection, it is necessary, in referring to Houston's order dated December 15, 1841, to correct a very gross error on the part of historians which has, so far as I am aware, never been challenged by critics. Yoakum,[4] in closing the chapter devoted to the year 1840, says:

The President's[5] health had been for some time very bad; and, getting no better, he obtained from the Congress a leave of absence, and about the middle of December retired from his official duties, leaving them to be discharged by the Vice-President.

That is all true, but in the succeeding pages Yoakum does not state plainly that Lamar afterwards resumed his duties as president, and the inference is left that his retirement was permanent, which was not the case. Thrall[6] makes a palpable error. He says:

The cares and responsibilities of office weighed heavily on President Lamar, and the severe strictures of political opponents affected his deeply sensitive nature, and he applied to Congress for permission to absent himself from the Republic. The request was granted, and during the last year the Government was administered by Vice-President Burnet.

[1]*Cong. Globe*, 33d Cong., 1st Sess., Appendix, 1081.
[2]Houston.
[3]1841.
[4]*A Comprehensive History of Texas*, I, 368.
[5]Lamar's.
[6]Thrall, *A Pictorial History of Texas*, 137.

The "last year" refers, of course, to 1841. It is, of course, too well known to require proof, that Lamar was the prime mover and cause of the Santa Fé Expedition of 1841, and that he furnished Col. McLeod with a proclamation to be given to the people of Santa Fé.[1] It is also well known that he was the promoter of the Yucatán alliance consummated in the months of July to September, 1841. Moore states in his pamphlet[2] that this alliance was originated and was carried out by Lamar in 1841. He did, on account of ill health, for a time retire from the presidential duties, but only for a time. His letter to Burnet implies also that it was only temporary; for it reads thus:[3] "Ill health has compelled me to ask of the Honorable Congress permission to retire from the discharge of official duty for the present." Bancroft falls into the same error; he says:[4] "The labors of office and the animadversions to which he was exposed, induced Lamar to apply to congress for permission to absent himself; and his request being granted, during the last year of his term, the government was administered by Vice-President Burnet"; and adds in a footnote:

From Dec. 15, 1840 to Feb. 3, 1841, the acts of congress were approved by David G. Burnet, after which date no signatures are attached to the acts passed in the copy of *The Laws of the Republic of Texas* in my possession, only the word "approved" with the date, being used.

This last statement, however, proves nothing, for in printing the laws passed during Houston's administration from 1841 to 1844 his signature never appears, though he did sign many of them. Those which he signed are, as the secretary of state explains,[5] simply marked "approved."

I have here devoted much space to proving that Lamar did act as president in 1841, because the historians so plainly infer that he did not, that the general reader and even the worker in Texas history

[1]Eugene C. Barker, in *University of Texas Record*, V, 159; Bancroft, II, 333.

[2]Moore, *To the People of Texas*, 29.

[3]Hobby, *Life and Times of David G. Burnet*, 23.

[4]Bancroft, II, 343.

[5]Gammel, *Laws of Texas*, II, 792.

is led astray. If their statements were accepted, of course Lamar had nothing to do with the Yucatán alliance of 1841; but, their statements being disproved, all doubt as to Lamar's having held the reins of government in 1841 are removed. The peaceful invasion of Texan territory by the Santa Fé expedition had its conception with Lamar, and became a calamity only because of circumstances over which he had no control. Had the mission been successful, he would have been heralded as the foremost statesman of Texas. The Yucatán alliance was timely and of great help to Texas, and has only been recorded with doubting language by historians because it was little understood by historians, and because of the bitter attacks made upon it by Houston in after years. Notwithstanding the great deference given to Houston's opinions, nearly all the historians give the Yucatán alliance and the conduct of the Texas squadron in Yucatán a left-handed compliment. Lamar never quit his station because he shrank from criticism, as historians have stated; on the contrary, in his own lifetime, an able biography of him appeared in a leading Texas publication,[1] and, according to it, he was willing that his reputation should stand or fall according to these two policies.

Commodore Moore remained at the port of Carmen, Laguna de Términos, from the tenth until the twenty-eighth of March, at which time, accompanied by the two schooners, *San Antonio* and *San Bernard*,[2] he sailed for Vera Cruz. He says:

. .. arrived off Vera Cruz on the 31st, and ran close in under the Island of Sacrificios to send in a boat to the United States Ship Warren. . . . I discovered that the Steamer under the Castle was raising steam, and the Schooner now under Mexican colors was warping alongside of her. I immediately run up the boat and began making preparations to give them a warm reception, (9 o'clock A. M.) standing out to get an offing, the wind being very light, and we being barely out of gun shot of the Castle. I remained near all day, passing once inside of one of the reefs forming the harbour, but they did not come out. The Warren sent a boat out to the ship, by the officer who came in her, I

[1]*Texas Almanac*, 1858, 109-114. The sketch was probably either prepared by Lamar or reviewed by him.

[2]Moore to Hockley, April 4, 1842, in Moore's *To the People of Texas*, 46-50.

learned . . . that Mr. Thomas Lubbock[1] who escaped from Mexico, had sailed but a few days previous . . . for Laguna to join me; that night I sent the *San Antonio* back to Laguna for Mr. Lubbock, and stood to the N. and W. in Company with the *San Bernard;* the following forenoon I captured the Mexican Schooner Doloritas *nine* days from Matamoras bound to Vera Cruz, she was very near the land when we discovered her, and the super cargo and part of the crew made their escape in the boat . . . —she parted company yesterday for Galveston, and in the afternoon I landed the Captain Mate and boy with all their private effects at Point Delgada. . . .

I herewith enclose all the quarterly returns of this Ship and the *San Bernard,* a correct chart of the sea coast of Texas, a correct chart of the bar and harbour of Pass Caballo with the Labacca and Matagorda Bays, and a plan of the proposed break-water, by which *twenty feet water* can be made at the bar at a comparatively trifling expense, and there is after getting in, one of the finest harbors in the world. . . .

On the 3rd inst., within a few miles of Tuspan, we captured the Mexican Sehr. "Dos Amigos," from Matamoros, bound to Tuspan, with a cargo of salt. I will dispatch her also to Galveston to-night or tomorrow, in company with the San Bernard, the Comd'r. of which vessel[2] will take this dispatch to the Seat of Government and return to Galveston with an answer and instructions for me, by the time I arrive there. I touch at Sisal to get *ten thousand dollars* which will be due on the 8th inst., when I will sail direct for Galveston, in pursuance of your orders of the 15th Dec. . . . there is every necessity of keeping the squadron at sea, and in a fighting condition, to prevent our Ports being blockaded and all communication cut off from the United States. Without the speedy return of our Navy on this coast, the navy of Yucatan will be captured or join that of Central Mexico, through fear, if nothing else.

In a letter of the next day,[3] he adds:

I feel it my imperative duty to urge upon the Department the necessity of fitting out the steamer Zavala, in order that we may keep the ascendency by sea and the communication open between Galveston and New Orleans.

[1] A member of the Santa Fé expedition.
[2] D. H. Crisp.
[3] Moore to Hockley, April 5, 1842, in Moore's *To the People of Texas*, 50.

Moore, in commenting upon his recommendation respecting the *Zavala* says:[1]

Nos. 18 and 19 . . . are letters from me to the Department; the latter[2] contains my recommendation to the government to fit out the *Zavala* which could *then* have been done at a small expense and saved from destruction, the most efficient vessel in the Navy; worth, $100,000, which has been lost to the country by the *wise economy* of government. . . . The wreck of the *Zavala,* now lying in Galveston harbor, is a melancholy evidence, of the *sort of economy* practised by President Houston!

In these remarks Moore is undoubtedly correct; for, by an act of the congress of Texas, approved by Houston,[3] the president of Texas was authorized to have the *Zavala* repaired, and at a later session another act was passed, also approved by Houston,[4] making an appropriation of $15,000 for the purpose. This authority Houston never used.

The following letter will explain the temporary discontinuance of the Yucatán-Texas alliance:[5]

His Excellency the Governor . . . has received notice that they[6] do not think of invading us at present, and that if they do invade at all it will not be for eight months or a year, for reason of the want of resources and the embarrassed position in which Gen. Santa Anna finds himself. The State can not continue paying all this time, eight thousand dollars monthly to the vessels under your command, as agreed with the Government of Texas, to which you are subject, and for that reason I inform you, without, however, considering the friendly relations being interrupted, which has been reciprocally preserved by both Governments; that, you can . . . retire with the squadron under your command, after the current month has expired. . . . The Governor does not doubt but that he can depend upon the assistance of Texas after the above indicated time has transpired.

Under date of April 22, 1842, Lemus adds:[7]

[1]Moore, *To the People of Texas,* 45-46.
[2]Moore to Hockley, April 5, 1842.
[3]Gammel, *Laws of Texas,* II, 791.
[4]*Ibid.,* 813-814.
[5]Lemus to Moore, March 29, 1842, in Moore's *To the People of Texas,* 53-54.
[6]The Mexicans.
[7]Lemus to Moore, in Moore's *To the People of Texas,* 55.

The want of funds has compelled the Treasury to give a bill for $4000 to complete the $12,208, which will be paid in thirty days after date, consequently Mr. Seeger has only received $8666.66 including the account of supplies, and an order for account of the Schooner San Bernard.

Commodore Moore now sailed for Galveston with the squadron; and arriving there May 1, 1842, and finding President Houston and the secretary of war and the navy, Col. Hockley, there, he personally handed the latter his final report of the cruise of the squadron, the most important parts of which are as follows:[1]

I parted company with the San Bernard on the morning of the 6th April, and in consequence of continued winds . . . did not arrive at Sisal until the morning of the 18th, when I met the San Antonio, she having on board Mr. Thos. Lubbock. . . . The same afternoon the brig of War Wharton arrived, and the next day I sent Lt. Comd'g. Wm. Seeger to Merida. . . . On the forenoon of the 23rd, the San Bernard arrived, when I received your communication of the 14th ult . . . And got underway—the brig Wharton, and schrs. San Antonio and San Bernard in company: the next afternoon we all anchored off Campeache. On the 25th, the Yucatan vessels of war, two brigs and two schrs.—went to sea, and as they passed us they lowered their flags *three times* which we of course returned. In the afternoon I received on board eight thousand dollars. . . . we all got under way at 1 o'clock A. M.; (26th.) In the afternoon parted company with the Wharton off the Arcas Islands and pushed on for this place, where I arrived to-day, and anchored at 4 o'clock— the San Antonio in sight astern, but the San Bernard not, she will be up tomorrow.

[1]Moore to Hockley, May 1, 1842, in Moore's *To the People of Texas*, 60-61.

J. C. CLOPPER'S JOURNAL AND BOOK OF MEMORANDA
FOR 1828.[1]

PROVINCE OF TEXAS.

Novr. 10th 1827—Departed Cincinnati on this evening on board the Steam boat Franklin for Louisville—Company for the same destination Messrs. N. Clopper, A. M. Clopper, E. N. Clopper Captn. Lyndsay—for this night's darksome series of conflicting emotions; why the spirit slumbered not, and the heart was ill at ease, vide: the records of Memory.

Nov. 11th. Sunday morning arrived at Louisville; Met Dr. G M Patrick and Mr. Gregg of Ky: who connected themselves with us under the firm of the Texas trading Association Remained here three days awaiting the departure of a steam boat— pleased with the Town's commercial appearance the picturesque wildness and grandeur of the falls and spirit of enterprize dis- coverable in the progress of the canal around them—wrote four letters—three to Cincinnati—two of which remain not at Wood- lawn of the Mound.

Nov. 14 This morning departed for N. Orleans on board the splendid Boat Amazon—our Compy. seven in all—Had a delight- ful passage down as far as St Helena on the Mississippi where the

---

[1]The original of this journal is in the possession of Edward N. Clopper, Cincinnati, a grandson of J. C. Clopper, who has kindly furnished the printer's copy, at the same time lending the original for editorial purposes and sending also the following sketch of its writer:
"Joseph Chambers Clopper was born in Chambersburg, Pennsylvania, January 11, 1802, and died in Cincinnati, on January 7, 1861. His parents, Nicholas Clopper of New Jersey, and Rebecca Chambers of Chambersburg, Were married in 1790 and had eight children, all of whom, except Joseph, died single. In 1829 he married Mary Este of Morristown, New Jersey, whose sister Hannah was the wife of David G. Burnet. Three children were born to them, two of whom died in infancy; their son, Edward N. Clopper, was superintendent of schools in Houston, Texas, at the time of his death in 1880. In 1818 Nicholas Clopper took his wife and children to Cin- cinnati, where he purchased land and built a house which is still the family homestead. A few years later he acquired land in Texas for speculation and ranching purposes, and spent considerable time in the province looking after his property. In 1827 he took his sons, Joseph, Andrew and Edward, with him to Texas, the following diary, kept by Joseph, being an account of their experiences during that visit.—E. N. C."

boat broke her shaft—the border and island scenery of the different rivers and streams generally undiversified, occasionally picturesque and beautifull. At the last named place were taken in tow by the La Fayette with a keel lashed to her opposite side—presenting such a wide front to the waters our progress was very slow affording sufficient time for the eye to delight itself with the prospective loveliness of the border country which increases in interest as we approached the great Southern depot—reached the City on the 28th instant.

Purchased a large flat as a depository for our freight and boarding house—father's residence at the Western Hotel—first night's supper oysters and oyster soup. A vast number of shipping in port—say three hundred sail, from most of the principal commercial countries. City stands on a flat plane secured from inundation by the river by a levee of sand and shells extending many miles up and down the river continually kept in repair within the corporation by hirelings slaves and criminals—streets unseemly and inconveniently narrow tho' mostly laid off at right angles— there are several streets of handsome breadth ornamented with trees and some fine brick buildings—tho' the greater part of the City is constituted of frame and these mostly very low houses about one and a half story. The public square fronting the river with the Cathedral at its rear-presents a very beautiful view rendered more picturesque as the building externally has much the stamp of antiquity awakening the eye of the mind to rest upon the time-stricken ruins of a castle of romance There are many handsome public buildings such as the new theatre, exchange the several banks etc. Population variant according to the periodical seasons when health or sickness most prevails—supposed in all migratory and stationary "from snowy white to sooty" to be between 40 and fifty thousand souls at this time, composed apparently of all tongues and kindred and people. The French language still prevails tho' the Americans (as in contradistinction those citizens who speak the English tongue are termed) are fast gaining the ascendency in manners customs style and the general character of a city or people.

New Orleans has a small artificial basin on the west side connected with Lake Pontchertrain by a canal which will admit coasting vessels freighting one hundred tons. The Sabbath is distinguished more as a day of amusements balls dances excellence and variety of the markets than as a day of sanctity and rest— very few stores are closed and drays and carts run without intermission. The French soldiery attend mass in the morning in full uniform and the rest of the day in parading and exercise at the guns Walked down with three or four of our Compy to the battle ground—five miles below the corporation—charmed with the elegance of taste displayed by gentlemen residents at their different mansions on the river—the eye rests with rapture on the beautiful groves and hedges of the orange tree in its survey of the fascinating scenery enriched by the profuse variety of fruits and shrubbery skilfully arranged and intermingled one with the other—reached the field of carnage—now covered with stalks of sugar cane and corn—the plane is here about one mile in breadth perfectly level and widening with the course of the river—the only vestige of that day's glorious triumph of *Freedom* is the intrenchment extending from the shore of the Mississippi to an impassable swamp;'being about one mile in length—this trench is about 10 or 12 feet in width by 4 or 5 in depth, in many places nearly filled—here then I stood and silently surveyed the scene for this was a *wide field* for meditation—at this point the gallant foe was found in heaps of slain—here "blood burst and smoked around"—here the cries and groans of the wounded and expiring were heard "as when a thousand ghosts shriek at once upon the hollow wind"—there the British chieftan fell and yonder stand the two lonely trees where his remains were embalmed as a sad solace for the afflictions of kindred spirits in a foreign land—at a distance of one hundred and fifty yards in the rear of the intrenchment is the beautiful seat when whence genl. Jackson viewed the battle raging, a spectator of the deeds of arms while Fame was weaving around his brow a chaplet of immortality too dazzling alas! for the visions of thousands boasting themselves discerners of the intrinsic merits of man—when shall we be able to discriminate and know that "it is not all gold that glitters"? that there are things apparently all glorious in themselves that shine but with a borrowed lustre— light that is not their own.

Returned. Were detained in Orleans much longer than we anticipated—often disappointed in our prospects of leaving a City with which we had already become most heartily disgusted—some of us continually presenting to others the infectious mien of dejected *Ennuis* To remove this made several visits to Miss C. W. an interesting and intelligent young lady with whom I became acquainted in Cin: a few years previous these visits were too ineffectual for frequent repetition—the eye—the ear—the taste for intellectual elegancies were agreeably entertained and delighted but ah! the Memory was but too much awakened and the heart grew sick—obtained some handsome specimens of this Lady's penmanship and poetic taste for my sister. Wrote six letters—four for Cin:—Query—Woodlawn of the Mound, hast thou *still* with thee more than an equal division?

Dec: 18th The Compy purchase three eighths of a small schooner the Little Zoe—burden 20 tons—20th. Cargo on board and Custom House clearance procured—spirits once more light and buoyant 22nd Saturday evening 5 o'clock—passengers all on board— "This hour we part—this hour our flutt'ring sails Spread their white bosoms to the gentle gales"—the breezes slowly die away— the spirits sink. Land of my love! how lone am I! Friends of my heart! how lost! As a Gondola that scarcely *wakes the tide* our little bark moves gently on toward her destined port—not so with the mind—the movements of its thoughts are retrograde and screened by a veil of "leaden gloom," far beyond lies the beautiful scenery on the constituent loveliness of which it delights to dwell and revel and feast upon the sweets of pensive retrospect—the stars are in brilliant glow—the wind from the N West grows high—about 11 o'clock at night under full sail the vessel strikes the shore where we are obliged to lie all night in great peril of our vessel as she lay in a whirlpool of the river recieving against her side huge logs and trees borne on a current of unusual rapidity. In the morning the crew and passengers fourteen men in all succeed in getting her off. Sunday—have pretty favourable breezes— scenery—nothing imposing, a flat prairie and swamp country on both sides—gratified with the majestic and beautiful appearances of many large vessels bearing for N Orleans under full press of canvass. Land to take in wood for our voyage—tormented almost to madness by swarms of sand flies—a Small insect or gnat more intolerable much than the musquito. This night strike the shore again a little below Fort Jackson; get off without damage cast anchor within sound of the roaring of the Sea. Monday morning the sun unclouded rises and a bland breeze from the west promises us a delightful entrance into the "vasty deep"—ascend the mast head—the ocean is seen on both sides the river—the land appearing as two great artificial banks or levees thrown up as barriers against the "meeting of the waters"—reach the Balize—river of great breadth—the eye is lost in its survey of extensive alluvial flats and watery surfaces—enter the S. West pass—most of the morning at the mast head charmed with the boundless and novel prospect—anxious for the moment when we should launch upon the broad bosom of the sea—met by a pilot boat are conducted through the nine feet pass at 12 o'clock, delightfully wafted away on the gently undulating billows of the ocean amidst the smiles of the elements and sportive exhibitions of innumerable porpoises. The Mississippi waters distinguishable for fifteen or twenty miles at sea. Mr. Gregg is very sick ere the land is out of view. Water has now a beautiful sea-green hue. Monday evening—out of soundings—the sea is now of the deepest indigo—the swells increase and billows roll confusedly as tho' there was an angry commotion at their unfathomable depths—the evening is yet without a moon and the stars twinkle and beam a soft and lovely lustre— a lively southern breeze springs up—our little bark glides swiftly o'er the waves—leaving apparently a fiery stream behind— this was to us a beautiful phenomenon—the vessel seemed to have stirred up myriads of animalcula that glowed in her wake as so many "sparks from smitten steel or nitrous grain the blaze"—the sea at this distance from shore is of the liveliest and deepest cerulean hue. Christmas day very heavy rain in the morning for several hours—exposed to it all. Mr. Gregg and W. ´sick and vomiting as for a wager. Sea pretty heavy—undulatory motion of the vessel very quick and sickening Father commences a course of severe vomitings—a large brig heaves in sight all sail set and coming ´fast upon us—begin to talk of powder lead guns and pirates. Brig nears us—hoists signal for us to come to—do so—find that she was a fine brig sixteen days from N. York bound to some point on Vermilion Bay with materials for the establishment of a Light-House. Captn apologises for our detention and sails off— clouds are dispersed and sun again appears—sea still running high—feel somewhat unpleasant myself as did the whole Compy— but none so bad as to vomit saving those above mentioned—⁻have no appetite for anything Looking at poor Gregg upon whose forlorn dejected countenance a smile had not dared to appear since his first greetings with the ocean. Strove all of us to rally each other on the comparative excellencies of this Christmas day's amusements pleasures and social happiness with the fair—saw some sea-fowl that seemed to have been driven off by the stormy winds—another unpleasant night is laboured through—sail on all Wednesday without any remarkable occurrence—saw some large trees which we determined should be and saluted them as old neighbours from the forests of Ohio and Kentucky—they were driving along with a fine breeze and strong current towards the shores of Texas tho' too tardily for us and we were again without a neighbour—our dogs three in number all sick and refuse to eat—but fight continually from pure *peevishness*.

Thursday morning feel a return of appetite feel a freshness in the breeze—the sea is of a green cast—about 9 o'clock the joyful cry of land is echoed round the deck   strain the eye and discern the breakers at the shore—great flocks of geese and ducks fly over us—think it to be Galveston island—coast along within sight—while sitting at breakfast a sudden squall of wind and heavy rain take us and turn over dishes and drench the whole of us—thought once we should capsize ere the sailors could furl sails   wind lulls in about an hour and rain ceased—clouds and fog disperse and we have a beautiful afternoon. Still in sight of land—come to an anchor early in the evening in 10 fathom water powerful current running parallel with the land. Saw the sun as he appeared in the act of engulphing himself—shortly after the lovely star of evening gracefully descended the horizon after him and bathed her golden locks in the western tides; "whilst high amidst her silent orb the silver moon rolled clear"—the breeze was bland and the surface of the waters unruffled—there was a magnificence in this scenery, an imposing grandeur that seemed to rivet the soul and interest it to exercise all its faculties in contemplation of Him who arrayed them in all their splendour and gave to each his mighty energies—there was a correspondent calmness on the mind —all was quietude—the Captn had gone to his repose when about 9 o'clock the wind suddenly rose   the Captn. was called and told the wind was favourable for sailing. The anchor is weighed—the sails set and we scud away—in about 15 minutes encounter a

severe gale from the N. West—the sea becomes fearfully tumult-
uous—gale increases—topsail is furled and sails reefed—billows
rolling to a prodigious height—vessel lying on her side and riding
majestically over towering waves—a dutch passenger's hat and
bible blown away he fastens himself to the ropes—we are all
stretched across the deck—water dashes over upon us from bow
to stern—suffer greatly from the cold—gale continues till morning—high winds till late in the day—find that we are blown off
about 20 miles from the coast—discover smoke in several directions—supposed to be from the fires of Indian hunters—wind still
from the land—beat up and down the coast till the evening of
the next day when we discover the mouth of the pass leading into
Galveston bay between the eastern point of Galveston island and
Point Bolivar—after striking on the bar discover the channel
leading into the harbour of the celebrated La Fitte this is a deep
and commodious harbour perfectly secure from any wind having
good anchorage—not knowing the channel we ran into a sand bank
under full sail, next morning found that our vessel was on her
side with not more than 18 inches water. Saturday evening four
or five of us went ashore with our guns and lay till morning on
the soft grass—not knowing that it was Sunday we rambled about
shooting at geese ducks and other waterfowl of the country—which
collect here in innumerable multitudes every morning to feed on
marine substances that are left on the beach by the tide Shot
some fine large red fish which with our fowl and oysters afforded our
craving appetites a banquet that was most exquisitely delicious
and savoury—not able to get our vessel off to day go on shore
again in the evening—kindle a large fire of drift wood—none
growing upon this point of the island—step a little distance to
a small bayou where we gather loads of oysters—roast them and
feast till feasting is a labour and we are invited to repose by "tired
Nature: sweet restorer—balmy sleep." Monday morning see deer
on the island—out shooting again—in the evening at flood tide
succeed in hauling out into deep water—lay at anchor till tuesday morning—favourable breeze from the South hoist Sail and
pursue the western channel running on the left of Pelican island,
so called from the vast number of that species of bird that are
continually seen on and about it—sailed many miles through
water of five feet depth our schooner drawing upward of four and

a half—saw the wreck of the Rising-suns—lost when father was in
this country last—discover the western pass leading into the ocean.
Galveston island is about 30 or 40 miles in length varying from
one to five in breadth and makes a fine hunting ground for several
small tribes of Indians—anchor for the night in seven feet water—
not much timber yet to be seen on the land—come in sight of the
wreck of the Mary a schooner of 100 tons burthen lost three years
since on Red fish bar—a dry shoal of sand pebbles and shells
reaching from one shore at Davis' point to the other fifteen or
twenty miles in length and forming the dividing line between
what are termed Galveston and Trinity Bays. This Bar is about
twenty five miles from Point Bolívar—it has several channels con-
necting the Bays the principal of which is about one mile from
Davis' point having five fathom water immediately in the channel
and a hard bar or shoal directly after passing through; upon
which we struck in four and half feet water and dragged over into
the Trinity considered the safest and handsomest Bay on all the
coast—discover Cedar Point directly ahead it being about four or
five miles to the right of the mouth of the rio San Jacinto for
which we were Steering anchored for the night about two miles
off the mouth in 8 feet water. In the morning are visited by three
men in a small boat—one of them (major Taylor) an acquaintance of father—get favourable news—are piloted by them into the
San Jacinto—strike on a bar at the entrance—haul off and anchor
for the night—go ashore on father's league known by the name
of Hunter's Point—a lovely spot of land surrounded by a beautifully picturesque scenery decorated with groves of cedar pine magnolia etc. presenting a perpetual view of evergreen scenery
and considered one of the handsomest situations in all the
Colony. The bay on one side—the meandering San Jacinto or
sacred hyacinth on another the back of it prairie and timber
standing in bodies and clusters like small islands of green upon
the broad waste of ocean—at this season the surface of the waters
are enlivened with vast shoals of water fowl from the majestic
swan to the smallest fowl of that class—are amused and gratified
in viewing them in their airy circles and graceful movements on
the streams. Shoot a number of different kinds which make dainty
dishes for our spare tables—get a pilot and sail up this beautiful
stream ten miles where we enter the mouth of Buffalo bayou—

this is the most remarkable stream I have ever seen—at its junction with the San Jacinto is about 150 yds in breadth having about three fathoms water with little variation in depth as high up as Harrisburg—20 miles—the ebbing and flowing of the tide is observable about 12 miles higher the water being of navigable depth close up to each bank giving to this most enchanting little stream the appearance of an artificial canal in the design and course of which Nature has lent her masterly hand; for its meanderings and beautiful curvatures seem to have been directed by a taste far too exquisite for human attainment—most of its course is bound in by timber and flowering shrubbery which overhang its grassy banks and dip and reflect their variegated hues in its unruffled waters these impending shrubs are in places overtopped by the evergreen magnolia rising in the grandeur of its excellence to the reach of deserved pre-eminence where it unfolds its far-scented magnificence; softening to the eye of admiration the dazzling lustre of its expansive bloom by agreeable blendings with the deep sea-green of its umbrageous foliage—the banks of this stream are secured from the lavings of the water by, what are here termed "cypress knees"—these are apparently exuberances of cypress roots and shoot up along the margin of the waters to the height of three and four feet and from 3 to 10 inches in diameter without leaf or branch; and so closely and regularly are they often found standing in lines as to resemble piles driven in purposely as security against the innovation of the tides—often along these shady banks have I rowed my little skiff and wondered if ever some Bard had consecrated its border shades by a correspondent flow of song—if some native Ossian had ever breathed forth in his artless strains the dictates of an inspired Muse. I thought of other streams immortalized, and thought that this might by its enchanting beauties give immortality to some future Bard—for it can not forever be "by fame neglected and unknown to song" and "creep inglorious like a vulgar stream."

Harrisburg is laid out on the west side of this bayou just below its junction with Bray's bayou—it is yet in the woods consisting of 6 or 8 houses scatteringly situated—the timber consisting principally of tall pine and oaks so excludes the prairie breezes as to render the Summer's heat almost intolerable, but this can be the case but for a short time—being situated at the head of navigation without any local cause for unhealthiness and surrounded by a vast quantity of timber which in this country must prove immensely valuable there is only wanted a population a little more dense and a few capitalists of enterprise and energy to render it one of the most important towns in the colony—here then we safely landed on friday the 4th. January 1828—we pass the winter in a small log pen our fire in one corner—have a great deal of rain for five or six weeks—no snow and very little frost—in all as to weather the most delightful winter I ever lived through. Shoulder our axes and build a fine large warehouse with a shed dining room—move across Bray's bayou into it—now feel ourselves comfortable—sitting in our own house—the work of our own hands and as the N. Western winds blow cool and chill encircling a large log heap at evening hour as a band of youthful brothers and as the spiral flames dispelled the gloom of night, so would we feel our cares our Secret griefs dissipated by the genial influence of social converse. "Home! sweet Home! receptacle of each fond tender tie that binds us to existence" this would be our theme. The winter passed away without the melioration of gentle woman's converse—there are it is true several married women—but these are seemingly of as rough a mould as their uncultivated and disagreeably rustic partners   there are but two unmarried females in the quarter, to me altogether, unpossessed of the *winning* graces of which their sex is so Susceptible. Several evenings the Doctr and myself made efforts to soothe "the savage breasts" with "concord of sweet sounds," but we found but little or no "music in their souls" By the middle of March have about two acres of ground cleared and planted in cane corn beans and a variety of garden vegetables   purchase a couple of houses and cut large timber for another—tear down those standing and construct with the whole a raft, consisting of four houses with board and stuff sufficient to roof them—collect our farming utensils kitchen furniture bedding etc and prepare for a voyage of 30 miles on a raft to the mouth of the San Jacinto at Hunter's Point—our league—Dr. Patrick myself and cook Frank compose the crew—first day's sail 1 mile— next day 2 by working hard at the oars frequently against wind and tide—second night endure a thunder storm—very heavy rain— cold and wet through—walking the raft a great part of the night— body ill at east—but mind solacing itself in far distant lands.

I go ashore and kill two fine fat turkies—catch a fish weighing about 20 lbs—live well while these last—fourth day we have sunk so that half our deck is under water—meet a canoe bound for Harrisburg send word for speedy assistance—same day meet the Schr. Pomona from Orleans for the same Port Send further intelligence of our *distress.*

Sunday—floating along. Sun beaming down upon us with almost intolerable violence land—our dog discovers a large rattle snake in the high grass—set fire to it—the wind rises and very soon the prairie for a considerable distance is one conflagration forming a truly appalling spectacle! in about half an hour great numbers of crows daws hawks and other carnivorous birds are hovering over this scene of destruction ready to devour the various animals found, ready roasted—a large alligator swims close up to the raft lands among the rushes—attacks our dog which escapes— fire two guns at him without any other effect than to drive him off—the fifth night after a day of toilsome labours land and lie down to rest—about midnight are roused by human voices—are boarded by Captn. Lindsay and Edward who had left Harrisburg that same evening at 8 o'clock and paddled a canoe 19 miles our whole distance in a voyage of five days—by this time our whole raft is under water except the two ends where boards were piled next day by hard labour against a strong wind reach the San Jacinto—1 mile from where we were overtaken—at this place is kept a ferry by Mr. Lynch—very hospitable and kind Yankees[1] acquaintances of Mr. Loring of Cin: here the surrounding country is very flat and void of timber immediately on the waters— we make our raft fast to a drifted tree and get into a yawl make for the landing and go to cooking supper—a heavy S. E. gale springs up—the tide rises several feet in a very short time and carries away our raft waves are rolling 3 or 4 ft in height— we all 5 in number man our boat and come up with the raft driving rapidly before the wind we jump on board waves dashing 2 or 3 feet over it a number of our logs are torn loose— are unable to get her ashore—our oars become unmanageable but one—are driven into old river—succeed in getting her behind a

---

[1]Perhaps the writer of the diary is thinking of Mr. and Mrs. Lynch. Cf. p. 57, below.

small point—by this time it is dark twilight—drive up close to an island of water flags. Lindsay and myself with the cable in hand jump in to the boat make to the flags—thinking to leap on dry ground I spring out am up to the middle in water a deep mud bottom thick set with rushes—am followed by Lindsay—drag our boat but find no diminution of depth—have some apprehensions of alligators—seen here from 10 to 12 ft in length—run a pole into the mud and make fast—get on board again—beds and utensils in the meanwhile put into the yawl by the balance of the crew—here we lay tossing all night in continual expectation of our raft going to pieces—toward midnight the whole heavens are wrapt in darkness—never did I witness so awful a scene—the thunder rolled and the forked lightnings glaring through the gloom made "night hideous"—thick "darkness visible"—the cloud burst over us—but already drenched we scarce heeded the descending torrents—about break of day the wind veered round to the N. west—then the billows struck us if aught more furiously—we knew this would soon blow out the tide and unless we escape soon our labours would be all lost to work we went with poles our raft which drew about $4\frac{1}{2}$ ft water dragging over the mud lifted and dropper alternately by the waves—almost despairing to get her out we redoubled our exertions Capn. Lindsay falls overboard—the sudden immersion into the cold water angrily dashing around him nearly proved fatal to him I reach him my pole and he gets aboard and to work again we get round the point in a shattered condition and reach the San Jacinto—wind and tide fair we construct a sail and pass on without breakfast or change of raiment. I should have mentioned that after being *cast away* and making the harbour above—we felt nearly exhausted and wanted our suppers—from which we had been so unfortunately driven about 1 mile. I agreed for one to venture the winds darkness and the tide after it—poor Patrick who was nearly spent and sick with fatigue—agreed to go as steersman—leaving Lindsay and Edwd. to watch I and Frank manned the oars—after turning the point and meeting the full force of wind and tide—we pulled our utmost for 10 minutes or more without any apparent gain— but persevering we got under the opposite shore and reached the goal of our wishes—taking a hearty glass and full rations we loaded and embarked again taking our faithful dog along who had

trustfully watched over the provisions during our absence—to continue—we past on prosperously down the San Jacinto for about
five miles when we struck on a bar   two or three jumping overboard
to their necks and the balance with poles we get off—our sail
still up we pass briskly down   we enter a small bay at the river's
mouth about 1 mile in breadth and several in length—here the
wind having greater Scope a Strong current and tide setting out
and the waves rolling higher than any we have yet passed through
we are apprehensive of two dangers—the one of being dashed to
pieces—the other of being carried out into the broad expanse of
the Trinity Bay—however not yet daunted we succeed by means
of our sail and oars in reaching our destined port an hour before
sun-set   after a voyage of one week precisely from Harrisburg,
we landed at Hunter's Point about the last of March—
and many an hour's talk and lively jest has this voyage afforded
us—young men who had thought themselves *brought up;* thus to
find that they in fact had "come down on a raft"—it was no
small matter for lively reflection and humourous sallies on the comparative merits of past and present situations—our descriptions
were to father rare food for merriment.   Father and Gregg who
had traveled down by land meet us on the beech—we accompany
them up to Doctr. Hunter's and spend the night

Turn to making improvements   get our houses out of the water
—establish ourselves in a small cabin about 10 ft square open all
around admitting a free circulation of sea breezes—continue here
about six weeks during which time we are hard labourers living
on coarse fair and subject to many inconveniences—we clear off
about an acre of woods and briers—fence in about two acres
plough dig and plant it—in corn potatoes and garden vegetables—
and finish putting up and roofing a fine warehouse

The Rights of Man arrives.   Gregg and Patrick return to Harrisburg.   Lyndsey and I remain a few days longer—here I receive
my first letters from the States four at once—am quite another
person   Such joys come not oft to gild the darksome days of the
wayworn traveller   One evening about an hour before sunset the
Capt. and I load a small canoe with our little household matters
fix up a sail take our dog Gunner aboard and set out for Harrisburg—we had not more than half crossed the little bay before
spoken of before a stiff southerly breeze springs—the white caps

begin to foam angrily around us and once pitched over the bow
of our frail little bark. I had command of helm and sail Captn.
sitting in the bow—breeze driving us along so as to create some
apprehensions lose my steering oar—fortunately find another in
the boat—night overtakes us—the breeze still brisk and lively—
see some swan and a flamingo—the most beautiful of birds that
float on water—deer also on the little islands that beautify the
lovely San Jacinto—driving on at the rate of six knots—we several times narrowly escape shipwreck upon snags and sawyers
reach Mr. Lynch's a little after his supper having sailed 10 miles—
they are very kind Mrs. Lynch is quite a respectable and amiable
woman—she and her husband came to this country in the same
vessel with my unfortunate and lamented brother Nicholas. She
spoke of him in the most flattering terms—departed Spirit of an
exalted mould I felt it was but a tribute due to thy excellent
worth!—next morning before 'tis light we sail—the wind soon
falls—and we have to ascend Buffalo bayou by force of paddles—
breakfast four miles above at Captn. Hiram's and reach Harrisburg at mid-noon—all well.

Find that Father and Edwd. had started some days previous
with a load of goods for Sanfelipe. The Doctr. Captn. myself
and cook Frank start with another waggon load for same place
about the last of April—which we reach the evening of secd day—
distance fifty odd miles—we passed over very little land of productive fertility most of the country being prairie we cross the
grand prairie—this prairie abounds with deer and Mustangs or
wild horses—it is beautiful to behold their lofty gambols and wild
manoeuvres unconstrained and unshackled by the thraldom of
Man. The grand prairie is here about 20 miles across its length
is said to be from 80 to 100 without a tree and scarce a shrub
to obstruct the view—it is all clothed with grass from one to
two feet in height the eye in its wanderings is lost for a resting
place and returns to the mind nought but the resemblance of a
boundless ocean—its billows, the pliant bendings of successive
swards before the unbroken blasts—its canopy the same cloudless
azure of the skies or dark pavilion of the threatening storm. After
passing through pine island, a small cluster of that species of
timber the first we reach for a distance of 15 miles and the only
watering place for the same distance we journey three miles be-

fore entering the Brazos bottom This is a low flat black rich soil from five to 6 miles wide well timbered and in many places covered with impassable Cane breaks—the greater part of this bottom is inundated by the overflowings of the Brazos River which happens at an average once in three years Sometimes two or three years in succession It is a stream of prodigious rapidity and great depth when full—it is scarce 100 yds in breadth at Sanfelipe from bank to bank. Sanfelipe is situate on the west bank on a high rolling prairie that here runs into the river it is composed of about 20 houses principally of hewn logs. Col Austin's is quite a commodious and respectable dwelling This town is centrally situated as the capital of Austin's Colony in latitude 29°, 45',—long. about 97°, 30'—there is a great deal of excellent land in its vicinity—much of it unfortunately subject to destructive overflows—it is also a fine stock country—the choice lands tho' for cotton and sugar on this river lie about 20 miles above and commencing perhaps at the same distance below, from them down to the sea board where lies the best land and being on tide much of it, is not inundated. Vessels do not yet approach nearer than within 60 miles of Sanfelipe—but at a small expense can be rendered navigable for small steam vessels the whole distance up 160 miles by water and 80 by land from the sea board. Sanfelipe can not be called a healthy place because of the inundations of country around by the River—this generally takes place in May— another cause is the prevailing South East winds blowing over a large portion of these stagnations must bear with it miasmata sufficient to affect of itself the health of the place it is thought that these causes may in a great measure be deprived of their baneful effects. There is however very little sickness prevailing this year—many attribute it principally to the great drought which commenced immediately after the overflow and still continues— notwithstanding these natural causes so powerfully operative against the colonial planter, there is more than one individual on this *Mississippi of Texas,* as the Brazos may be well termed if small things may be compared with great, who will turn out more than 100 bales of cotton and sugar cane proportionally—it is thought there will be a sufficiency of sugar made this year to supply both Colonies—Austin's and De Witt's—tho' in the former alone the census of last Spring makes a total of 3000 souls

There are several planters already engaged in erecting sugar mills and they have resolved to dispose of it at 10 cts   this is cheaper than it can be sold at here by purchasers and shippers from N. Orleans.   Many have their cotton gins in operation and the establishment of a cotton factory is already agitated.   Here also is raised some of the fattest and most delicious beef and bacon in the world at no expense nor trouble, the grass of the prairies and mast of the bottoms makes it all.   Salt is made abundantly and sold remarkably low and the waters abound with the finest fish, oysters, crabs turtles etc—the forests with Buffalo deer bear etcetera.   The Society of Sanfelipe is fast improving.   The laws are becoming better known and more rigidly enforced and the Colony fast disgorging itself of that corruption and moral depravity so prevalent in the first establishment of colonial communities   The colonists have no fixed code of Laws as yet—their legal   proceedings are regulated after the common and municipal laws of the United States of N. A. what statutory provisions they have hitherto recd. from Saltillo, Capital of the State of Coahuila and Texas, are modelled after the Civil or old Roman Laws—it being a constitutional provision there shall be no other Courts than Courts military and ecclesiastical—this is bringing into practice here the Code of Louisiana.   The young Society of Sanfelipe consists of two or three married ladies young and old 3 or four widows young and old, two or three young ladies—these compose the first class or *higher circle* and very respectable and measurably interesting folks they are; from amongst whom as the head of the *Ton* I would name Mrs. Long—widow of Genl. Long, shot in the City of Mexico six or eight years since—a short sketch of this lady must suffice for them all.   In person, she is tall forming what is called a beautiful figure, presenting the conformation of a delicate female endued with the energies of masculine vigour yet moving with a grace that is truly and wholly feminine—her countenance tho' not expressive of the fire of genius nor the striking energies of more than ordinarily effective talents yet is highly interesting—her features are regular—her aspect smiling— her eyes sparking her tongue not too pliant for a female being kept in admirable subjection to her excellent understanding—almost ever pouring forth the vivifying humours of her lively spirit and consequently very engaging in all her conversations—as she will now command all your sympathies in an artless and moving detail of personal privations and sufferings such as the hearer is ready to believe few such frames ever encountered and lived under —now she will fascinate her auditor by the ease and fluency with which she can descant upon general topics—addressed by the beau the fop or gallant, he does not find her out of her *forte*—a gay widow of about 35 she is agreeable where and when and as the manner and disposition of her company requires.   She has one daughter—a beautiful little girl of about 12 or 13. Mrs. Long is now residing with her brother in Law—Majr. Calvit at the mouth of the Brazos.   The most respectable portion of the male Society consists of about eight or ten—Married, batchelors and young men—four or five of whom are lawyers.   Col. Austin is a small spare little old batchelor without any remarkable intellectual qualifications, of rather a dry and reserved disposition tho' possessed of excellent common sense and considerable general information; altogether well qualified to be the founder of a Colony.

Mr. Gregg withdraws from the Co. and connects himself with some connexions of his on the Guadaloupe. We purchase thirty odd beaves and make preparations all of us except Andw. who remains at Harrisburg to drive them to San Antonio market—are prevented by the rise of the Brazos from crossing them   I volunteer to return to the mouth of the San Jacinto for necessary articles that had been neglected.   Young Eaton from Chilicothe Ohio accompanies me as far as Harrisburg.   We have a large Bayou to cross—at this time filled by back water from the river and widened 100 yds he plunges in and 30 steps from shore he and his horse become entangled—he swims out and with great difficulty the horse is saved—presently there come up a couple of Spaniards, we construct a small raft of brush etc to bear our saddles baggage etc drive in our horses and swim over.   These Spaniards were soldiers of Genl. Teranne's[1] escort—commissioner of the Mexican Republic, to meet at Nachitoches the United States commissioner for the purpose of determining the dividing line between the two Governments.   This Geul.'s escort consisted of 35 soldiers—and a number of attendant mechanics and servants— also a botanist and astronomer   they were several weeks at San-

[1]Terán's.

felipe. The Genl.'s coach was a remarkably curious construction—
after the fashion of the capital city—what that fashion is or was
can not be understood without a view of the indescribable machine
—suffice it to say that the long vista which discovers to the mind's
eye the gradual advancement of civilization arts and sciences
show'd me the unseemly vehicle standing in its proper place—a
splendid specimen of the ingenuity and cunning workmanship of
man when the last shades of the dark ages were vanishing from
before the dawning of the intellectual world. It was of a prodigious
size two or three feet wider than ours—constructed of huge pieces
of timber much carved inlaid and plated with silver—the hinder
wheels larger than those of Cin.:[1] and those before little superior
to that of a wheel-barrow—but to our journey—we travel on wet
and cold as night approaches, roads very muddy, drop down in the
midst of the Grand Prairie spread our blankets and slumber the
night away—next evening reach Harrisburg after a complete soak-
ing from a heavy shower—next day pass on alone—have another
bayou to swim—reach the Point—vegetables and peas we had
planted, flourishing finely—had a long search thro' the cedar
groves after a small pocket book supposed to have been dropped
by me, and which for its etc etc was thought invaluable—find it not.
Next day Dr. Hunter accompanies me Swim again the Bayou, a
large Alligator floating near—a very invigorating circumstance—
travel on till we reach the bayou near the Brazos—here we have
to raft and swim again—push on a new track thro' the Brazos
bottom—darkness overtakes us—never was I in such a dismal
place—nothing but a small horse path—the large cane meeting
above our heads form one continual arch—the eyes kept mostly
closed and body bent forward to force a passage—reached the
river almost famished find it swollen to an unusual height and far
extending over the lowlands. by means of a canoe the ferryman
takes us to his little hut surrounded by water—gives us some
supper—in the morning enter Sanfelipe having rode 160 miles

About the middle of June the river has fallen and the bottom
becomes passable Captn. Lindsay Dr Patrick and hirelings cross
over to collect our beeves—weather very hot and oppressive
—great difficulty in driving cattle thro' the bottoms—get

[1]Cincinnati.

but a few over at one time—the others escaping and getting back.
I am taken down with the fever—company return for the cattle
Edward in company—they drive them 20 miles up the river to
cross—my fever continues have Shakes or chills—am visited by
Mrs. Calvit and Mrs. Long in our Hall of Batchelors—my feelings
for such kindness were indescribable—the first females I had seen
from the first attack—am considerably restored by it and in a few
days after walking about—cattle are most of them bro't over.
In course of a week I set out with the Captn. to hunt the remainder we get lost in the bottom finally get out—discover the
cattle—set out again and in one day ride 50 miles thro' the scorching, treeless prairies—and two days in the dismal wilds of the
Brazos bottom at length get all our cattle over the river   Dr.
Patrick has a slight attack and recovers—about the 1st of July
my dear brother E—and I are attacked with the fever brot. on
by our extreme exposures and fatigues—on the 5th Lyndsay and
Patrick start with the cattle for San Antonio—on the 4th July a
great ball is given about 20 miles off—made up by subscription
of the colonists in honour of that day so glorious for what they
still feel to be *their Country*—my dear brother and I lying lonely
side by side on our cheerless palates none but father with us—
on the night of the 5th I receive a letter dated 7th April   it were
vain to attempt an expression of its effects situated as we were—
two days after I am able to ride about and gather strength very
rapidly—am able to attend on brother—he is able to ride a little
morning and evening—thirsday evening he called at Mrs. Wil-
kin's—presented Miss Jane with a couple of sheets of favorite
songs—friday morning 11th he rides about 1 mile to a Spring and
back—falls on his palate quite exhausted—for several days previous to this in my solitary rides over the prairies—I seemed to
have a presentiment that his death was near at hand—the thought
was ever in my mind—had he complained of suffering and audibly
mourned his afflictions—I should have felt more easy—but no,
no like the solemn stillness that precedes the tempest—so did he
seem to be awaiting the dissolution of soul and body—the patience
of the Christian—the pious resignation of the believer being beautifully exemplified in and throughout his last series of afflictions—
his fever continued rising till about the middle of the day—father
and I sat by him—he could not speak without the greatest pain—

father asked him where he felt most pain—with broken catches he answered "throughout—my—whole—system." Shortly after he became somewhat delirious—got up and walked into a room for water—lead him back—he sat up—I sat behind him and supported him for awhile on my breast in an agony of sorrow—father groaned aloud as he contemplated us. I laid him down—he complained of a great pain in his limbs—rose up and sat again—looked at father and exclaimed—"the lambs ought to be gathered." I was sensible at the time that his rational powers were affected by the fever, yet was this exclamation to me a consoling indication of what but a short time previous had been the joyous tenor of his thoughts. Dr. Nuckols arrives—attempts to stimulate, but the hand of Death was already on him—father and I both called on him—he became roused—we asked him—did he know the Dr.—from the manner in which he turned his head and looked upon him I was satisfied he was perfectly sensible—father and I had hold of his hands—he then turned his eyes on his beloved father for a few minutes—then turned them on me with a feeble farewell pressure of his cold hands—withdrew his eyes—fixed them on the heavens and in a few minutes we percieved that he breathed no more. Farewell! Edward, thou most dutiful and affectionate of sons; thou tenderest of brothers—truest of friends—most guileless of the children of men—short were the wanderings of thy pilgrimage, but they were toilsome mingled with sorrows—leading from the home of thy kindred—thou hadst no mother, no Sister, no gentle voice of womankind to smooth thy passage to the tomb, but thou hadst the tenderest of fathers the most affectionate of brothers. O, Edward thou hadst Him who sticketh closer than a brother—so that we rejoice in believing that, tho' thou hast fallen asleep in a far distant land—far from "the scenes of thy Juvenile days"—one of a little community budding in the wilderness—, "thy last days were thy best days." "Let me die the death of the righteous and let my last end be like his!"

He died on Friday evening about an hour and half before Sunset. Saturday evening was buried attended by all the citizens male and female who had had an opportunity of knowing how to appreciate his merits and who with one sentiment of respect paid this last mournful tribute to the worth and memory of the amiable the youthful stranger. Sunday I write the melancholy circum-

stances to my dear, only brother.　Father and I commence boarding at Mr. Whiteside's—in a few days father takes sick—he took
my hand and with tearful eyes said—"I fear we have been here
too long"—what a volume did these few words speak to my soul!
upon which a deadly apathy had seemed to have siezed.　I did
not weep I did not speak—but stood alone like a blasted trunk
already stripped of its branches braving the thunderbolts heedless
of the storm—with the attention of the Dr. and timely use of
restoratives he is stirring about in a week's time.　Isack B. Desha
is lying in the house at same time sick and a prisoner—he had
been apprehended some weeks previous for the murder of a Mr.
Early from Ohio whom he followed to this country for his
money　they land on our league at the mouth of the San Jacinto
last spring when we were at work there—they then came on to San
felipe where they remained till we arrived　Desha called himself
Parker.　He and Early then started alone for San Antonio—at Gonzales (90 miles from Sanfelipe) Desha was alone—staid a few
days there and went on to San Antonio—returned to Sanfelipe
sick—told different tales as to Early and was shortly after apprehended.　On the 23rd father is able to ride　about sunset same
day we start for San Antonio—father with a brace of pistols and
I with a rifle leading a pack mule—we travel by moonlight till
one o'clock and lay down in the prairie till morning　about mid-
day reach Judge Cumming's on the Colorado—father is quite exhausted and overcome by the excessive heat of the sun　remain
here till next day.　Judge has a fine young orchard of peach trees—
peaches just ripening—has a rich and valuable farm prairie; and
bottom land finely timbered.　Start again—cross the Colorado—
this is another rapid stream somewhat less than the Brazos—and
very seldom overflowing its banks—it is a much shorter river than
the Brazos and the country much healthier—we put up at Mr.
Beeson's—this part of the Colorado is about 25 miles from the
Brazos and becoming quite populous　as well as the last named
stream it has a grist mill on it and the frame of a saw mill—
meet with a large company of Tonkaway Indians at Beeson's—a
friendly small tribe.　Journey on thro prairie land five miles to
Scull creek—so called from a murder there committed 6 or 7
years since—find no water　a dismal savage looking place—turn
my head around and see an Indian with his rifle close up behind

father—tell him of it   he turns round and salutes him   find him
to be a Tonkaway hunter—he soon strikes off into the woods and
we pass on through a country thinly covered with post oak   find
no water till we have travelled 17 miles from Beeson's—this is
the first branch of the Navidad (nativity)   here we unpack, turn
out our horses, strike up a fire cook our breakfast and dinner—
rest about 3 hours—start again cross the main branch of the Navidad, a small branch at this distance from the gulph into which
it empties—good timber on it—continue on through a post oak
country, soil generally thin and sandy tho' well clothed with grass,
reach the main branch of the rio La Vaca (cow river)   this is
also a mere branch and forms the western boundary of Austin's
colony—the dividing line between him and Dewitt   cross it and
ascend a high and extensive prairie—the view here is almost
boundless the breeze is strong, bracing and delightfully exhilarating.
Father fancied he could almost taste its sweetness—the eye is
charmed with the loveliness and grandeur of the prospect that
here so opens on it—the deer and wild horses playing before us—
the latter more especially with arched necks lofty heads their
manes and tails given to the winds the regularity of their movements with a sudden wheel like thought and the wild terror issuing from their nostrils—all tending to remind us of Job's war
horse "clothed in thunder and swallowing up the ground"   these
give an animation and lively zest to the scenery that makes the
whole superior far to description—these prairies are interspersed
with what are termed islands of timber charmingly variegating
and destroying what would otherwise be a monotony of undula-
tions in the prairie—we cross a second branch of the last named
stream—a mile further and we camp at the third fork—we lie
under a large tree with a fine fire—the wolves keeping a terrific
howling around us throughout the night—this is the principal Indian range—many have been robbed of money and horses—in the
morning have a strong pot of Coffee and start—this day travel
thro' the loveliest country I have ever seen—the greatest stretch
of my imagination never pictured a scene to be compared with
this   we cross a 4th and fifth branch of the La Vaca—the last
of which stands in deep pools of the purest sweetest clearest water
I ever beheld   I stood on the bank and on the clean white rock
about 10 ft below the surface I could have seen a pin—these pools

are full of trout and sunfish—it is a most pleasing and grateful thing to contemplate them throwing in little matter to them and seeing them darting about thro the amber-like fluid—art has had nothing to do here   Nature seems to have chosen this region for her own fanciful pleasure works.

After passing this last branch of the La Vaca we ascend a very high prairie   the scenery here as much surpassed the former day's as that did any I had before seen.   I will not attempt to describe but only say that there are in Cin: about half a dozen young persons ladies and gentlemen whom I then wished with me—they are lovers of the sublime and the beautiful and with such—how delightful would have been the pictures of that day, as they seemed freshly touched by the inimitable hand of Nature   we ride on about 9 miles through this high prairie land when we enter post oak roads which continue on to Gonzales on the rio Guadaloupe   we arrive at Peach creek within 8 miles of Gonzales   here we find 6 or 7 men from Sanfelipe come to this place purposely to search for the bones of Early.   Our Compy. had found part of his clothes in said creek as they passed on—we stop and get coffee and venison—these men had found a scull bone but nothing more we saddle up and go on over a stony piece of ground for several miles then thro' a most lovely post oak woods open green with long grass and abounding with deer—by sunset reach Gonzales— find Captn. Lindsay and Dr. Patrick lying prostrate with raging fevers—they had been there in that situation nearly a week—the Captn. was lying on a scaffold in a little arbor of trees the Doctr. on the loft of a miserable hut burning up with the sun and fever.—father continues with them a couple of days—is much recruited and starts on with a traveller after the cattle—which a few days previous had been driven on by Mr. Gregg and hirelings. I remain to nurse the sick.   Doctr. more particularly becomes fearfully alarmed—after two weeks—Mr. Urban's goods come on— we get the Captn. into one waggon—the Dr. is sufficiently recovered to ride on horseback in Co. with the waggons   I start—have a wild animal to ride a pack to manage and the sick to attend to— but the fatigues the exposures—privations of natural rest that I was compelled to undergo—is past—and will not be attempted here in detail—we were seven days from Gonzales to San Antonio— distance 76 miles—the Country between those two places is principally a wild Sandy broken woodland country indifferently watered, commencing with the Guadaloupe—a narrow but deep and rapid stream—of great length and pure limpid waters. Gonzales stands on its banks—the Capital of Dewitt's Colony composed of 6 or 7 log pens—two leagues westward of the Guadaloupe runs De Witt's western boundary line—making the whole Colony between 40 and 50 miles in breadth and 100 in length running down to within 10 leagues of the sea coast—it contains a great deal of beautiful country—high rolling and healthy tho but a comparatively small portion is of great fertility. On the river St. Marks, which empties into the Guadaloupe 3 miles above Gonzales there are many great mill seats the water power being very great—this Colony contains but few settlers nor can it be expected to flourish under its present Empresario—Col. De Witt. This man has been raised among the pioneers of the western states—is well acquainted with Indian manners customs and modes of warfare—his has ever been an unrestrained life with regard to morals and religion—his situations have necessarily exposed and as it were compelled him to class and associate with those bold independent and but too loose and dissipated tho' brave and dauntless Sons of Liberty—introductors of civilization. Yet has the Col. been much in refined society—his education is considerable and his natural powers of intellect strong and vigorous—sufficiently so to render him well qualified for his station—but alas dissipation [and] neglectful indolence have destroyed his energies and are rendering in a great measure abortive the efforts of his colonizing assistants—he is tho' much of a gentleman and like his most excellent Lady is very kind and hospitable to Strangers. To our journey—we come to no more streams till we reach the Sewully[1] (Buffalo river) fifty miles from the Guadaloupe—what water lies between is only that which is found standing in deep holes formed by drains or sluices by which the superabundant waters are carried off in rainy seasons—these holes are 12—13 and 16 miles apart,—and between the two last named rivers the country is high and mostly sandy and thinly wooded—there is one stretch of 8 or 9 miles which seems to be one immense hill of the finest unmixed sand. I could compare our march thro' it to noth-

[1]Cíbolo.

ing but a slow journeying thro' a deep dry frosty snow—tho' widely differing in several respects—the excessive labour and fatigue to our animals—and the suffocating heat—it was early in Augt. we travelled along here — these Summer skies are un-clouded—and the Sun's powerfully reflected heat was preserved unchanged in temperature by the stinted growth of post oak, black Jack and Hickory, that stands low bushy but thinly over this great scorching sand bank. I really think the burning wastes of Africa would be but little more intolerable to the thirsty traveller, were it not for the grassy verdure which I found to my astonish-ment every where growing in luxurious bunches out of this seem-ingly sterile unproductive portion of the earth—these bunches spring up at distances of 1—2 and 4 ft so that when the eye is placed near to the earth the whole country seems one compact sur-face of the most beautiful green—we were nearly a whole day getting thro' this *fluid earth,* admitting the term, for the sake of *expression.* It was in this dreary region I feared we should have to bury Captn. Lindsay—and such were the Dr.'s apprehensions would be his own fate—here also and every additional day seemed to prove to me that my own constitution had undergone a radical revolution—for notwithstanding my weakness at Gonzales and labours daily and nightly—my copious perspirations, I seemed daily and almost hourly to strengthen and even to fatten—these causes tho' much more lightly operative ever produced contrary effects in the summer seasons in the more northern latitudes where I resided—upon the whole, as a result—I really feel myself al-ready acclimated tho' not yet wedded to Texas

We lie two days at the Seawully[1]—this Stream has but little water in the Summer or dry seasons its valley extends to a con-siderable distance on each side—is rich in soil and no doubt a healthy country—it is entirely unsettled My patients experience a change greatly for the better—I take the Dr. into the river, in the height of his fever and give him a complete bathing—Start on again—meet some of the drivers of our cattle from St. An-tonio—inform us of Mr. Gregg's extremely low state and that on the banks of the Seawully they expected to dig his grave—from this stream on about 10 miles we pass over a lovely country abound-

[1]Cíbolo.

ing with deer bear mustang etc—we then traverse a barren broken country for five or six miles, when we enter upon what is here called Musquite prairie—this is a very thin soil producing a short delicate nutritious grass—the Musquite tree seems to be a species of the honey locust, bearing a resemblance in the leaf and producing a long delicate thorn—also a sweet pod, in shape like that of the small black-eyed pea—the trunk and growth of the branches are more after the form and appearance of the peach—and indeed at a distance the whole prairie or country seems like one immense peach orchard—now on the decline having outlived Earth's giant race who strode over this region dropping a seed at every 10-yard-stride. The first appearance of this tree in travelling westward from the States is at Peach Creek near Gonzales—we cross the Salou[1] a small stream within five miles of San Antonio—Musquite prairie continues the earth here is covered with small smooth grey flint stones from an ounce to two or three pounds in size—the land is ascending for a couple of miles when we are on an exceeding high country—two miles further and we come to a Spanish fort and magazine commenced some years since and left unfinished—this stands on the summit of the circular ridge within one mile of San Antonio commanding a view of the town and the vast plain on which it stands—from this spot San Antonio has a very striking resemblance to one of Uncle Sam's handsomest and largest country villages—the curious traveller feels stimulated to urge on his jaded steed satisfied from this *first blush* that he shall be transported with a nearer view of its proportions its lofty domes—its elegant simplicity and natural beauties—he hurriedly descends the eminence in a fever of body and mind—comes to a little canal which he beholds with rapture extending itself abroad o'er the thirsty land and watering beautifully verdant and flourishing fields of corn—enters a regular avenue of huge cotton wood trees—thinks of the grand Avenue leading to U. Sam's house—asks who it was who so slandered this people by saying that they are but little superior to the lowest grade of the human family—surely the labour and utility of these canals—the beauty and taste displayed in the planting of this avenue is a flat contradiction to it all—he passes on—thro' the midst of this friendly shade—on the right stands a massy pile of ruins—for what purpose were

[1]Salado.

these stones piled one upon another and why were they thrown down—this he discovers was one of the strong holds of Popish delusion, in which the Royalists in 1810-11 sought refuge from the avenging fury of the Patriots who battered down the mighty walls with their cannon—it is now a garrison—A few yds before him he sees the exceedingly serpentine San Antonio, coming winding around the town and gliding by as if hurried with important despatches to the Gulph of Mexico—he looks with mortification and disgust at the order of architecture which suddenly presents itself on his left he crosses the little river and beholds the same wigwam style of building which constitutes the principal part of the town—he proceeds on finds that the streets intersect each other very irregularly presently enters the public Square this is laid off at right angles being about 150 by 300 yards in the centre of which stands the Church—a large clumsy stone building—that seems to have been standing for Centuries. It has a steeple of the same materials, very well modelled of octagonal form—in this is hung 2 bells kettle-toned and of different sizes—these have their tongues tied with ropes and are made to bellow most horribly by two barbarous boys who stand close by and jirk these engines of torture to the utter dismay and confusion of the astounded stranger perhaps 40 times per diem—this Church has also a skylight dome at the opposite end. In the midst of this Square the traveller stands and contemplates the buildings around him—he had before entering been disgusted with their dwellings that [he] first met— being formed of branches of the Musquite tree set up end ways in all the zigzag varieties of their growth having the interstices daubed with mud—these *hollow squares* are thatched over with the swamp flag and stand ready to receive their inhabitants who carry in a few chests a palate or two and some dried skins and the mansion is furnished. But the public square presents to the strangers eye a more solemn picture each side is formed of one unbroken solid wall except where the streets pass thro'—these walls have doors at neighbourly or family distances opening into what may more properly be termed cells than rooms—as few of them have windows—none indeed have sashes nor is their a pane of glass in the town—they seem more like port holes than windows—having bars like a prison grate; or dark shutters—these walls show no roof above them but seem to stand as we may suppose do the ruins of an earth-shaken or sacked and burnt City after the buildings had been battered down to the last story by a destroying and victorious enemy—these walls are about 18 or 20 ft in height   the roof is invisible from the outside—is formed of huge cedar logs as rafters on which are laid small boards—these beams have a descending inclination from the back walls outwardly so as to rest upon the front walls about $2\frac{1}{2}$ ft below their height.   the roof is then covered with a cement from 8 inches to a foot in thickness from off which the rain is conducted by wooden troughs passing thro' the walls and projecting 3 or 4 ft into the Square.   Thro' this square and the heart of the town runs a canal for the purpose of watering the garden lots, as the water by small outlets may be conducted from this to all parts of the place—the traveller hears around him a confusion of unknown tongues, the red natives of the forests in their different guttural dialects—the swarthy Spaniard of a scarce brighter hue— the voluble Frenchman—a small number of the sons of Green Erin—and a goodly few of Uncle Sam's Nephews or half expatriated sons—he feels himself now for the first time in his life a stranger truly in a foreign land and enters a door for a short residence that he may discover something more of this people— but what he has seen we will let him make known in his own proper person. I find that Father has obtained a house and opened his goods. Mr. Gregg is convalescent, tho' like Lyndsay and Patrick continues in a very debilitated state—business tolerably brisk profits moderate—some difficulty in dealing with the Mexicans, not understanding their language—form an acquaintance with two or three families—become some what a favourite with our landlady who has two pretty daughters—accompany them several times to the fandangos—waltzes and reels the principal forms of dance among them—always performed in the streets. Men do not select their partners—this is more gallantly left to the ladies—the former placing themselves in a line on the floor and when the latter arise and face the object of their choice—it sometimes happens that two or more make the same selection and then there is a good deal of elbowing among the fair ones—there are always managers to regulate matters—often solicited but never participate in the intricacies and mazes of their figures—delicacy forms but a small part of female character in San Antonio—their

very language seems almost to forbid the cultivation of this most
beautiful of the Graces—unmarried girls are very vigilantly kept
from all intercourse whatever with the other sex unless one of the
parents be present—soon as married they are scarcely the same
creatures—giving the freest indulgence to their naturally gay and
enthusiastic dispositions, as if liberated from all moral restraint—
The complexion of the native mexican is a shade brighter than
that of the aborigines of the country—the men are not generally
well formed in feature or person—are extremely ignorant in all
the advanced arts of civilization—the majority not being able to
read—they are astonishingly expert in the management of horses—
not surpassed perhaps by any other people on the Globe.   They
are completely the slaves of Popish Superstition and despotism—
distinguished for their knavery and breach of faith   The softer
sex are generally handsome in person and regular in feature and
of rather a brighter hue than the men eyes black, sparkling, holding most intelligent converse when disposed in the still language
of the affections—wear long black hair handsomely adjusted into
curls and puffs on public occasions—they are remarkably addicted
to dress and Jewelry and on festal occasions appear as richly arrayed as any females I have ever seen—exhibiting no small degree
of taste and are certainly among the vainest of their sex.   But
all this show lasts no longer than till they reach their homes, where
they instantly appear as if they might soon be numbered on the
Charity list.   The Gochapines[1] or European Spaniards that dwell
among them are exceptions to these remarks.   These are mostly
intelligent and wealthy—became acquainted with a daughter of
one of them.   And often have I regretted my ignorance of their
bewitching language.   She was of the middle size her person of
the finest symmetry—moving through the mazes of the fandango
with all the graces that distinguish superiority of person of mind
and of soul—her face was perhaps not sufficiently oval to be of
that form most admired as the model of beauty—her features were
beautiful forming in their combination an expression that fixed
the eye of the observer as with a spell—her complexion was of
the loveliest—the snowy brightness of her well turned forehead
beautifully contrasting with the carnation tints of her cheeks—a

[1]*Gachupines.*

succession of smiles were continually sporting around her mouth her pouting cherry lips were irresistible and even when closed seemed to have utterance—her eye—but I have no such language as seemed to be spoken by it else might I tell how dangerous was it to meet its lustre and feel its quick thrilling scrutiny of the heart as tho' the very fire of its expression was conveyed with its beamings. I felt lonely and sad as a stranger in that place and a vision so lovely coming so unexpectedly before me could not fail to awaken tender recollections and altogether make an impression not soon to be forgotten.

The 16th of Sept. the anniversary of the Declaration of Mexican Independence was celebrated with a great deal of order and unanimity and considerable enthusiasm of feeling. A stage was erected in the public Square very much resembling a huge bedstead with a tester and curtains reaching down like drapery to the platform and made fast to the four posts at the tops of which were flying their own National flag that of The United States, of Great Britain and of France—while that of Old Spain formed a carpeting for the stair case ascending to the stage. The Soldiery and citizens both ladies and gentlemen paraded the streets in the afternoon in the evening an oration was delivered from the stage by a Priest—was told it was an excellent and patriotic composition—but I thought badly delivered and apparently with but very little effect on the multitude—a large table was set covered with wines and other liquors, sweetmeats etc *"pro bono publico."* The Square was then lighted up with lamps and candles and every thing cleared off for the enjoyment of the "dearly loved fandango" five or six setts at it at once.—never before did I witness so large a collection of such happy beings. Thus passed off their day of Independence

Continue to be myself "chief cook and bottle washer" for our company of Invalids in San Antonio—have some amusements in teaching the girls A. B. C—and learning their language with them—old lady no longer afraid to trust them to my discretion— have opportunities of witnessing their manner of living. Every family has in the yard an oven built in form of a cone solely for the purpose of roasting the heads legs and tails of animals—on such occasions all the connexion round, are invited, skins are spread on the earth—when these delicacies are thrown down in the centre of the waiting circles, and every one that is fortunate enough to have a knife makes a lively use of it till the whole head is fairly demolished and as many of the legs as can be possibly crowded after it.   When they have to pay for their meat in market a very little is made to suffice a family   it is generally cut into a kind of hash with nearly as many peppers as there are pieces of meat—this is all stewed together.   The way in which they obtain their bread is worthy of notice.   They raise only Indian corn—this is soaked in lime or ley till the rind of the grain is taken off   it is then ground on a concave stone about 12 inches wide and 20 in length with legs cut to it 6 or 8 inches long—the hinder being somewhat longest so as to give the stone an inclination from the body of the grinder—a handful of corn is laid on this and masticated with another stone resembling a roller but cut so as to fit the concavity   this operation is always performed by the women, and in a kneeling posture—they generally go over it a third time—if they wish to treat their friends with very white bread the whole family gather round the pot of corn and grain by grain bite off the little black speck at the end of the germ— when the dough is already[1] a small portion at a time is taken and patted in the hands till thin as a flannel cake—this cake making operation is always accompanied with tunes and words that seem peculiarly to chime in with the patting ceremony   it reminded me very much of our tuneful ladies in a *finery starching* scene.   These cakes are baked on sheet iron and when eaten hot with butter or gravy are very palatable—but soon get tough—they answer the natives for spoons with which they all dip into the same dish of meat and peppers prepared as above—one spoon not lasting longer than to supply with two mouthfuls when a new one is made use of.   Very few families are supplied with the common necessary kitchen and household utensils—not even with chairs—sitting on skins spread upon the earthen floors of their dwelling   thus live the commonality throughout the northern provinces of Mexico.

The population of San Antonio is differently estimated from three to five thousand—they must rapidly improve with their increasing intercourse with the Americans.   There is kept up here a garrison of three or four hundred soldiers for the defence of the

[1]All ready.

place against the Indians but more particularly that very powerful tribe the Cumanches who are supposed to be 6 or 7,000 warriors strong and are continually at war with the Mexicans in some one part of the Province of Texas Saw about 20 or 30 of this tribe, who came in to trade—they are fine looking men—and the largest in frame considered collectively, I ever saw—are remarkably proud and overbearing toward the Mexicans whom they heartily despise Allways on horseback in their travels and warfare—are expert horsemen—use the bow the lance and the shield not having many firearms among them—their mode of attack is generally by arranging the lances in front, the guns in the center and bows in the rear—their horses at full speed accompanied with the fury and yellings of demons—they are among the bravest and most warlike of the Mexican tribes—friendly in their disposition toward Americans and dreading the deadly rifle. The Lapans[1] are a branch of the Cumanches and the next most formidable tribe in Texas. These two tribes range from the Brazos River to the Rio Grande and the mountainous country south of Santa Fee but are rarely known to molest American traders in those countries. Have abundance of figs peaches and melons here—very little attention paid to the cultivation of fruits tho' it is a climate very congenial to most of tropical productions—fall from a grape tree very seriously hurt—sell off our goods at auction—make arrangements for journeying to the east. Take a ride with Captn. Lindsay toward the head of the San Antonio river which rises 6 or 7 miles above the town or rather gushes a full sized river of the lesser magnitude from under one of the immense hills north of the town. We become bewildered among the hills woods and ravines and are disappointed in seeing the romantic spectacle but feel in a measure compensated by witnessing a few miles farther N the most picturesque and pleasing scenes of country that ever gratified our views—immense hills—extensive vales—barren rocks—luxuriance of verdure—deer starting up from before us and bounding over the adjacent landscape—blue mountains towering in the distance, as it were to shut out the view of infinitude—the whole lovely in its original wildness, and most impressively imposing in sublimity. Such is the scenery around San Antonio—forming an immense

[1]Lipans.

and complete ampitheatre 6 or 7 miles in diameter, within which nearly the whole plain is a rich and productive soile and may be watered at any time of the year by canals of little expense from the San Antonio river—and certainly there never was a stream better calculated for the purpose of manufacturing machinery— but all is in the possession of a people too ignorant and indolent for enterprise and too poor and *dependent* were they otherwise capacitated. Begin to understand the "common parlance" of the place tolerably well. Landlady and girls most willing to assist me—am asked all about *my country*—how far to it—how many relations I have—what religion they profess—tell them some were Roman Catholics—greatly delighted. By the by this family are pretty strict in the observance of their forms—repetitions of "Our fathers"—"Ave Marias"—"Credos" etc for indeed the religion of this place is understood by very few if any as a gracious affection of the heart and soul but a mere requisition of personal mortifi- cation in form of penances etc. Old lady very anxious to know when I would visit her country again—tell her perhaps in two or three years—informs me by that time her prettiest daughter will be marriageable and wished I would bring her some Jewelry with me—gives me a brass ring with a blue glass sett as a remembrance from her daughter whose delicate fingers at the same time were ornamented with more than one of gold—put it carefully in my pocket however, seemingly much flattered by the *distinguished* compliment.

On the evening of 3rd October leave San Antonio for Sanfelipe on the Brassos. Mr. Gregg having started some days previous with a company Father, Doctr. Patrick, Captn. Lindsay Myself and a traveller forming our Company. As we ascend the hill one mile from town look back and behold the sun taking *his departure* also behind the *western* hills—not a cloud to hinder the *warm* greeting of his farewell beams—the evening was as tranquil and serene as I ever witnessed—our hearts danced within us and our mouths spoke the gladness thereof—not even the great distance the toils and dangers that lay between us and our homes—could lessen the joyousness of our feelings—for we felt for the first time that the slow measured steps of our horses were *now* bearing us *toward* the land we loved best. Camp about 8 miles from town where we overtake a large company with silver and mules for

Louisiana—next day reach the Seawully[1]—meet two or three Mexican families moving to San Antonio with a small stock of horses cattle and hogs—they were making a part of their supper from a polecat—which caused a considerable space between their camp and ours these are beautiful little animals to look at and very numerous—tho' too offensive for near approach when they choose to make themselves so. Loose[2] our horses. See vast numbers of deer in the search after them. When found 'tis very late in the day—do not overtake the drovers till late in the night—in a woody country—tis very dark—discover their fires—come up and prepare our suppers Keep a guard out—about midnight are alarmed by the guard who came in from his post with the report that there were Indians or other persons heard going off at speed through the woods and thought that some of *our* horses were stolen. Captn. and Doctr. are too fatigued to accompany me. I mount a horse kept up for emergencies and after considerable riding discover and get all ours collected—meanwhile great preparations going on at the Camp for a desperate defence of the silver, et cetera,—morning at length arrives—father quite unwell from his exposures to the heavy dew and fatigues through the night—are consequently late starting—nothing particular in this days journey—meet a large drove of beeves for San Antonio market—reach the Guadaloupe and enter Gonzales about sunset—propose resting here a day or two—finished a letter to Rebecca and sent it by Mr. Burnet. Several small log habitations erected here since our last visit. With recruited spirits recommence our journey—reach Peach Creek, the dismal scene of Early's murder by Desha. Meet an old hunter who takes us to the spot where he had a few days before found the bones of that unfortunate traveller—they had been very much scattered and some broken by the wolves—he had discovered all but the scull and collected them together for the purpose of exhibiting and then burying them—reach that branch of the La Vaca which forms the dividing line of Austin's and De Witt's Colonies—find a house erecting. pitch our camps for the night. Catch some large sunfish from the limpid stream. Camp the second night three miles West of Scull

[1]Cíbolo.
[2]Lose.

Creek—hear bear in the night gathering mast from the live-Oak. Next day cross the Colorado and camp near Judge' Cumming's—arrive safely at Sanfelipe the day following—friends all well—continue here about one month—meanwhile brother Andw. visits us from Harrisburgh—is considerably recruited in flesh and spirits. Succeed badly in making collections. Father and I about the middle of November start for the mouth of the Brassos to meet a vessel expected from Galveston Bay—not yet arrived—hear of her detention by a Mexican cruiser sent on this coast for the capture of smugglers—become acquainted with the families of Doctor Wells and Mr. Bell—much pleased with them intelligent and amiable people. Father concludes not to return to Cincinnati before the ensuing Spring—but that I should go on soon as the vessel might be prepared to sail. In consequence return immediately to Sanfelipe to make new arrangements (60 miles). Return again with trunk and effects accompanied by Captn. Lindsay —meet with father—proceed southwardly to Brassoria—a town newly laid out on the Brazos about 18 miles direct from the sea coast—on tide water and well situated to flourish with the population of the country, having an exceedingly rich and extensive fertile country around and excellent schooner navigation—contains 4 or 5 dwellings and a store a duel fought here the day before with rifles—no blood shed. Go on down to Mr. McNeal's[1] within 7 miles of the Sea—this is the most intelligent industrious and hospitable family met with in Texas—hold a considerable number of Slaves and cultivate cotton to a pretty large extent—having a large and valuable gin of their own. Family consists of the Father and Mother—five sons, all grown but one, and a lovely daughter of 16—the beauty of the Colony. We continue in this amiable domestic circle 3 or 4 weeks anxiously awaiting the arrival of the vessel—pass off the time very agreeably in viewing the country deer hunting—bee hunting—grape gathering etc etc—get no tidings of the Schooner father and I start once more for Sanfelipe—I having determined to go on by land—reach Mr. Bell's—rainy season commences. Captn. John Austin arrives with a schooner of 60 tons purchased at N. Orleans to trade from the

[1]McNeel's.

Colony round the Mexican coast. We journey on through the rain and are two days in travelling to Mr. Brown Austin's[1]—a distance that in dry weather when the waters are low may be rode in 4 hours. Monday morning 15th Decr. take an early breakfast and start for Mr. Little's about 30 miles over a very flat sandy prairie country—travel all day thro' bogs quicksands and water—have to lie down on the wet prairie till morning am fatigued and wet to the neck with walking and wading my poney having given out— we suffer from the cold N. W. Decr. blasts, not having materials to keep up a fire—travel on next day striving to head the almost innumerable ravines and creeks which were overflowing their banks and a large portion of the flat country find it impossible to make our point that day—conclude to steer another direction and if possible reach Mr. Huff's on the St. Bernard by night—get into almost impassible bogs—horses can not carry us through—dismount and wade through mire and water for miles—father nearly exhausted and myself but little stronger not having had a mouthful to eat since sun rise the day before—get within a mile of Huff's by night—find it impossible to cross Snake Creek it being nearly a quarter of a mile in breadth—deep—full of growing timber vines and floating logs—turn out our horses, strike a fire and camp for the night—toward day commences raining—make a tolerable shelter from it. In the morning attempt to swim my horse through—fail and return and make a raft of logs with which I succeed after an hour of excessive toil in effecting a passage over— have a mile further to walk thro' high grass and heavy rain before reaching the house. Make a voracious meal of corn bread coffee milk and fat bacon having fasted fifty odd hours under constant bodily exertion exposed to wet and cold—got a suffiency for father and started off again thro' the rain taking a different rout as directed making the distance a mile greater—reach the camp abt. 12 o'clock—find father busy in restoring his fire which the rains had nearly extinguished despite of his efforts—his endurance of personal fatigue and exposure was matter of astonishment to me— he also makes a pretty hearty *break-fast*—we saddle up once more and reach Mr. Huff's—where next day a traveller arrives bearing

[1]A brother of Stephen F. Austin.

a letter with information that the expected Schr. Rights-of-Man had entered the Brazos—remain two days here with Father who has pretty well recovered from the effects of our memorable journey—having made our arrangements and plans and received his counsel and blessing we part in the firm persuasion of meeting again the ensuing Spring or Summer where above all earthly places we most delighted to dwell in thought.

NOTES AND FRAGMENTS.

MRS. NELLIE STEDMAN COX.—Mrs. Cox was the daughter of Ebenezer Hiram Stedman and Mary Warner Steffee. She was born on March 24, 1855, at Stedmantown, Franklin County, Kentucky. In 1874 she was married to Cornelius C. Cox, a wealthy ranchman of Lagarto, Texas, who had served in the navy of the Republic of Texas, and in the army of the Confederate States during the war between the States. She donated to the Texas State Historical Association a manuscript autobiography of her husband, in recognition of which, she was made one of the first life members of that Association. Mrs. Cox removed from Texas to Kentucky a few years ago, returning to Texas in the spring of last year. She died at the home of her sister in law, Mrs. Harmon Stedman, at Corpus Christi, July 7, 1908. Mrs. Cox was also a member of the Daughters of the Republic of Texas, a charter member of the Texas Woman's Press Association, and a pioneer in free kindergarten work in Texas.

ADELE B. LOOSCAN.

THE LAMAR PAPERS.—The Thirty-first Legislature passed an act providing for the purchase of the Lamar Papers. Under this authority the Governor purchased these valuable historical manuscripts on July 20, 1909, and had them placed in the State Library. The Lamar Papers number between 2500 and 3000 pieces, which vary in size and extent from a mere slip to that of a volume containing several hundred pages. The collection includes data and manuscripts collected by Lamar, and letters and documents either written by or addressed to Lamar. The character of the contents of this collection and its voluminousness are explained by two facts: first, Lamar held important offices in the Republic of Texas, being secretary of war under Burnet, vice-president under Houston, and president from 1838 to 1841; secondly, Lamar planned to write "a faithful account of the origin and revolutionary struggles of the Republic, that the children of the patriots, while they are in the full enjoyment of the independence bequeathed to them, may the more watchfully guard and valiantly defend the precious boon purchased with the price of their father's blood."[1] The papers were purchased direct from the daughter of Ex-President Lamar, Mrs. Loretta Lamar Calder, of Beaumont, Texas.

E. W. WINKLER.

THE TEXAS LIBRARY AND HISTORICAL COMMISSION.—Among the laws passed by the Thirty-first Legislature is that creating the Texas Library and Historical Commission. Notwithstanding that this law is a conservative piece of legislation, it took much hard work to secure its final passage.

The Texas State Historical Association was organized in 1897. In 1899 a bill was introduced into the Legislature which provided for the creation of a Texas State Historical Commission. The commission was to be composed of the Commissioner of Agriculture, Insurance, Statistics and History, and two other persons, members of the Texas State Historical Association, to be appointed by the Governor. The Commission was to have control of the State Library. The law then governing the State Library was to continue in force under the Commission. This bill passed the Senate.

The Texas State Library Association was organized in 1902. This association, with the co-operation of the Federation of Women's Clubs and the State Teachers' Association, drafted a bill which was introduced into the Legislature in 1903. The bill provided for the creation of a State Library Commission, which was to be composed of five persons to be appointed by the Governor, and whose duties it was to establish traveling libraries and otherwise encourage free public libraries. It was to have no connection with the State Library. The bill passed to engrossment in the Senate.

A bill similar to that of 1903 was again introduced in 1905. The name of the commission was changed to Texas Library Commission and the commissioners were to have control of the State Library. This bill met with opposition, and made little progress.

Nothing daunted the Texas State Library Association with its allies introduced in 1907 the bill of the previous session in much amplified form. The principal changes being the continuation in force of the law governing the State Library and the provision for

---

[1] An extract from the introduction to the projected history of Lamar.

a legislative reference section in the State Library. This bill failed to pass.

The bill introduced in 1909 embodied the substance of the bills of 1899 and 1907. However, the clause relating to traveling libraries was eliminated during its passage. The bill as finally passed provides for the creation of the Texas Library and Historical Commission, to be composed of three members appointed by the Governor and two members ex-officio—the Professor of History in the University of Texas and the Superintendent of Public Instruction. The duties of the Commission are as follows: (1) to control and administer the State Library, to collect materials relating to the history of Texas and the adjoining States, to preserve, classify and publish the manuscript archives, to encourage historical work and research; (2) to aid and encourage public libraries, and (3) to aid those who are studying the problems to be dealt with by legislation. The Commission held its first meeting on March 30, 1909, and is composed of Dr. George P. Garrison, Professor of History in the University of Texas, Chairman; Mrs. J. C. Terrell, Fort Worth, Vice-Chairman; Major George W. Littlefield, Austin; Hon. Richard Mays, Corsicana; Hon. R. B. Cousins, Superintendent of Public Instruction, and E. W. Winkler, State Librarian and Ex-officio Secretary.   E. W. WINKLER.

THE QUARTERLY

OF THE

TEXAS STATE HISTORICAL ASSOCIATION

VOL. XIII.   OCTOBER, 1909.   No. 2

*The publication committee and the editors disclaim responsibility for views
expressed by contributors to* THE QUARTERLY.

THE NAVY OF THE REPUBLIC OF TEXAS.

ALEX. DIENST.

IV. \

THE SECOND NAVY OF TEXAS

XIII.   THE MUTINY ON BOARD THE SAN ANTONIO.

On the evening of February 11, 1842, there occurred a mutiny
on the Texan war vessel *San Antonio,* which had just arrived from
Sisal and was lying in the Mississippi River opposite the city of
New Orleans. When the principal officers had gone ashore, the
seamen in some way procured liquor and drank themselves into a
state of intoxication. Their suspicious conduct was noted by the
officers left on board, who began to prepare for an emergency, but
did not suspect a mutiny. The sergeant of marines asked M: H.
Dearborn, officer in charge of the deck, for permission to go ashore.
Dearborn replied that no officer then on the vessel was authorized
to give such permission and advised the sergeant to wait until the
captain returned. The sergeant continued to argue the point; and
Lieutenant Charles Fuller, who was for the time in charge of the
vessel, came on deck and inquired the cause of the disturbance.
Some of the men told him that they wished to go ashore. He
then ordered the sergeant to arm the marine guard. This was
done, and the sergeant probably gave arms to the crew also. He
then approached Lieutenant Fuller and, after having first attempted to strike him with a tomahawk, shot and killed him. As

Fuller's body lay on the deck, it was beaten with muskets and cut-lasses; and two midshipmen were wounded in attempting to protect it. The mutineers then shut up the officers in the cabin, lowered the boats, and went ashore; but they were followed, and several of them were arrested, six at once, and others later.[1]

Soon afterwards the *San Antonio* sailed to join Moore's flagship, the *Austin,* on the coast of Mexico, carrying two of the mutineers and leaving nine in jail at New Orleans. On its arrival, Moore ordered the trial of these two by a court-martial, which convened on the *Austin,* March 14. One of them was sentenced to be hung, and the other was given further time to get evidence from New Orleans. These proceedings were approved by the Texan government.[2]

After Commodore Moore went to New Orleans to refit in May, 1842, he entered into a correspondence with Governor Roman of Louisiana concerning the prisoners remaining in jail there, and was informed that a requisition from President Houston would be needed to secure their surrender. The requisition was accordingly issued on September 12, 1842, and on September 15 Moore was directed to order a court-martial to try the accused as soon as the testimony of witnesses could be procured. The name of one of the mutineers was omitted in the first requisition, and a special requisition for him was issued on October 29.[3]

The prisoners lying in jail were surrendered to Moore just before he sailed for Galveston, April 15, 1843, and in accordance with the previous orders of President Houston a court-martial was ordered, which convened on board the ship *Austin* on April 16, at one o'clock. The court was composed of Commander J. T. K. Lothrop, president; Lieutenants A. G. Gray, J. P. Lansing, Cyrus Cummings, and T. C. Wilbur, with Surgeon T. P. Anderson as judge advocate. The prisoners were tried on the following charges: first, murder and attempt to murder; second, mutiny; third, desertion.

Of the prisoners, Seymour Oswald, sergeant of the marines, had escaped before the party was surrendered to Moore, and Benjamin

---

[1] See the *New Orleans Bee,* February 12; *The Picayune,* February 13; the *New Orleans Commercial Bulletin,* February 14; the *Telegraph and Texas Register,* February 22.

[2] Moore, *To the People of Texas,* 47, 48, 51.

[3] Moore, *To the People of Texas,* 93, 95, 99, 100, 105.

Pompilly had died in prison, confessing on his death-bed that he had killed Lieutenant Fuller. The court proceeded to the trial of Frederick Shepherd, boatswain of the *San Antonio*. After the examination of several witnesses, Joseph D. Shepherd, one of the mutineers, turned State's evidence upon a promise of pardon by the president. But for this the prosecution might have failed, as the principal witnesses perished in the ill-fated *San Antonio,* which was lost in the Gulf early in September, 1842. The testimony of Shepherd developed the fact that the mutiny had been planned and agreed to by the crews of the *San Antonio* and *San Bernard,* while these vessels were off the eastern coast of Yucatán in January, 1842. It was proposed to sell the *San Antonio* to the Mexican government. Circumstances forced the postponement of the mutiny till the *San Antonio* reached New Orleans.

The verdict of the court-martial after a careful trial is recorded in the following document, which was signed by every member of the court:

TEXAS SLOOP-OF-WAR AUSTIN,
August 18, 1843.
COMMODORE E. W. MOORE:

Sir: We, the President and members of the court-martial, convened for the trial of Frederick Shepherd and others, have the honor to transmit to you the accompanying documents, being a true record of the evidence and minutes of the court.

In discharge of the painful duty and the awful responsibilities imposed upon us, we have endeavored to confine ourselves strictly to the law governing courts-martial, and to the evidence that has been brought before us, and we have duly deliberated upon the verdicts returned.

In the trial of Frederick Shepherd, we are of opinion that there is no evidence before the court to prove that he was aware that a mutiny was to take place, or that he was in a situation to aid or assist in quelling one on the night of its occurrence. We have, therefore, found the prisoner *not guilty,* and recommend his discharge.

Of the prisoners Antonio Landois, James Hudgins, Isaac Allen, and William Simpson, we have only to say that we deem the evidence elicited at the trial of each and every one of them sufficiently clear and distinct to convict them each of the various charges and specifications preferred against them, and have therefore sentenced them to death.

We beg to call your attention to the evidence in the case of

William Barrington, from which you will find that he was deeply engaged in the mutiny on board the *San Antonio;* but it appears in the evidence that he informed one of the officers that it was to take place. In consequence of this information, the court has sentenced him to receive one hundred lashes with the cats.

Of the evidence in the case of John Williams and Edward Keenan, we think it unnecessary to make any comments. Williams, you will find, is strongly recommended to mercy.

Very respectfully,

Lothrop,
Gray,
Lansing,
Cummings,
Wilbur.[1]

In carrying out the sentence of the court-martial, Moore proceeded with due formality. On April 22, William Barrington was punished with one hundred lashes on the back. On April 25, Moore had the sentence of each mutineer who had been given the death penalty, together with the laws governing the navy, read to him before the assembled officers and crew, and warned him to be ready to die the next day. On that day, when all were assembled and the necessary preparation had been made, he told the prisoners of his duty to see the verdict executed; and that, as it was his first experience of the kind, he hoped it would also be the last. At noon the ship was hove to, and the four who had been condemned to death were hanged at the yard arm. Prayers were then read over each separately, and the bodies dropped into the sea.[2]

The conduct of Moore in executing the sentence of the court-martial which he had ordered was characterized, in a communication addressed to him by Secretary of War and Marine G. W. Hill, as murder; and, for this and other alleged offenses, he was, by order of President Houston, dishonorably discharged from the naval service of the Republic.[3] The action of the president, however, was sharply censured by a House committee of investigation of the Eighth Texas Congress; and, as to the charge of murder, a court-martial provided for by the same Congress declared Moore not guilty.[4]

[1]*Cong. Globe*, 33d Cong., 1st Sess., 2160.
[2]See *Cong. Globe*, 33d Cong., 1st Sess., 2160; THE QUARTERLY, VII, 223.
[3]Moore, *To the People of Texas*, 182-183.
[4]See p. 118 below.

XIV. MOORE'S EFFORTS TO FIT OUT THE FLEET AT NEW ORLEANS
AND HIS AGREEMENT WITH YUCATÁN.

While Commodore Moore was awaiting orders at Galveston after his return from the Mexican coast, he received the following communication from the secretary of the navy regarding the *Progreso :*[1]

DEPARTMENT OF WAR AND MARINE,

Com. E. W. Moore,   Galveston, May 3rd 1842.
     Commanding Texas Navy.
SIR.—
His Excellency, the President, has instructed me, for reasons appearing to him upon the petition and showing of the party interested, to direct that the prize schr. "Progreso," lately captured and sold, be permitted to pass the blockade, at present maintained, on the part of this Government, against the ports of Mexico on the Gulf, and to *enter any one* of said ports without hindrance or molestation by the navy of this Republic. . . .
     I have the honor to be,
               Very respectfully,
                 Your most obedient servant,
     Signed.   GEO. W. HOCKLEY,
                 Secretary of War and Marine.

Moore says the *Progreso* took advantage of this passport, and sailed under Mexican colors from New Orleans with four hundred kegs of powder while he was there, and that he could easily have captured her but for his orders. About the same time, Moore received another order from the secretary of war and marine which follows :[2]

DEPARTMENT OF WAR AND MARINE,

Commodore E. W. Moore,   3rd May, 1842.
     Commanding Texas Navy.
     Sir,—You will proceed forthwith to the Port of New Orleans, United States, to refit—the Schooners San Bernard and San Antonio will proceed to Mobile for the purpose of receiving such supplies as will be furnished by our Consul at that place[3]—the officers necessary for the committal of the mutineers on board the San Antonio will proceed from Mobile to New Orleans for that purpose.

---

[1]Moore, *To the People of Texas*, 61.
[2]Moore, *To the People of Texas*, 62.
[3]Moore says that the consul at Mobile was unable to furnish any supplies.

Convoy will be given to all transports of troops from Mobile or New Orleans to Corpus Christi. . . .
I have the honor to be,
        Your most ob't servant,
Signed.   GEO. W. HOCKLEY,
                                    Secretary of War and Marine.

A third order to Moore bearing the same date as the two already given[1] directed him to enforce the blockade ordered by President Houston on March 26, 1842. The causes leading to the proclamation of this blockade of the Mexican ports are given in the introductory part of a pamphlet issued by President Houston as follows:[2]

My Countrymen:—Repeated aggressions upon our liberties—the late insult offered by a Mexican force advancing upon Bexar—and the perfidy and cruelty exercised towards the Santa Fe prisoners, all demand of us to assume a new attitude—to retaliate our injuries, and to secure our Independence.

The attempt to secure peaceable recognition of independence from Mexico was found to be futile. In a letter written to Barnard E. Bee on February 6, 1842,[3] Santa Anna said:

I fully appreciate the problematic conditions of Texas; and I have before me the entire series of its consequences. I believe war to be necessary. I believe it a measure indispensable to the salvation of Mexico, and that her government will not faithfully perform her duties, if she does not strain her resources to the utmost, boldly to enforce a full confession of her justice.

Commodore Moore remained a week at Galveston, and pursuant to orders left on the 8th of May to fit out his vessels to enforce the blockade. He remained on board the ship *Austin,* and took with him the schooners *San Bernard* and *San Antonio.* To equip and provision the vessels and to pay the officers and men required a great deal of money, and Texan credit was low, but, while Moore

---

[1]Moore, *To the People of Texas*, 63. The order is printed with the date May 3, 1843, but a note on page 201 corrects the date to 1842.
[2]*Address of the President to the People of Texas*, Apr. 4, 1842.
[3]See *Austin City Gazette*, March 23, 1842.

had many promises of pay, he received very little cash. According to his own account he used of his private means and credit $34,-700 ;[1] and in later years his claim was allowed by the Texan Congress.

About one month after reaching New Orleans Commodore Moore was almost ready to sail; but on June 6 Commander Lothrop joined the squadron with the *Wharton* and brought the following instructions from Secretary Hockley :[2]

You will furnish Commander J. T. K. Lothrop with such men and provisions as you can procure for the brig Wharton, and procecd with the squadron under your command, with the *utmost possible despatch,* to enforce the blockade of the Mexican ports, in accordance with the Proclamation of His Excellency the President.

The *Wharton* had only nine seamen on board, was without provisions and ammunition, and would require an additional outlay of six thousand dollars to prepare her for the cruise. Though he had already strained his credit, Moore attempted properly to equip this vessel, meanwhile sending his brother to Texas for one-half of the appropriation of twenty thousand dollars made for the navy by the last Congress. In the letter which his brother bore Moore said :[3]

. . . not *one dollar* of this amount do I contemplate throwing into circulation, but if I had it I would be able to raise a sufficient amount here on my own paper, using the Exchequer bills as collateral security.

So fully did Commodore Moore rely on receiving this small amount for such an important enterprise, that he shipped two-thirds of a crew for the *Wharton,* contracted for provisions, arranged the manner of payment, and had arrived at the certainty of being able to sail with the whole squadron in ten days after his brother's return, if his mission proved successful. We may imagine his dis-

---

[1] Moore. *To the People of Texas,* 67. In this pamphlet Moore publishes many letters to prove that Houston, while ostensibly advocating war and anxious for the navy to proceed to sea, withheld the money appropriated for the purpose.

[2] *Ibid.,* 71.

[3] *Ibid.,* 72.

appointment when his brother returned, and he found that in place of the long-promised means, a shadow had been sent in the shape of President Houston's bond or obligation to pay over on Moore's requisition exchequer bills, when signed, to the amount of ten thousand dollars. The explanation sent along was as follows:[1]

The President directs me to say . . . that he has pledged himself, in the papers, that no further issue shall be made of Exchequer bills until the meeting of Congress.

The bond was absolutely worthless to Moore, and meanwhile what he had procured for the squadron was fast being consumed, and his engagements for future supplies were forfeited. Two hundred and thirty seamen had been shipped for the four vessels; but at the announcement of the failure of the government to send any funds the officers were disheartened, the seamen commenced deserting, and there was every prospect of a complete failure of the expedition. In this extremity Moore left at once for Texas, and returned the worthless bond of President Houston. He arrived at Houston July 2, 1842, and was at once closeted with the secretary of the navy. Among other documents he placed the following in the hands of the secretary:[2]

Mobile, 26th May, 1842.

Sir—Captain Seeger of the schooner of war San Antonio, visits Merida for the purpose of receiving the money for the draft of ($4000) four thousand dollars, given me last month.

I have also authorized Captain Seeger to make an arrangement with His Excellency the Governor, and yourself, for an additional amount of money to enable me to reach your coast at an early date, better prepared for a longer stay, and I sincerely hope that the Government of Yucatan can aid me.

I have the honor to be,

Very respectfully,

Your obedient servant,

Signed   E. W. MOORE,

Commanding Texas Navy.

To the Hon. PEDRO LEMUS,

Secretary of War and Marine,

Merida—Yucatan.

[1]Moore, *To the People of Texas,* 72, 73.
[2]*Ibid.,* 76.

This letter clearly indicates that Moore was looking to Yucatán to renew the alliance and to help the Texan navy; and the secretary of war and marine and President Houston were well aware at this time, both from documents and from personal interviews, of his plans. Yet there is no word of disapproval or of protest. This should be remembered in connection with the subsequent condemnation of Moore for the adoption of such a policy without giving notice of his intention to the proper department.

On July 5, Moore addressed a communication to the secretary of the navy[1] in which among other matters he drew attention to the fact that for the past two years nearly every officer had served without receiving pay, that many seamen when their time expired had to be discharged without pay, and that not an officer in the navy had a commission. He also said that the *Zavala,* which was lying in Galveston harbor unfit for service, must be repaired at once and caulked and put in the docks at New Orleans; "if she remains where she is with the water in her, the worms will destroy her in six or eight weeks." Agreeably to his recommendation, these matters were at once brought to the attention of Congress and suitable relief was given by it. Appropriations were made for the support of the navy, for repairing the *Zavala,* and for carrying out other recommendations made by Moore;[2] but as Houston would do nothing, all proved unavailing. The *Zavala,* which he was to repair, he allowed to become a wreck.

Moore says[3] that he remained in Houston from the 2d to the 23rd of July trying vainly to get twenty thousand dollars that had been a short time before appropriated by the Texan Congress for the support of the navy. On the latter date he called on President Houston, who expressed his gratification at having just had the opportunity to sign another bill making an additional appropriation for naval purposes of $97,659. Houston then asked Moore when he would return to New Orleans, and Moore replied that it was useless to return "without the means of raising money to sustain the Navy." The president then refused to put the twenty thousand dollars Moore was asking at his disposal, but offered to

[1]Moore, *To the People of Texas,* 78-79.
[2]Gammel, *Laws of Texas,* II, 813.
[3]*To the People of Texas,* 82-85.

give him a bond to be used in raising money on the faith of the appropriation. Moore said that money could not be procured in New Orleans by any such arrangement; that he had nearly exhausted his means and credit to sustain the navy and would go no further till he saw a disposition on the part of the authorities to aid him; and that he would return to New Orleans at once, "disband the Navy and leave the vessels to rot in a foreign port, as officers and men could not be kept on board without rations." The next day he wrote Houston a letter stating the necessity for his having the amount of the appropriation, and soon after he was furnished with exchequer bills to cover the whole of it except a small amount that had already been expended. But he found with the sealed orders which were given him, and which were not to be opened till he reached New Orleans, instructions to the effect that he was not to sell the bills outright, but only to hypothecate them, their value being thus seriously reduced.

The commodore arrived at New Orleans on July 31. He found the ship *Austin* leaking seventy-three inches a day, and at once made arrangements to put her in dry dock; other repairs were also needed on her and the *Wharton*. He now opened his sealed orders respecting the future action of the navy and found a proclamation of blockade for the Mexican ports, which was to be in force three days after its publication by him in the New Orleans newspapers. One of the reasons given in the proclamation for its promulgation was that a former proclamation of blockade[1] had been suspended, with a view to refit the vessels necessary for its effectual enforcement.[2] It is likely, considering the time of Moore's arrival in New Orleans, that the proclamation was published early in August, 1842. On August 19, he writes to the secretary of the navy that "he has not yet succeeded in negotiating for funds to get to sea. The pressure in the money market is unprecedented, and Texas liabilities are almost worthless." On September 7, he reports having made some progress, but still lacks money; and asks that the *San Bernard,* then at Galveston under command of D. H. Crisp, be repaired so as to join the squadron. She was not repaired, but was blown ashore by a storm in the month of September.

[1]That of March 26, 1842.
[2]Moore, *To the People of Texas*, 88-89.

On September 26, Moore received from Acting Secretary of War and Marine M. C. Hamilton a communication, dated September 15, containing the following statements and instructions:[1]

I enclose herewith, a copy of Proclamation, issued by His Excellency the President, revoking the order of blockade, published in March last, in reference to the ports on the coast of Mexico. Your "sealed orders" [for the renewal of the proclamation], dated 27th July, from this Department, are by consequence rescinded, and are hereby countermanded . . . You will not however, relax your exertions in consequence of it, nor will your activity on the Gulf be in the smallest degree impeded thereby. . . . You will proceed to sea without further orders; and . . . open your "sealed orders," which are herewith transmitted.

The proclamation revoking that of the 26th of March gives for its reasons that:[2] "treaties of recognition, amity and commerce have been concluded with Her Majesty's Government of England, in which stipulations are entered into embracing the recognition of Texian Independence by Mexico:" and "that mediation is now employed, as well as an offered mediation by the Government of the United States of the North." And it goes on to state that, these countries being desirous that the blockade should cease, Texas, being under many obligations to them, therefore revokes the order of blockade; and only Mexican war vessels and vessels bound for Mexican ports laden with contraband of war will be liable to capture.

The sealed orders enclosed with the secretary's letter were opened by Moore on April 19, 1843, after leaving the bar of the Mississippi, and he found that they directed him to cruise up and down the Mexican coast capturing all Mexican vessels he might fall in with, "both armed and merchantmen," and capturing cities and laying contributions upon them. They contained the following general statement: "The Department having great confidence in your capacity and discretion as well as your knowledge of international law, deems it unnecessary to give more detailed or particular instructions."

A letter from Moore of October 14 reports, among other things,

[1]Moore, *To the People of Texas*, 95.
[2]*Ibid.*, 96.

that on October 1 two midshipmen, F. R. Culp and George R. White, had fought a duel in which Culp was mortally wounded; and that on October 11 Captain Robert Oliver, commanding the marine corps, had died on board the sloop of war *Austin* of congestive fever. The same letter states that Moore has made every effort to raise funds, without success. On October 26 he again writes to the department that he cannot get to sea if the government does not furnish him with the means, that the terms of many of the seamen are expiring, and that unless they are paid it will be useless to endeavor to ship another crew. On November 5, Moore received a communication from the secretary of war and marine dated October 29, which said, among other things:

With respect to the detention of the squadron, I am instructed by His Excellency the President, to say, that he regrets it exceedingly—that it was very much to be wished that it could have been upon the Gulf; but that all the funds placed by Congress at the disposition of the Government for that branch of the public service, have already been placed at your command.[1]

Moore comments on this statement as follows: "Strange as it may appear, *not one dollar* of the $97,659 appropriated in July 1842, *had been or has ever been to this day placed at my command.*" In a communication from Hamilton to Moore, dated January 2, 1843, this assertion is acknowledged. Moore says, "The evident intention of this paragraph in the letter, was to impress the belief on the minds of the members of Congress while in 'secret session,' (which was no doubt then resolved on by His Excellency) that I had received the whole of both appropriations. . . . Moreover, I have been informed by several members that such was their conviction."

Hamilton's letter of October 29 goes on to say:

Nothing has been received in reference to the schooner San Antonio since she sailed for the coast of Yucatan in August last. Has she since returned?

If you cannot with the means at your command, prepare the squadron for sea, you will immediately with all the vessels under your command sail for the port of Galveston.

[1]Moore, *To the People of Texas*, 100, 101, 104.

This last clause contains the "order" to which President Houston in his proclamation of March 23, 1843,[1] refers as that for Moore's return to Galveston. This is the order that according to the proclamation was reiterated in the other orders that were disobeyed, and is the text for the various charges made against Moore of contumacy, disobedience of orders, mutiny, and piracy. If the reader examines the order critically, he can see that it was a provisional order for Moore to return to Galveston, if he found it impracticable to carry into execution the government's positive orders to prepare for operations against the enemy, which was still the desire of the government. Moore states that if this had been an unequivocal order for his return to Galveston, he would have been fully justified in postponing the execution of the order; for the enemy was daily expected upon the Texan coast, and the government of Texas would certainly not wish him to return to sea when unprepared to make such a defense as the vessels under his command ought to make.[2]

On November 19, 1842, Moore received from Acting Secretary Hamilton a letter, dated November 5, 1842, in which appears the following:[3]

Nothing can now be done with the San Bernard until appropriations are made for her repair. I much fear she is lost to the Government, and from accounts there is much reason to fear that the San Antonio is also lost, with those on board. If so, and it is impossible to fit out the two remaining vessels for efficient service, they had much better be in Galveston harbor than in a foreign port. With the hope, however, that some kind fortune may have enabled you to accomplish your purpose, I have the honor to be, etc.

The inference to be drawn from this, which is another of the "orders" cited in Houston's proclamation of March 23, 1843, is that if by any good fortune Moore can get his vessels to sea and cruise on the Mexican coast, he is to do so and the government will rejoice; but if not, then he is to come to Galveston.

The fears expressed regarding the *San Bernard* and *San Anto-*

---

[1] See *ibid.*, 168-170.
[2] Moore, *To the People of Texas*, 102, 103; THE QUARTERLY, IX, 22-24.
[3] *Ibid.*, 107.

nio proved to be only too true. On September 22, 1842, Lieutenant
D. H. Crisp writes Commodore Moore:[1]

The gale   . . .   drove me on shore and left me here in two
and a half feet water. . . . I am getting everything out
and putting on board the Galveston. . . . I am rather short-
handed, having but 20 men, and four on the "list." . . . I
think it will take me about two weeks from this to get
afloat. . . .

October 24, Crisp writes Moore again, saying:[2]

I presume the best plan will be to repair her [the *San Bernard*]
thoroughly and launch her— . . . at present I am doing
nothing to her—my provisons will last about three days more, and
then unless I hear something from the department I shall be
obliged to discharge my men.
The navy appears to be *hard up,* and I think we are finished. . . .
I hope we may hear something from the "San Antonio" by the
next arrival—I much fear that gale which drove me ashore capsized her—with my yards down it laid me on my beam ends, and
I believe would have capsized me if she had not driven
ashore. . . .
The boat has just arrived from Houston, and brought me no
news from the department. . . . so I shall be obliged to discharge my men immediately, and when the officers have eaten up
the rest, I presume they must discharge themselves.

From the *Archer* Crisp wrote on November 2 that he had received a letter from the Department informing him that nothing
could be done for him, and that he must do the best he could. On
November 8, Moore sent Lieutenant Crisp from New Orleans such
rations as he needed. These extracts from the letters of Crisp will
serve well to show to what straits the naval officers were put to
secure even the necessities of life.
The third of the "orders" cited by Houston in his proclamation
against Moore was dated November 16, 1842, and was received
December 1.[3] It simply instructs him to "carry out the instruc-

[1]Moore, *To the People of Texas,* 108. Crisp's letter was written from
the *San Bernard.*
[2]*Ibid.,* 110.
[3]See Moore, *To the People of Texas,* 111.

tions heretofore issued by the department, under date of 29th October and 5th November." Commodore Moore, on December 2, 1842, made reply to this letter, saying among other things:[1]

The San Antonio sailed from Galveston on the 27th August first for Matagorda and then for the coast of Yucatan—she having on board *over three months* provisions. . . . I did not mention her having sailed or the nature of her cruize, deferring it until her return, which I have been anxiously expecting for more than a month—but from news received from Campeche, two days since, up to the 15th November she had not been heard from, and I very much fear that she foundered or was capsized in one of the three heavy gales of September and October. The object of the cruize was to reconnoiter off the coast of Yucatan, and in the event of the people of that country holding out against the troops of Santa Anna, Lieu't Com'g Seeger was to communicate with the Governor and endeavor to obtain funds to fit out the Navy.

I received a letter from the Secretary of War and Marine of Yucatan in the early part of November, from the tenor of which I have been expecting funds from that quarter, but . . . I fear that nothing can be expected, . . . for the enemy are upon them by both sea and land. . . .

I have been compelled to discharge within the last month about *thirty men,* whose term of service have expired, and had not *one dollar* to pay them off; . . . and on the 14th inst. there are not more [than] *six* men in both vessels whose term of service will not have expired. Under this state of things the department will see the utter impossibility of moving the vessels from their present anchorage without means to ship seamen, . . . neither can towage or pilotage be obtained on the credit of the Government. . . .

If I had money to ship a crew and purchase the balance of our provisions and clothing . . . I could sail in a few days, and as the enemy are now on the Gulf (blockading Campeche) . . . I would not hesitate attacking them with this ship and the brig Wharton—every officer in the service is anxious, exceedingly anxious, to get off.

In this letter Commodore Moore also sends to the auditor the returns of the pursers, N. Hurd and F. T. Wells, up to the quarter ending October 1, 1842. And again he speaks plainly of his desire to form an alliance with Yucatán, and indicates that Comman-

[1]Moore, *To the People of Texas,* 112.

der Seeger is there for that purpose as he has been at a previous time during Houston's administration. Afterwards Moore was denounced as a traitor for carrying out this plan; but the statement of his wish to do so evokes for the time no criticism whatever.

On the same day that Moore sent this letter to Texas, the acting secretary of war and marine sent a letter to Moore at New Orleans, which President Houston in his proclamation represents as the fourth order that was disobeyed. The letter merely states:[1] "Sir:—When you shall have arrived at Galveston and prepared your returns, as heretofore instructed, you will immediately proceed to this place, and report to the department in person." In reply to this fourth order, Moore writes December 19:[2]

I forward the muster rolls of the sloop "Austin" and the brig "Wharton" by which the department will see how many men we have to take care of the vessels. I am still making every exertion in my power to raise money to ship a crew and get out of the river; nothing from Yucatan since last I wrote—have definite information that the Mexican steamer "Montezuma" is on her way to Vera Cruz.

On January 12, 1843, Moore received from the navy department the fifth order named in the proclamation as having been disobeyed. It is dated January 2, 1843, and reads:[3]

Your communication of the 19th ult, enclosing muster rolls of ship Austin and brig Wharton has been received. Any expectations that may have been entertained of realizing or in any manner making available the appropriation of the extra session of Congress, will certainly end in disappointment. It was subject, from the first, and still is, to such contingencies as to render it a dead letter on the statute books. . . . You will, therefore, report in conformity (if practicable) with your previous orders, at Galveston.

It should be noted that the last order rests on the condition "if practicable," and that the letter transmitting it acknowledges receipt of the muster-rolls which Moore had sent to prove the im-

[1]Moore, *To the People of Texas,* 116; the letter was received December 14, 1842.

[2]Moore, *to the People of Texas,* 116-117.

[3]*Ibid.,* 117.

practicability of moving the vessels at that time. He had also become involved by the use of his credit to obtain supplies. It was apparently impossible, unless by the use of his already overstrained private resources, to move the vessels even to Galveston. The only hope that remained was that Yucatán, now closely besieged by Mexico, would advance the means for defeating the common enemy. Through two friends Commodore Moore received aid to dispatch a very fast pilot-boat, the schooner *Two Sons,* to Yucatán with a proposition to the governor of that state. It was dated on the sloop of war *Austin,* New Orleans, January 17, 1843, and the most essential part of it is as follows:[1]

His Excellency, the Governor of Yucatan. Sir—
. . . In the latter part of August last, I dispatched the schooner of war San Antonio to Yucatan with letters to His Excellency, Governor Mendez, containing certain propositions on my part, the tenor of which were, that if the government of Yucatan, would send to me the sum of $20,000 to fit the vessels under my command for sea, I would pledge myself to sail forthwith for your coast and protect it from the invading force of the Government of Santa Anna . . .   The object in sending this communication to you now, in this manner, is to renew those propositions . . . if your Excellency will send to me by the schooner which conveys this, the sum of $8,000, I will, as soon after its reception as the utmost haste and dispatch will admit of, sail for your coast, [and] attack forthwith our common enemy, who are now blockading your ports. . . .

E. W. MOORE.

This proposition was favorably received by the governor of Yucatán, and Colonel Martin F. Peraza was sent to New Orleans with the money for which Moore had asked and with authority to conclude an agreement whereby Yucatán might obtain the services of the Texan fleet. The agreement was signed at New Orleans, February 11, 1843.[2] It was quite similar to the one that President Lamar had made with Peraza, as the agent of Yucatán, September 17, 1841.[3] The essence of it was that on condition of receiving from Yucatán money enough to get the Texan fleet to sea, Moore should

[1]Moore, *To the People of Texas,* 119-121.
[2]A translation is given in Moore, *To the People of Texas,* 125-126.
[3]*Ibid.,* 17.

sail as promptly as possible to Campêche and attack the Mexican squadron which was then blockading that port; and that after capturing this squadron he was to continue his coöperation with the Yucatecan government until the Mexican army should also be forced to surrender, for which service he was to receive eight thousand dollars per month. On February 24, Moore wrote to Acting Governor Barbachano of Yucatán[1] that he hoped to sail within a week.

The next day, however, arrived Colonel James Morgan and William Bryan, who had been appointed by President Houston commissioners to carry into effect a secret act for the sale of the Texan navy passed by the Texan Congress January 16.[2]

By the same steamer that brought them, Moore received a letter from Secretary of War and Marine Hill, which he opened in the presence of Colonel Morgan. It contained the sixth and last order cited in President Houston's proclamation of March 23 as having been disobeyed. On January 27 a letter was presented to Commodore Moore from the commissioners, enclosing another letter from the department of the same date as that previously received. The letter from the commissioners read:

New Orleans, Monday 27th February, 1843.
Sir:—You will receive herewith a letter from the Hon. Secretary of War and Marine of the Republic of Texas in regard to the vessels of the Republic under your command in this port: and we should be glad to receive your report with as little delay as practicable.

We have the honor to be,
With every respect,
Your obedient servants,

J. Morgan,

Signed

Wm. Bryan.

To Commodore E. W. Moore,
Commanding Texas Navy.

---

[1]Moore, *To the People of Texas*, 129.

[2]There was a third commissioner, Samuel M. Williams, appointed, but he did not serve. The secret act has not been found; its provisions can only be inferred from the act of February 5, 1844, repealing it (Gammel, *Laws of Texas*, II, 1027), which refers to it as authorizing the sale of the navy.

The enclosed order read:

DEPARTMENT OF WAR AND MARINE,
Washington, 22nd January, 1843.

To Commander J. T. K. Lothrop,
Or officer in command of Navy,

Sir:—Immediately upon the reception of the order you will re-port the condition of the vessels, the number of officers and seamen under your command, to Wm. Bryan, Sam'l M. Williams and James Morgan, who have been commissioned by the President to carry into effect a *secret act of Congress with regard to the Navy,* and you will act under and be subject to the order of said commissioners, or any two of them, until you receive further orders from this department.

I have the honor to be,
Your obedient servant,
Signed   G. W. HILL,
Secretary of War and Marine.

[Endorsed:]
Received February 27.

Moore was recognized by the commissioners as the officer in command of the navy, and therefore as the proper recipient of the order they enclosed to him. But they had previously delivered him an order bearing the same date—January 22—from Secretary Hill directing him to leave the Texan vessels under command of the senior officer present and report without delay to the Department of War and Marine at Washington. Moore's explanation of his conduct in the premises is that he followed a well known military rule in obeying the order received last, there being no priority of date.[1]

Everything that passed between Moore and the commissioners was apparently harmonious; no serious misunderstanding seems to have arisen; they seem to have had entire confidence in Moore and to have acquiesced in his every suggestion; and there is no protest on record from either Morgan or Bryan. According to the orders Moore had received and obeyed, he was to be guided by what any two of them agreed upon. There was no friction, and they agreed on all matters. Then, was not everything done in a legal way? And if any one was to blame, was it not the commissioners rather

[1]Moore, *To the People of Texas,* 130-132.

than Moore? Their instructions read that "should sickness or any other cause prevent the commissioners from acting jointly, they or either of them, may act in all things separately and singly, but not adversely."[1] Another point in their written instructions was as follows: "Should Post Captain E. W. Moore, not forthwith render obedience to the orders of the department with which you are furnished, you will have published in one or more newspapers, in the city of New Orleans my proclamations."

On March 10, Moore wrote a letter to the secretary of war and marine[2] fully explaining his plans and purposes and his obligation to comply with his agreement with the Yucatán government. The arrangement, he said, was one greatly to the advantage of Texas, and could be ended any time that Texas so desired.

On April 3, 1843, Moore received from Acting Secretary of War and Marine Hamilton, in a letter dated March 21, 1843, the following order:[3]

In consequence of your repeated disobedience of orders, and failure to keep the Department advised of your operations and proceedings, and to settle your accounts at the Treasury, within three, or [at] most six months, from the receipt of the money which has been disbursed, as the laws require, and as you were recently ordered to do, you are hereby suspended from all command, and will report forthwith, in arrest, to the Department in person.

On receipt of this Commodore Moore at once wrote the following letter to the commissioners:[4]

TEXAS SLOOP OF WAR AUSTIN,
New Orleans, April 4th, 1843.
Gentlemen—

The communication, dated 21st March, from the Department of War and Marine, was handed to me by one of you on the evening of the 3rd instant, and as there has been and is a singular erroneous opinion in the mind of the Executive in relation to my acts and motives, both of which are most seriously impugned, in order

[1]*Cong. Globe*, 33d Cong., 1st Sess., App., 1081.

[2]Moore, *To the People of Texas*, 137-138.

[3]Moore, *To the People of Texas*, 139-140.

[4]Moore, *ibid.*, 140. See also *Cong. Globe*, 33d Cong., 1st Sess., 2166; Moore, *Doings of the Texas Navy*, 11-13.

to preserve the Navy, (now ready for sea, with the exception of a few seamen) and save my own reputation, it is absolutely necessary that the tenor of the communication referred to above, should not be known to *anyone* until we arrive at Galveston, for which place I will sail direct, as soon as I get to sea; on my arrival, I will proceed in person to the Seat of Government agreeably to orders, and on my arrival at that place I feel assured that I can satisfy His Excellency the President, that so far from having any disposition to disobey orders, I have used every possible exertion to get the vessels in such a condition that I could venture on the Gulf. . . .

My "sealed orders" having been countermanded and others issued, I would be pleased if both, or either of you take passage to Galveston in the ship with me. . . .

I have the honor to be,
With high regard,
Your obedient servant,
E. W. MOORE,
Commanding Texas Navy.

Messrs. J. MORGAN and WM. BRYAN, New Orleans.

This letter gave entire satisfaction to the commissioners, and they united in the desire that Moore retain command of the vessels.[1] That the commissioners were entirely satisfied with Moore's action is shown by the fact that neither of them thought it necessary to publish Houston's proclamation; and they assured Moore that they were empowered by the president to act separately when it was not convenient for them to act jointly.[2] They made this statement to Moore, as he says, because he hesitated to act on the authority of one; and this he claims to have satisfied him.

XV. ENGAGEMENTS OF TEXAN AND MEXICAN NAVIES OFF THE
YUCATÁN COAST AND HOUSTON'S PROCLAMATION
AGAINST MOORE.

Commodore Moore left New Orleans with the ship *Austin* carrying eighteen guns and a complement of 146 men, and the *Wharton* with sixteen guns and 86 men, on the 15th of April, 1843. He was accompanied, in obedience to his invitation, by Commissioner James Morgan; and with him went also Colonel William G. Cooke, afterwards adjutant general of Texas. He arrived at the Balize on

[1]Moore, *To the People of Texas*, 139.
[2]*Ibid.*, 142.

the 17th, and was there detained by the fog until the 19th. On the 18th the American schooner *Rosario* arrived and anchored near him, having had a passage of three and one-half days from Campeche. She brought intelligence of the capitulation of the Mexican troops under General Barragan, near the city of Mérida, and of the division of the Mexican squadron, the *Montezuma* being off Telchac. On leaving the mouth of the Mississippi, the direction of the cruise was changed, at the suggestion of Colonel Morgan, from Galveston to Yucatán. The reasons for this were given by Morgan himself in his testimony before the court-martial by which Moore was afterwards tried.[1] In answer to questions from Moore, he said that while the Texan vessels were still within the Mississippi River, there came on board the *Austin* the captains of two vessels who stated that they were just from Campêche; that the Mexican and Yucatecans were about to settle their difficulties; that Barragan and Lemus had capitulated; and that Ampudia was understood to be planning an expedition against Galveston. The witness had therefore hazarded the responsibility of suggesting to Moore to go by Yucatán, on the way to Galveston, to prevent if possible the formidable invasion of Texas that Houston had predicted. He expressed his conviction that Moore, without this suggestion, would have gone straight to Galveston. In a letter to Moore, dated June 3, 1843,[2] which harmonizes, so far at goes, with the evidence given before the court-martial, Morgan states that he wrote from the Balize near the mouth of the Mississippi to his colleague Bryan, who was still at New Orleans, not to go to Texas at once, nor to write to the Department of War and Marine till he heard further from Morgan himself; for information obtained on the outward voyage might turn the squadron again towards Galveston. And Moore says that he and Morgan had received, just before leaving New Orleans, information that they regarded as credible to the effect that Mexico had pledged herself to England, in case she failed to prove her ability to reconquer Texas by taking Galveston before May 15, to agree to an armistice.[3]

Moore now sailed direct to Yucatán, and being much delayed by

[1]Moore, *Doings of the Texas Navy*, 12-13.
[2]Moore, *To the People of Texas*, 171-172.
[3]*Ibid.*, 145-146.

adverse winds, arrived at Telchac April 27, one day too late to meet the *Montezuma.* On the next afternoon he communicated with Sisal, where he learned that the *Montezuma* had passed but a short time before. On the evening of the 29th, he anchored within fifteen miles of Lerma, and the following morning at four o'clock got under way. [1]At daylight the *Austin,* under Moore's command, and the *Wharton,* under Captain Lothrop, discovered two large steamers, two armed brigs, and two armed schooners bearing down, evidently to attack them. The Texan vessels prepared for action and headed directly for the enemy. At 7:35 the Mexicans began firing. Some of the shot passed over the Texan vessels, and some fell short, but none reached their aim. At 7:50 the Texans began replying, and the engagement lasted till 8:26, when the Mexican vessels passed out of range of the Texan fire.

Moore then cast anchor within seven miles of Campêche. At 11:15 the two steamers again approached, and the fight was renewed between them on one side and the *Austin* and *Wharton,* assisted by two schooners and some gunboats belonging to Yucatán, on the other. At 11:40 the Texans, finding that their shot did not reach the Mexican vessels, again ceased firing. At 1 p. m. a few more shots were exchanged, but the distance made them ineffective. In the course of the engagement, the *Austin* was struck by one shot, which did no great damage. The *Wharton* had two men killed and four wounded. The Mexican vessels fared worse, losing fourteen men killed and thirty wounded. The *Guadalupe* had seven killed, and a number wounded.[2]

The relatively great loss in killed and wounded on the Mexican vessels is accounted for to no small extent by the fact that they carried much larger crews than the Texan vessels. They should have inflicted far more damage than they did; for the *Montezuma, Guadalupe* and *Eagle* carried in the aggregate four 68-pounders; six 42-pounders; two 32-pounders; and six 18-pounders, all Paix-

[1]For the account of the engagement which followed, see Moore, *To the People of Texas,* 151-153.

[2]Midshipman Alfred Walke, Journal (MS. in Texas State Library) for April 30. Captain Cleveland, chief officer of the *Montezuma,* died about the time of the engagement. According to Moore (*To the People of Texas,* 157), his death occurred on April 29 and was due to yellow fever; but Commissioner Morgan, in a report to Secretary Hill dated May 9, 1843, says it was understood that Cleveland was killed.

han guns; besides, the Mexican fleet had the inestimable advantage of possessing two steamers. The vessels of the Yucatán squadron joined those of Texas during the fight, and in any estimate of relative strength must, of course, be counted with them. While the combined fleet carried two guns more than the Mexican, the broadside was very much lighter. Colonel Morgan testified[1] that the entire crew of the Texan vessels considered the affair a jubilee occasion, and the only regret was that they could not close with the Mexicans and fight it to a finish. He adds that both Commodore Moore and Captain Lothrop managed and fought their vessels handsomely. The wounded men of the *Wharton* were sent to the hospital at Campêche and were soon able to be about.

On Tuesday, May 2, Moore, after giving his crew one day's rest, endeavored to bring the enemy into action; but with their three steamers,—for they had now been re-enforced by the arrival of the *Regenerador*—they were able to keep directly to the windward of him and out of firing range. Moore maneuvered for three days without bringing the Mexicans to action; but on the afternoon of May 5 several ineffective shots were exchanged. On the 7th, a few minutes after sunrise, he undertook to close with the Mexican vessels; but they fled under steam and soon left the *Austin* and *Wharton* behind. Not a shot was fired during the day. In order to give his crew a little rest, Moore ran into Campêche on the afternoon of May 7 and anchored, waiting for a breeze to resume his maneuvers, while the Mexican ships anchored off Lerma, some six miles away. On the 10th he took advantage of the opportunity to send a dispatch to Secretary Hill[2] acquainting him with the doings of the squadron.

Moore found on reaching Campêche that an armistice existed between Yucatán and Mexico, and that a treaty of amity was being negotiated under the impression that the Texan squadron would not come to the relief of Campêche. The naval battle of April 30 prevented the completion of the arrangement. While the vessels were at Campêche, the governor of Yucatán offered the loan of two long 18-pounders for the *Austin* and one long twelve for the *Wharton,* which Moore was glad to accept, and which proved very

[1]Moore, *Doings of the Texas Navy*, 18.
[2]Moore, *To the People of Texas*, 149.

useful in the action that came a few days later. With the consent of the governor, these two guns were afterwards brought to Galveston.

On May 16, Moore succeeded in engaging the Mexican squadron again, and this time there was much sharper work.[1] The firing was begun by the Mexicans at 10:55, with the *Austin* about two and a half miles distant, the *Wharton* about one-fourth of a mile further, and the Yucatán squadron in shore near these two. At 11:05 the *Austin* replied with its long eighteen, and the *Wharton* began firing also. The engagement soon became warm and lasted until 3 p. m., when the *Guadalupe* ceased firing, and the Mexican vessels could no longer be brought to close quarters. In the course of the fight, the *Austin* was considerably damaged and lost three men killed and twenty-one wounded. The minutes of the action state that at one time Moore ran his ship directly between the *Montezuma* and the *Guadalupe* in seeking to close with them. The *Wharton* lost two men killed by the bursting of a gun, but was not struck by the Mexican shot at all. The Mexican vessels suffered greatly. The *Montezuma* was badly damaged, and the *Guadalupe* almost disabled; and the loss in killed and wounded on the two vessels, according to the testimony of an English deserter from one of them, amounted to 183.[2] In this fight, owing to the short range of its guns, the Yucatán squadron took no part. The Texan vessels threw a much heavier broadside than the Mexicans; but, inasmuch as the distance at which the greater part of the firing took place made all except the long range guns unavailable, little can be inferred from the gross comparison. As Moore expressed it, the Paixhan 68-pounders of the Mexican vessels were tremendous guns, and the "hum" of their missiles was a "caution."

Among those killed in this engagement was Frederick Shepherd, who was one of the men charged with mutiny on board the *San Antonio,* but was acquitted. He was captain of a gun on board the *Austin,* and behaved himself with such gallantry as to win from Moore the strongest commendation.

On June 1, 1843, Colonel Morgan came on board the *Austin* from Campêche, bringing with him a proclamation by President

[1]Moore, *To the People of Texas,* 160-162.
[2]Walke, MS. Journal, entry for May 16, 1843.

Houston. This proclamation, though dated March 23, was not published until May 6, 1843. It is as follows:

PROCLAMATION.

BY THE PRESIDENT OF THE REPUBLIC OF TEXAS.[1]

Whereas, E. W. Moore, a Post Captain commanding the Navy of Texas, was, on the 29th day of October, 1842, by the acting Secretary of War and Marine, under the direction of the President, ordered to leave the port of New Orleans, in the United States, and sail with all the vessels under his command, to the port of Galveston, in Texas: and whereas, the said orders were reiterated on the 5th and 16th of November, 1842: and whereas, he, the said Post Captain, E. W. Moore, was ordered again, 2nd December, 1842, to "proceed immediately and report to the Department in person": and whereas, he was again, on the 2d January, 1843, ordered to act in conformity with the previous orders, and, if practicable, report at Galveston: and whereas, he was again on the 22d of the same month, peremptorily ordered to report in person to the Department, and to "leave the ship Austin and the brig Wharton under the command of the senior officer present:" and whereas, also, commissioners were appointed and duly commissioned, under a secret act of the Congress of the Republic, in relation to the future disposition of the Navy of Texas, who proceeded to New-Orleans in discharge of the duties assigned them and, whereas, the said Post Captain, E. W. Moore, has disobeyed, and continues to disobey, all orders of this government, and has refused, and continues to refuse, to deliver over said vessels to the said commissioners in accordance with law; but, on the contrary, declares a disregard of the orders of this government, and avows his intention to proceed to sea under the flag of Texas, and in a direct violation of said orders, and cruize upon the high seas with armed vessels, contrary to the laws of this Republic and of nations: and, whereas, the President of the Republic is determined to enforce the laws and exonerate the nation from the imputation and sanction of such infamous conduct; and with a view to exercise the offices of friendship and good neighborhood towards those nations whose recognition has been obtained; and for the purpose of according due respect to the safety of commerce and the maintenance of those most essential rules of subordination which have not heretofore been so flagrantly violated by the subaltern officers of any organized government, known to the present age, it has become necessary and proper to make public these various acts of disobedience, contumacy

[1]Moore, *To the People of Texas*, 168-170; *Cong. Globe*, 33d Cong., 1st Sess., App., 1082.

and mutiny, on the part of the said Post Captain, E. W. Moore; Therefore: I, Sam Houston, President, and Commander-in-Chief of the Army and Navy of the Republic of Texas, do, by these presents, declare and proclaim, that he, the aforesaid Post Captain, E. W. Moore, is suspended from all command in the Navy of the Republic, and that all orders "sealed" or otherwise, which were issued to the said Post Captain, E. W. Moore, previous to the 29th October, 1842, are hereby revoked and declared null and void, and he is hereby commanded to obey his subsequent orders, and report forthwith in person to the Head of the Department of War and Marine of this Government.

And I do further declare and proclaim, on failure of obedience to this command, or on his having gone to sea, contrary to orders, that this Government will no longer hold itself responsible for his acts upon the high seas; but in such case, requests all the governments in treaty, or on terms of amity with this government, and all naval officers on the high seas or in ports foreign to this country, to seize the said Post Captain, E. W. Moore, the ship Austin and the brig Wharton, with their crews, and bring them, or any of them, into the port of Galveston, that the vessels may be secured to the Republic, and the culprit or culprits arraigned and punished by the sentence of a legal tribunal.

The Naval Powers of Christendom will not permit such a flagrant and unexampled outrage, by a commander of public vessels of war, upon the right of his nation and upon his official oath and duty, to pass unrebuked; for such would be to destroy all civil rule and establish a precedent which would jeopardize the commerce on the ocean and render encouragement and sanction to piracy.

In testimony whereof, I have hereunto set my hand and caused the great seal of the Republic to be affixed.

Done at Washington, the 23 day of March, in the year of our Lord, one thousand eight hundred and forty-three, and the Independence of the Republic the eighth.

Signed, SAM HOUSTON.

By the President.

JOHN HALL,
    Acting Secretary of State.

On reading the proclamations both Morgan and Moore determined that it would be improper to attempt further hostilities against the enemy, and agreed to sail for Galveston immediately on receipt of sufficient powder to fight their way back if molested. The governor of Yucatán had none to spare; but he sent to New

Orleans at once and procured what was necessary for the two vessels and for his own troops. This took several weeks. On the 25th of June the Mexican squadron left the Yucatán coast in the night, and the Texan fleet was in undisputed possession of the Gulf of Mexico. On the 28th of June the Texan vessels left Campêche and on the 30th arrived at Sisal. After remaining at Sisal a week and making such collections as were still due from Yucatán to Texas and paying all accounts made by himself and crew, Moore left the Yucatán coast with the thanks of the people of that country and their best wishes for his future welfare. After stopping at the Alacranes a few hours to catch turtles for his men, who were in need of fresh provisions, the vessels sailed for Galveston and arrived on the 14th of July, 1843.

Thus gloriously for Texas was the Yucatán expedition ended and the object of the cruise attained. The Texan navy rode in triumph upon the Gulf, and Galveston and Texas were free from apprehensions of an attack or invasion from Mexico by sea. That the outcome was so unfortunate for some of its worthy leaders, was no fault of theirs; and notwithstanding the shame brought upon them by Houston, the great majority of the people of Texas applauded and endorsed what they had done.

Notwithstanding Houston in his proclamation states, "that this Government will no longer hold itself responsible for [Moore's] acts upon the high seas," the government of Texas did nevertheless so hold itself responsible; and he, himself, be it said to his credit, afterwards approved two joint resolutions for the relief of certain disabled seamen, marines, and landsmen wounded in the action of the 16th of May off Yucatán.[1] Among the number awarded half pay for life were Dick Streatchout, Thomas Atkins, John Norris, Thomas Barnet, George Davis, James Brown, and Terence Hogan; while Andrew Jackson Bryant was to have the same pension, so long as his disability from wounds should continue.

[1]Gammel, *Laws of Texas*, II, 976-977, 1011.

XVI. DISMISSAL OF MOORE, LOTHROP, AND SNOW FROM SERVICE, AND TRIAL OF MOORE.

President Houston in his proclamation demanded of all nations in amity with Texas "to seize the said Post Captain, E. W. Moore, and bring . . . [him] . . . into the port of Galveston, that . . . the culprit or culprits [may be] arraigned and punished by the sentence of a legal tribunal." Yet, strange as it may seem, the president was averse to doing this, when the culprit presented himself; and it was only by Moore's own persistent efforts that he was able to get himself tried at all. On the day of his arrival at Galveston, July 14, he addressed a note to H. M. Smythe, sheriff of Galveston county, saying that, as he had been proclaimed by the president of Texas a pirate and an outlaw, he had voluntarily returned and now surrendered himself for the purpose of meeting the penalties of the law. The sheriff replied on July 15 that, as he had not been asked to take cognizance of the matter, either by the president or by any judicial authority, he did not conceive it incumbent upon him to do so.[1]

While Moore was yet on board ship, after reaching Galveston harbor, he received also a note from J. M. Allen, mayor, saying that the citizens and military of the city wished to give him a hearty welcome and begged that the hour of his landing might be fixed in accordance with their purpose. When he came ashore, he was received with the firing of cannon and the applause of crowds. He made a speech denying that he had disobeyed orders; and Colonel Morgan, who landed with him, also addressed the assembled throng, declaring that he assumed the responsibility for the cruise, and that under similar conditions he would do the same again.

On the 17th of July Moore reported his arrival to Secretary Hill; and on the 21st of July he wrote again, saying, among other things.[2]

I am . . . anxious to appear before the tribunal which his excellency, the President, has expressed so much solicitude to the world to have me brought before.[3]

---

[1] For both letters, see Moore, *Doings of the Texas Navy*, pp. 20-21.

[2] For both letters, see Moore, *To the People of Texas*, 179-180.

[3] In this letter, Moore reports also the death of Lieutenant J. P. Lansing at Sisal on July 3.

On July 25, Moore received a letter, dishonorably discharging him from the Texas navy.[1]   The charges recited in it are identical with those given in the proclamation of March 23; but in addition, he is charged with piracy, for having acted as commander of the vessels after being suspended, and with murder, for carrying out the sentence of the court-martial in the case of the mutineers of the *San Antonio.*   On the same day William Bryan and William C. Brashear informed Moore by letter that Commissioner James Morgan had been discharged on April 3 and Brashear appointed in his stead; also that Commander J. T. K. Lothrop and Lieutenant C. B. Snow were discharged from the naval service of the Republic of Texas, and that Moore was authorized to turn over the command of the ship *Austin* to the senior lieutenant on board. Captain Lothrop was to turn the brig *Wharton* over to Lieutenant William A. Tennison.[2]   The charges against Lothrop were disobedience, delinquency, and contempt of his superiors in refusing to assume command of the navy on the arrest of Moore, April 3, 1843, or to recognize and obey the order of the Department of War and Marine to the effect.   Concerning this, Moore says:[3]

As an evidence of the *extraordinary* course which the government has ventured to pursue, in order to crush her victims, I will relate the fact, that the President has *dishonorably* discharged a patriotic and meritorious officer, in consequence of *his failure to execute an order which he never saw*—and the authorities *knew* this fact when the discharge was penned!!   The circumstances were these: A *sealed* letter was handed to Captain J. T. K. Lothrop in New Orleans, from the Commissioners, and was withdrawn by one of them (Col. J. Morgan) a few minutes afterwards, *before the Captain* went on board of his vessel (where it is customary to open special communications.)   It was returned, with the *seal unbroken,* when solicited by the Colonel who expressed himself pleased that it had not been read, as circumstances had arisen, which rendered its delivery no longer necessary.   He gave no intimation of the character of the communication to Capt. Lothrop.   All this was done by Col. Morgan with the full concurrence of the other commissioner (Mr. Wm. Bryan.)   It now[4] appears that the *sealed letter* con-

[1]Moore, *To the People of Texas,* 182-183.
[2]*Ibid.,* 181.
[3]*Ibid.,* 10-11.
[4]September 21, 1843, the date of Moore's pamphlet.

tained an order appointing Capt. Lothrop to the command of the squadron in my place—and he has been *dishonorably discharged* from the service, for not thwarting the *Government Commissioners,* by ousting me from my command in compliance with a commission or order, which he has *not* seen to this day!!

Lieutenant Snow was dishonorably discharged for leaving the *San Bernard* in Galveston, when—as Moore claims—he was literally starved out by the policy of the government, and was going to join the squadron at New Orleans, carrying with him and depositing with Moore some small arms, which were liable to be stolen from the vessel he abandoned.

Moore and Lothrop, and apparently Snow also, acknowledged receipt of the communications dismissing them from the service. Moore had already, in his communication of July 21 to Hill, expressed his readiness and anxiety for trial; and, in his letter of July 28 acknowledging receipt of the notice of his dismissal, Lothrop, after protesting against his treatment, continued as follows:[1]

I claim and demand, a fair and impartial hearing for the charges brought against me, and as His Excellency and the Department have not thought proper to render me that common justice I shall at the proper time appeal to a higher tribunal.

Seeing that President Houston said nothing, in his annual message of December 12, 1843, concerning the dismissal of Moore, Lothrop, and Snow or the charges against them, Moore appealed to Congress. He gained his point; the naval committees of the House and Senate of the Eighth Congress made a joint report[2] that was a complete vindication of Moore's character and conduct. Extracts from it follow:

In this case, Captain Moore was dismissed from a service in which he had made great sacrifices in sustaining the honor and reputation of his country, and deprived of a high and honorable station, which he had dignified by his official conduct and deportment, without a trial or even the semblance of a trial; and if such a course can be sustained or even excused in the functionary pur-

[1]Moore, *To the People of Texas,* 179-180, 188-189.
[2]*House Journal,* 8th Tex. Cong., 348-361.

suing it, it must be under the provisions of some positive law. . . .

The undersigned know of no law that justified it. . . .

If, then, there is found no authority in the Constitution for the exercise of the power which was brought into action on this occasion, the committee are at a loss to know from whence it was derived. If there is any statute which confers it, the undersigned have been unable to discover it; but in their researches upon the subject, they have found a statute, which expressly declares, that it shall not hereafter "be lawful to deprive any officer in the military or naval service of this Republic, for any misconduct in office, of his commission, unless by the sentence of a court martial." This law . . . has never been repealed. It was therefore in full force and operation on the 19th of July, 1843, when Commodore Moore was dishonorably dismissed, and deprived of his commission . . ., "by the order of the President," without "sentence of a court martial."

So direct and palpable a violation of the positive provisions of a statute well known to the Executive at the time he gave the order, cannot be justified. . . .

The undersigned, however, cannot discover in the papers and documents submitted to them, the grievous offenses and crimes imputed to Captain Moore in the letter from the Secretary of War and Navy, conveying to him the order of the President for his dishonorable discharge. . . .

With regard to the first charge, the undersigned have found abundant evidence . . ., showing that he [Commodore Moore] had expended more money for the use of the navy, than he is charged with having received; they therefore consider this charge as wholly groundless. . . .

And thus the committee went through all the charges against Moore, finding them all practically groundless. On the seventh and last charge of "piracy" they comment in their report as follows:

Without investigating this new and singular species of piracy—a species which seems to have escaped the knowledge of most, if not all, the elementary writers on international law, the undersigned deem it only necessary to say, that the facts submitted to them do not sustain the charge. . . . Captain Moore was in command of the squadron by the authority of the commissioners, which command, conferred as it was by lawful authority, was a full and entire removal, for the time being, of the suspension and arrest, which was intended to be imposed by the order of the 21st of March, 1843. . . .

But whether Captain Moore was guilty of treason, murder, and piracy, or not, it forms no justification, in the opinion of the undersigned, for the violation of a positive statute in dishonorably dismissing him from the service without a trial, or an opportunity of defending a reputation acquired by severe toils, privations and hardships, in sustaining the honor and glory of the flag under which he had sailed and fought. If he were guilty, the courts of his country were open for his trial and punishment, and he should immediately upon his return have been turned over to those tribunals; and if not guilty, it was worse than cruel, thus to have branded with infamy and disgrace, a name heretofore bright and unsullied on the pages of our history; and to have driven from our shores, as an outcast upon the world, one whose long and well tried services, all appreciate and approve.

The undersigned, therefore, recommend the adoption of the accompanying resolution,

> JOHN RUGELEY,
> JAMES WEBB,
> WM. L. HUNTER,
> H. KENDRICK,
> J. W. JOHNSON,
> LEVI JONES.

The resolution recommended in the report, after reciting "that it is due to Post Captain E. W. Moore, to have a full, fair and impartial investigation of the charges," provides that, as a court-martial composed of naval officers cannot be convened, it is made the duty of the secretary of war and marine to convene, as soon as practicable, a court-martial composed of the major general of the militia, at least two brigadier generals, and other officers next highest in rank, who are to constitute a naval court-martial. It was passed by Congress, and Houston approved the resolution itself,[1] if not the finding. The court was composed of Major General Sidney Sherman, Brigadier General A. Somervell, Brigadier General E. Morehouse, Colonel James Reily, and Colonel Thomas Seypert; with Thomas Johnson as judge advocate. The trial commenced August 21, 1844, and closed December 7, 1844; and the decision was made public through the press January 11, 1845. The charges against Moore were willful neglect of duty,

---

[1]Gammel, *Laws of Texas*, II, 1030.

with six specifications; misapplication of money, embezzlement of public property, and fraud, with three specifications; disobedience to orders, with six specifications; contempt and defiance of the laws and authority of the country, with five specifications; treason, with one specification; and murder, with one specification. The court found him guilty under four specifications of the charge of disobedience, and not guilty of all the other charges. The report of the joint naval committee of the two houses of the Eighth Congress will show that the orders included in the four specifications of the third charge were in part conditional, and that the others Commodore Moore could not carry out and so reported upon the receipt of them.[1] Thus it will be seen that out of twenty-two specifications Moore was found not guilty of eighteen, and guilty, but in manner and form only, of four. Not guilty was the real verdict of the court and of the people, and it was so recorded by the only historian[2] that mentions the court-martial proceedings. Houston himself considered it a full and complete victory for Moore as evidenced by his vetoing the findings of the court with the statement, "The President disapproves the proceedings of the court in toto, as he is assured by undoubted evidence, of the guilt of the accused in the case of E. W. Moore, late Commander in the Navy."

XVII.   FINAL DISPOSITION OF THE VESSELS OF THE NAVY.

When Moore and Lothrop returned on the 14th of July, 1843, to Galveston, with the *Austin* and the *Wharton,* the Texas navy had come to an end so far as active service is concerned. It is true, however, that officers were still on the pay-roll, and if the occasion had come for the use of the vessels they could have been used with much effect. That the navy was intended to be used offensively if necessary, may be gathered from the provisions of an act approved February 5, 1844, authorizing the secretary of war and marine to contract for keeping the navy in ordinary.[3] The

[1]*Cong. Globe,* 33d Cong., 1st Sess., 2166; Moore, D*oings of the Texas Navy,* 23.

[2]Thrall, *Pictorial History of Texas,* 618: "The parties charged were honorably acquitted." By using the word "parties" Thrall probably means to include Lothrop and Snow; but these, of course, were not tried.

[3]Gammel, *Laws of Texas,* II, 1027.

contract in the case of the ship *Austin,* the brigs *Wharton* and *Archer,* and the schooner *San Bernard* was to continue for one year unless those vessels should be required for the public service; and in that case the contractor was to be paid according to contract. It was further provided that the act approved 16th January, 1843, authorizing the sale of the navy, should be repealed.

Several writers have stated that the sale of the navy was never attempted; they probably gained this impression from the fact that the vessels remained in possession of the Republic. But the sale was attempted, as the following extract from an interesting and undoubtedly true account of it will show:[1]

All kinds of dire threats were made against any nation or individuals who should have the temerity to bid on the vessels. As the time drew near things waxed to the boiling point. Companies were organized and armed for battle to protect the country from the outrage to be perpetrated upon it. At last the day of sale arrived, the city was full of excited people, and Captain Howe was on hand with his battalion all in uniform and armed to the teeth. At about 11 A. M. an officer of the Republic appeared at the place of sale and announced the property for sale to the highest bidder. The people waited in breathless anxiety and with thumping hearts to see who was going to offer to buy. But after a short suspense it was knocked off to the Republic of Texas. You can imagine the effect of dropping a piece of ice on a white hot iron. The temperature went down like when a blue norther strikes the country. I venture to say; that the warlike spirit of Galveston has never been at so high a pitch, nor never been cooled off so suddenly since.

Lieutenant William A. Tennison was placed in charge of the vessels in ordinary and remained so until late in September, 1844, when, on account of sickness, he was relieved of the command, and William C. Brashear was commissioned to take charge of them, Tennison being directed to report to him. Those who have followed the history of the annexation of Texas to the United States can easily understand why the navy was not needed after being placed in ordinary. It was because the United States government itself undertook the protection of Texas against Mexico from the day on which the treaty of annexation was signed, and because,

[1]Emeline Brighton Russel, in *Galveston News,* October 20, 1901.

just previous to that event it ordered a naval force to the Gulf for the purpose. The promise that such action would be taken was made by W. S. Murphy, the United States *chargé* in Texas, soon after the statute providing that the Texan fleet should be laid up in ordinary was passed.[1] The navy of Texas was therefore no longer a necessity; and it was left in ordinary until annexation took place.

The joint resolution by which annexation was effected provided that the Texan navy should be ceded to the United States. The transfer was made by Lieutenant William A. Tennison, who was then in command of the vessels, and he states that it took place in June, 1846. He was left in charge till August, when, finding that he was not recognized as an officer of the United States government, he turned the vessels over to the care of Midshipman C. J. Faysoux.[2] The vessels transferred were the ship *Austin* of twenty guns, the brig *Wharton* of eighteen guns, the brig *Archer,* eighteen guns, and the schooner *San Bernard,* seven guns.[3]

XVIII. THE OFFICERS OF THE TEXAS NAVY.

When Commodore Moore and Captain Lothrop were discharged from the service by President Houston, the officers of the Texas navy, with but three exceptions, through sympathy with the discharged officers, and as an expression of their displeasure, tendered their resignations. No notice was taken of their action by the Department of War and Marine, and they were virtually in the situation of officers on leave of absence, without pay or the right

[1]Tyler, *Letters and Times of the Tylers,* II, 287-288.

[2]Tennison's Journal, folio 394, p. 1. There have been found at Washington only three papers relating to the transfer: 1 a list of officers of the Texan navy and a statement of pay due them; 2. an abstract of unpaid bills for supplies furnished the navy from February 16, to May 11, 1846; 3. a muster roll of the officers attached to the navy in ordinary, February 16, 1846.

[3]Thrall is in an error when he says, page 340, that the *San Jacinto* was one of the vessels transferred. The *San Jacinto* was lost in 1840 (see THE QUARTERLY, XIII, 26). He is also in error in stating that the *San Bernard* was destroyed in 1842 in a storm; she was only badly damaged and was later repaired. Finally, he is mistaken in saying that the *Zavala* was wrecked in the same storm. She was in bad repair early in 1842 and was run ashore on the flats in Galveston harbor to prevent her sinking. There she was permitted to lie until the worms made her unfit for repairs, when she was broken up and sold in 1844 (Moore, *Doings of the Texas Navy,* 6). Brown, II, 199, copies Thrall's errors.

to engage in any livelihood.[1] When annexation was consummated, they fully hoped to be attached to the United States naval establishment on the strength of the clause in the treaty of annexation providing that Texas, when admitted to the Union, should cede to the United States, among other means of defense, her navy. To the destruction of all their hopes, the Navy Department at Washington interpreted this to include only the vessels, and not the officers. Commodore Moore and others of the officers at once prepared a memorial and presented it to the House of Representatives, and it was referred to the committee on naval affairs. The committee, after carefully investigating their claims, reported a bill for their incorporation into the navy of the United States in comformity with the terms of the resolutions of annexation which formed the compact of union between the United States and Texas.[2] The method proposed was to repeal the limitation fixed by the statute of August 4, 1842, upon the number of officers and give the president authority to appoint the Texan officers to places in the service, with the proviso that these extra places should not be continued longer than they were held by the incumbents for whom they were specially provided.[3] The officers of the United States navy were bitterly opposed to this measure and appointed Commanders Buchanan, Dupont, and Magruder to direct their opposition. Their position was that the proposed arrangement would have the effect of elevating Moore, Tod, and others, who had been only lieutenants while they were in the United States navy, over those who were at that time their superiors; and of giving still others marked promotions without their having undergone due probation service. They interpreted the word "navy" in the resolution of annexation as meaning vessels only, and not including officers. This interpretation was in harmony with the opinion of the Supreme Court of the United States in the case of one of the Texan officers who had endeavored by *mandamus* to compel Secretary Mason to pay him his salary as an officer of the United States navy.[4] In this argu-

[1]Moore, *To the People of Texas*, 190, 191.

[2]*House Reports*, 31st Cong., 1st Sess., II (Serial No. 584), Rep., 288.

[3]Buchanan, Dupont, and Magruder, *In relation to the Claims of the Officers of the late Texas Navy*, 1.

[4]Brashear *vs*. Mason, 6 Howard, 92, 99, 100.

ment Buchanan, Dupont, and Magruder undoubtedly had the better of the Texans. But when they attempted to deal with the history of the Texas navy their statements are successfully challenged by Moore, and their arguments shown to be fallacious.

Special objections were raised to the appointment of either Moore or John G. Tod as an officer of the United States navy. A bitter fight was made against Moore on the ground that his dismissal from service by President Houston barred him from any participation in the benefits of the bill, even if it should be passed. In the midst of the controversy, a pamphlet containing, among other documents prejudicial to Moore, a copy of the message of President Jones vetoing a bill to return to him a portion of the money he had advanced for the use of the Texas navy on the ground that he was a defaulter, appeared in Washington. The publication and circulation of this pamphlet Moore attributed to Houston,[1] and in answer he wrote his *Doings of the Texas Navy.* In reply to the denial of his status as an officer of the Texas navy at the time of annexation, and to the charge of being a defaulter, Moore adduced the resolution of the Senate of Texas adopted June 28, 1845, declaring that his trial by court-martial was "final and conclusive";[2] and two resolutions by the House adopted the same day, one of which declared that the finding of the court fully entitled him to continue in his place as commander of the Texas navy, and the other that the thanks of the Republic were justly due him and those under his command in its service.[3]

As to Tod, the United States naval commanders thought he was not justly entitled to be included in the list of officers connected with the Texas navy at the time of annexation, inasmuch as his commission as captain in the navy of Texas from June, 1840, was made out after the United States flag was flying over the Capitol building in Texas. Tod was given his rank by President Anson Jones, who was a bitter enemy of Commodore Moore. Jones interpreted Houston's act dismissing Moore as final and appointed Tod to take his place; and the United States officers claimed that, as Tod had never been confirmed by the Senate, his commission

[1]*Doings of the Texas Navy,* 3, 32.
[2]*Senate Journal.* 9th Tex. Cong., 2d Sess., 75.
[3]*House Journal,* 9th Tex. Cong., 2d Sess., 86.

was a nullity. In order fairly to present Captain Tod's position, it is necessary briefly to recount some facts of his career.[1] It will be recalled that Moore had charged Tod with negligence when acting as agent, in allowing poor wood to be used in the construction of the *Austin*. Tod evidently sought redress at the hands of the Texas Congress, for shortly afterwards we find, upon the petition of Captain John G. Tod, a concurrent resolution introduced and passed thanking Tod for "his faithful and important services rendered to the country," and requesting the president to order a copy of the resolution to be read at the navy yard, on board each public vessel in commission, in the presence of officers and crew, and to be entered upon their log books. The president promptly sent a message vetoing the joint resolution of thanks to Tod; but the resolution was reconsidered January 31, 1842, and passed over his veto.[2] There is nothing to show whether or not Moore had to swallow this bitter pill. Captain Tod served Texas as a naval officer until 1842, when, at his own suggestion, in order to curtail the expenses of the government, he yielded his position. In later years when the Texan officers received back pay, Captain Tod was denied the benefits of the arrangement, the secretary of the navy insisting that his commission was void. Texans, however, would not admit the point, claiming that annexation was not fully consummated until the Republic of Texas yielded its power and authority to the State of Texas, which took place on February 19, 1846. Repeated resolutions of thanks and endorsements from the Texas Congress show in what high esteem Captain Tod was held in Texas; and at the request of the Texas senators and representatives Tod was at last paid equally with the other officers connected with the Texas navy at the time of annexation.[3] He died in 1878.

The efforts made during the years 1847 to 1850 to get any favorable action from the government of the United States toward Texas naval officers ended in failure. In 1852 the endeavor was renewed; a joint resolution was passed by the Texas Legislature once more instructing the Senators and requesting the Representa-

---

[1]See THE QUARTERLY, XIII, 9, 10, 11, 12, 35.

[2]*Senate Journal*, 6th Tex. Cong., 138, 139, 195, 198.

[3]Gammel, *Laws of Texas*, VI, 1063; *House Reports*, 46th Cong., 2d Sess., IV.

tives to use their influence to procure the incorporation of the officers into the navy of the United States reciting that "they are justly entitled to the same, as well from the construction of the terms . . . [of the treaty], as from their high characters, personal and professional, and the zeal, fidelity, patriotism, and valor with which they sustained the cause of this country during her struggle for Independence."[1] This effort came near being successful, but like the others it finally failed. It was not until 1857 that the few remaining Texan officers received any recognition from the government. The twelfth section of an act approved March 3, that year,[2] reads as follows:

And be it further enacted, That the surviving officers of the navy of the Republic of Texas, who were duly commissioned as such at the time of annexation, shall be entitled to the pay of officers of the like grades, when waiting orders, in the Navy of the United States, for five years from the time of said annexation, and a sum sufficient to make the payment is hereby appropriated . . .; *Provided,* That the acceptance of the provisions of this act by any of the said officers shall be a full relinquishment and renunciation of all claim on his part, to any further compensation on this behalf from the United States Government, and to any position in the Navy of the United States.

The survivors benefited by this act[3] were E. W. Moore, commodore; Alfred G. Gray, Cyrus Cummings, William A. Tennison, Charles B. Snow, and William Oliver, lieutenants; John F. Stephens and Norman Hurd, pursers; and the widow of Lieutenant A. J. Lewis. To this list must be added the name of Captain Tod, whose pay was turned over to his estate in 1883. Another claimant put in his appearance in 1858. This was Commander P. W. Humphries,[4] who was recognized by the Texas Legislature as entitled to the rank of commander in the navy of the Republic from July 3, 1839, to the date of annexation and entitled to pay the same

[1]Gammel, *Laws of Texas,* III, 1005; *Cong. Globe,* 33d Cong., 1st Sess., 2170.

[2]*Cong. Globe,* 34th Cong., 3d Sess., App. 427.

[3]The list of beneficiaries is taken from Tennison's Journal, folio 296, p. 4. I can find no list elsewhere. While this is not dated, it reads: "Officers who received pay from the U. S. Gov't," and could only apply to this act.

[4]Gammel, *Laws of Texas,* IV, 1152.

as other officers. The midshipmen were barred by the secretary of the navy, and today the only survivor, so far as I know, George F. Fuller, of Ozone Park, New Jersey, is prosecuting his claim under the act of 1857.

It is a pleasure to note the kindly deed of the United States in thus assisting the former naval officers of Texas, who were almost without exception ill used by Texas, or rather by those in power in Texas. It must be acknowledged, however, that as a matter of right they had not the shadow of a claim against the United States. Even if the interpretation of the word "navy" in the resolution of annexation were construed to include the naval officers, the navy had been practically disbanded when Moore returned from Yucatán, and the officers sent in their resignations. That they should take advantage of annexation to put in a claim was natural; but the officers of the United States navy were right in opposing their admission, and Congress was generous when it allowed them five years' pay.

Below is a list of the officers of the second navy of Texas, which was furnished on application of Commodore E. W. Moore by Adjutant General C. L. Mann. Their appointments were confirmed by the Senate on July 20, 1842, and by order of George W. Hockley, secretary of war and marine, they were to take rank as their names appeared in the list. The dates of their commissions are given, and it is stated whether they were dead or alive on July 31, 1850. It will be noted that over half of them died within the short period of eight years.

Edwin Ward Moore, Post Captain, Commanding

....April 21, 1839, Alive
J. T. K. Lothrop, Commander...............July 10, 1839, Dead
D. H. Crisp, Lieutenant.....................Nov. 10, 1839, Dead
Wm. C. Brashear, First Lieutenant..........Jan. 10, 1840, Dead
William Seeger, Second Lieutenant..........Jan. 10, 1840, Dead
Alfred G. Gray, Third Lieutenant...........Jan. 10, 1840, Alive
A. J. Lewis, Fourth Lieutenant.............Jan. 10, 1840, Alive
J. P. Lansing, Fifth Lieutenant............Jan. 10, 1840, Dead
George C. Bunner, Lieutenant...............Jan. 10, 1840, Dead
A. A. Waite, First Lieutenant..............Sept. 10, 1840, Dead
William A. Tennison, Second Lieutenant.....Sept. 10, 1840, Alive

William Oliver, Third Lieutenant............Sept. 10, 1840, Alive
Cyrus Cummings, Fourth Lieutenant........Sept. 10, 1840, Alive
C. B. Snow, Lieutenant...................,.....Mar. 10, 1842, Alive
D. C. Wilbur, Lieutenant.....................June 1, 1842, Dead
M. H. Dearborn, Lieutenant....................July 1, 1842, Dead
R. M. Clark, Surgeon..........................Nov. 22, 1840, Dead
Thomas P. Anderson, Surgeon..............Sept. 10, 1841, Dead
J. B. Gardner, Surgeon.................,..July 20, 1842, Alive
Norman Hurd, Purser......................Jan. 16, 1839, Alive
F. T. Wells, Purser........................June 10, 1839, Dead
J. F. Stephens, Purser............,........Sept. 21, 1841, Alive
W. T. Brennan, Purser.....................July 21, 1842, Dead

On Brennan's death, James W. Moore was appointed to take his place. In the list of those officers who petitioned Congress to be incorporated in the United States navy, appears the name of William E. Glenn,[1] "late master of the line of promotion." This carefully prepared list, added to the names mentioned in the body of the work, constitutes the *personnel* of the body of officers of the Texan navy.

A few additional notes regarding some of these may be of interest. William Seeger was commander of the *San Antonio* when she was lost. A. J. Lewis died some time in the fifties. William A. Tennison was alive in 1858. Thomas P. Anderson, surgeon, had a son, Philip Anderson, who was living in Galveston in 1900. Mrs. R. W. Shaw of Galveston is a granddaughter of Norman Hurd. The midshipmen, being boys at the same time, have naturally been the last survivors. Of these Major John E. Barrow died in New York in 1902; W. J. D. Pierpont died in December, 1903. Of all the officers of the Texas navy, but one is alive today, Midshipman George F. Fuller, of Ozone Park, New Jersey. Com-

---

[1]In Fuller's "Sketch of the Texas Navy" (THE QUARTERLY, VII, 223, 226), this name appears as "Wm. H. Glenn." Fuller also includes Robert Bradford and Edward Mason as midshipmen on board the *Austin* in 1842 and 1843 and Middleton on board the *Wharton,* and mentions that Dr. Peacock acted as assistant surgeon to Dr. Anderson of the *Austin.* He also states that in Walker's time, Faysoux commanded the whole Nicaraguan navy, consisting of one schooner with which he blew up the whole Costa Rican navy, consisting of one brig. Faysoux was afterwards mate of the *Creole* in its Cuban expedition, his commanding officer being Lewis, formerly third lieutenant of the *Wharton.*

mander Lothrop died in 1844 at Houston. Just before his death
he took command of the steamship *Neptune,* running between New
Orleans and Texas. But one name remains, and the tale is closed.
Edwin Ward Moore finally procured from the Texas Legislature
the passage of three acts providing that he should be paid for his
services and reimbursed for his expenditures on the navy. It appears that by joint resolution approved by the governor January
24, 1848,[1] $11,398.36½ was allowed him. February 23, he
was allowed a claim of three thousand five hundred dollars for
commanding the navy.[2] Finally on February 2, 1856, was passed an
act for his relief,[3] by which the treasurer was authorized to pay him
$5,290.00, "Provided the said Moore shall first file with the treas-
urer a full and final release against the Republic and State of Texas
for all demands." It has been asserted that he never received these
moneys granted him by Texas. He at any rate received the compliment of having a county named for him in the state. Very little
is known of him after 1837, but he made New York his home. He
came to Galveston in 1860 and erected the old post-office building
in that city. He took no part in the Civil War, and died in Virginia in 1865.

There is no question that Commodore Moore should be classed
as one of the heroes of Texas; and this narrative may fitly be closed
with the tribute paid him by the foremost officer of the Confederate
navy:[4]

With an energy and ability possessed by but few men, he took
hold of the discordant materials which Texas was collecting for the
formation of a navy (a work, generally, of time and much patient
toil), reduced them to system and order, and presented to the
world the spectacle of a well-organized marine, bearing the flag of
a Republic, not four years old!

[1] Gammel, *Laws of Texas*, III, 334-335.
[2] *Ibid.*, 351.
[3] *Ibid.*, IV, 371.
[4] Semmes, *Service Afloat and Ashore During the Mexican War*, 49.

THE CLOPPER CORRESPONDENCE, 1834-1838.[1]

NICHOLAS CLOPPER TO J. C. CLOPPER.[2]

San Jacinto, 9th April 1834.

My Dear Son

. . . .

A Mr. Thompson from New York is now arrived here via N. O and says one of the Gentn who contracted for my point,[3] 1600 acres at $2, is coming on prepared to pay and improve it handsomely.

You ask wheather we have any protestant preaching, and say you are told that all denominations are tolerated. We have never yet had preaching on our section, but there are a few travelling preachers of difft sects, who preach occasionally but it can not yet in a proper sense be said they are tolerated, but the general expectation is that this will be the case. We are not yet organized in a State Govt. on this subject there appears to be more division than was at first apprehended. Colo Austin is not yet returned, he had started from Mexico, and was brot back and retained a prissoner owing to some expressions in a letter written by him to his friend in Texas,— how this Business will terminate we can not tell, the people are divided among themselves and we have many lofty minded men, who are aspirants to Office. Yet upon the whole Texas must flourish in the end. Men of Capitall and enterprise are continually

[1]The originals of the letters belonging to this correspondence are in the possession of Mr. Edward N. Clopper, of Cincinnati, and were sent by him with the Journal of J. C. Clopper for publication in THE QUARTERLY. The Journal was published in the number for July, 1909. The parties to the correspondence were Nicholas Clopper, his sons Joseph C. and A. M. Clopper, and Mrs. A. L. Wilson. See THE QUARTERLY, XIII, 44, note. The place to which all the letters are directed is Cincinnati. The omitted passages consist partly of relatively unimportant personal details, and partly of expressions of religious feeling. Most of the notes and endorsements quoted were probably made by Mrs. Mary Este Clopper, wife of J. C. Clopper.

[2]Endorsed on back "Received May 25, 1834"; and, in a different hand, "after Husband's very severe illness at Beechwood," the words "very severe" and "Beechwood" being underscored twice, and the word "illness" once.

[3]I. e., what was then called Clopper's Bar or Clopper's Point, and is now known as Morgan's Point. It is at the northwest extremity of Galveston Bay, between that and the arm of it known as San Jacinto Bay.

coming out, etc. . . . We shall have the new buildings ready soon and land fenced for Corn etc. Doctr P. has built and improved about 10 miles above Capt. Lyndsay is at work on Trinity, but we expect him daily, to assist on our buildings, he talks of going to Kentucky this Season. You will write immediately on Rect of this, as I think June will arrive before we get away. I send much love to Mary and the girls[1] and our friends generally, and particularly to Mr Ludlow and family, Dr. Willson and family, etc Continue to pray for us. And will write soon.

Yr affectionate father

N. C.[2]

A. M. CLOPPER TO NICHOLAS CLOPPER.

Highland Cottage 2nd. Jany.—1836.

Dear Father,

I recieved your letter dated 5th September about a fortnight ago from Doctr. Patrick, who got one at the same time. I was truly glad to hear of your good Health and that of my Brother and Sisters. I wrote to you about the last of Septr. it being the first chance I had by way of Nacogdoches. I hope you have recieved it 'ere this the Country is in such a state at this time that there is no business done; the Texonians have taken Lababia, and march'd from thence to San Antonio. on the 5th. last month they compell'd Genl. Cos to surrender, whose army being 1100 strong, and that of the Americans about 600. we have to regret the loss of one of our bravest Citizens, Col Milam, who was shot in the forehead while passing across the street. Edward Burleson is commander in chief, F. W. Johnson Commanding Col. American loss at San Antonio, about 8 kill'd and several wounded, Mexican loss about 300 kill'd and a good many wounded. John Iiams had been at San Antonio. on his return he told me that Dimmet[3] and one other man was taken near Labahia by the Irish, and put in Irons and sent to Matamoras. a few days ago I mention'd it to G. F.

[1] Nicholas Clopper had four daughters: Rebecca, Ruhamah, Mary Ann, and Caroline, none of whom married. The first two died in 1845, and the last two in 1875.

[2] On the margin of the sheet, with index referring to these initials, is the note: "*Died* Decr., 1841, aged 76."

[3] Captain Philip Dimitt.

Richardson. he told me it was not true, that Dimmet was now stationed at Lababia for the purpose of keeping it in possession. Col. Morgan has arriven about a fortnight ago with two Schooners laden with Goods, who told me he had reciev'd a letter from you dated in November, that you were in good health which I was glad to hear. he was advised at the Balize not to come here at present as they thought it dangerous that he would be taken by Mexican Cruisers. he then ask'd his men if they would be willing to fight, should they be attack'd. they said they would. he then purchas'd an eighteen Pounder, Muskets, Cutlasses and every thing necessary, and came out in company with the Schooner Pennsylvania and brig Durango[1] bound for the Brazos as far as Galveston. after those two had left them they discover'd a Sail in sight suppos'd to be the Montezuma. she made off and they got in without molestation. his large Vessel call'd the Flash,[2] intends sailing for Orleans in a few days, therefore I embrace the present opportunity of writing by her. the Col. did not bring his family with him, he brought out Governor Zavala's family who live at Singleton's place. Còl. Morgan inform'd me that 9 tenths of the United States is with us, that there is about 10000 coming out here in the course of a few months all hot for fighting. sooner than not have a fight that they will go to Mexico. the Americans here intend marching to Matamoras and taking it. I have seen Stephen Richison and he does not appear willing to have the Land referr'd to Arbitrators [He said] that he had once offer'd to do it, and Davis was then displeas'd that he was as that time hard run but he has now got out of his difficulties and does not think it right that he should wait any longer. he told me to let you know. Doctor Patrick told me he thought it a dull chance to get anything done at present, that there is no business doing now, owing to the present state of the Country   this Stephen Richison told me also. there is now lying at Galveston an armed Schooner of 12 Guns from Baltimore

[1]The *Durango* was soon afterwards pressed into the Texan service, for which indemnity was demanded by the United States government and paid by Texas. See Garrison, *Texan Diplomatic Correspondence*, Part I (*Annual Report of American Historical Association for the Year 1907*, Vol. II), p. 271; *U. S. Treaties and Conventions*, 1078.

[2]In reference to the *Montezuma* and the *Flash*, see THE QUARTERLY, XII, 175, 193-5, 197-8, 252.

call'd the Invincible[1] she has come out to protect the coast, and Lynch told me that Col Macomb has gone on to New York to purchase 4 Vessels with arms and ammunition, 6—32 pounders 4—twelve pounders and some 6 pounders for the protection of the coast they intend fortifying Galveston this spring. I inform'd you in my last latter of the failure of our crop owing to the ants and worms and sickness of Britton and myself also. I am now enjoying good health at present, except occasional attacks of the Rheumatism. Doctr. P. intends living at the Point the Present year which is now call'd New-Washington.

Bancroft went to the army and has return'd a few days ago I have not seen him there is no person to be had to do any thing at the present crisis I should be glad to see you out here as soon as practicable. there is now living at sloop point a Mr. Seymour and family from New York very clever people he had selected his land near Robinson's[2] Colony last year but does not like to move there at present he says he would like to purchase one or two hundred acres for a residence on the Bay. I told him I would write and let you know whether he could have it off of the land adjoining Dr. Ps. and Col. Morgans. he wish'd to buy 50 or 100 acres from me but I wont sell at the new house. I shall expect an answer on the reciept of this. and now my Dear Father may God grant you every happiness this world can bestow while here on earth and at last that you may be reciev'd up to the Mansions of bliss where there is Joy and pleasures forevermore. this prays.

your affectionate Son,

A. M. CLOPPER

Remember me with love to Brother and Sisters friends etc. Mr. Burnet and family are well.

Edward Este is determin'd not to write untill he recieves letters

---

[1] See THE QUARTERLY, XII, 201-2, 252-261.
[2] Robertson's.

NICHOLAS CLOPPER TO J. C. CLOPPER AND SISTERS.[1]

Highland Cottage San Jacinto 5th Jany 1835

My dear children

In my last, I mentioned the death of Mrs. Jackson the sister of Mr W. Willson who was living in our house at the point. in a few weeks after Mr. Willson himself was taken off leaving a young and amiable wife, and two Children one an infant. Mrs. W. has had severe and hard trials, but has been wonderfully supported, under them, and bears up under them like a Christian. She is now living in the house with us   we have an excellent house wench, and live as one family in peace and quietness. in the Spring her calculation is to return to her friends in Boston, and we calculate to go together as far as N. Orleans, and perhaps to Cincinnati. if so she will rest a while with you. your letter dated 27 Septm. enclosing one from Mrs Bowering came duly to hand, inclosing a Letter to Miss Elizabeth B Jack at Mr T Hopes informing her of a legacy left her in England. this information they recieved long since, and Mr. Hope her Step-Father, went from here to England some 18 Mo since, as I understood with power, to recieve the same, and has not yet returned, and it is thought will not again return. when I was last in Sanfelipe, I saw Capt Christman,[2] who married a daughter of old Mr Hope. I asked him about Miss Jack. he said she was living in his family and was well, and has had the benifit of schooling etc, and that she was a fine girl etc. Capt C. lives high up the country, say 150 miles so that it is not very probable, that it will be in our power to deliver the letter before we go to [the] U. S. in that case shall inclose it to her.

I was a few days since at Mr. Burnetts. they are all well   Mrs. B. says she has written frequently, and has not been favd. with any Letters for a length of time, and her Brother E[3] says the same Edward E. has been but little with us owing as he says, to the

---

[1]This letter and the next are written on the same sheet. It is directed simply to J. C. Clopper, but the contents, as well as the addresses within show the letters were intended for both himself and his sisters. On the back of the sheet is written "received March 7th, 1835."

[2]Chriesman.

[3]Edward Este.

Judge being so much from home, makes it necesary for him to re- main with his Sister. Colo. Austin has not yet returned from Mexico, but writes favourably on the whole. our country is im- proving, and settlers continue coming in. the Harrisburgh Steam Mill, land and Lotts is now selling at Auction, and we under- stand is going off at good prices. the purchasers principally Strangers. . . .[1]

N. Clopper.

A. M. CLOPPER TO J. C. CLOPPER AND SISTERS.[2]

My Dear Brother and Sisters,

It is with pleasure I take up my pen to address you with a few lines, knowing that it is the only mode we have of communicating our Ideas to one another. Father and I were both taken sick on the 16th Septr. and remained so about seven Weeks. I was badly salivated; so much so that I had recourse to the slate to make my wants known, my tongue being all raw, and swelled to such a de- gree, that I could with difficulty, get it out of my mouth. . . .

Father has sold 1600 Acres off of the Hunter League the Point[3] included at $2.00 p Acre, 1-3 to be paid down, 1-3 in twelve months, the balance in two years. Edward Este has been to see me. he told me that you J. C. C. had written his Brother a very severe letter, and wishes you to write him, and let him know whether he answer'd it, and if so, to let him know the sum and substance of it. I have not returned his visit yet, but expect to do so ere long. I hope I shall be able to pay you all a visit in the Spring. . . .

your affectionate Brother,

A. M. Clopper.[4]

---

[1] In the part of the letter here omitted. Mr. Clopper indicates his in- tention to return to Cincinnati in the spring. Following this part is a note which reads as follows: "Came—made 2 trips after that the last one in 1840—returned with Caroline July, 1841—died in December, 1841."

[2] See note 1, p. 132.

[3] See note 3, p. 128.

[4] Written at the end of this letter is the note, apparently referring to A. M. Clopper, "he died in 1853."

A. M. CLOPPER TO NICHOLAS CLOPPER.[1]

Highland Cottage 17th October 1836.

My Dear Father,

I reciev'd your letter on the 14th inst. by the hands of Doctor Patrick, and it was truly gratifying to me, to hear of your recovering and gaining strength. I hope there is many days if not years, for you yet of happiness here below (comparatively speaking.) I hope to see you once more at least in this world, and at Death; to meet you with all my dear Brothers and Sisters, in the mansions of Glory, and join in singing the praises of our dear Redeemer, throughout the boundless ages of eternity. I just got home from the Island of St Louis which lies between the west end of Galvezton and the main land. I have been station'd there for about five months for the purpose of carrying Express to Velasco and back, and another would take it on to the east end' of Galvezton. I have now been six months in the service. the brown mare Phillis was taken to San Antonio last fall   I have never seen her since, and as soon as Tomlin came in I lent him Tartar to ride to Matagorda, and the people press'd him from him into the service, so he told me. he then went on board the Independence[2] and remain'd there a few months. the last I heard of him he was in Orleans, and I'm inclin'd to think he has gone on to Boston. I had been riding Fidelle a few days on the express, before the battle of San Jacinto and shortly after the battle, I hobbled her out near Brinsons, in the care of Adam Smith, untill I could go down to Galvezton Island to get my chests which I had put on board of the Schooner Flash, to go to New Orleans, and from thence to Cincinnati, and when I return'd home, our Cavalry had taken my mare off to the army, so that I have not a single animal to ride. I will now endeavour to break the roan filly. my dear Father I have been very unfortunate. I had a furlough to come home from the Island about 3 months ago from the President, and I had to return again in the course of fifteen days and from the reports of the Enemy's coming on again in a large body in a short time, I thought best to

---

[1]This letter and the next are written on the same sheet, which is directed to Nicholas Clopper.

[2]See THE QUARTERLY, XII, 203, 265-275.

box up all the papers and Deeds, and bury them, [being] afraid to trust them with any person on this side of the Bay. Doctor Patrick was then living at Anahuac, and I had no way of sending them to him. my Canoe has also been press'd into the service, and immediately I came home, I dug it up and open'd it, and found them all nearly ruin'd. I have been ever since I came home which was on the 12th inst. opening and drying the Papers with the greatest care I possibly could. some of them are very much torn and scarcely legible. I shall never bury again even for the shortest time. Mrs. Wilsons Transfer to Doctor Patrick was also amongst them and is nearly ruin'd, though the signers names are all to it. I was very much hurt to find them in such a condition. Doctor Patrick is now gone to Columbia and will return in a few days. he will then write to you. I saw Colonel Morgan day before yesterday, and I told him you would allow him six pct in Orleans on the same bank or place or which was most convenient to him. he told me he would take 12½ or the Hammer'd Dollars are ready for you here at any time, he says that they are 8 pct. and then freight and risk in the bargain. he told me he reciev'd your letter and will answer it. when you write to Mrs. Wilson tell her I have written 3 letters to her, and intend writing in a day or two. I am very much in want of Provision and Cloathing. I wish you could send me two Bbls flour 100 lbs. Coffee and Sugar according. our army will suffer unless they can obtain supplies shortly from the U. S. a rifle would be very acceptable at this time. I will endeavour to see Mr. Barnet[1] as soon as I can. God bless you my dear Father.

A. M. CLOPPER.

A. M. CLOPPER TO J. C. CLOPPER.[2]

18th October 1836.

Dear Brother,

I recieved your letter under date 20th April directed to Doctor Patrick and myself on the third July and was very sorry to hear of Father's illness, but your letter bearing date Septr. 1st was truly

---

[1]Plainly written, but possibly intended for Burnet.
[2]See note 1, p. 134.

gratifying to hear of Father's recovery. it appears you wish to know the reason why I was not in the battle. I will relate it to you; sometime in march I started on my way to the Army which was then station'd at the Colorado. I had got as far as San felipe. I there saw Jack Roark who told me that there was a letter for me at his mothers from the U. S. and that it felt very heavy as if there was money in it. I then went to my Captain Daniel Perry, and told him that I should like to get it, before I Join'd the Army, knowing that it was either from you or my Father. he consented and told me to return as quick as I could. the people were then moving off as fast as possible. San felipe was full of waggons with families, and on my road to mrs. Roarks away below Staffords, nearly every family from Sanfelipe to her house was gone. I then tho't it necessary to go home and see if it was the case there, as I was within a days ride, so as to secure my papers. I then rode down to the point very early in the morning and Colonel Morgan invited me to stay untill after breakfast that he wish'd to see me. I then staid. he told me at the table in the presence of Mrs. Mather, Miss Johnson, Mrs. Patrick and Adam Smith, that he wish'd me to ride Express, as he was acquainted with me and knowing that I was acquainted with the President that he would prefer me to any other and that I could render double the service to the Government in this way, to that of being in the army. I told him that I was ready to start back next morning to the army, and had promis'd my Captain to return. he told me he would have that fix'd. I then told him if any one told me that I accepted it through cowardice I would immediately quit it and go to the army. he then wrote a letter by me to the secretary of State Saml. Carson for me to ride and I have been in that service ever since. Colonel Rusk Secretary of War, wrote a Note to Captain Perry why I was detain'd I was then satisfied. there was a good many tories on the trinity viz. Judge Williams, Doctor Whiting, Bloodgood and many others. I have now given you my reason for not being in the army if you think it a sufficient one you will inform me in your answer to this Doctor Patrick intends writing shortly and will give you all the news. tell Rebecca to send me a few pair winter Socks, 4 Shirts, as I am short, both in clothes and provision. . . . Mrs. B's youngest child died at Velasco a short time ago. the eldest had like to have died also, is now recovering. Provision is very high, Corn from 3 to 4 Dollars a Bushel and money very scarce and hard to get, it is my wish to go in[1] if I can possibly do so. Col Morgan told me he would give $1.50 pr Acre for the Land adjoin[ing] him and Patrick if I would let him have it now, before he goes to the States. I told him I could not take it. Capt Spillman holds the Island that he's living on at $10,000 Dollars. I think it best to hold this a little longer. I have not had time to look over the Cattle since I came home therefore can give no account. expect to write again shortly.

Your affectionate Brother
A. M. Clopper.

A. M. CLOPPER TO NICHOLAS CLOPPER.

Highland Cottage 18th Decr. 1836.

Dear Father,

I saw Capt. Wm. P. Harris yesterday and he told me that he will start for N. Orleans in the course of a few days on board of the Kosciusko. I therefore embrace the opportunity of writing. I had written about a month or six weeks ago to Joseph pr Schooner Flash. I hope he has reciev'd it 'ere this. I wish you to send me 2 Barrels of Flour 100 lbs Coffee and ½ Bbl Sugar as soon as possible. Provision is very scarce and hard to be got. Flour is now selling at Lynch's at $18 pr Bbl, and I am told it is 20 on the Brazos. Sugar 20 cts pr lb. and no money to be had Corn very scarce $1.50 pr Bushel on the Brazos there is none to be had in our neighborhood tell Rebecca not to forget what I had written to her for I am told that there is 25000 Mexicans on their march and will be here early in the Spring. St. Anna and Col Almonte cross'd at Lynch's ferry about 3 weeks ago on their way to the City of Washington, escorted by Majr. Patton Col. Hockley and Col Bee to make a treaty. I hope and trust that we shall have Peace by Spring, that we may be able to attend to our own affairs. Burnet told me at the runaway scrape or in other words last Spring that he would write to you in a short time I have never seen

---

[1]I. e., to return home. See note 1, p. 138.

him since. I have no horse that I can ride as yet   I am not able
to give you an account of the stock as yet   I rather think there is
a good many of them missing.   some people lost all their Stock.
I am fearful unless peace is made shortly or a sufficient force
[comes] from the U S. that we shall not be able to contend with
so large a force.   last fall Col. Morgan ask'd me what I would
take per acre for the land laying between his, and Cedar Bayou.
I told him $1.50   he then thought it too high.   he now wants it,
and I told him I would not take it.   he has purchas'd Doctor
Patrick out at 1.50   Mr. Reynolds was over there some time ago
(Anahuac) where Morgan resides.   he return'd to my house and
told me that Morgan told him that he was determin'd to have that
land at that price that you told him that he might have as much
land as he wanted at $1.50 per acre and I am determin'd that he
shall not have it.   he has been trying to scare me into measures,
by telling me that the Mexicans will be on and take all my stock
etc, as if I could not risk as well as he can.   I have since been
offer'd more.   I was thinking from Reynold's talk perhaps Morgan
might write to you, and try to bargain with you for it.   I told him
that I should keep it myself, unless he gives me a good deal more
for it.   The Seat of Government is now at Columbia and will
shortly be removed to the Town of Houston, 6 miles above Harrisburg on Buffaloe Bayou at John Austins place   that place is purchas'd by the Allen's the same Allen that was about purchasing the
point from you.   they have agreed to build a house that will cost
$10000 Just to have Government there for three years.   should
Government then be removed elsewhere the House will then revert
back to the Allens.   this of course will enhance my Property.
should peace be made by spring, I intend if possible to go in.[1]
tell the Girls I have got a small box of Shells ready to take to
them.   I hope Sister mary has got home   tell her that Edward
is well and is keeping Batchelor's hall, at Majr. Burnets place.
the Majr. and his Lady is now living at Velasco   Wm P. Harris
told me yesterday, that Majr. B and family intends coming to my
House immediately to stay till spring, will then remove to Houston as soon as he can build.   he talks of selling his place as he

[1]See note 1, p. 137.

never intends living there again, upon the account of Scott and Lynch they are enemies to him. I think a good deal of Burnet now. he told me that he would do any thing for me, that was in his power with pleasure. him and his Lady have been very clever to me indeed I always make their house my home when there. do not forget to send me the articles I have nam'd if possible. times are very hard here at present.

Now my Dear Father I must bid you adieu. May God of his infinite mercy bless and protect you through life and grant you yet many days of happiness here below and at last recieve you to himself and oh! God! grant that we may all meet around thy throne, whenever thou see'st fit to take us home is the prayer of your affectionate Son

A. M. CLOPPER.

A. M. CLOPPER TO NICHOLAS CLOPPER.

Highland Cottage 1st March 1837.

Dr. Father,

I reciev'd your letter dated 10th December per Mr. Stratton on the 1st February and was much gratified to find that you are still in the land of the living. The Schooner Flash will start in a day or two for N. Orleans, and Mr. Stratton if he can get a passage in her, intends returning to Orleans. he is much pleas'd with this part of Texas, and would like to stay. he thinks that there is to much wind here, but Orleans would agree with him much better; you wish to have a full account of the cattle, which I am unable to give you as yet. I only got home in october last from public Service which was upwards of six Months and I have had no animal to ride I have rode the Roan filly a little but had to turn her out on account of the grass being so very bad, and no Corn to give her that she fell away very fast. she pitches pretty bad, however I intend taking her up again shortly and breaking her complete. I hardly think the Mexicans got any of my Cattle, but still I have miss'd several, and two or three of the Cows died, Pink, Calico and Whiteface. I intend collecting them as soon as I possibly can. Kate looks thin, the two Colts look tolerable well I have got the Cow pens between this and Spilman's well broke up, and intend planting them in pumpkins and Corn I have made but little fence. if I can possibly get any person to come and make me 4 or 5000 rails, I intend doing it; as I am not able to work now as I have done, on account of Rheumatic pains. I have had no chance to get my upper House finish'd yet and I am afraid there will be a dull chance of getting it done this season as every person appears to be flocking to Houston. I am told they are building there rapidly. Col. Morgan told me yesterday that Lotts were selling at Houston as he understood at $1000, that there had been something like thirty sold, if I recollect aright. I inform'd you in my last where Houston lies, and who was the purchaser's the Messrs. Allens, one of them has purchas'd Sloop Point. I told Col. Morgan that one of your friends wish'd to purchase a Lot, and ask'd him his price, he told me 1st choice $500—2d 300—3d 200 and so on down as low as $25, but if he would put up a two story frame building he might have one of the first choice for $100, and so on in proportion, if a one story building, the Lots would be higher. I also told him that hammer'd Dollars would suit you as well as any. he replied that they were ready. he then ask'd me if you had sent his note on. I told him it was likely you had, and I expected he would find it at the House of Messrs. Sloo & Byrne. I told him should he go in by the way of Cincinnati that you would be very glad to see him, and where you reside he said he would do so should that be his route. the highest I have been offer'd for the Greenfield tract as yet is $1.50 by 2 persons, Col Morgan for one. he has purchas'd Doctor Patricks part at that price. I dont wish to sell it yet. Mr. Stratton told me to hold on a while and not sell yet, that there was a Gentleman on board of the Vessel he came out in, that told him as soon as the affairs of Texas become settled that there was a great many of the Mississippi Planters coming out to purchase farms, that they had worn theirs nearly out that they were determin'd to have places here. this Gentleman heard numbers conversing in this way in N. Orleans, and he thought that it would break up the state of Mississippi. I therefore think it Best to Defer the sale of it a while longer. I think I can do much better with it here, nor you can there, I therefore wish you not to sell it, as you have given, the disposal of it to me. I therefore consider it mine. if I cannot sell it for more than your friend offers, I will write and he shall have the preference. I have some Idea who it is. the Buildings at N. Washington were all burnt by Santa Anna himself; except the Corn Crib that I built. Col Morgan is now about putting up a large 2 Story frame Building I have not secur'd any land on the Brazos yet and Mr. Tomlin I expect has gone to Boston I have not seen him since last July and know not whether I shall ever see him again or not I have not heard from Mrs. Wilson for a long time if you have heard lately let me know how she is. I was very thankful to you for the things sent and Garden seeds I planted the Onions a fortnight ago they are now growing handsomely. And now my dear Father I must bid you Adieu, may God in his providence increase your days on earth at least a few years longer that we may be enabled to see each other face to face again that you may be restor'd to perfect health should it be otherwise order'd Lord grant that we may all meet at the right hand of God, is the prayer of your affectionate Son,

A. M. CLOPPER.

Love to Sisters and friends.

Mr. Mather was here in the latter part of Jany. he lives on chocolate. he came over to Col. Morgans for provision, and on his way home one of his Oxen died. he tyed the other to a tree, the other side of Choats, and took his Saddlebags to go home, but never reach'd there. his saddlebags was found near willow branch, it being high, and I rather suspect he was drown'd, as he could not swim.

Col. Mc. Comb Mov'd his family out here last summer. his wife died last fall. about a week ago he cut his throat with a razor, and has left 5 Children the eldest a daughter 17 or 18 yrs old. I believe you knew him.

I expect Majr. Burnet and Lady at my house shortly to spend a few Months untill as I understood he can build, which will be at Houston.

A. M. CLOPPER TO NICHOLAS CLOPPER.

Highland Cottage 27th June 1837.

Dear Father,

I wrote you per Steam Boat Constitution, in the fore part of the present month, stating that Mr. Burnet had been at my house a few days previous.   he reciev'd your letter written in February fav'd per Mr. Bamford.   I also reciev'd several at the same time with one from Mrs. Wilson, she was well and desir'd to be remember'd to you.   Mr. Burnet told me that it was impossible to get any thing done ever since the war began.   he told me that he would write a long letter in answer to yours immediately, as he pass'd through Harrisburg.   Martin Allen was with him.   he got Darius Gregg and had that League of Land survey'd, and it came out exactly right so as to take in Martin Allens land to the lower half.   Mr. Callaham told me he never saw a man more pleas'd than Mr. Allen was.   I saw Gregg a short time ago   he told me he gave the notes of it to Allen.

I have been to see Majr. Burnet lately, relative to my getting a Petition for the Land that my Brothers was to have gotten.   he told me that it could not be done and that he thought it very doubtful whether you could hold your League as you had left the Country.   I told him that you had been rendering all the assistance for Texas that you possibly could at Cincinnati, that you had furnish'd ½ Ton balls for the Cannon that came from there etc.   he said that might make a difference.   I went up to Houston and show'd my discharges to the President, and he told me that they were not made out right, that I must have them made out correct against next Congress, which I shall get Majr. Burnet to do.   the weather has been remarkably dry for six or seven weeks past, so much so that the sun has parch'd nearly every thing up   I rather think that crops of Corn will be short on account of the Drouth   I have not been able to get scarcely any thing done.   I have been afflicted with Rheumatic pains more or less this whole season.   from the tone of your last letter I am daily looking for you and Rachel.   I hope you will bring some Corn, Flour, Coffee and Sugar with you as those articles are very much needed.   a few Mackerel would be an excellent relish and very acceptable.   at the time of the runaway scrape the Mexicans enter'd my House, and took what provision I had, and some of the Tories or negroes I know not which, stole my sieve, plates Cups and Saucers, Knives and forks, milk pans etc, broke me up in the house Keeping line.   should this reach you before you start, I wish you to bring such articles with you also cŏoking utensils, viz. Pots, skillets with covers, and Dutch Oven large enough for roasting Geese Ducks etc—Washing Tubs.

I have understood that Montezuma and some other General who are Liberals, have gain'd a decided victory over Bustamente. the Land office has been clos'd by the consultation of 1835 and was to have been open'd the 1st June 37. it still remains clos'd, it will not be open'd before the 1st October. Kate and Colts look well—the Cattle look well also. there has several of the Cows died. I believe there has been but few lost by the enemy. I wish you would bring me out some good Chewing Tobacco, 10 or 12 lbs. at least. I have been offer'd 2.50 per acre for the Greenfield tract. I think I can get three in a short time. I have understood that Ritson Morris has sold the $\frac{1}{2}$ of his League on Clear Creek for 12 thousand Dollars. I intend to sell some Land the first good opportunity so as to enable me to purchase a couple of negro fellows and a house Girl for I am not able to do much myself. I have understood that Negroes are very low in Tennesse and alabama this Season, that some of the best Hands have been purchas'd as low as three hundred Dollars and from that to four. there is but very little sickness here at present as far as I can learn. your friends here are all well. My best love to Brother and Sisters and all enquiring friends. tell Sister Mary I should be much gratified to recieve a few lines from her. now my Dear Father may [God] Grant you a safe and speedy return to Texas, and many happy days here on earth, and at last a safe transmittance to his heavenly Kingdom is the sincere prayer of your affectionate Son—

A. M. CLOPPER.

MRS. A. L. WILSON[1] TO NICHOLAS CLOPPER.

Roxbury, Sept. 18, 1838.

My Dear Sir

I should have answered your letter immediately on receiveing it, but as I was uncertain about the money requisite for my journey, I thought it best to wait until I could write with certainty; which I was about doing, when I received a letter from Dr. Patrick on

---

[1]Concerning Mrs. Wilson, nothing has been learned further than what appears in this correspondence.

Friday last, dated Houston August 1st. After speaking very affectingly of the death of his wife, whom it seems took the Small Pox in May, of which she lingered (or rather a consequent disease) untill July 31st when her eyes were closed forever on things of mortality, Fatigue and want of rest he says brought on an inflamation of the liver of which he is but just recovering being so weak as not to be able to sit up but part of the day. But I presume you have heard from him long ere this. He mentions advising me to return to Texas, but as I do not intend making it my Home and the law prohibits foreigners from holding lands and as there is some risk in having it held in trust it might be advisable to sell. He says if I come to this conclusion my affairs can be settled without my coming to the country. He likewise says he was doubtful whether my title to the League could be obtained without my being in the Country, but he has obtained a Certificate in which (if nothing new takes place) a Patent must issue as soon as they have a president that will sign them. Houston still refuses to sign any, but Lamar who it is supposed will succeed him is in favour of carrying into effect the land law, so that we may expect patents for our lands some time next Spring I have written almost word for word of what he says that you may be the better able to advise me. . . .

(Mrs.) A. L. Wilson.

JAMES H. C. MILLER AND EDWARD GRITTEN.

EUGENE C. BARKER.

In the summer of 1835 James H. C. Miller and Edward Gritten strove earnestly, each in his own way, to check the increasing misunderstanding and friction between Texas and Mexico which culminated in the Texas Revolution. For this history has ill requited them, characterizing the former as a traitor and the latter as a spy.[1] Of Miller this judgment is too harsh, and of Gritten it is entirely unfounded.

Little, in fact, is known of Miller. John Henry Brown with unnecessary fervor congratulates himself for his inability "to name the State of the Union that gave him birth," because "the commonwealth is not responsible for such involuntary stains upon its escutcheon."[2] He settled at Gonzales, in De Witt's colony, between 1831 and 1835.[3] He was a physician; and, from the fact that on at least one occasion he commanded a party of old settlers in an expedition against the Indians,[4] one might conclude that he was a man of recognized ability and consequence.

In considering the charge against Miller two things should, in justice to him, be borne in mind: (1) that upon settlement in Texas colonists, constructively at least, swore allegiance to the gov-

---

[1]Yoakum says of Miller (*History of Texas*, I, 344): "But there were spies at San Felipe, watching and reporting to Ugartechea the movements of the war-party. Dr. James H. C. Miller, of Gonzales, . . ." Brown says of him (*History of Texas*, I, 352): ". . . there was a spy in the camp at San Felipe, one who had in a short residence at Gonzales made a favorable impression, but who now developed the loathsome attributes of a tory and a traitor. This disgrace to our race was known as Dr. James H. C. Miller. . . . This creature was doing the foul work of a spy for Ugartechea."
Of Gritten Yoakum says (I, 341, note): "There remains now but little doubt of his treachery"; and Brown says (I, 310): "Gritten developed into an enemy of Texas." Gritten has recently suffered the additional misfortune of being made the "villain" of an historical novel (*The Lone Star*, by E. P. Lyle).

[2]Brown, *History of Texas*, I, 352.

[3]See map 4 in Rather, *De Witt's Colony*, THE QUARTERLY, VIII, following p. 192.

[4]See Brown, *History of Texas*, I, 284-285.

ernment and became Mexican citizens; and (2) that in the spring of 1835 the Texans were sharply divided on the question of their future relations with Mexico. A small, but very active, party wanted to establish the independence of Texas; while the great majority of the people desired to continue the existing relations, but had not yet made up their minds what to do in case of a radical alteration of the republican constitution of the country, which Santa Anna showed some signs of tampering with. A few had reached the conviction that until it became clearly evident that the proposed changes would work a real hardship upon them it was their duty to submit. Miller and his fellow-townsmen of Gonzales were of this opinion, and so, it might be remarked in passing, was the staunch patriot, David G. Burnet.[1] In March and April some of the men who favored secession from Mexico became involved in what their contemporaries regarded as a questionable land deal with the legislature of Coahuila and Texas; and when the general Congress quashed the sale, and Santa Anna dispersed the legislature, they sought to alarm the colonists by declaring that those acts were only the beginning of a comprehensive policy of oppression. It is possible that they sincerely believed this; for, having been recently in the interior, they were better informed of the threatening political outlook than those who remained at home. Many colonists, however, believed that private motives prompted their warnings and gave them little attention. Toward the end of June some military correspondence was intercepted at San Felipe which seemed to disclose a plan on the part of the government to throw an overwhelming army into Texas, and this, seeming to confirm the dire prophecies of the war party, produced a momentary flurry of general excitement during which William B. Travis, with a small company, attacked and captured a Mexican garrison at Anahuac, commanded by Captain Tenorio. But shortly afterwards the government explained that the object of sending troops to Texas was to establish the custom houses and protect the country from the Indians, and this assurance enabled the conservatives to regain the ascendancy, so that by the middle of July they were making vigorous efforts to prove the loyalty of Texas to the government. Public

[1]See the *Texas Republican*, September 19, 1835.

meetings passed pacific resolutions, and a representative committee of delegates from San Felipe, Columbia, and Mina drew up an address and appointed two commissioners to lay it before General Cos at Matamoras with assurances of fidelity to their adopted country.

This was the situation when, on July 25, Miller wrote to J. W. Smith, of Bexar, suggesting that if Colonel Ugartechea would now demand the arrest of the foremost agitators, the colonists would probably give them up. The letter was in part as follows:

. . . All here is in a train for peace, the war and speculating parties are entirely put down, and are preparing to leave the country. They should *now* be demanded of their respective chiefs —a few at a time—at first, Johnson, Williamson, Travis, and Williams,—and perhaps that is enough. Capt. Martin once revolutionary, is now, thank God, where he should be, in favor of peace and his duty, and by his influence in a good degree has peace been restored. But now they should be demanded—the moment is auspicious. The people are up. Say so, and oblige one who will never forget his true allegiance to the supreme authorities of the Nation and who knows that until they are dealt with, Texas will never be at quiet. Travis is in a peck of trouble. Dr. James B. Miller disclaims his act in taking Anahuac and he feels the breach.

Don Lorenzo de Zavala is now in Columbia trying to arouse [the people] etc have him called for and he also will be delivered up. Williamson, Johnson, and Baker are now on a visit to him, and no doubt conspiring against the Government.

Fail not to move in this matter, and that *quickly,* as now is the time.[1]

These names demand a word of explanation. Colonel Ugartechea, for whom the letter was ultimately intended, was the superior military officer in Texas; F. W. Johnson and S. M. Williams had figured prominently in the recent land speculations; Travis had led the assault on Anahuac; R. M. Williamson had just delivered a war-like fourth of July oration; Mosely Baker was an outspoken member of the war party; and de Zavala was a political refugee from Mexico. The order had already been given for the arrest of de Zavala, and on August 1, before he heard of Miller's letter, Gen-

---

[1]A copy of this letter, certified by Andrew Ponton, *Alcalde* of Gonzales, is to be found in the Texas State Library; it is partially and inaccurately printed in Brown, *History of Texas,* I, 303.

eral Cos sent from Matamoras a demand for the surrender of
Travis.[1]   It thus appears that Miller was advising little that the
authorities were not already determined to do.   He did, however,
encourage Ugartechea to act more promptly than he might otherwise have done, for on July 31 the latter issued an order for the
arrests.[2]

Miller's own statement of his motives as avowed in the letter may,
I believe, be frankly accepted.   He took his oath of allegiance seriously, he was a Mexican citizen; he, with the majority of the colonists, desired nothing more ardently than peace; he was convinced
that the country could never be tranquil until the agitators were
suppressed; and therefore, in his own mind, both as a loyal Mexican
and as a well-wisher of his fellow-Texans, he was justified in urging the measures which he thought would most effectually accomplish that end.   That he misjudged the means for doing this is
beside the mark.

The colonists refused to make the arrests, public opinion changed
during August and September, and on October 2 hostilities began
with the battle of Gonzales.   Miller's letter had been no secret, and
the change in popular feeling brought condemnation upon him.
This he so keenly felt that, in October, he published a long article,
explaining his motives and pleading for justice.[3]   After briefly
reviewing recent political conditions, he declared that in the beginning the war party was composed largely of the men who had
been interested in the land speculations, and hence the inference
was natural "that their zeal and patriotism had to excite them
something of a private nature."

. . .   And indeed the whole country from one end to the other
with the exception of a very limited number of individuals, seemed
resolved on peace on any honorable terms, and expressed full confidence in the good faith of the Government in its relations with
us. . . .   With the people, I thought it [the war party] was
trying to wheedle us with fancied dangers. . . .   When I say,
with the people, I say what I mean, for I heard hundreds of persons
and in all parts of the country, say, that if they took their rifle into

[1]Cos to *Ayuntamiento* of Columbia, August 1, 1835.   Austin Papers.
[2]Ugartechea to Tenorio, July 31, 1835.   Bexar Archives.
[3]See the *Texas Republican,* October 3, 1835.

hand, at all, it would be to go and take *the agitators of the public peace* (some confined themselves to the *speculators)* and deliver them to the Government,—and I may safely appeal to the generous minded people of Texas, whether at that time nine-tenths of them did not at least feel if they did not speak this.

Miller went on to say that several persons, both private citizens and public officials, knew and approved the contents of his letter; that they expected Ugartechea's order for the arrests by a particular mail, and had made preparations to execute it. Some of the colonists interpreted his advice to Ugartechea to call for a few at a time as implying that in the end he wished many to be arrested. This, Miller explained, was entirely wrong. He hoped, on the contrary, by naming a few men, whom Ugartechea was already determined to demand, to divert his attention from all others. He acknowledged that his personal relations with some of the men named were not cordial, but denied that he had been actuated by any motive of private revenge. He believed that the government now had ruinous designs upon Texas, and declared that in the present circumstances he would be the last man to advocate the surrender of any one to the authorities.

This is the whole of Miller's case. He opposed the war party, and placed himself squarely on the side of the government. A less honest or a more politic man might have avoided such an unequivocal declaration of principles; but want of diplomacy can scarcely be regarded as treason, or candor as the mark of a spy. It is natural enought that in the heat of conflict his attitude should have been misunderstood; but it is cause for regret that writers of our history have not been more judicial than his contemporaries.

Miller's end is as vague as his beginning. Brown declares[1] that he left the country in 1835, never to return. The records of the Land Office do not show that he ever acquired any land in Texas, and it is probable that his sojourn here was brief.

From July, 1835, to October, 1836, the record of Gritten is fairly complete, and it is one of useful and even honorable service to Texas. He is said to have been an Englishman, long a resident in Mexico, and to have first visited Texas in 1834 as secretary to

[1]*History of Texas,* I, 285.

Colonel Almonte, who was in that year commissioned by the government to make a statistical report on Texas.[1] Yoakum adds the information that he was the brother-in-law of J. M. Carbajal, a respected citizen of De León's colony, in the present county of Victoria.

It is just possible that Gritten remained in Texas after the departure of Almonte. At any rate, a letter of his in the Bexar Archives indicates that he had been some time in the country before the beginning of July, 1835.[2] During July and August he devoted himself unsparingly to the task of restoring confidence between the colonists and the government, and apparently held for a while some sort of commission from Ugartechea to report on the state of public opinion in the settlements. An extract from the letter mentioned above and another found in a dispatch of Colonel Ugartechea to General Cos afford all the information that is obtainable on this point. Gritten wrote on July 5 to Ugartechea: "According to what Dr. Miller has told me, you want me to give you a description of public opinion in this district; and I shall also indicate the rumors that circulate here. This I do, thinking to render a service to my country. And I shall be happy if I am able to avert in this part of the republic fighting and blood-shed, which would be regretable as much for the nation in general as for Texas in particular." On the 7th, Ugartechea writing of Gritten to General Cos said: "I have allowed to this individual, who has constantly behaved himself with loyalty and good faith, a soldier to accompany him to San Felipe" to investigate the imprisonment of a Mexican courier and the seizure of his dispatches. The half dozen long letters which within the next two weeks Gritten wrote to Ugartechea are among our most valuable sources for the history of the period, and without the support of other evidence confute the charge against him of treachery to the interests of the colonists.[3] They tell Ugartechea that the great majority of the

[1]Yoakum, *History of Texas*, I, 341, note; II, 44-45; Brown, *History of Texas*, I. 310, 448-450.

[2]Gritten to Ugartechea, July 5, 1835. Bexar Archives. The letter is printed in *Publications* of the Southern History Association, VIII, 345-348.

[3]These letters, dated July 5, 6, 7, 9, 11, 17, 1835, are all in the Bexar Archives; and all except the last are printed in *Publications of the Southern History Association*, VIII, 345-456, *passim*.

Texans are peaceable, law-abiding Mexican citizens, and urge the adoption of conciliatory measures by the authorities, while at the same time saying plainly that the introduction of a large body of soldiers into Texas would unite all parties against the government. One extract will suffice to illustrate the burden of Gritten's advice: "With benevolent measures the passions of the people may be calmed, which could not be done by force, . . . This munici- pality [Gonzales] and that of Mina are working as hard as they can to banish the bad impression caused by the lack of confidence. . . . I do not doubt that all these steps will be successful; and I intend for the good of this country to second them."

Through Gritten's influence the municipality of Gonzales on July 7 passed resolutions of loyalty to Mexico,[1] and on the 17th the joint committee from San Felipe, Columbia, and Mina, referred to above, chose him as one of the two commissioners to wait on General Cos and explain the pacific attitude of the mass of the col- onists. The other commissioner was D. C. Barrett. At the very outset of their journey to Matamoras they encountered a courier from Colonel Ugartechea ordering the arrests already mentioned. Realizing the effect that this might have on the people, they de- tained the courier at Gonzales, while Gritten hastened on to Bexar and tried to persuade Ugartechea to revoke his order. The latter not only refused to do this, but assured Gritten that it would be useless to talk to Cos of loyalty until the colonists manifested the sincerity of their protestations by surrendering the offenders. Some days later a letter from Cos confirmed this prophecy, and the commissioners went no further. Barrett returned to his home at Mina, and Gritten remained at Bexar, where he continued to act as a mediator between Ugartechea and the colonists.[2]

From this time on Gritten identified himself with the Texans. On July 28 he had technically become a colonist himself by ob- taining certificates for a league and a quarter of land in Milam's

[1]MS. in *Texas State Library.*

[2]For the basis of this paragraph see: Brown, *History of Texas*, I, 300; Bancroft, *North Mexican States and Texas*, II, 162; Wooten (Editor), *A Comprehensive History of Texas*, I, 168-171; Barrett and Gritten to Cos, August 9, 1835, Bexar Archives; *Texas Republican*, September 19, 1835.

colony.[1] From his position at Bexar he was able to keep the people authoritatively informed of events in Mexico, and the wonder is that he was not regarded as a spy by Ugartechea. September 8 he wrote Barrett[2] that it had become evident that the government was determined upon harsh disciplinary measures in Texas, and that the people must submit or be prepared to resist. In connection with this letter Stephen F. Austin, who had just returned from his long imprisonment in Mexico, gives his estimate of Gritten, saying: "I place more reliance on what he says because he has made so many exertions to affect an amicable reconciliation. . . . I think he has been faithful to the people here and fear that he will get into prison."[3]

On December 11, the General Council, which was the legislative branch of the provisional government established at the beginning of the revolution, showed its confidence in Gritten by electing him collector of the port of Copano, but Governor Smith declined to sign his commission, declaring that he had always considered him a spy.[4] Nevertheless, Matthew Caldwell was at that very time writing to Smith in commendation of Gritten's general efficiency in the commissary department of the army, and calling particular attention to a recent important performance of his in carrying ammunition to the Texan army while it was besieging Bexar.[5]

In March, 1836, he was working in the printing office of the *Telegraph and Texas Register,* at San Felipe.[6] On the 25th of that month a subscription was started soliciting land donations for the government, and Gritten pledged a quarter of a league—one-fifth of all that he had.[7] In July we find him acting as translator and interpreter in the prize case of the schooners *Comanche* and *Fanny*

[1]Land Office Records, Vol. 16, pp. 329, 393.

[2]A copy of the letter, certified by Stephen F. Austin, is in the Lamar Papers in the Texas State Library.

[3]Austin to Grayson, September 19, 1835 (copy). Austin Papers.

[4]Brown, *History of Texas,* I, 449. See also THE QUARTERLY, V, 308, note 2.

[5]Caldwell to Smith, December 19, 1835. Miscellaneous documents relating to the Treasury, 1835-1836, in Comptroller's Department.

[6]Borden to Burnet, March 24, 1836. MS. in Texas State Library. Financial Affairs.

[7]A printed broadside, in the Texas State Library. Formerly file No. 351.

Butler, which had been captured by Texan naval vessels, and President Burnet at the same time said that until a few days before Gritten had been in the employ of the government since April.[1] On September 19, Gail Borden congratulates Austin on having the services of Mr. Gritten, who "can do more business in the Spanish than any person I know of."[2] The last trace of him that has come to my notice is a receipt for forty dollars paid him by the government on October 11, 1836, for his services as translator in the case of Bartholomé Pajes, who was accused of trying to rescue Santa Anna from his imprisonment in Texas.[3]

This evidence, though fragmentary, is sufficient to exonerate Gritten of the imputations against his honesty. Two additional points should be mentioned: Miss Rather assures me that in studying the sources for her history of *De Witt's Colony* she arrived at the same opinion of Gritten as that which I have outlined above; and Professor Bolton, who has extensively explored the Mexican archives, tells me that though he has seen there an abundance of correspondence from spies in Texas none of it is from Gritten. This is negative evidence, but it helps to strengthen the case already presented.

My notes on Gritten have been taken incidentally as I gathered material on the general subject of the Texas revolution, and that I cannot follow him beyond the end of 1836 may merely be due to the fact that my minute acquaintance with the archives extends no further. It does not necessarily signify that his career in Texas then closed.

[1]Comptroller's Department. Military Service, 2d Series, No. 602.
[2]Austin Papers.
[3]Comptroller's Department. Military Service, 2d series, No. 618.

NOTES AND FRAGMENTS.

THE FORSYTHS IN TEXAS.—Among the Forsyths in Texas may be mentioned the following:

Captain Cyrus Hamilton Forsyth, born Portland, Maine, 1812; died of yellow fever in Galveston, Texas, 1839. He was with Major Montgomery and was a volunteer captain in his command or on his staff in the battles for the establishment of the Texan nation. There is the name Forsyth on the monument to the heroes of Texas at Galveston. He was unmarried and left no issue. He was a son of Captain Thomas Forsyth (who had been educated as the heir of his uncle, Dr. Matthew Forsyth, Viscount de Fronsac of the Royal French Navy, a citizen of Normandy, France) by Sallie, daughter of Captain John Pray, whose wife was Mary, daughter of Colonel John Hamilton of North Carolina. Colonel Hamilton had raised a regiment for the crown in 1776 and was on the staff of the Marquis of Cornwallis. His first American ancestor was Hon. Matthew Forsyth, Viscount de Fronsac and a seigneur of Canada, a sketch of whom appeared in the *American Historical Magazine* of Jan. 1908. Colonel Hamilton was a relative of Governor John Forsyth of Georgia.

Joseph Forsyth, sometime marshal of Dallas, descended, I believe, though I am not certain, from the Kentucky branch of the same Scottish family, whose first ancestor (John Forsyth) came to Kentucky through the north of Ireland about 1754. He died as the result of wounds received at Wellington, Kansas, where he alone and unaided quelled two cowboy riots. An eye-witness relates that the cowboys were "shooting up" the town, and every one was afraid; but Marshal Forsyth went to the corner of the street, took off his hat and emptied his spare cartridges in it and held up the entire gang as they came along. He killed three of the rioters and was mortally wounded himself, but he quelled the riot.

The Hon. Thomas Scott Forsyth, nephew of Captain Cyrus Hamilton Forsyth, was a journalist in Dallas, Marshall and other towns in Texas, 1906-8.

Are there others of the name who are worth recording?

X. Y. X.

THE QUARTERLY

OF THE

TEXAS STATE HISTORICAL ASSOCIATION

VOL. XIII.   JANUARY, 1910.   No. 3.

The publication committee and the editors disclaim responsibility for views expressed by contributors to THE QUARTERLY.

RECOGNITION OF THE REPUBLIC OF TEXAS BY THE UNITED STATES.[1]

ETHEL ZIVLEY RATHER.

THE MOVEMENT FOR INDEPENDENCE.

When Texas in the fall of 1835 found herself at war with Mexico, her first step, after putting the country in a state of defense, was to cast about for aid.   Two alternatives were presented to her: she might either ally herself with the Mexican Liberals, who were also in rebellion against the centralized government of Santa Anna; or she might declare independence, and trust to the United States for assistance to sustain it.   What she did was to experi-

---

[1] A thesis presented to the faculty of the Yale University in part fulfillment of the requirements for the degree of Doctor of Philosophy, May, 1908.   This paper does not claim to be a complete study of the relations between the United States and Texas which led to the recognition by the former of the independence of the Republic of Texas in 1837.   There should be some material on the subject in the records of the Department of State at Washington, to which I have not had access; while the archives in the City of Mexico would doubtless throw much additional light upon the relations between the United States and Mexico during this period.   The most valuable and complete sources, however, have been available (see bibliography, pp. 254-255).

My acknowledgments are due to Mr. Worthington C. Ford, formerly of the Library of Congress, and to Mr. Richard Rathbun, assistant secretary of the Smithsonian Institution, for courteous assistance in the use of materials in the Library of Congress; and especially to Professor George P. Garrison and Dr. Eugene C. Barker of the University of Texas, Professor Herbert E. Bolton, of Leland Stanford University, and Professor J. S. Bassett, of Smith College, for valuable suggestions and indispensable help.

ETHEL ZIVLEY RATHER.

ment with each course in turn; and the revolution falls thus into two phases—first, an effort to restore the "republican principles" of the constitution which Santa Anna had overthrown; secondly, a struggle for independence. Some emphasis has been laid upon the conscientiousness of the Texan colonists during the first period in adhering to their obligations to Mexico and the reluctance with which they finally threw off allegiance to their adopted country. It is no doubt true that, rather than engage in a war whose issue was at best doubtful, the majority of the colonists would have preferred to continue the old relationship with Mexico under the constitution, if peace might thereby have been restored. But in tracing the relations between Texas and the United States at this time, one is forced to question whether the Texan leaders were as sincere during the first months of the revolution in their loyalty to the constitution of 1824 as they were later on in the acknowledged war for independence; whether more confidence either in their own strength or in help from without might not have led earlier to an unqualified declaration of independence. In the fall of 1835, however, they felt that help from some quarter must be forthcoming—that alone they were incapable of resisting the forces that had already suppressed similar uprisings in other provinces throughout Mexico.

The Consultation at San Felipe, which was called partly for the purpose of determining what course to pursue, decided, November 6, against a declaration of independence by a vote of thirty-three to fifteen. On the next day a report defining the position in which Texas stood was brought in by a committee appointed for the purpose, and unanimously adopted. It stated that:

Whereas, General Antonio Lopez de Santa Anna, and other military chieftains, have, by force of arms, overthrown the federal institutions of Mexico, and dissolved the social compact which existed between Texas and the other members of the Mexican confederacy; now the good people of Texas, availing themselves of their natural rights,

SOLEMNLY DECLARE

1st. That they have taken up arms in defence of their rights and liberties, which were threatened by the encroachments of military despots, and in defence of the republican principles of the federal constitution of Mexico, of eighteen and twenty-four.[1]

2d.   That Texas is no longer morally or civilly bound by the compact of union; yet, stimulated by the generosity and sympathy common to a free people, they offer their support and assistance to such of the members of the Mexican confederacy as will take up arms against military despotism.

3d.   That they do not acknowledge that the present authorities of the nominal Mexican republic have the right to govern within the limits of Texas.

4th.   That they will not cease to carry on war against the said authorities whilst their troops are within the limits of Texas.

5th.   That they hold it to be their right during the disorganization of the federal system, and the reign of despotism, to withdraw from the union, to establish an independent government, or to adopt such measures as they may deem best calculated to protect their rights and liberties, but that they will continue faithful to the Mexican government so long as that nation is governed by the constitution and laws that were formed for the government of the political association.

6th.   That Texas is responsible for the expense of her armies now in the field.

7th.   That the public faith of Texas is pledged for the payment of any debts contracted by her agents.

8th.   That she will reward, by donations in lands, all who volunteer their services in her present struggle, and receive them as citizens.[2]

Throughout the rest of this year and the beginning of the next, the General Council of the provisional government[3] remained at least nominally faithful to this declaration. On the other hand Provisional Governor Smith was from the first an ardent advocate of an immediate declaration of independence; and it is to this

[1]The Mexican republic, so-called, which Santa Anna had just overthrown was established in 1824. Its constitution was modeled largely after that of the United States (Garrison, *Texas,* 98).

[2]Gammel, *Laws of Texas,* I, 522.

[3]One work of the Consultation was the organization of a provisional government. "The scheme adopted was double, one part providing for a civil and the other for a military organization; and both of them were triumphs of potential confusion and conflict of authority. The civil government was to consist of a governor and lieutenant-governor elected by the consultation, and a council made up of one member from each municipality elected by its delegates. The governor and council had ill-defined and practically coördinate powers, . . . and there was no provision against deadlocks" (Garrison, *Texas,* 197-198).

difference of opinion that the long and undignified quarrel between the governor and the Council has been ascribed.[1]

The attitude of the Council on this subject is no doubt partly responsible for the general impression that in the fall of 1835 the majority of the Texans, known as the conservatives, were reluctant to withdraw allegiance from Mexico—that, in spite of their declaration to the contrary, they did feel still under moral obligation to remain faithful to the constitution of 1824.[2]   Stephen F. Austin, also, repeatedly offered support for such a belief.   In a report made to the provisional government, November 30, 1835, after explaining at some length that the volunteers had taken up arms in defence of the constitution of 1824, he continued thus:

I have faithfully labored for years to unite Texas permanently to the Mexican confederation. . . . There was but one way to effect this union with any hope of permanency or harmony, which was by admitting Texas into a state of the Mexican confederation. . . .

The people of Texas desired it; and if proofs were wanting (but

[1]Smith, "The Quarrel Between Governor Smith and the Council of the Provisional Government of the Republic," in THE QUARTERLY, V, 295. The subjects of dispute as enumerated in this article were as follows: (1) the question of aiding Colonel Gonzales, a Mexican Liberal; (2) the change in the manner of drawing drafts on the treasurer, so that the council might vote money without the governor's consent—in anticipation perhaps, of Smith's opposition to assisting the Mexican Liberals; (3) the relations with General Mexía, another Mexican Liberal; (4) the call of a convention, in order to declare independence; (5) the appointment of D. C. Barrett and Edward Gritten, members of the Council, and prominent opponents of Smith, respectively as judge advocate general of the Texan armies, and as collector of the port of Cópano; (6) the Matamoras expedition, undertaken on the basis of coöperation with the Mexican Liberals.

[2]The declaration of November 7 was entirely illogical. It stated that Texas had taken up arms in defense of a union from which she herself had practically withdrawn. In referring to the confused statements in this document Austin speaks apologetically thus:

"The general consultation of Texas was elected at a time when the country was distracted by popular excitements, produced by the diversity of opinions which naturally resulted from the disbelief of some that the federal system would be destroyed, or was even attacked, the excited and intemperate zeal of others, and the general want of certain information in all. It could not be reasonably expected that a body elected under such circumstances, would be entirely free from the conflicting opinions that prevailed amongst their constituents, or that a clear and positively definite position would be taken by it" (Austin to Barrett, December 3, 1835, in *Telegraph and Texas Register*, February 27, 1836; also in Wooten, *A Comprehensive History of Texas*, I, 566).

they are not) of their fidelity to their obligations as Mexican citizens, this effort to erect Texas into a state affords one which is conclusive to every man of judgment who knows anything about this country.

'The object of the Texans, therefore, in wishing a separation from Coahuila, and the erection of their country into a state, was to avoid a total separation from Mexico by a revolution. . . .[1]

Later on, also, in explaining the action taken by the Consultation of San Felipe, Austin again said:

The majority of Texas, so far as an opinion can be formed from the acts of the people at their primary meetings, was decidedly in favor of declaring in positive, clear and unequivocal terms, for the federal constitution of 1824, and for the organization of a local government, either as a state of the Mexican confederation, or provisionally, until the authorities of the state of Coahuila and Texas could be restored. This measure was absolutely necessary to save the country from anarchy, for it was left without any government at all, owing to the dispersion and imprisonment of the executive and legislative authorities, by the unconstitutional intervention of the military power. Some individuals were also in favor of independence, though no public meeting whose proceedings I have seen, expressed such an idea.[2]

Even William H. Wharton, one of the most radical advocates for independence, in speaking of the November declaration, said: "I do not blame the Consultation for their declaration. They were not empowered and it was not in the contemplation of those who elected them to make any other."[3] Morfit, the agent sent out in the summer of 1836 by President Jackson to examine into the condition of affairs in Texas, also reported, August 22: "The Texans assert that this resistance was not because they even *then* [that is, after Cos's invasion] wished to separate from the confederacy, but,

[1]Wooten, *A Comprehensive History of Texas*, I, 562-563.
[2]Austin to Barrett, December 3, 1835, *ibid.*, 566.
[3]Wharton to Archer, November 29, 1835, in Brown, *History of Texas*, I, 428. There is some conflict as to the date of this letter. It was printed in an undated circular as an enclosure in a letter from Archer to the editors of the *Telegraph and Texas Register* and in another circular, likewise undated, as an enclosure in a letter from Archer to the editor of the *Texas Republican* (both in Austin Papers). In the first case it is dated November 26, and in the second November 28.

on the contrary, because they were desirous to bring back the Government to the terms of the constitution of 1824."[1]

Despite such authorities, an examination of the private correspondence of the time, principally Austin's own, and other documents that were not intended for the Mexican eye leads one to the conclusion that the declaration of November 7 and all acts in conformity thereto were not altogether the results of loyalty to the constitution of 1824, but were dictated largely by policy. William H. Wharton, in declining his appointment to go as commissioner to the United States,[2] testified to the fact that it was expediency that governed the action of the Consultation. Referring to the indefinite attitude assumed by the November declaration he said: "It was generally thought, and I then thought it a matter of policy so to declare. It was thought (by a majority over a very strong minority) that a declaration for the constitution would neutralize the prejudices or enlist the sympathies and assistance of the Federal party of the interior in our favor; and also that under such declaration we could obtain the requisite loans, etc., from the capitalists of the United States."[3] James W. Robinson, one of the prominent members of the Consultation and who afterward became Lieutenant-Governor of the provisional government and ex-officio president of the General Council, writing from the Consultation on November 3, 1835, said: "How the convention will decide is uncertain, but the probability is in favor of the constitution as a matter of policy only, as all agree we must go, sooner or later, for independence."[4] Robinson, it must be remembered, was also of the radical party, and his statement may be somewhat biased. But it is a well-known fact that the first report of the committee of the Consultation,[5] which John A. Wharton presented, November 4, was an absolute declaration of independence. This was even adopted; but on the recommendation of Houston, tradition says, it was reconsidered, and the declaration of November 7

[1]*Senate Docs.*, 24 Cong., 2 Sess., I, No. 20, p. 7.
[2]See below, p. 168.
[3]Wharton to Archer, November 29, 1835, in Brown, *History of Texas*, I, 428.
[4]Robinson to Frost Thorn, November 3, 1835, cited by Yoakum, *History of Texas*, II, 12, footnote.
[5]See above, p. 156.

took its place.[1] The motives that influenced the Consultation in making this change were no doubt the same as those expressed in a report sent in to San Felipe, November 9, by the Jurisdiction of Liberty. It said:

In behalf of their fellow citizens they [that is, the committee appointed to make the report] state that a premature declaration of independence would be inexpedient and injurious, that a temporary provisional organization of Government with a carefull attention to the development of events is the best policy; that a precipitious cesesion from the Mexican Republic might incur the reprehension, and wean from us the sympathies of many friends in the North.[2]

Another argument in favor of the interpretation of the declaration of November 7 as a measure purely of expediency is the striking analogy between the present situation and that of 1832. At that time a struggle was going on in Mexico between Bustamante, who had set up a tyrannical form of government, and Santa Anna, then posing as the champion of the Constitution of 1824. In the meantime hostilities had broken out at Anahuac between the Texan

[1]The *Journals of the Consultation* in the printed form in which they now exist (Gammel, *Laws of Texas*, I. 507-548) state simply that on November 4 Wharton, from this committee, "made a report." That this is an expurgated edition of the Journals there is much internal evidence to show. But, aside from this, the circumstances under which the Journals were published would naturally lead one to expect as much. December 25, 1835, when the quarrel between the governor and the council concerning the coöperation with the Mexican Liberals was at its height Barrett, who was perhaps the most radical of Governor Smith's opponents, presented a "corrected copy of the Journals of the Convention" [Consultation], and this "revised Journal" was ordered printed (Gammel, *Laws of Texas*, I, 507. 693). Yoakum, *History of Texas*, II, 12, footnote, is authority for the statement that a declaration of independence was first adopted and then reconsidered. He bases his information upon another copy of the journal, page 51—probably the original. Garrison, *Texas*, 195, suggests that the declaration of November 4 may be among the archives in the state house, but it has not yet been discovered.

[2]Extract from a letter addressed to the Provisional Government by the Committee of Safety of the Jurisdiction of Liberty, November 9, 1835, in minutes of the General Council, November 15 (MS), Austin Papers. It was printed in *Proceedings of the General Council*, for November 16 and appears in Gammel, *Laws of Texas*, I, 554. This is another illustration (see above, note 1) of the revision which took place before printing. Besides having the spelling and the punctuation corrected, the printed copy reads, simply, "that a precipitate secession from the Mexican Republic might incur reprehension." Evidently it was the desire of the Council to eliminate anything that would savor of independence.

colonists and Mexican troops stationed in Texas. The report had reached Mexico that it was a move on the part of the Texans for independence. Mejia, of the popular party, immediately made a truce with Bustamante's troops, and set out to Texas to suppress the rebellion. It would be well, the Texans thought, to have some excuse to give for the disturbances. They therefore drew up what were known as the Turtle Bayou resolutions, declaring in favor of Santa Anna and the Constitution of 1824. Mejia was well satisfied with these expressions of loyalty. "He was received with great ceremony at Brazoria and immediately presented with the blessed resolutions. Nothing further was needed to prove to him that the conduct of the Texans had been entirely innocent and praiseworthy."[1] It was not strange, therefore, that in 1835 the Texans called to mind an expedient that three years earlier, under similar circumstances, had served them so effectively.

In 1835, however, a large proportion of the Texans were actually contemplating independence. But the problem of securing immediate aid against Santa Anna confronted them. The Mexican Liberals held out flattering inducements.[2] The other source, the United States, from which they were ardently hoping to receive help, was far less certain. Besides a precipitate declaration might meet with the disfavor of their neighbor on the north,[3] whose good will above all it was essential to retain. Under considerations such as these many of the radicals were induced to temporize, with the mental reservation that independence should be the ultimate aim,

[1]Garrison, *Texas*, 178-179.
[2]Smith, "The Quarrel between Governor Smith and the Council," in THE QUARTERLY, V, 299-300.
[3]As a matter of fact good use was made later on of the "forbearance" of the Texans at this time. Even Wharton, in an appeal made before a public meeting in New York, April 26, 1836 (see below, p. 186), laid considerable emphasis upon this point. He says, "Even after all this [that is, Cos's invasion, etc.], they did not declare independence. No, on the 7th of November last, while flushed with various and signal triumphs over the central mercenaries, the people of Texas, in solemn convention, declared for the constitution of 1824, and pledged themselves to aid with their fortunes and their lives in its restoration. On the second of March, however, finding that all parties in Mexico had united against them, . . . they then declared their absolute independence" (*Address of the Honorable Wm. H. Wharton*, April 26, 1836, Austin Papers).

And in this desire it is safe to assume that a great number of the so-called conservative party also shared.

There can be no doubt that Stephen F. Austin was influenced by such considerations, and his attitude throws perhaps the truest light upon the situation in the fall of 1835. He was at the time the recognized leader of the conservatives; and he has subsequently been held up as the one man who to the last was faithful to every possible obligation to Mexico. To all outward appearance this was true. In his zeal to coöperate with the Liberal party he even incurred the suspicion of some of his own fellow citizens—so much so that he was spoken of contemptuously as a "Mexican." Though a man remarkable for his fairness in dealing with others, his opposition to a declaration of independence in the fall of 1835 led him into bitter and unjust denunciations of his opponents—a thing that he deeply regretted afterward.[1] But the principle at stake was not loyalty to Mexico, however reluctantly he may have renounced allegiance to his adopted country when such a step became necessary. The controlling motive of his life was the welfare of his colony; and on his return from Mexico, he undoubtedly felt that the radical party, in precipitating the revolution, was endangering the very end they had in view, namely, independence. That he, too, however, had become convinced that independence must be the ultimate result, there is abundant evidence to show; and this perhaps explains the apparent inconsistency of his attitude in the fall of 1835. In a personal letter to a cousin, written August 21, 1835, from New Orleans on his return from a two years' imprisonment in Mexico, he gives the clearest exposition of his views. Having been kept in close confinement in Mexico, he was as yet unaware of the recent developments in Texas. He had, however, as he says in this letter, already come to the conclusion that the best interests of Texas demanded that she become a part of the United States. He had foreseen that the Anglo-American colonization of Texas, if unchecked, would result inevitably in her separation from Mexico, which he considered but the preliminary step to annexation to the United States. As a means of hastening the process he planned

[1] See below, p. 165, note 5; p. 173, note 1.

to induce a great immigration during the winter of 1835-6—'with passports, so long as the door was legally open; should it be closed, it would then be time enough to force it open, if necessary.' The immigrants should of course be slaveholders, in order to harmonize with their neighbors in the slaveholding states. When this had been accomplished, he expected "the violent political convulsions of Mexico to shake off Texas as a gentle breeze shakes off a ripe peach." The importance of Texas to the southwest he believed would appeal to all reflecting men, but especially to Jackson and the Senate. In the meanwhile, however, everything should be governed by *"prudence* and an *observance of appearances."* "The Mexicans," he says, "are a strange people. *Appearances* mean everything to them even though they know they are being deceived. They have high ideals of national dignity, but will sacrifice national dignity and national interest, too, if it can be done so as not to arrest public attention. The more the Anglo-American population of Texas is increased the more readily will the Mexican government give it up; and the more Texas *seems* to oppose a separation from Mexico the less tenacious will Mexico hold to it."[1]

Again, after the decision to join the Mexican Liberals had been

[1]Austin to a cousin (probably Mrs. Mary Austin Holley), August 21, 1835, Austin Papers. Compare this with Austin's attitude as expressed in a letter to Capt. Henry Austin, written shortly after the passage of the law of April 6, 1830. After deploring this law he goes on to say that all the settlers had been growing sincerely attached to the Mexican government. He does not know, he says, what the ultimate fate of Texas is to be, but for himself he is opposed to union with the United States except under certain guarantees, among which he would insist upon the perpetual exclusion of slavery from the country. A much earlier expression of the same opinions regarding Mexico that are contained in Austin's letter of August 21, 1835, is found in a letter written in cipher by Poinsett to Clay, July 27, 1825 (cited by Reeves, *American Diplomacy under Tyler and Polk,* 62). Poinsett says:

"I find that there exists great apprehension in the minds of the people of this country that the government of the United States contemplates renewing their claim to the territory north of the Rio Bravo del Norte, and it may be of some importance to consider their great sensibilities on this subject. It appears to me that it will be important to gain time if we wish to extend our territory beyond the boundary agreed upon by the treaty of 1819. Most of the good land from the Colorado to the Sabine has been granted by the state of Texas and is rapidly peopling with either grantees or squatters from the United States, a population they will find difficult to govern, and perhaps after a short period they may not be so averse to part with that portion of their territory as they are at present."

made, Austin wrote: "Every possible aid should be given the Federal party in the interior; but it should be done as auxiliary aid, in conformity with the 2nd article of the declaration. By doing this the war will be kept out of Texas. The country will remain at peace. It will fill up rapidly with families, and there will be no great need of a standing army."[1]

The importance of these statements lies in Austin's powerful influence. All things considered he was, without doubt, the first man in Texas. The newspapers quoted him; the private correspondence of the time also attests his popularity. Expressions such as the following were frequent: "All eyes are turned towards you . . . Texas can be wielded by you, and *you alone;* and her destiny is now completely in your hands. I have every confidence that you will guide us safely through all our perils."[2]

Soon after his arrival in Texas, however, Austin saw that his plan for separation from Mexico[3] would never have time to materialize. The war, indeed, was upon them. It had come, he said, much sooner than he had expected when he left Mexico or New Orleans.[4] Still he was opposed to declaring independence. The centralized government had succeeded in crushing similar rebellions throughout Mexico. Texas would do well to look to her resources before defying the strength of the "Napoleon of the West," as Santa Anna styled himself. A declaration of independence would turn against her even the Federal party with whom there was yet an opportunity to unite. If this union were effected the war might be kept out of Texas and prevented from assuming a "national" character.[5] In the meantime every nerve should be strained to put the country in a state of preparation.

As a part of their effort in this direction there would be nothing

[1]Austin to Johnson, Parker, Barrett, Robinson, Hanks, Sublett, and Hoxey, December 22, 1835, Brown, *Life of Henry Smith*, 177-180.
[2]W. B. Travis to Austin, September 22, 1835, Austin Papers.
[3]See above, pp. 163-164.
[4]Austin to Grayson, September 19, 1835, Austin Papers.
[5]Austin to Houston, January 7, 1836, *Telegraph and Texas Register*, February 27, 1836; Austin to F. W. Johnson, Daniel Parker, D. C. Barrett, J. W. Robinson, Wyatt Hanks, P. Sublett, and Asa Hoxey, December 22, 1835, in Brown, *Life of Henry Smith*, 177-180; Austin to R. R. Royal, December 25, 1835, *Ibid.* 249-253. These last two letters cited were the result of a party warfare in which Austin allowed himself to become involved. See below, p. 173, note 1.

amiss in applying to the United States, also, for sympathy and material aid. Even before hostilities began, Austin had said, "If there was any way of getting at it I should like to know what the *wise men* of the United States think the people of Texas ought to do."[1] Later on, only a week after the Consultation that had declared for the constitution had adjourned, Austin wrote, "The fate of Texas depends mainly on this—we ought to get united to the U. S. as soon as possible, it is the best we can do."[2]

Nothing can be more natural than this promptness with which the minds of the Anglo-American colonists reverted to their mother-country when friction began with the Mexican authorities. Often throughout the whole colonization period there was clearly discernible among the Texan pioneers a longing for the laws and institutions they had left, and a consequent impatience at the clumsy machinery of Mexican government. There was no congeniality between the two peoples. A newspaper article signed "Jefferson" and printed in the *Telegraph and Texas Register*, expresses sentiments toward the Mexicans which must have been typical. In comparing the Texan revolution with the American revolution of 1776 the writer said:

We separate from a people one-half of whom are the most depraved of the different races of Indians, different in color, pursuits and character; and *all* of whom are divided from us by the insurmountable barrier which nature and refined taste have thrown between us—a people whose inert and idle habits, general ignorance and superstition, prevents the possibility of our ever mingling in the same harmonious family; and if possible, could only be done by self-degradation. . . . *we* separate from a people who not only neglected us, but drained our little resources, and threw every obstacle in the way of our advancement and prosperity. . . . [a nation] not sufficiently stable to assume a character, and consistent, in her different convulsions, only in treachery, tyranny and imbecility.[3]

This article appeared in February, 1836, and was written prob-

---

[1]Austin to a cousin, August 21, 1835, cited above, p. 163.
[2]Austin to Perry, November 22, 1835, Austin Papers.
[3]*Telegraph and Texas Register*, February 27, 1836.

ably by Wharton,[1] who was then on his way as commissioner to Washington. Its object had been to show the futility of further attempts to coöperate with the Mexican Liberals. But, though Wharton was unaware of the fact, it was unnecessary. During the first two months of 1836 even the most ardent adherents to the principles laid down in the November declaration had been won over, and when the convention met at Washington, Texas, March 1,[2] a declaration of independence was a foregone conclusion. On the next day, indeed, the declaration was made, and seven weeks later, on the battlefield of San Jacinto, the independence of Texas became a reality.

EFFORTS TO SECURE RECOGNITION.

1. *The work of the first commission.*

The Texans realized that one of the first essentials in carrying on a successful revolution was money. In his inaugural address the chairman of the Consultation, Dr. Branch T. Archer, had stated: "It will be necessary to procure funds . . . in order to carry on the war in which we are now engaged; it will, therefore, be our duty to elect agents to procure those funds."[3] November 12, five days after the expedient of declaring for the constitution of 1824 had been adopted, the Consultation decreed that a commission, consisting of Stephen F. Austin, Branch T. Archer, and William H. Wharton be dispatched to the United States furnished with such instructions as the governor and the council might deem necessary.[4]

These instructions were not issued until nearly a month later, and Austin seems to have feared their power would be limited to soliciting financial aid only. He is said to have expressed an un-

---

[1]In his correspondence with the Texan Government Wharton refers to two pamphlets, one signed "Curtius," the other "Jefferson," which he had written and sent to Congress (Wharton to Governor Smith, February 7, 1836. Garrison, *Dip. Cor. Tex.*, I, 65; Wharton to Austin, January 15, 1837, *ibid.*, 176).

[2]When the Consultation had adjourned, November 14, 1835, it had been resolved "to meet on the first day of March next, unless sooner called by the governor and council "(Gammel, *Laws of Texas*, I, 548).

[3]Gammel, *Laws of Texas*, I, 511.

[4]*Ibid.*, 534.

willingness to go at all, unless vested with authority to treat with the government for annexation.[1] Wharton at first definitely declined his appointment, but for a different reason. He was one of the recognized leaders of the radicals, as Austin was of the conservatives, and he was loud in his demand for an immediate declaration of independence. The attitude assumed by the Consultation was much too indefinite, he claimed, to induce capitalists to lend pecuniary aid. Moreover, the declaration was of such a nature as would lead to the belief that the revolution was simply an internal domestic quarrel, and on that basis the United States would refuse to interfere. He advised that a convention meet, January 15, of the coming year to declare independence and sell Texas to the United States if practicable.[2]

The delay in providing instructions seems to have been due largely to doubts as to just what duties, aside from raising money, should be laid upon the commissioners, and the authority by which they should be sent out. A select committee appointed for the purpose of deciding this question reported November 21:

that upon considering the matter, they are unable to find any acts of the Convention, or of this Council, whereon to base instructions for the conduct of said agents, or any "data" which can guide your committee in an opinion of their duties, but from all the information they can obtain, your committee have concluded, that the agents should receive their instructions from the Executive; but in order to enable the Governor to give the necessary instructions, an ordinance should first be originated by the Committee of State, and passed and approved, defining in general the powers and duties of the agents, and make it the duty of the Executive to give such instructions as will be conformable to the resolutions of the Convention and the ordinances of the General Council, made with reference to the subject in view when this office was created. But your committee can not advise that the Committee of State be instructed upon this subject with propriety, until

[1]M. A. Bryan, Austin's nephew, to his father and mother, November 30, 1835, Austin Papers.
[2]Wharton to Archer, November 29, in Brown, *History of Texas.* I, 428. Wharton finally accepted the appointment (Journal of the Council, 108, cited by Yoakum, *History of Texas* II, 36). Yoakum also had access to a copy of the Journal of the Council different from that printed in Gammel, *Laws of Texas,* I.

the reports of the several committees on the Military, Navy, and Finance have been received and passed.[1]

Two weeks more were consumed in trying to frame an ordinance creating a loan of one million dollars, for which the commissioners were to negotiate.[2] Finally, December 4, Provisional Governor Smith, in his message to the General Council, took up the matter thus:

It must be acknowledged by all, that our only succour is expected from the East, where as yet we have not dispatched our agents, sufficient time has elapsed since the rising of the Convention, for them, by this time, to have arrived in the United States. They have called on me, in vain, day after day, time after time, for their dispatches, at least some of them, and they are not yet ready. I say to you, the fate of Texas depends upon their immediate dispatch and success. Why then delay a matter of such vital importance, and give place to minor matters which could be much better delayed? Permit me to beg of you a suspension of all other business, until our Foreign Agents are dispatched.[3]

Accordingly, on the next day an ordinance was passed authorizing the governor to issue to the commissioners[4] instructions as follows: they were to negotiate a loan of one million dollars and receive donations for Texas; to purchase supplies for the government, such as munitions of war, provisions, war vessels, etc.; to appoint agents for the government in the principal cities, subject only to themselves; to grant letters of marque and reprisal; and finally to open communications with the United States government relative to the political situation of Texas, under such instructions as the governor might deem prudent, in the present revolutionary condition of Texas and Mexico.[5] On the 7th the governor's formal

[1]Gammel, *Laws of Texas*, I, 31.
[2]Barker, "Texas Revolutionary Finances," in *Political Science Quarterly*, XIX, 628.
[3]Gammel, *Laws of Texas*, I, 623-624.
[4]Both Austin and Wharton had decided to go. The personal enmity, which had long existed between them and which had been augmented in the fall of 1835 by their differing views toward declaring independence, did not wear away until after they had worked together for a while in New Orleans (Austin to McKinney, January 21, 1836, Austin Papers).
[5]Gammel, *Laws of Texas*, I, 956-958.

commission authorizing the negotiation of the loan was issued,[1] and on the 8th the commissioners' private instructions were drawn up.[2]

It was this latter document which conferred upon the commissioners their diplomatic authority. After giving directions concerning the armed vessels that were to be fitted out and sent from New Orleans, the supplies to be purchased there, the loan and the donations that might be tendered, the instructions continued:

Finally, you will proceed to the City of Washington, with all convenient speed endeavoring at all points to enlist the sympathies of the free and enlightened people of the United States in our favour by explaining to them our true political situation and the causes which impelled us to take up arms; and the critical situation in which we now stand. You will approach the authorities of our Mother Country, either by yourselves, or confidential friends; and ascertain the feelings of the Government toward Texas, in her present attitude. Whether any interposition on the part of that Government in our favour can be expected. or whether in their opinion, any ulterior move on our part would to them, be more commendable and be calculated to render us more worthy of their favour, or whether by any fair and honorable means, Texas can become a member of that Republic. If not, if we declare Independence, whether that Government would immediately recognize and respect [us] as an independent People. Receive us [as] allies, and form with us a treaty of Amity both offensive and defensive. If all should fail on the part of the Government, or a refusal to intermeddle in our difficulty, You will immediately notify this Government whether good or bad, of your success,[3] and govern yourselves accordingly. On the failure of success with the Government, you will redouble your energies in arousing the sympathies of the Patriotic citizens of the north to rally to our assistance.[4]

[1]Commission issued by Governor Smith, December 7, 1835, Austin Papers; also in Garrison, *Dip. Cor. Tex.*, I, 51-52

[2]Private Instructions, December 8, 1835, Austin Papers; also in Garrison, *Dip. Cor. Tex.*, I, 52-54.

[3]What is meant, evidently, is "If all should fail on the part of the government, and there should be a refusal to intermeddle in our difficulty, you will immediately notify this government of your success, whether good or bad."

[4]Garrison, *Dip. Cor. Tex.*, I, 53. The wording of these instructions seems to imply that the Texans expected that in some way annexation might be accomplished before recognition was secured. They would not have objected at this time as they did later on (see below, p. 230) to a cession of Texas by Mexico to the United States, previous to recognition.

It must not be supposed that enthusiasm for the Texan cause lay dormant in the United States until the coming of Austin, Archer, and Wharton. The Mexican invasion of Texas created the most intense excitement throughout the country. Spirited meetings were held in New Orleans, Mobile, Montgomery, New York, Boston, and doubtless in many other cities.[1] Volunteers from the United States had already enlisted in the Texas service,[2] and a contribution of $7,000 had come from New Orleans.[3] September 1, 1835, Henry Meigs of New York wrote to Austin:

A sympathy almost universal, exists for your welfare and that of your colony.

The Govemt of the U. S. cannot disobey the public opinion, which will insist upon your safety and well being so long as you exhibit that temperate and just view and conduct which you have always done.

In a later letter, September 29, 1835, he said:

The U states are looking to your course with deep interest. It is not possible to separate you from them long. Every political, religious and commercial tie exists between them and you.

And again, November 15.

Public sentiment is aroused for your cause. We know that you are Bone of our Bone! and Flesh of our Flesh! that none but a Republican Government can exist over you! . . .

Govermt can hardly do for you what private opinion and zeal is already active in doing. . . .

The Secretary of State (a few days ago) told me that there was but one result for your affairs—and that was, a natural and inevitable connection with the policy and Interests of *your country the United States.*[4]

John P. Austin, also, writing from New York, November 8, 1835,[5]

[1]John P. Austin to S. F. Austin, November 8, 1835, Austin Papers; *Telegraph and Texas Register*, January 30, 1836.
[2]Minutes of the General Council, November 15, 1835, Austin Papers; Gammel, *Laws of Texas*, I, 554-558.
[3]Barker, "Texas Revolutionary Finances," in *Political Science Quarterly*, XIX, 616.
[4]All three letters in Austin Papers. In the third Meigs speaks of his "intimate connection with the Secretary of State," whose remarks, here quoted, are interesting in view of Forsyth's later attitude toward Texas. Meigs was a brother-in-law of Forsyth.
[5]Letter cited in note 1 above.

to his cousin, Stephen F. Austin, after dwelling upon the "general and increased interest throughout the U. States" in favor of Texas, and the disposition shown to render "prompt and efficient aid," went on to relate a conversation held with an individual "direct from Washington—an old and intimate friend of President Jackson—who said the president had no disposition to interfere with any present aid given by the citizens of the United States, provided they did not openly violate the laws of nations." Moreover, he stated that orders had been sent to Pensacola for men-of war to cruise in the Gulf of Mexico and that a sloop-of-war was being fitted out with all possible dispatch at Philadelphia to sail in a week or ten days to cruise between Tampico and the mouth of the Mississippi, "which," he added, "will be very much in your favor and a great protection to vessels bound into any of your ports." After such repeated assurances, it was quite natural, in spite of the neutrality proclaimed by the United States,[1] for the Texans to look confidently for material aid from their kinsmen on the north. Stephen F. Austin, in December, 1835, wrote that there would probably be thousands of volunteers from the United States in Texas within a few months.[2]

The commissioners reached New Orleans New Year's Day, 1836.[3] Their work began most auspiciously. Indeed no one was

[1]See below, p. 210.

[2]Austin to Johnson, *et al.*, December 22, 1835, in Brown, *Life of Henry Smith,* 177-180.

[3]Report of Austin, Archer, and Wharton to Burnet, July 21, 1836, Garrison, *Dip. Cor. Tex.,* I, 111-112. There is a conflict of evidence about the date of their arrival in New Orleans. On January 2, Barrett, chairman of the committee on the state and judiciary, in a report recommending that the commissioners remonstrate with the United States concerning a plan to transport the Creek Indians to Texas, says:

"that they cannot but express much surprise that our public agents have so long delayed to proceed to the fulfillment of the objects of their appointment; that, however, the Government may feel inclined to receive and respect the counsel of these gentlemen, and that of all others interested in the fate of Texas, yet duties of a different character having been assigned to our public agents to the United States of the north, it cannot be expected that they will devote their time to instructing the Government at home; when as agents of that Government they have higher and more important duties, which they are pledged to perform abroad. . . .

"Your committee therefore advise that the Governor be requested immediately to communicate instructions to the said commissioners, as to the necessity of proceeding with all possible despatch to such points in

more surprised than the commissioners themselves at the enthusiasm they found to exist. Austin wrote that it was a thousand fold greater than he had dreamed it would be. He was now convinced that Texas could obtain from the United States all the help she needed, and it was upon this assurance that he united for the first time with Archer and Wharton in the demand for an immediate and unanimous declaration of independence.[1] To make his conversion the more complete, news from Mexico stated that the Federal party had joined Santa Anna to invade Texas. If this were true, to adhere to the declaration of November 7 could do no possible good. On the other hand, the indefinite position in which it placed Texas had already done injury and would ruin the cause, except for the confident expectation that the new convention would soon meet and declare absolute independence.[2]

Austin confessed now that his own impulses had long been to see Texas free from the "trammels of religious intolerance, and other anti-republican restrictions." But he had hesitated, he said, on account of the responsibility he felt in colonizing Texas, to precipitate others into the situation which this involved, until convinced that they would be sustained. The information he had ac-

the United States of the north as shall enable them with the greatest certainty to effect the objects of their mission" (Gammel, *Laws of Texas,* I, 723-724).

It seems strange that a committee of the General Council should have been ignorant as to the movements of the commissioners; but Austin, at least, if not his colleagues also, had spent some time in Quintana previous to their departure from Texas, which could not have taken place earlier than December 25 (Austin to Johnson, *et al.* December 22, 1835, in Brown, *Life of Henry Smith,* 177-180; Austin to Royall, December 25, 1835, *ibid.* 249-253). It would have taken several days for the Council at San Felipe to learn that they had gone. The evidence certainly seems to point to the correctness of Austin's statement that they reached New Orleans on January 1.

[1] Austin to Houston, January 7, 1836, in *Telegraph and Texas Register,* February 27, 1836; Austin to Capt. Henry Austin, January 7, 1836, in Gen. Stephen F. Austin's Letter and Memorandum Album, 1836, Austin Papers. In this letter Austin deplores the fact that he went to New Orleans by water instead of overland as it carried him through Quintana where he became involved in party warfare—a thing he had always tried to avoid. It was while in Quintana that he wrote the letters of December 22 and 25 (see Brown, *Life of Henry Smith,* 177-180; 249-253) in which he bitterly denounces the advocates of an immediate declaration of independence—especially Wharton (see above, p. 163).

[2] Austin, Archer, and Wharton to Governor Smith, January 10, 1836. Garrison, *Dip. Cor. Tex.,* I, 55-57.

quired on this subject since leaving Texas had fully satisfied him.[1]
Elaborating these views in a letter to his cousin, Henry Austin,
he said:

> We can get all the aid we need to sustain our independence and
> I think it will not be difficult to procure the recognition of the
> U. S. Gov't. Nothing is wanted but union and concert of action
> and of purpose at home and an unqualified declaration of inde-
> pendence at once. That of 7th Nov'r has been made an absolute
> declaration of independence, by the acts of the Mexicans by sub-
> mitting to centralism and of the Gov't. in invading us, and no act
> of that government for the sale or transfer of Texas to any one, can
> be or ought to be, in any manner valid, or obligatory on the people
> of Texas. . . .
>
> I had no idea before I left home of the deep and general interest
> that is felt for the cause of Texas, or of the influence which my
> opinions seem to have in this country—had I known it sooner, I
> should have been less cautious than I have been about precipitating
> the people of Texas into a declaration of independence. The re-
> sponsibility, however, would have been very great on me had I
> contributed to involve the settlers whom I had been instrumental
> in drawing to that country, before I was certain they would be sus-
> tained. I am now confident they *will* be fully and promptly sus-
> tained in their independence, and that the sooner such a declara-
> tion is made the better. Besides, the reasons for leaving open any
> door, however small, for a re-union with Mexico have ceased, for
> all parties have united against us.[2]

Indeed Austin became so imbued with the American spirit of
expansion that he suggested that the declaration of independence
prescribe no limits on the southwest or northwest, leaving the field
open for expansion beyond the Rio Grande, "and to Chihuahua and
New Mexico."[3] Wharton was not so ambitious. From Nashville
he wrote Governor Smith that it was his belief that to fight for

[1]Austin to Houston, January 7, 1836, in *Telegraph and Texas Register*,
February 27, 1836; also in Wooten, *A Comprehensive History of Texas*, I,
570-571.
[2]S. F. Austin to Henry Austin, February 14, 1836, in extracts of letters October 14, 1830—February 14, 1836, Austin Papers.
[3]Austin to Houston, January 7, 1836, in *Telegraph and Texas Register*,
February 27, 1836, also in Wooten, *A Comprehensive History of Texas*,
I, 570-571.

anything beyond the Rio Grande would "damn us beneath all depth in hell."[1]

In addition to the friendly interest manifested, another cause for congratulation, the commissioners felt, was that, in spite of the fact that Texas, according to her own declaration, was nothing more than a seceded state of the Mexican confederation, with no credit and no wealth except her lands, there were still found individuals who were willing to advance money with which to finance the revolution. A short time after their arrival in New Orleans two loans were negotiated, the first for $200,000, the second for $50,000. To be sure, the terms upon which these loans were secured were not all that could have been desired. The lenders, or holders of the scrip, had the right to take in return lands in Texas at fifty cents an acre. The most objectionable feature was that the lenders were allowed to choose their lands, priority of selection being reserved to subscribers of the first loan; and no further sales of lands by the Texan government were to take place until this choice was made. Moreover, in the case of the first loan, after the first payment, which was to be 10 per cent of the whole, had been made, the lenders had the right to withhold further payment, if they so desired.[2] The second loan was supposed to be a cash payment.[3] In other words, these so-called loans were nothing more

[1]Wharton to Governor Smith, February 7, 1836, Garrison, *Dip. Cor. Tex.*, I, 66.

[2]Printed copies of these terms are among the Austin Papers. The following were the subscribers to the first loan: T. D. Carneal, L. Whiteman, Paul Anderson, and J. F. Irwin all of Cincinnati; J. N. Morrison of Maysville, Kentucky; Robert Triplett of Yellow Banks, Kentucky; and George Hancock of Louisville, Kentucky; W. F. Gray of Fredericksburg, Virginia; J. S. Brander of Pittsburg, Virginia; and Alfred Penn of New Orleans. In the case of the second loan twelve subscribers were from New Orleans, three were from Virginia, and two were from Kentucky. It would be instructive to attempt to discover how much the interest felt for Texas in some sections of the United States was due to the influence of individuals who had invested heavily in Texas lands. Barker, "Land Speculation as a Cause of the Texas Revolution," in THE QUARTERLY, X, 95, says, "In 1836 the Texans contracted several loans on the public land, and there is material to warrant the belief that those who advanced the money were ready, if the revolution had continued long enough, to enlist volunteers for the cause."

[3]Gouge, *Fiscal History of Texas*, 53, says the amount actually received was only $45,820. Austin estimated that it would yield but $40,000 cash (Austin to McKinney, January 21, 1836, Austin Papers). This may have been written inadvertently, as undoubtedly was the following

than gigantic land speculations, whereby five hundred thousand acres of the choicest lands in Texas were to be secured at fifty cents an acre.[1] But they meant about sixty thousand dollars in cash for Texas, and were therefore duly gratifying. Moreover, the interest was only eight per cent, though the commissioners were authorized to offer as much as ten.[2]

In communicating the transactions to the government the commissioners reported enthusiastically: "Some of the best informed persons of this place confidently assert that this loan insures the triumph of our cause and the independence of Texas. That in New Orleans, so near us, and so well acquainted with our situation, confidence enough should exist in us to induce a loan, speaks volumes in our favor and will give confidence everywhere else." The "hundreds of capitalists," they continued, "who would soon be in possession of stock in this loan would feel as much interest in Texas as those who had long lived there. As evidence of this fact the subscribers had already offered to send to Texas five hundred men, officered, armed, and equipped, to serve throughout the war under easy terms as regarded reimbursement when the war was over." In conclusion they said: "Disposing of our land at fifty cents pr. acre for the purpose of getting money so particularly indispensable at this moment, appears to us very fortunate. In fact rather than have missed the loan, we had better borrowed the money for five years and given them lands in the bargain."[3]

statement regarding the first loan: "We have effected a loan for $200,-000, but only get 20 pr. cent advance at this time" (Austin to Perry, January 18, 1836, Austin Papers).

[1]Barker, "Texas Revolutionary Finances" in *Political Science Quarterly*, XIX, 629.

[2]Gammel, *Laws of Texas*, I, 948. For the ratification of the first loan the commissioners pledged the faith of the country; for the second they pledged their individual property.

[3]Austin, Archer, and Wharton to Smith, January 10, 1836, Garrison, *Dip. Cor. Tex.*, I, 56-57. Unfortunately the Texan authorities were not of the same opinion. They were glad to get the money at first, but opposition to the terms of the loan was soon manifested, and it grew stronger during the term of the government *ad interim*. A compromise was proposed, but a subsequent act of the Texan government destroyed the monopoly which the stockholders in the original loan had hoped to enjoy, so they declined to buy more land. The matter was not finally closed until the summer of 1838 (Barker, "Texas Revolutionary Finances," in *Political Science Quarterly*, XIX, 631-632). This unfortunate squabble did much to injure the credit of the young republic.

Another piece of enterprise on the part of the commissioners during their stay in New Orleans deserves notice. This was the designing of a flag for Texas, which was intended as an appeal both to England and America for recognition. Austin first planned a flag, a draft of which was sent to Gail Borden, January 18, 1836.[1] This design was submitted to the commissioners and modified In this form Professor Garrison describes it as follows: "It had —or was meant to have—the thirteen stripes of the United States flag, with the red changed to blue, and in the upper left-hand corner, instead of stars, was the British union with red stripes on a white field. On the flag was a sun encircled by the motto Lux Libertatis, and on the face of the sun was the head of Washington, underneath which were the words, 'In his example there is safety.' "[2] The flag was not accepted by the Texas authorities, but this "mute appeal . . . [of the Texans] to their near and still nearer of kin which lay in joining the British Jack to the stripes of the American Union was at once proud and pathetic."[3]

The rest of the work of the commissioners in New Orleans consisted in supervising the purchase of supplies;[4] providing for the equipment of the schooner *Ingham,* late revenue cutter, for the service of Texas; appointing William Bryan general agent of the government at New Orleans, and Edward Hall purchasing agent; authorizing T. D. Owings to raise troops for Texas in Kentucky; and instructing A. J. Yates to go to New York to purchase a steam vessel to defend the Texas coast.[5] Wharton left on the 17th for

[1]Austin to Borden, January 18, 1836, Austin Papers. Professor Garrison identifies as this design a drawing of a flag found some years ago among the Nacogdoches Archives (in the Texas State Library). He also shows that the flag presented to Moseley Baker's company at San Felipe in February, 1836, was in all probability made after this pattern. (Garrison, "Another Texas Flag," in THE QUARTERLY, III, 170-176). There is another draft of the flag in the Austin Papers, which, although now separated from the letter to Borden, was doubtless originally filed with it.
[2]Garrison, "First Stage of the Movement for the Annexation of Texas," in *The American Historical Review,* X, 73-74.
[3]Garrison, "Another Texas Flag," in THE QUARTERLY, III, 176.
[4]A. Houston, quartermaster-general, to commissioners, January 10, 1836, Austin Papers.
[5]A. J. Yates to Austin, Archer, and Wharton, January 14, 1836; Austin and Archer to Henry Smith, January 26, 1836; Austin and Archer to Yates, January 21, 1836; Austin and Archer to Colonel Owings, January 18, 1836; all in Austin Papers, the last two also in Garrison, *Dip. Cor. Tex.,* I, 59-62.

Nashville. Austin and Archer remained in New Orleans through-out January.

During the next two months the commissioners slowly made their way toward Washington. They were greatly delayed on account of the frozen condition of the roads and rivers and the illness of Austin and Wharton at Nashville.[1] It had been their intention before leaving Texas[2] and while in New Orleans[3] to return home in March, perhaps in time for the March convention. By March 3, Austin and Archer had gone no further than Louisville, Kentucky, and Wharton was still ill in Nashville. Before they could reach Washington the convention undoubtedly would have declared independence and organized a permanent government. The provisional government which they represented would then no longer exist, and in that case their present credentials would be worthless at Washington. A failure on their part to receive recognition as commissioners, they realized, would be disastrous. In order now to enter into negotiations concerning recognition, it was absolutely necessary to have an official copy of the declaration of independence and new instructions from the convention. They were therefore in no haste to proceed until these documents should have been forwarded to Washington.[4] By the latter part of the month

[1]Wharton to Governor Smith, February 7, 1836, Garrison, *Dip. Cor. Tex.* I, 65-66; Austin, Archer, and Wharton to Governor Smith, February 16, 1836, *ibid.*, 66-69; Austin and Archer to the Governor of Texas, March 3, *ibid.*, 72-73.

[2]See Barrett's report, January 2, 1836, given above, p. 172, note 3, in which he says, "Already one-half of the time allotted to the fulfillment of the trust committed to them is expired."

[3]Austin, Archer and Wharton to Governor Smith, January 10, 1836, Garrison, *Dip. Cor. Tex.* I, 57.

[4]Austin and Archer to the Governor of Texas, March 3, 1836, Garrison, *Dip. Cor. Tex,* I. 72-73, a rough draft of which is among the Austin Papers; Austin, Archer and Wharton to the Government of Texas, April 6, 1836 (its date should have been April 5; see Yates to Allen, April 5, Garrison, *Dip. Cor. Tex.*, I, 79, and Wharton to Austin, April 6, *ibid.*, 80-81), Garrison, *Dip. Cor. Tex.*, I, 79-80. In this last letter the commissioners report:

"Knowing that we could not effect anything with the money market, or with the Government, until we received an absolute declaration of Independence by Texas, and special powers and instructions to present it, we purposely delayed getting to Washington until such time as we thought we would certainly meet with the declaration, and also with the appointment of some one of us, or somebody else, to lay the matter before the Government officially."

it was reported that the commissioners had arrived at their destination.[1]

But in the meantime they had not been idle. In all the larger cities[2] they addressed enthusiastic gatherings, with the direct result that hundreds of volunteers, armed and equipped by contribution, flocked to Texas.[3] Even the ladies of Nashville offered the means with which to equip one company.[4] Resolutions, praying the recognition of Texas, were drawn up at these meetings and sent to Congress. Money, too, was offered on such advantageous terms[5] that the commissioners were encouraged to recommend to their government the issue of scrip bearing only five per cent interest and redeemable in tracts of 640, 320, and 160 acres at $1.00 per acre, to be located after all land claims had been definitely and finally settled.[6] Indeed from the time they reached New Orleans until they arrived in Washington the commissioners wrote always in the same cheerful tone. From Nashville, February 16, they reported to Governor Smith: "It is with the most lively sentiments of gratitude toward the patriotic and generous citizens of this free

[1]G. C. Childress to President Burnet, March 28, 1836, Garrison, *Dip. Cor. Tex.* I, 74; Austin, Wharton, and Archer to William Bryan, March 31, Austin Papers.

[2]Their route lay through Nashville, Louisville, Cincinnati and Pittsburg.

[3]The great majority of these volunteers, however, did not reach Texas until after the battle of San Jacinto, and their presence in the country then proved to be a great menace.

[4]Austin, Archer, and Wharton to Governor Smith, February 16, 1836, Garrison, *Dip. Cor. Tex.* I, 66-69; Austin to Owings, February 12, 1836, *ibid.*, 69-70.

[5]For some reason, though, nothing came of it; for Burnet, in an article written August 10, 1836, printed in the *Telegraph and Texas Register*, August 26, 1837, says that the commissioners traversed the United States from New Orleans to New York and (excluding the loans secured in New Orleans) were able to raise only $10,000, which came from New York (see below, p. 186). They were offered $50,000 in Mobile on the same terms as the New Orleans loan, but they then believed money could be secured to better advantage (Austin, Archer, and Wharton to Governor Smith, February 16, 1836, Garrison, *Dip. Cor. Tex.* I, 67). As another method of raising money the commissioners upon the recommendation of H. R. W. Hill, whom they had appointed as Texan agent in Tennessee, decided to have the Texan government issue treasury notes. Without awaiting the consent of the government they proceeded to take the necessary steps (Austin, Archer, and Wharton to Governor Smith, February 24, 1836, *ibid.*, 71).

[6]Austin, Archer, and Wharton to Governor Smith, February 16, 1836, Garrison, *Dip. Cor. Tex.*, I, 67-68. Compare these terms with those of the first loan as given above, p. 175.

and happy land, and with renewed confidence in the triumph of our cause, that we inform you, of the universal and enthusiastic interest which pervades all ranks and classes of society in every part of this country in favor of the emancipation of Texas."[1] Upon two things only, they urged, did the success of the cause depend. There must be union and harmony at home, and the March Convention must make a decided and unanimous declaration of independence. If these ends were achieved, the recognition of Texas, they believed, would follow.[2]

From the standpoint of recognition the important results of the work of the commissioners on their way to Washington in the spring of 1836 were: (1) their own personal letters to President Jackson and to friends in Congress; (2) pamphlets containing information concerning Texas, and printed addresses which they themselves had delivered, copies of which were forwarded to Washington; and (3) the resolutions and memorials which, through the instrumentality of the commissioners, as has been noted,[3] were drawn up at public gatherings and sent to Congress.[4] As will be indicated later on,[5] these last documents and similar ones that came from other sections of the United States did far more toward bringing the question of recognition before the authorities in Washington than did any of the commissioners until Wharton was sent back in the fall of 1836.[6]

There are only two of these printed addresses which remain on record to illustrate the kind of appeals the commissioners made to the people. One is that of Wharton's delivered later on in New York, April 26.[7] The other was given at this time by Austin,

---

[1]Austin, Archer, and Wharton to Governor Smith, February 16, 1836, Garrison, *Dip. Cor. Tex.*, I, 67-68. A letter written May 24, 1836, by A. M'Call, a "sensible writer of Virginia," as Yoakum calls him, says: "Austin is doing wonders among us for his country; he is a Franklin in patience and prudence" (Yoakum, *History of Texas*, II, 175).

[2]Austin to Barrett, February 18, 1836, Garrison, *Dip. Cor. Tex.*, I, 70-71, where the title is given "Austin to [Smith(?)]".

[3]See above, p. 179.

[4]Wharton to Governor Smith, February 7, 1836, Garrison, *Dip. Cor. Tex.* I, 65-66; report to Austin, Archer, and Wharton to President Burnet, July 21, 1836, *ibid.*, 111-112.

[5]See below, p. 213.

[6]See below, p. 222.

[7]See below, p. 186.

March 7, to an unusually large audience at the Second Presbyterian Church of Louisville, Kentucky. Wharton's address is more
eloquent, perhaps, but Austin's is more worthy of note, because it
deals with definite facts, is more logically written, and is better
calculated to appeal to more varied interests.[1]

After outlining briefly the history of the colonization movement
and the origin of the revolution, with a view to showing the justice
of the Texan cause, Austin went on to speak of the present situation of Texas. The declaration of November 7, 1835, he said, was
"an absolute Declaration of Independence—a total separation from
Mexico."[2]   But it was Mexico and not Texas who had forced this
situation; it was she who had trampled under foot the Constitution of 1824 and broken faith. The object which Texas now had
was *freedom,* which she might obtain either as an independent republic or as a part of the United States. To the United States,
in either case, Texas looked for help. This the citizens of the
United States ought to render for the following reasons: Patriotism called for it—the Texan cause was the same holy cause of
light and liberty for which their forefathers, the founders of the
great American republic, had fought and bled. Philanthropy
urged it—the emancipation of Texas would not only give to her the
principles of self-government, but would open the way for a
'stream of light and intelligence to flow from the great northern
fountain over the benighted regions of Mexico.' Precedent justified it—even the Greeks and Poles had received encouragement
from the United States in their struggle for liberty. Finally cold
calculating policy approved the wisdom of it—the people of the

[1]Copies of these addresses are among the Austin Papers. Austin's
address was reprinted with Wharton's (New York, 1836). There is nothing to show where Austin's was first published, but the date of its first
publication must have been before April 26, as Wharton on that date
quotes from a printed copy (see Wharton's address, p. 14). Moreover
the separate copy among the Austin Papers is apparently the one used by
Mrs. Holley in preparing her book, *Texas,* published, 1836. (See address
as reprinted in Holley, *Texas,* pp. 253-280; also manuscript note on fly
leaf of the pamphlet, Austin Papers).

[2]It is an interesting comment upon the demand public opinion in the
United States was making for the independence of Texas to see the commissioners, especially Austin, thus interpreting the declaration of November 7. Simultaneously with this interpretation they were pleading
with the home government to declare independence.

south and west must look to their interests. "By filling it [Texas] with a population from this country, who will harmonize in language, in political education, in common origin, in everything, with their neighbors to the east and north. . . . Texas will become a great outwork 'on the west, to protect the outlet of this western world, the mouths of the Mississippi, as Alabama and Florida are on the east; and to keep far away from the southwestern frontier —the weakest and most vulnerable in the nation—all enemies who might make Texas a door for invasion, or use it as a theatre from which mistaken philanthropists and wild fanatics, might attempt a system of intervention in the domestic concerns of the south, which might lead to a servile war, or at least jeopardize the tranquility of Louisiana and the neighboring states.

"This view of the subject," he concluded, "is a very important one, so much so that a bare allusion to it is sufficient to direct the mind to the various interests and results, immediate and remote, that are involved." In so "directing the mind" Austin little realized that he was helping to kindle passions which were destined to prevent for more than a decade one of the aims he had in view— annexation; and which were to have their influence, at least indirectly, in postponing until the next year the other object of his mission to Washington, namely, recognition.

From the time of their arrival in Washington, late in March, things began to look gloomy for the commissioners. Contrary to their expectations no dispatches were awaiting them from Texas. That independence had been declared they had learned through the newspapers,[1] but it was quite useless for them to present themselves to the authorities, devoid as they were of official information and the necessary credentials. This was all the more harassing as they were led to believe that the congress then in session was inclined to look favorably upon the objects they had in view.[2] April 6, they reported:

We have received the Declaration through the papers, but we have not received it officially, and it is therefore useless to us. The Gov-

---

[1]Austin, Archer, and Wharton to the Government of Texas, April 6, 1836, Garrison, *Dip. Cor. Tex.*, I, 79-80.
[2]Wharton to the Governor of Texas, April 9, 1836, Garrison, *Dip. Cor. Tex.*, I, 81-82.

ernment will not act upon it, until it is presented to them by some one with ministerial powers from the same Convention that made the declaration. When presented in this form, with evidence of our Capacity to maintain our Independence, we believe this Government is prepared to recognize us, and if we wish, to admit us into this Union, on liberal principles, if the people of Texas wish it. But they require a Minister with full powers to treat on the subjcet. If we had had these powers, Texas would have been, by this time, recognized, if not admitted into the Union.[1]

Three days later Wharton wrote:

Since the meeting of the new convention we have had no correspondence with the Texas Government. We have seen the declaration in the papers but this government will take no notice of it until it is presented by an agent with *credentials* from the present government. Let me urge the vesting of some one with plenipotentiary powers without *One Moments delay*. He must be here before this congress adjourns. They I think are favourable. The next may have a preponderance of Northern and Eastern jealousy and Abolition. Let our Minister be instructed and empowered to negotiate a treaty for the admission of Texas into this union if such which God Grant is the wish of Texas. . . . Do attend if you have not done it already to sending on a Minister immediately with ple[n]ary powers to treat for the admission of Texas into this Union. Probably 2 or 3 agents would be better.[2]

A. J. Yates, writing from Baltimore after Austin had joined him, also attested the friendly spirit at Washington. He said:

Everything at Washington appears very prosperous and the Congress and Government are all ready to recognize us and if desired by us to receive us on favorable terms into the Union. The Commissioners can not present themselves officially however untill they receive despatches subsequent to the adoption of the Declaration of Independence. They have received the most marked attention in Washington and both parties are warmly in our favor. I have had several conversations with the President and several of the Cabinet and members and find all unanimously ready to do all they can for us.

If the Government had done their duty on the declaration of Independence and forwarded the necessary powers and instructions to

---

[1]Austin, Archer, and Wharton to the Government of Texas, April 6, 1836. Garrison, *Dip. Cor. Tex.*. I, 80.

[2]Wharton to the Governor of Texas, April 9, 1836, Garrison, *Dip. Cor. Tex.*, I, 81-82.

the Commissioners Congress would have decided the matter before this time.[1]

Wharton complains to Burnet, April 23, that though he had "written to the government a dozen times . . . [he had] not received one line since the 20th of February last,"[2] and on the next day Austin writes Bryan, the New Orleans agent, "you and you *alone* have written to us, from the Government of Texas, we have not received one word, not even one."[3]

To make matters worse unofficial reports from Texas were far from encouraging. News had come that the Mexicans were again invading the country,[4] and rumors were afloat of the unseemly quarrel between the governor and his Council.[5] Realizing that nothing could be done in Washington under their present instructions, and knowing that the situation in Texas demanded the immediate aid of money and men, the commissioners decided to separate and devote their attention for the present to securing these material necessities.[6] On April 5 Austin set out to visit Baltimore, Philadelphia, and New York, while Archer on the next day left for Vir-

[1]A. J. Yates to A. C. Allen, New Orleans, April 5, 1836, Garrison, *Dip. Cor. Tex.*, I, 79.
[2]Wharton to Burnet, April 23, 1836, Garrison, *Dip. Cor. Tex.*, I, 87.
[3]Records of the Department of State, Book 34, p. 422.
[4]Wharton to Austin, April 7, 1836, Austin Papers; Austin to Bryan, April 24, 1836, Records of the Department of State, Book 34, p. 422.
[5]Report of Austin, Archer, and Wharton, July 21, 1836, Garrison, *Dip. Cor. Tex.*, I, 112; Wharton to the Governor of Texas, April 9, 1836, *ibid.*, 81-82. In this letter Wharton makes the following appeal: "If our invaders prevail or if *anarchy* and confusion and violence among the inhabitants should arise then *Texas will not be recognized.* On this you may rely. For Gods sake for our wives and childrens sake and our bleeding countrys sake let harmony and union prevail as among a band of *brothers.*"
[6]For this purpose J. M. Wolfe had already been dispatched, March 31, to Charleston, S. C., with instruction to travel through the Southern States (Austin, Archer, and Wharton to Wolfe, March 31, 1836, Austin Papers and Dip. Cor. Tex. with U. S., MSS). He visited Alabama, Mississippi, Louisiana, Tennessee, Kentucky, Ohio, Virginia, Pennsylvania, New York, New Jersey, South Carolina, Georgia. His chief success lay in getting memorials sent to Congress. The money raised was used in sending volunteers to Texas (Wolfe to Congress of Texas undated, *ibid.*) In attempting to raise money the commissioners were as much hampered by the failure of the Texan government to send them official information as they had been in their diplomatic capacity. "Capitalists would not lend under the November declaration," Wharton reported (Wharton to the Governor of Texas, April 9, 1836, Garrison, *Dip. Cor. Tex.*, I, 82).

ginia. Wharton alone remained in Washington to keep in touch with the government.[1]

From New York Austin made one other attempt to secure the active support of the United States as a nation. In sheer desperation at the repeated disasters which had befallen his country, he threw aside all ceremony, and on April 15 addressed an almost frantic appeal to "Andrew Jackson, Martin Van Buren, Richard M. Johnson, John Forsyth, Lewis Cass, T. H. Benton and to any member of the cabinet, or Congress of all parties and all factions of the United States." He asked first that some of the $37,000,000 surplus in the United States treasury be devoted to the Texan cause; and second that Jackson and Congress come out openly and make the war what it alraedy was *sub rosa*—namely, a national war.[2] Of course nothing came of it. Richard M. Johnson, to whom it seems to have been sent, although apparently an ardent sympathizer with Texas, in his reply expressed his opinion that it would be "useless, at this time, to get our Government to go into the contest as a nation."[3] Jackson, who also inspected the document, indorsed on the back of it the following: "The writer does not reflect that we have a treaty with Mexico, and our national faith is pledged to support it. The Texians before they took the step to declare themselves Independent, which has aroused and united all Mexico against them ought to have pondered well—it was a rash and premature act, our neutrality must be faithfully maintained."[4]

Austin spent nearly two months on his journey through Baltimore, Philadelphia, and New York.[5] By the middle of May he was

[1] Yates to Allen, April 5, 1836, Garrison, *Dip. Cor. Tex.*, I, 79. Austin, Archer, and Wharton to the Government of Texas, April 6, 1836, *ibid.*, 80; Wharton to Austin, April 6, 1836, *ibid.*; Austin to Burnet, June 10, 1836, *ibid.* 98.

[2] Austin to Andrew Jackson *et al.*, April 15, 1836, Jackson MSS., also Austin Papers.

[3] Johnson to Austin, April 18, 1836, Austin Papers.

[4] Jackson MSS.

[5] Austin, from Baltimore, to a cousin, April 7, 1836, manuscript letter in a pamphlet containing Austin's address at Louisville, March 7, 1836, Austin Papers; Austin from Philadelphia, to Biddle, April 9, 1836, Austin Papers; Austin from New York to Jackson *et al.*, April 15, 1836, *ibid.*; commission of Yates given by Austin and Wharton, New York, May 9, 1836, *ibid.*

back in Washington,[1] which city he left May 24 for Texas.[2]   If Archer went to Richmond as he planned,[3] he returned immediately, for, on April 26, all three of the commissioners attended a very enthusiastic meeting at Masonic Hall in New York City.   Samuel Swartwout, who was an ardent friend of Texas, presided.   Wharton was the orator of the day, and "in a strain of sublime and touching pathos" he appealed for sympathy and aid.   Austin and Archer also spoke, and the result was a series of resolutions expressing deep interest in the cause and declaring it to be to the "honour of a free and powerful nation like the United States, to be the first to take her [Texas] by the hand, and acknowledge her independence." Committees were also appointed to receive donations and to confer with the commissioners as to the best way of lending efficient aid.[4]

It was about this time, and no doubt due to the joint efforts of the commissioners in New York, that negotiations were made for a loan of $100,000 on terms similar to the New Orleans loan, except that the present subscribers had the privilege of taking Texas lands at twenty-five instead of fifty cents an acre.   The commissioners were not particularly enthusiastic over this arrangement, but as has been pointed out,[5] its terms were perhaps as good as those made in New Orleans, since, in the latter case, the expense of issuing stock certificates and of surveying the land was to be borne by the Texan government; in the former, by the lenders themselves.   Only ten per cent of this New York loan was ever paid.[6]   The commissioners admitted that this was all they counted upon getting, since they did

[1]Austin and Wharton from Washington to James Treat, May 16, 1836, Austin Papers.

[2]Austin to Houston, June 16, 1836, cited by Yoakum, *History of Texas*, II, 177.

[3]See above, p. 184.

[4]*Texas, Address of the Honorable Wm. H. Wharton*, New York, April 26, 1836, Austin Papers.   An account of the meeting is also published in this pamphlet, 54-56.

[5]Barker, "Texas Revolutionary Finances," in *Political Science Quarterly*, XIX, 634.

[6]Treat to Austin, July 30, 1836, Austin Papers; article by President Burnet, August 10, 1836, in *Telegraph and Texas Register*, August 26, 1837, cited above, p. 179, note 5.   Barker, "Texas Revolutionary Finances," in *Political Science Quarterly*, XIX, 634, says only $7000 of this ten per cent can be accounted for.

not expect the loan to be ratified "unless the prospects of Texas were gloomy even to desperation."[1]

Wharton and Archer remained in the United States for some time after Austin's departure, but practically nothing is known of their work during this period. Finally they embarked together on the *Independence*,[2] and reached Texas about the middle of July.[3]

In the meantime Austin, on his way home, had stopped for a few days in New Orleans. The tone of his correspondence now, con-trasted with the enthusiasm with which he had written from here at the beginning of the year, tells the story of his disappointment at the outcome of the mission. The fault he charges to the Texan government alone. Conditions in Washington he had considered most favorable, and the commissioners had not been wanting in zeal. But they were rendered helpless by the negligence of the authorities at home. In a letter to President Burnet from New Orleans, June 10, Austin said:

I fully believe that nothing is wanting at Washington, to procure an acknowledgment of our independence but *official information,* of the true state of things at home. That is, evidence that a govt *de facto* is regularly organized and in operation and able to sustain the independence of Texas—that the Mexicans have been defeated, and driven out of Texas, (if the latter be the fact) or if not driven out, how far they have retreated. What is the force of the Texas army, what that of the enemy, their relative position, and the situa-tion of the country generally. All this should be sent *immediately* in an *official* form to the representatives of Texas in Washington (Childress and Hamilton,[4] including Wharton should he still be there, or either of them who may be there) with instructions to lay it before the Govt of the U. S., without delay and apply for a rec-ognition of our independence.

[1]Report of Austin, Archer, and Wharton to President Burnet, July 21, 1836, Garrison, *Dip. Cor. Tex.*, I, 112.

[2]Treat to Austin, July 30, 1836, Austin Papers.

[3]Austin's Letter and Memorandum Album (1836), p. 25, *ibid.*

[4]Childress and Hamilton were the first representatives of the govern-ment *ad interim* (see below, pp. 194-195). While in New Orleans, Austin met Collinsworth and Grayson (Austin to Ficklin, October 30, 1836, Austin Papers), the commissioners of the government *ad interim*, who had been appointed, May 26, to supersede all others. It may have been here that Austin learned for the first time of their appointment, as the letter re-calling him and his colleagues was written May 27, three days after his departure from New York (see below, p. 202).

If such documents as the above had been received by the representatives of Texas before I left Washington, I believe that I could have brought on our recognition. The feeling there is decided and ardent in our favor and no time should be lost in making a proper use [of it].[1]

Six days later he wrote to Houston:

I shall do all I can to procure the annexation of Texas to the United States, on just and fair principles. . . . The first step is, a recognition of our independence; that done, the way is clear and open. If *official* reports in manuscript of all the principal facts in regard to the political and military state of things in Texas had been sent by the executive government of Texas to our agents at Washington, I could now have had the recognition of our independence to take home. Nothing but the want of such *official documents* was wanted when I left Washington. I believe that a report from you, signed by yourself, would have been fully sufficient. There were no accounts of the battle of San Jacinto, except those in newspapers. . . . I am of opinion that our independence will be acknowledged, and that Texas will be admitted into these United States, if they are regularly asked for.[2]

So thoroughly convinced was Austin of the correctness of his opinions concerning the attitude of the United States authorities toward recognition,[3] that one of his first acts upon reaching Texas was to lay before President Burnet the absolute necessity of keeping in close touch with the commissioners who now had charge of the work. An entry in his private memorandum says:

The day I arrived at Velasco (late in the evening of 27th June) I represented to president Burnet the great importance of writing officially once a week if possible to the representatives of Texas at Washington City in the U. S. and stated it as my opinion that the omission of this govt in not furnishing to their representatives, whoever they might be, official reports of the battle of San Jacinto and of the organization of the Texas govt. and general situation of the country etc had been fatal to the interest of Texas, as I believed that our independence would have been acknowledged by the U. S. Govt. and Congress if those official documents had been sent

---

[1]Austin to Burnet, June 10, 1836, Garrison, *Dip. Cor. Tex.*, I, 98.

[2]Austin to Houston, June 16, 1836, cited by Yoakum, *History of Texas*, II, 177.

[3]What grounds Austin had for his convictions will be indicated below, pp. 212-218.

on in time. Nothing of the kind was ever sent on—those of us, (Austin, Wharton, Archer, Childress and Hamilton) who were in Washington received nothing, not even one word from their Govt. and had nothing to operate with, in their exertions to procure a recognition of our independence, but newspaper accounts and private letters from individuals in Texas and N. Orleans etc   I was assured that Grayson and Collinsworth (the present representatives of Texas at Washington City) should be regularly written to, and on the 9th July president Burnet wrote to them (by the schooner Comanche bound to Orleans) and enclosed certified copies of Gen. Santa Anna's letters to Gen. Jackson and Gen. Urrea, and of the treaties of 14th May etc.[1] I wrote to them at the same time. . . . I gave it as my opinion [concerning] the importance of official reports from the head of each department of the Govt. relative to the state of the public affairs of the respective branches and that such reports should be published and sent officially to the reps. of Texas in Washington to be used there in support of our application for independence, etc.[2]

On the next page of this memorandum book is this entry: "July 20—Went to Velasco to meet B. T. Archer and W. H. Wharton (who had returned a few days before from the U. S.) for the purpose of making a return of our mission to the U. S. as commissioners   We made our report and rendered an account of all the monies we had recd. and disbursed for Texas, and accompanied the [account] with all the original vouchers, which were passed to the Auditor for examination."[3] The following is the report as it was rendered, July 21:

Being appointed by the Convention of November last Commissioners for raising funds and other purposes in the United States in prosecution of our duties we arrived in New Orleans on the 1st of January 1836. On reaching the city we found that the government of Texas was without funds or credit, and that the quarter

---

[1]On July 25 the following documents were copied by Ramón Martínez, Columbia, Texas, and sent to Jackson, reaching him September 28: Santa Anna to Filisola, April 22, 1836; Filisola to Santa Anna, April 28, 1836; Santa Anna to Filisola, April 30, 1836; Santa Anna to Filisola, May 14, 1836; Filisola to Santa Anna, May 25, 1836; Treaty of Velasco, May 14, 1836; all in Jackson MSS.

[2]Austin's Letter and Memorandum Album (1836) p. 24, Austin Papers. The incoherence of the language here is due to Austin's failure to read through his rough memorandum after certain erasures and insertions had been made.

[3]*Ibid.,* p. 25.

Master of the army and other agents were wholly unable to procure the requisite supplies of arms ammunition provisions etc.   Under these circumstances we promptly exerted ourselves to make a flat loan at a fixed rate of Interest.   This, however was wholly impracticable.   Capitalists would not lend at any interest without obtaining lands in payment.   Impelled by the urgency of our situation we effected a loan with Robert Triplett and others which has been submitted to and modified by your Excellency and Cabinet.

We are free to admit that the terms of this loan were not such as we would have dictated—but we are bold in asserting that a loan could not at that time have been effected on better terms and we saw that the immediate procurement of funds was indispensable. This being accomplished we started for Washington City through the Western States, making it our business to hold [meetings] at prominent points, for the purpose of explaining the justice of our cause, of obtaining Volunteers and procuring memorials and petitions to the Congress of the United States for the recognition of the Independence of Texas.   In addition to this we furnished the Members of congress with our printed addresses and essays in which we endeavored to develope and defend the origin principles and objects of the contest in which Texas and Mexico are engaged.

On reaching the Eastern Cities new obstacles presented themselves.   The unhappy and violent differences between the late Governor [Smith] and his council were known and magnified.   It was also believed that the convention of March would not declare for Independence and added to all this, we as commissioners had no power to sell the public lands.   In a short time the fall of the Alamo, the Massacre of Col Fanins command, the retreat of our army, the supposed rising of the Northern Indians, the nonratification of the first loan and the neglect of the present Government to correspond with us and ratify our powers and appointment, presented insuperable difficulties.   We were consequently only enabled to obtain a loan in New York on very disadvantageous terms, which has been submitted.   Our main object in effecting this loan was to obtain the 10 per cent.   We did not bind ourselves to recommend its ratification and did not expect that it would be ratified unless the prospects of Texas were gloomy even to desperation.   Subjoined is an account of our receipts and disbursements.[1]

The net results of their six months' labor in the United States were (1) three loans, which had yielded to the Texan government something like \$75,000, and donations to a very much smaller

[1]Garrison, *Dip. Cor. Tex.*, I, 111-112.

amount; (2) recruits of volunteers for Texas;[1] and (3) widespread enthusiasm in the cause, which manifested itself in memorials and petitions to Congress praying the recognition of Texas.

It will be seen that in their report the commissioners confine themselves to the material side of their work. They do not even suggest that they had gone out in any diplomatic capacity, and the note of disappointment that is clearly discernible throughout the report is obviously due to their failure to accomplish anything in this direction. They no doubt had correctly interpreted the interest aroused in Congress by means largely of resolutions sent in from various sections throughout the country; and they give it as their conviction that, had they received the coöperation of the home government, recognition at this time would have been secured. If the possibility of the immediate recognition of Texas existed at all, it lay in this first session of the twenty-fourth Congress. It must be borne in mind, however, that not until March 2, when independence was declared,—indeed not until April 21, when it was won at San Jacinto,—was the situation in Texas such as would at all have justified this measure. However favorably, therefore, the whole of Congress in the spring of 1836 might have been disposed to look upon recognition, conservatism alone might have prevented any immediate action in the matter. By the time Congress assembled for its second session, December 5, 1836, other forces were at work upon whose existence the earlier commissioners had never reckoned.

2. *The work of the second commission.*

During the six months' absence of the commissioners in the United States important events had occurred in Texas. The long quarrel between Governor Smith and his Council had sapped all the energy of the provisional government, so that during the last seven weeks of its unworthy history it existed in name only. From January 18 to March 11, when it adjourned *sine die,* the minutes of the Council almost invariably read: "The Council met pursuant to adjournment. A quorum not being present, adjourned. . . ."[2] When the Convention assembled at Washington, March 1,[3] all at-

[1]See above, p. 179.
[2]Gammel, *Laws of Texas,* I, 254-265.
[3]See above, p. 167.

tention was concentrated there, and the General Council soon ceased to be.

The first work of the Convention was to declare independence. Its next was to draw up a constitution and organize a permanent government. Pending the adoption of the constitution and the election of officers for the new government, a government *ad interim* was necessary. By an ordinance passed March 16, the day before the Convention adjourned, this was created,[1] and David G. Burnet was placed at its head.

But it was not only in civil affairs that changes had taken place. When the commissioners left Texas in the previous December, there were no hostile forces north of the Rio Grande. In the spring of the year, however, Texas had been again invaded, and the series of disasters that had followed—the fall of the Alamo, the capture of Goliad, and the six weeks' retreat of Houston's army—were no more than might have been expected from the disorganized state of the army and the government. But the tide had turned, April 21, at San Jacinto, and not only had the whole Mexican force practically been annihilated, but Santa Anna himself was the prisoner of the Texans. Moreover, on May 14, two treaties had been made between him and the Texan authorities. According to the first or open treaty, Santa Anna had agreed that all hostilities should cease, and that the Mexicans should withdraw beyond the Rio Grande; by the second treaty, which was secret, he agreed to have the independence of Texas acknowledged by Mexico, to accomplish which he was to be liberated immediately and allowed to embark for Vera Cruz.[2] In accordance with this second treaty an attempt had been made to release Santa Anna. This, however, had raised such a storm of opposition that he had been again placed in confine-

[1]Executive Ordinance, March 16, 1836, Gammel, *Laws of Texas*, I, 1053-1054; Kennedy, *Texas*, II, 502-504. This is the only official document that I have been able to find relating to the establishment of the government *ad interim*. Yoakum, *History of Texas*, II, 73, refers to manuscript journal of the convention for the election of officers.

[2]Austin's Letter and Memorandum Album (1836), pp. 18-23; copies are also found in Yoakum, *History of Texas*, II, 526-528; Brown, *History of Texas*, II, 62-65. Article 4 of this treaty, which became of great interest later on, says, "A treaty of commerce, amity, and limits, will be established between Mexico and Texas, the territory of the latter not to extend beyond the Rio Bravo del Norte."

ment, and when Austin reached Texas, late in June, the Santa Anna excitement, as it was called,[1] was at its height. Some went so far even as to plan to take Santa Anna to the army and have him court-martialed, but against such a step wiser counsels prevailed.

It is not surprising that the makeshift government, which during the winter and spring of 1835-6 had shown itself so incapable of managing home affairs, should have proved itself also remiss in regard to its foreign agents. Indeed any statement which the provisional government could have made to its agents at Washington would have tended rather to disprove than to establish the fact that Texas was a *de facto* government. Besides, it was not to be expected that the United States would take any step toward recognition, seeing that Texas herself had made no definite claims to independence.

But, after the March Convention had declared independence and organized the government, it was natural to suppose that the question of recognition would be pushed forward with energy. Austin, Archer, and Wharton, although commissioned merely to feel the pulse of the government concerning recognition and annexation, confidently expected, as we have seen, to be intrusted by the Convention with the work of carrying through these measures. And such it seemed at first would be the case, at least so far as recognition was concerned; for, on March 7, only five days after independence was declared, it was resolved by the Convention:

That a committee of three members of this body be appointed to inform our commissioners now in the United States that we have declared independence, and to urge upon them the necessity of using their utmost exertions to bring about as soon as possible the recognition of the independence of Texas, by the Congress of the United States of the north, now in session.[2]

If this had been done—if the government *ad interim,* after independence was declared, had drawn up the proper credentials for the Texan agents and followed these up with evidences that Texas had organized her government—the commissioners, at least, believed it possible that the unrestrained enthusiasm of the country

[1]Austin to Ficklin, October 30, 1836, Austin Papers.
[2]Gammel, *Laws of Texas,* I, 848.

at large for Texas might have prevailed, and that Congress, before adjourning for the summer, might have felt disposed to recommend unqualified recognition, and perhaps annexation as well.

But no further step was taken by the Convention, and the policy pursued by the government *ad interim* in its attempt to establish diplomatic relations with the United States is accountable only when one takes into consideration the great inexperience of the youthful republic. Instead of confirming the commission of Austin, Archer, and Wharton and sending them official information, first, of the declaration of independence, March 2, and, second, of the defeat of the Mexicans, April 21, a new set of commissioners was chosen after each of these events, and in neither case were the credentials issued adequate. This may be better understood by realizing that the Texans selected in each instance their most prominent and capable public men, who, they apparently thought, should thereafter be left to their own discretion, rather than hampered by unintelligent instructions from home. Only through experience in Washington did these agents gradually come to a realization of the equipment expected of them by the United States authorities. The situation, therefore, throughout the term of the government *ad interim* was this: The first set of commissioners, Austin, Archer, and Wharton, finding that the first thing necessary was official information that independence had been declared, spent their time, while awaiting this, in the effort to secure material aid for Texas; the second set, Childress—chairman of the committee that had reported the declaration—and Hamilton, and later on Carson, the secretary of state, were all witnesses of independence, but were enbarrassed chiefly by want of official accounts of the battle of San Jacinto; and finally, Collinsworth—Carson's successor as secretary of state—and Grayson, the attorney-general, superseding all other commissioners, were equipped with copies of the declaration and treaties with Santa Anna, but arrived in Washington after the adjournment of Congress, and bore credentials that were objected to because of their informality.[1]

In accordance with the authority conferred upon Burnet as president of the newly established government *ad interim* "to appoint

[1]See below, p. 204.

Commissioners to any foreign power,"[1] one of his first acts after
the adjournment of the Convention was, March 19, to name George
C. Childress as special agent, in conjunction with Robert Hamilton,
"with plenary powers to open a negotiation with the cabinet at
Washington, touching the political rights of the Republic; inviting
on the part of that Cabinet a recognition of the Sovereignty and
Independence of Texas, and the establishment of such relations between the two governments, as may comport with the mutual interest, the common origin, and kindred ties of their constituents."[2]

The wording of this commission is such as to imply that Childress
and Hamilton were not looked upon as agents with coördinate
powers. Moreover, in a rough draft of the commission[3] the words,
"in conjunction with Robert Hamilton," are inserted between the
lines, while the rest of the document remains in the form in which
it was first written for Childress alone—indicating clearly that
Hamilton's name was included as an after-thought. The official
letters written to them after their departure, also, go to show that
Childress was regarded as the superior diplomatic agent; and one,
at least, though addressed to Childress and Hamilton jointly,
speaks to Childress directly and only refers to Hamilton in the
third person.[4]

Several reasons for this discrimination suggest themselves. In
the first place, if the work of securing recognition was to be entrusted to some new person, Childress was perhaps the logical man.
He had been a member of the Convention of 1836 and chairman of
the committee appointed to draft a declaration of independence,
and the composition of that document has been ascribed to him.
Moreover, for Childress's success in Washington, much reliance
was based upon his former intimate acquaintance with Jackson.[5]
It may have been, too, that the government, even at that time, had
it in mind to entrust Hamilton primarily with the duty of securing

[1]Article 14 of Executive Ordinance, March 16, 1836, Gammel, *Laws of
Texas*, I, 1054.
[2]Dip. Cor. Tex. with U. S. (MSS.); also see Garrison, *Dip. Cor. Tex.*, I,
73-74.
[3]Dip. Cor. Tex. with U. S. (MSS.).
[4]Garrison, *Dip. Cor. Tex.*, I, 76-78.
[5]Carson to Childress and Hamilton, Garrison, *Dip. Cor. Tex.*, I, 77.
Childress was a native of Tennessee, and it was here, no doubt, that he
had known Jackson.

financial aid. At any rate he could have done very little diplomatic work, for shortly after he reached Washington Samuel Carson[1] arrived, bringing with him a commission for Hamilton issued by the government, April 2, instructing him to negotiate a loan for the purpose of supplying the army.[2]

It was not the intention of the Texan government that these commissioners should supersede Austin, Archer, and Wharton, whose appointment had been practically confirmed, so far as the government *ad interim* was concerned, shortly after independence was declared.[3] But the question as to the relation of the two sets of agents was not raised until after Childress and Hamilton had left Texas. They had gone as far as Nachitoches, Louisiana, when Childress wrote back to Burnet, March 28:

> I see from the newspapers, here, that Messrs. Austin, Wharton and Archer are supposed to be now at the City of Washington acting as Commissioners under the authority conferred upon them by *the late* provisional Government. If when Mr. Hamilton and I shall have arrived there we should find these gentlemen acting in the same capacity it would place both us and them in a very awkward situation. Will you please, in conjunction with the Cabinet, take this matter into consideration and take such steps with regard to it as you and they may think proper.[4]

April 1, before this letter could have reached him at Harrisburg, the secretary of state, Samuel P. Carson, wrote:

> It is desirable by the President and Cabinet that the Commissioners, Messrs. Austin, Archer, and Wharton, appointed by the provisional government should be associated with yourself and Mr. Hamilton and their aid and exertions requested in obtaining a recognition of our Independence.[5]

There was really little necessity to have settled the matter. Childress and Hamilton did not reach Washington until some time

---

[1]See below, pp. 198-199.

[2]Carson to Houston, November 28, 1836, Garrison, *Dip. Cor. Tex.*, I, 146-147. This commission was issued in accordance with article 9 of the Executive Ordinance of March 16 (see above p. 49) which gives the government power to create a loan of not more than one million dollars.

[3]See above, p. 193.

[4]Childress to Burnet, March 28, 1836, Garrison, *Dip. Cor. Tex.*, I, 74.

[5]Carson to Childress and Hamilton, Garrison, *Dip. Cor. Tex.*, I, 76-77.

between May 28 and June 10,[1] while Austin, who had become discouraged, had started for Texas, May 24.[2] Wharton probably coöperated with them for a while,[3] but he and Archer also soon left Washington.

Childress and Hamilton seem to have expected that after their departure more specific instructions regarding their efforts to secure recognition, as well as financial aid, would be drawn up and forwarded to them. In his letter from Nachitoches, March 28, Childress said: "Please have us furnished with instructions with regard to our political and pecuniary missions."[4] In his communication to the commissioners, April 1, however, Carson had written: "The objects of your mission were so fully explained to you before your departure by the government that nothing further on that subject need be said. I hope to join you in a short time after this reaches you when full explanations will be given."

Nevertheless, on the same day a document called "Private Instructions" was drawn up, but the additional light that it threw upon their course of action was of doubtful value. According to its direction the commissioners were to "hold the freeest and fullest conversation with the President and Cabinet officers . . . but should there be any reluctance on the part of the Sec of State to hear . . . a dignified elevation due to this Republic must mark . . . [their] course." These so-called instructions go on to explain: "Your own minds will suggest the course most proper to pursue as the govt cannot anticipate occurrences which might make it necessary to deviate from strict instructions and therefore leave to you the management of the subject with full confidence that the dignity and honor of your country will be fully maintained and advanced."[6]

On the same day an informal note was addressed by Carson to

---

[1]Wharton to Austin, May 28, 1836, Austin Papers; Childress and Hamilton to Burnet, June 10, 1836, Garrison, *Dip. Cor. Tex.*, I, 99-100.

[2]See above. p. 186.

[3]Austin to Burnet, June 10, 1836, Garrison, *Dip. Cor. Tex.*, I, 98-99; Wharton to Austin, May 28, 1836, Austin Papers.

[4]See above, p. 196.

[5]This letter, it will be noted, answered in a way both requests made by Childress on March 28, but it was impossible at that time for a letter from Nachitoches. to have reached Harrisburg in four days.

[6]Carson to Childress and Hamilton, April 1, 1836, Garrison, *Dip. Cor. Tex.*, I, 77.

Secretary of State Forsyth, introducing the commissioners and asking that they be presented also to Jackson and the Cabinet "in such a manner as may be suited to the station they occupy."[1] This attempt at a letter of credence and the "private instructions"—both of which were forwarded after the departure of the commissioners—together with their original commission, which they had carried with them, apparently constituted their only credentials.

In regard to at least one other matter they were given explicit directions, which they received in the form of a confidential letter from Carson. The rumor had come that Gorostiza, the Mexican minister plenipotentiary at Washington, had been authorized to sell Texas to the United States. Against any such assumption of authority over Texas on the part of Mexico the commissioners were to enter their solemn protest, in justification of which they were to set forth the Texas declaration of Independence.[2]

Carson had promised that he would shortly join Childress and Hamilton. Having found it necessary on account of ill health temporarily to give up his duties as secretary of state, he had been directed by President Burnet, April 1, to spend his vacation in Washington where he was to coöperate with the commissioners there "in procuring a *recognition* from the government of our *Mother* Country . . . [taking] in charge a general Supervision of all the interests and concerns of Texas in that country."[3]

Childress and Hamilton went together as far as Nachitoches, where they separated planning to meet again in Washington the

[1]Carson to Forsyth, April 1, 1836, Records of the Department of State, Book 34, p. 22; also in Garrison, *Dip. Cor. Tex.*, I, 78.

[2]Carson to Childress and Hamilton, April 1, 1836, Garrison, *Dip. Cor. Tex.*, I, 76-77. Wharton also says that the sale of Texas by Mexico was at first supposed to be Gorostiza's business. Wharton was consistent throughout in protesting vigorously against any purchase by the United States of a quitclaim to Texas previous to the recognition of Texas by the United States (Wharton to Austin, December 2, 1836, *ibid.*, 149).

[3]Burnet to Carson, April 1, 1836, *ibid.*, 75. This appointment of the secretary of state to go on such a mission was unwise. Wharton wrote Austin that Jackson had said it in some measure justified Gorostiza's designation of the Texas government as a fugitive government (Wharton to Austin, June 2, 1836, Austin Papers). June 6, a few days after Carson passed though Nashville, Tennessee, J. N. Bryan of that place wrote a personal letter to Van Buren setting forth the intense interest felt throughout the Western States in the welfare of Texas and recommending his friend Carson as a man well informed on the Texas situation (Bryan to Van Buren, June 6, 1836, Van Buren MSS.).

first of May.[1]   Carson followed them soon after their departure, but was so delayed by illness that he did not reach that city until June 22.   Their work on the way up was similar to that of the first set of commissioners and productive of like results.   April 18, Childress reported: .

We have been endeavouring (with some success) to create as much interest as we can at these points in the South and West which we have touched at, and shall continue (through the press and otherwise) to *agitate* the United States as much as possible. You will have received before this reaches you accounts of the public meetings and proceedings at Natches and other places.   So far as I can see the South and West is kindling into a *blaze* upon the subject.   So great is the interest felt upon the subject, and so numerous are the applications by letters from individuals, editors etc for information . . . that . . . we have . . . been under the necessity of employing upon our own responsibility a *Secretary* to the *Mission*.[2]

June 1, Carson wrote to Burnet from Nashville:

The enthusiastic bursts of feeling every where in this country exceeds anything I have ever witnessed.

The spirit in Congress is fine   I send all the papers I can to let you see what is passing there.   Public Meetings are getting up in all directions petitioning Congress to recognize our Independence. A bold move has been made in my native county (Burke No Ca) in our favor. . . .

. . . I am induced to believe that we should send on from this country every Volunteere we can. I am acting on that principle and shall not relax my efforts unless advised to do so by the Govt.

He then goes into detail concerning companies that are to go to Texas under General Dunlap and Captain Grundy.[3]

But in regard to recognition Childress says:

We are not sanguine of getting an *immediate* recognition of the Independence of Texas from the Government of the United States, but will open a negotiation and continue it untill crowned with success, unless otherwise instructed by your Excellency and the Cabinet.   It is of great importance, I conceive, to obtain it as soon

[1]Childress to Burnet, April 18, 1836, Garrison, *Dip. Cor. Tex.*, I, 85.
[2]Childress to Burnet, April 18, 1836, *ibid.*, 85.
[3]Carson to Burnet, June 1, 1836, *ibid.*, 93.   See also below, pp. 210-211.

as possible as the moral effect in our favour would be great in the United States. Many persons who now feel scruples in volunteering to take a part in the internal conflicts of a *foreign* country would freely do so if the independence of the party with which they sympathize was recognized by the Government of their own country.[1]

This apparent subordinating of the question of recognition to serve material ends is readily understood when one recalls the fact that at this time the military situation was at its worst. Unless the tide were turned not only the claims for recognition but independence itself would be a thing of the past.

As soon as the commissioners reached Washington they laid their credentials before Secretary of State Forsyth. Then came accounts through the newspapers of the battle of San Jacinto and the capture of Santa Anna. For some days they eagerly awaited official reports of these events, expecting apparently that the question of recognition would thereupon be settled forthwith.[2] But no communications from the government came, and finally, June 10, upon the basis of the unofficial accounts, they presented to Forsyth the claims of Texas to recognition as a *de facto* government. These communications were never answered.[3] At the same time they wrote begging Burnet to forward official reports and stating the absolute impossibility of acting without them.[4]. Carson also, upon his arrival, urged the same thing. He said:

In the total want of communications, from the Government, with regard to the reasons which actuate them, and indeed as to their whole policy and action except as I gather it from Newspapers and letters from individuals of Texas written to their friends in this country, I am at fault how to act and indeed frequently subjected to mortification, because of my inability to answer questions put by our best friends here, and who wish to shape their course in conformity to the wishes and measures of Texas.[5]

[1]Childress to Burnet, April 18, 1836. Garrison, *Dip. Cor. Tex.*, I, 85.

[2]*Niles' Register*, L, 336; Childress and Hamilton to Burnet, June 10, 1836, Garrison, *Dip. Cor. Tex.*, I, 99-100.

[3]*Debates in Cong.* 24 Cong., 1 Sess., 1891.

[4]Childress and Hamilton to Burnet, June 10, 1836, Garrison, *Dip. Cor. Tex.*, I, 99-100. The commissioners suggest that these communications may have been interrupted on account of the risings of the Creek Indians of Alabama. But it is likely that none were sent.

[5]Carson to Burnet, July 3, 1836, *ibid.*, 102.

Nothing more is heard of the efforts of Childress and Hamilton to establish diplomatic relations with the United States. About the time of their arrival in Washington new commissioners, Collins-worth and Grayson, had been chosen by Burnet, and Childress and Hamilton soon learned that their services were no longer required.[1] In a report from Washington Carson says: "I must conclude this communication with the expression of my entire approbation of the course and conduct of our agents Messrs. Hamilton and Childress, and also of the various efforts of the agents of the Provisional Government, whose reputation, as Gentlemen and Patriots, stand very high in this country."[2] But the commissioners themselves doubtless felt, as had their predecessors, that they had labored in vain, whereas, except for the neglect of their own government, their efforts might have been productive of good results.

3.   The work of the third commission.

On May 26, 1836, only two months after the appointment of Childress and Hamilton, all previous commissioners were recalled and James Collinsworth and Peter W. Grayson were sent by the government *ad interim* to Washington to solicit: (1) the intervention of the United States to stop the war upon the basis of a recognition of the independence of Texas by Mexico; (2) the recognition of the independence of Texas by the United States; and (3) the annexation of Texas to the United States upon certain specified terms.[3]

[1]See below, p. 202; also Carson to Houston, November 28, 1836, Garrison, *Dip. Cor. Tex.*, I, 145.

[2]Carson to Burnet, July 4, 1836, Garrison, *Dip. Cor. Tex.*, I, 103.   The efforts of Hamilton and Carson to secure financial aid were also unavailing.   Carson (*ibid.*) says: "Mr. Hamilton is in Philadelphia, feeling the pulse of the Capitalists, and will proceed to New York. It appears, from his correspondence, that a recognition by this Government of our Independence is made a sine qua non by Capitalists." Finally in the midst of their efforts they received notice through the New Orleans papers of Burnet's proclamation of June 10 (see *Niles' Register*, L, 395), revoking the authority of all Texan financial agents except Toby Bros. of New Orleans, whereupon they immediately ceased work (report of Carson to Houston, November 28, 1836, Garrison, *Dip. Cor. Tex.*, I, 147).   This proclamation was necessary, because the number of agents and sub-agents had grown so numerous that many frauds were being perpetrated.   But it tended for the time being to discredit the Texan government.

[3]For the complete commission see Garrison, *Dip. Cor. Tex.*, I, 89-91.

The reason for appointing these commissioners to supersede all other diplomatic agents seems not to have been due to dissatisfaction with the work of the latter. In recalling Austin and his colleagues, May 27, the secretary of state, William Jack, explained the motives which actuated the government. He said:

I am instructed by the President and Cabinet to inform you that inasmuch as important changes have recently occurred it has been deemed necessary to dispatch to Washington two commissioners for the purpose of representing this Government there. It was conceived most advisable to select gentlemen who are now in this country, because they could be more fully informed of the views of this Govt. and the wishes and interests of the people. These Gentlemen are Peter W. Grayson and James Collinsworth. Esqrs. to whom you will be pleased to communicate any valuable information which you may possess, affording them at the same time ever possible facility in consummating the objects of their mission.

In recalling you the President and Cabinet are not unmindful of your disinterested efforts in the service of your country, but have acted on the conviction that at this crisis of affairs commissioners fresh from Texas, would from their more intimate knowledge of her present wants and policy be able to represent her more efficiently at Washington.

The confidence which your country reposes in you is entirely unimpaired, and you will be received with heartfelt greetings of gratitude upon your return.[1]

The important changes here referred to are the defeat of the Mexicans at San Jacinto, the capture of Santa Anna, and the treaties of May 14; and, as in the case of Childress, the government now chose men best fitted to give official testimony of these events. Throughout the term of the provisional government Collinsworth had served as chairman of the Military Committee. Later on, he, as secretary of state of the government *ad interim,* and Grayson, as attorney-general, had both signed the treaties with

[1] Secretary of State Wm. H. Jack, to Austin and others, May 27, 1836, Garrison, *Dip. Cor. Tex.*, I, 91-92. Another copy of this letter is among the Austin Papers. It is addressed to Austin only and is dated May 29. Austin had left Washington before this letter was written (see above, p. 186). To just what "others" the letter of recall was actually sent it would be difficult to say. Archer, Wharton, Childress, Hamilton, and Carson were all in the neighborhood of Washington at the time when it should have arrived.

Santa Anna. However unwise a change of agents in Washington may have been, the Texan authorities undoubtedly felt that the men who had left Texas at the period of her greatest despondency were incapable of representing correctly, as eye-witnesses could do, the complete victory of the Texans and the utter defeat of the enemy.

The question naturally arises why these men were not instructed to coöperate with the others, as in the case of Childress and Hamilton. So far as the records show there had been no conflict of authority between the Washington agents. But the government had been led to see the inexpediency of the wholesale appointment of agents, which until this time had gone on unchecked. It had been the policy of the commissioners sent out by the government to appoint agents in all places visited. These in turn had appointed sub-agents, and so on. In the case of financial agents, this had resulted in numerous frauds, since almost any one might claim an appointment and accept donations tendered for the cause. Accordingly, Burnet, on June 10, 1836, issued a decree revoking all agencies of this kind except that of Toby Brothers in New Orleans.[1] The recall of all diplomatic agents then in the United States, just two weeks previous to this decree, may have been in line with the same general policy.

On July 8, four days after the adjournment of Congress, Collinsworth and Grayson arrived in Washington. They found Jackson on the point of leaving for the Hermitage, his home at Nashville, Tennessee. In an informal interview the president gave them to understand that a secret agent had been sent to Texas to secure information,[2] and that nothing could be done until his return. Forsyth was non-committal. Annexation, he admitted, was a favorite measure with Jackson when it could be brought about with propriety, and at his request the commissioners drew up a careful statement of the terms upon which Texas desired admission, which was at once forwarded to the president.[3] This, however, was all the satisfaction that could be obtained from him; and, feeling that little could be done in Washington during the summer, Col-

[1] *Niles' Register*, L, 395.
[2] See below, p. 220.
[3] Collinsworth and Grayson to Forsyth, July 14, 1836; Forsyth to Jackson, July 15, 1836, both in Jackson MSS.

linsworth decided to go to Nashville to converse more at length with Jackson. Grayson planned at first to go to Louisville, but concluded to remain in Washington, hoping to ópen official communication with the authorities there.[1]

Before anything could be done in Washington, however, it was necessary to have new credentials, since those the commissioners carried were not drawn up in proper form. July 15, Collinsworth and Grayson had written:

Should it be desired that we should longer represent our government here, it will be necessary to make out new commissions and forward them to the last named places, as those we have, have been deemed inadmissible in consequence of having no seal. It will be seen by reference to our constitution that in the absence of a seal of state the President may use his own private seal.

There is a further Omission on the part of the address to the President and secretary of State in omitting to state even the country they are from.[2]

August 2, Grayson, who was then alone in Washington, repeated this request for new credentials:

We feel a good deal embarrassed for the want of the proper letter of credence, that is to say, one made out with all the requisite formalities of a *Seal,* etc. Mr. Forsyth politely gave us to understand, that he would be happy to see us at any time we might desire to converse with him; but left us to infer pretty plainly that we were not in strictness, *accredited Agents,* on account of the informality of the papers conferring our authority.[3] He intimated moreover, that some advise from our Government addressed to this, was at least of formal necessity, in regard to the persons

---

[1]Collinsworth and Grayson to Burnet, July 15, 1836, Garrison, *Dip. Cor. Tex.,* I, 110-111; Grayson to Burnet, August 2, 1836, *ibid.,* 117-118; Grayson to Secretary of State Jack, August 11, 1836, *ibid.,* 121-122.

[2]Collinsworth and Grayson to Burnet, July 15, 1836, *ibid.,* 111.

[3]Forsyth, in reporting this interview to Jackson, said: "My call for their authority was answered by the production of papers similar to those given to Childress and Hamilton issued by Mr. Burnett but without seals, pointing to this .radical defect, I told them that their powers must be put into proper order before anything could be done with them officially. . . . From a long and free conversation with them I learned that they had no instructions or authority to do more than talk about the terms upon which Texas ought to be admitted into the Union—these terms to be hereafter considered and discussed and confirmed or rejected by the Texan Gov't. or such modifications made as should be deemed expedient" (Forsyth to Jackson, July 15, 1836, Jackson MSS.).

previously here in our character, whose functions have ceased by our appointment.

If we are to continue here, of the necessity of which you and your associates in the Government will of course judge from circumstances presenting themselves, I have to request that all these formal particulars I have mentioned will receive their proper attention. Besides this I would suggest that it will be proper to have made out and sent on to us a regularly authenticated Copy under the Seal of the State, of that portion of the Ordinances of the Convention, which established the present Government ad interim.[1] This is necessary to show its regularity, since in the Constitution proper as printed, nothing appears, that has any reference to the present Organization.[2]

For nearly three months after the first letter was written Grayson waited in Washington, but no new credentials from Texas came.[3] Finally, becoming exasperated, he withdrew to Louisville. From there, November 3, he addressed letters to Burnet and to Austin expressing his indignation. "I came here," he said to Austin, "a few days ago, from a sort of necessity, to await further communications from Texas if any are intended."[4] To Burnet he said: "Some ten days ago I arrived at this place from Washington, where I had remained until the 11th ulto., expecting to receive the credentials of our commission, in the form which had been pointed out by Maj. Collinsworth and myself, as necessary to give us official intercourse with this government. Not receiving them as I had been expecting and being not a little weary of my *unrecognized character* at Washington, I concluded to come to this place

[1] See above, p. 192.

[2] Grayson to Burnet, August 2, 1836, Garrison, *Dip. Cor. Tex.*, I, 117-118.

[3] This, however, was due, in large measure at least, to the poor means of communication and not altogether to remissness on the part of the Texan government *ad interim*. August 10, Burnet wrote Collinsworth and Grayson that he had not yet heard of their arrival in Washington (*ibid.* 120). Four official letters at least had preceded this communication: Burnet to Collinsworth and Grayson, June 20, 1836 (missing; see Burnet to Collinsworth and Grayson, July 8, 1836, *ibid.*, 104; and Grayson to Burnet, August 2, 1836, *ibid.*, 117); Burnet to Collinsworth and Grayson, July 8, 1836 (*ibid.*, 104-108); Jack to same, July 23, 1836 (*ibid.*, 112-114); Burnet to same, August 9, 1836 (*ibid.*, 118). By the time the commissioners' letter of July 15 reached Texas, the September elections were imminent, the result of which Burnet's next official communications announce (Burnet to Grayson, September 12, 1836, *ibid.* 122-123; Burnet to Collinsworth, September 12, 1836, *ibid.*, 123).

[4] Grayson to Austin, November 3, 1836, Austin Papers.

and await the determination of my Government on the subject of its further intercourse with this. A few days more I take it for granted, will bring us information whether our services will be longer required in this Country."[1]

In these letters he also stated what in his opinion was the status of the recognition question. The reason he assigns for the delay in recognition was not quite the same as that previously given by the other commissioners. They had thought it necessary only to establish the fact that Texas was independent. Grayson believed that the United States was more conservative than that, and would wait until assured that independence could be maintained. Moreover, he had come to realize that the question of annexation complicated the matter. In his letter to Austin he said:

On the subject of recognition I think Gen Jackson will still wait a little to observe the *course and character* of *civil affairs in Texas;* this being the only matter at present upon which any real doubt or solicitude remains; our Independence of Mexico being pretty generally looked upon as *established.*

The great misfortune of the delay to recognize consists in its bringing too near together, for the action on them by this Government of the two questions—*recognition* and *annexation.* A *decent* time you know ought to transpire after the disposition of the one before the taking up of the other, for reasons which will readily occur to you.

In his letter to Burnet Grayson said recognition would take place *"at the earliest moment that circumstances would at all justify it in the eyes of the world."* But while he believed that the two questions should be separated he felt that Jackson was favorable to both. August 11, he had written: "There is in my mind no doubt that the present Administration, *can carry the measure of* Annexation. Genl. Jackson feels the utmost solicitude for it and we know how much that will count."[2] He now repeated that from undoubted authority he knew the president was warmly inclined "to adopt such a course . . . as would the soonest bring about *all the objects"* with which he and Collinsworth had been charged —namely, recognition and annexation.

[1]Grayson to Burnet, November 3, 1836, Garrison, *Dip. Cor. Tex.,* I, 123-124.
[2]Grayson to Jack, August 11, 1836, *ibid.,* 122.

Collinsworth, who had spent nearly two months in Nashville in negotiation with Jackson, felt equally sure of Jackson's position, but he also foresaw complications. In a report of his work made from Brazoria, November 13, 1836, after his return to Texas, he says:

Without pretending to have received any official information upon the subject, . . . I think [I] may safely hazard the opinion that the present ex[ec]utive of the United States *is in favor* of all the measures contained in our instructions. Should the present government [that is, the permanent government under Houston][1] believe in the same policy, I cannot too forcibly impress upon them the necessity of dispatching some one forthwith vested with plenary powers to the court of Washington, as in my opinion much may be endangered by delay to bring these matters before the approaching session of the Congress of the United States at an early period of its session.[2]

Five days previous to this in a hastily written note to Austin he had even gone so far as to sketch the terms upon which he believed annexation might be secured. He said:

I am satisfied that an union of Texas with the U States may take place this winter upon the following basis. The Gov. of the U States to assume our debts to endow liberally academies colleges etc.

The object of the U. States is the jurisdiction over the soil, its value is of no object to them.

But no legislation on private claims will under any circumstances be admitted. All claims must be settled according to the laws under which they were acquired.[3]

The mission of Collinsworth and Grayson ended rather abruptly. While the former was in Nashville attempting to negotiate with Jackson[4] and probably while the latter was still in Louisville awaiting some answer to his communications from that

[1]See below, p. 221.
[2]Collinsworth to the President of Texas, November 13, 1836, *ibid.*, 126.
[3]Collinsworth to Austin, November 8, 1836, Austin Papers.
[4]November 13, Collinsworth in his report of his work, from Brazoria, says: "On the 21st of Oct last I recd the enclosed letter marked A [evidently referring to Burnet's communication of September 12, see below, p. 208, note 1] which I considered as finally ending any pretence of authority on my part to act as an agent of this government, and I accordingly set out for this place the next day" (Garrison, *Dip. Cor. Tex.*, I, 126).

place, letters from Burnet arrived announcing the fact that the September elections had been held, and informing the commissioners that the new Congress would doubtless at an early date take up the question of the appointment of an agent to Washington.[1] Thus the term of this commission expired with the government *ad interim,* and the status of the question of recognition was as yet practically undisturbed, so far as any efforts on the part of the Texan agents were concerned.

4. *The work of the friends of Texas in the United States Congress.*

From the foregoing sketch of the work of the first three sets of commissioners it will be seen that it was the opinion of those who had labored in Washington during the first session of the twenty-fourth Congress that only the lack of official information to show that Texas was *de facto* an independent government had prevented recognition. Collinsworth and Grayson had carried with them all the evidence of this kind that was believed to be necessary, but they had arrived in Washington during the recess of Congress—a time when it was impossible to effect anything. They also felt, however, that as nearly as they could determine the spirit generally was favorable; and Jackson, they believed, was anxious for both measures—recognition and annexation.

Questions like these, therefore, naturally arise. To what extent were the commissioners right in their interpretation of the situation at Washington? Were they so misled by the enthusiasm for Texas expressed by private individuals throughout the country, especially throughout the Southern States which they had traversed, that they naively assumed that the government of the United States would feel equally disposed to champion their cause? Did they see only their own limitations as commissioners, and fail to detect other less obvious but perhaps equally formidable obstacles in the way of immediate recognition? To a certain extent this may have been the case. But, on the other hand, was there not some justification for their belief that the questions of recognition and even annexation were seriously discussed by the United States

[1] Burnet to Collinsworth, September 12, 1836, Garrison, *Dip. Cor. Tex.,* I, 123; Burnet to Grayson, September 12, 1836, *ibid.,* 122-123.

authorities in the spring and summer of 1836? There are at least three circumstances that seem to indicate that this was true. These are (1) the well known desire of the United States to secure Texas; (2) the evidence furnished by the congressional debates that the complication in regard to the slavery question, while clearly discernible, was as yet comparatively unimportant; (3) the actual corroboration in the debates of the opinions expressed by the commissioners.

Almost from the time that the United States definitely surrendered Texas by the treaty of 1819, it was the open policy of the government to regain in some way the lost territory. The undertaking was first entrusted to Poinsett, who spent two years, 1825-7, attempting to extend the boundary so as to include the whole, or at least a portion, of Texas in the United States. This failed, and in 1827 he was instructed to treat for a cession of the desired section for the amount of one million dollars, which later on was increased to five millions. Thus two more years were consumed, and at the end of this time Poinsett was recalled. During the greater part of Jackson's administration, that is, from 1829 to 1836, Anthony Butler was the representative of the United States in Mexico. "It was a seven years' period of cheap trickery in which, on the one hand, Mexico was led to believe that the United States government would descend to any level to accomplish the cession of Texas, and on the other, Jackson was encouraged by hopes of a cession which came to nothing."[1] There can be no doubt that the relations between the United States and Mexico during this period hastened the Texan revolution.

Upon Butler's recall, Powhatan Ellis was sent as *chargé*, instructed to press certain claims of American citizens against Mexico. The time was most inopportune—Mexico was torn by revolution—and the result was that, in November, 1836, Ellis demanded his passports. Just previous to this, in October, Gorostiza, the Mexican minister to United States, having become exasperated by what he regarded as a refusal of the United States government to enforce neutrality, had withdrawn from Washington.[2] Thus, for

[1] Reeves, *American Diplomacy under Tyler and Polk*, 68-69.
[2] The immediate cause of his withdrawal was the occupation of Nacogdoches by a detachment of troops sent out by the United States general, Gaines (see below, pp. 211-212).

the present, all diplomatic relations between the United States and Mexico were suspended.

The events of this decade, thus briefly sketched, would seem to warrant the assurance of the Texans generally that the United States authorities would welcome the opportunity of pronouncing Mexican dominion in Texas at an end, and would gratefully accept so valuable an acquisition in case Texas chose to relinquish her independence and join the Union. Nor did the sympathy and the illegal but open assistance of the people of the United States at large tend to destroy this confidence. Naturally when war broke out the United States had at once assumed a neutral attitude. In his seventh annual message at the opening of Congress, December 7, 1835, Jackson had said:

Aware of the strong temptations existing and powerful inducements held out to the citizens of the United States to mingle in the dissensions of our immediate neighbors, instructions have been given to the district attorneys of the United States where indications warranted it to prosecute without respect to persons all who might attempt to violate the obligations of our neutrality, while at the same time it has been thought necessary to apprise the Government of Mexico that we should require the integrity of our territory to be scrupulously respected by both parties.[1]

But laws in support of neutrality could not easily be enforced, and a rather striking illustration will show how on at least one occasion these instructions were observed. While Carson was in Nashville on his way to Washington in June, 1836, he wrote to President Burnet concerning certain volunteers who had enlisted in the Texan cause:

Seventy men are now ready to leave under Captn Grundy who is the *prosecuting atty.* for the United States for this District, and has *formal orders* to arrest and prosecute every man who may take up arms in the cause of Texas or in any way *Violate* the neutrality of the U. S. He says he will prosecute any man under his command who will take up arms *here* and he will accompany them to the boundary line of the U. S. to see that they shall *not violate her neutrality* and when there, if the boys think proper to step over the line as *peaceable emigrants* his authority in this Govt will

---

[1]Richardson, *Messages and Papers*, III, 151; *Debates in Cong.*, 24 Cong., 1 Sess., 1424.

cease and he thinks it highly probable that he will take a peepe at Texas himself. Thus you see how the neutrality of this Govt. is *preserved* by her civil officers.[1]

Against such violations of national faith Mexico repeatedly protested, and the United States government as often reasserted its neutrality and disclaimed any responsibilty for the conduct of private individuals. But, however sincere the intentions of 'the authorities at Washington, there seems to have been little disposition in some sections of the country to take such proclamations seriously,[2] as is witnessed by the large number of volunteers that flocked to Texas. To discourage such immigration Gorostiza, on April 1, 1836, served notice that Mexico would hold herself responsible for no engagements or debts made by the revolted Texans, nor would she consent to any alienation of her national lands in Texas.[3] Such declaration was, of course, of absolutely no effect.

But the climax came, as Gorostiza thought, when the executive authorities at Washington refused to punish the actual invasion of Texas by United States troops. General Gaines had been stationed by the United States authorities at Fort Jessup near Natchitoches, Louisiana, with orders to preserve peace along the frontier, especially to hold the Indians in check.[4] He was also given permission to go as far as Nacogdoches if the hostilities of the Indians should make such a step necessary. In April, in response to a message that a force of Indians and Mexicans had united and were approaching Nacogdoches, he advanced his troops as far as the Sabine.[5] July 4, Austin wrote asking Gaines to guarantee the treaties with Santa Anna of May 14, and suggesting that his occupation of Nacogdoches would end the war.[6] August 4, Gaines on

[1] Carson to Burnet, June 1, 1836, Garrison, *Dip. Cor. Tex.*, I, 93.

[2] For one report in regard to Jackson's attitude, illustrating this, see above, p. 172. Also for an interesting account, from the Mexican standpoint, of the conduct of the United States throughout this period, see Tornel, *Tejas y los Estados-Unidos de América en sus Relaciones con la República Mexicana* (1837).

[3] Declaration of Gorostiza, April 1, 1836 (Garrison, *Dip. Cor. Tex.*, I, 74-75.

[4] By the treaty of 1831 between the United States and Mexico each had agreed to restrain incursions of its border Indians into the territory of the other. Texas was claiming the benefit of this treaty.

[5] Carson to Burnet, April 14, 1836, Garrison, *Dip. Cor. Tex.*, I, 83-84.

[6] Austin's Letter and Memorandum Album (1836) pp. 9-13, Austin Papers.

the basis of insufficient instructions refused to guarantee the fulfillment of the treaties,[1] but hearing of an Indian uprising, he had in the meantime sent a detachment to Nacogdoches. Ever since May, Gorostiza had been protesting against the authority given Gaines to cross into Texas, and now, after futile remonstrances with the authorities at Washington, who seem to have had no official notice, before September, of Gaines's movements,[2] he summarily demanded his passports, October 15. These events, naturally, were followed with keen interest by the Texan commissioners; and, in view of the assurances they personally had received in regard to the friendliness of the government, it is not surprising that they were confident of immediate recognition and of annexation, as well, provided they desired it. They sincerely believed that their entrance into the Union depended mainly upon the vote of the Texans themselves. And in the light of the occurrences the next ten years, one smiles at Wharton's eagerness in the spring of 1836 to return home in order to *persuade* the leading Texans to consent to annexation. He had just heard that Houston was opposed to such a step, and fearing the influence of the hero of San Jacinto he was anxious to see Houston before the latter's opinions were generally known. He therefore wrote Austin, May 28, that he would leave the work in Washington to Childress and Hamilton and return to Texas to exert such influence as he had with Houston. "I feel it more important than all other things in the world," he said, "[that] the present Senate should act upon the question of annexation. . . . If we first get the leading men in favour of it in Texas will all go right. . . ."[3]

But if this was the psychological moment to urge recognition and annexation it was allowed to pass. One can not read the debates in Congress from April 26, when the question of recognition was first

[1]Gaines to Austin, August 4, 1836, Austin Papers.
[2]September 4, Jackson wrote two letters to Gaines acknowledging communications from him dated August 11 and July 21 concerning (1) Austin's request in regard to the treaties with Santa Anna, and (2) rumors relative to the Indians. Jackson replied to the first. that the Mexican authorities had long since served notice that no act of Santa Anna's since his capture would be held binding on the Mexican government; to the second, that he should march his whole force to Nacogdoches if convinced that circumstances demanded such a step (both letters in Jackson MSS.).
[3]Wharton to Austin, May 28, 1836, Austin Papers.

discussed in the Senate,[1] until Congress adjourned, July 4, without being impressed, as the commissioners were, by the apparent failure on the part of Texas to take any initiative whatever in the matter. Memorials and petitions from various sections of the United States were continually arriving, but the commissioners from Texas were rendered impotent by want of the proper equipment. Indeed, it is worthy of note that, without exception, the discussions on the question throughout the first session of Congress were provoked, not by the efforts of the commissioners, but by these memorials and petitions from interested citizens of the United States.[2] The presence of the commissioners in Washington seems to have attracted very little attention in Congress. May 23, two months after Austin, Archer, and Wharton first arrived in Washington, Senator Morris, of Ohio, asked where were the authorized agents of Texas. Those gentlemen who were there as agents, he believed, had shown no credentials from the authorities of Texas. When he acted in the capacity of a representative he desired something official upon which to act. In reply Walker of Mississippi, an ardent friend of Texas, asserted that the Texan commissioners were public and accredited agents, not the less respectable because they were once American citizens.[3] On the same day Webster of Massachusetts, urging the Senate to avoid premature recognition, declared that as soon as Texas felt that she had a government she would naturally present her claims to her neighbors.[4] One other reference is made to the commissioners. In the course of this same debate, Senator Walker speaks of them as the young Franklins from Texas, who

[1] On May 16 Walker of Mississippi refers to a discussion on the subject which he says took place April 22, but evidently he has in mind the debate of April 26.

[2] Named in the order in which these documents were presented to Congress, they were as follows: To the Senate, April 26, proceedings from a meeting in Cincinnati; May 9, memorials from citizens of Philadelphia; May 16, resolutions of a meeting in Burke County, North Carolina; May 23, proceedings of a meeting at the court house of Warren County, Mississippi; June 13 a memorial from Shelby County, Kentucky, and resolutions of the legislature of the State of Connecticut; June 24, a memorial from a portion of the citizens of Louisiana; June 27, proceedings of meeting at Nashville, Tennessee; to the House, May 30, a memorial from a congressional district in Ohio; June 6, a memorial from the District of Columbia; June 27, a memorial from a meeting at Nashville, Tennessee.

[3] *Debates in Cong.*, 24 Cong., 1 Sess., 1529.

[4] *Ibid.*, 1527-1528.

perhaps had already presented their credentials.[1] It is true the commissioners considered that their business was not so much with Congress as with the executive, but, if they had been in a position to push the work, Congress would no doubt have acted more vigorously.

To be sure, opposition to Texas as a slave holding country was already in evidence, and it grew stronger as the session progressed. As early as May 7 a debate on the subject arose in the House. John Quincy Adams, aroused by the operation of Gaines on the Texan frontier, referred to it as an attempt to conquer Texas and re-establish slavery, which had been abolished by Mexico. He was opposed to any such addition to the United States. Thompson of South Carolina in reply deplored the inopportune introduction of slavery into the debate, especially by the gentlemen who had negotiated away Texas. It had been said, he claimed, by the enemies of Adams, at the time when the treaty of 1819 was drawn up, that a leading motive for ceding to Spain this valuable territory was to prevent the addition it would make to the slaveholding interests of the United States. Thompson regretted that Adams by his present attitude should have confirmed such a statement. Adams thereupon explained his great reluctance to enter into the treaty, claiming that he was the last man in the cabinet to agree to it; upon which the discussion as regards slavery was dropped.[2]

Two days later in the Senate Moore of Alabama regretted the disposition of some of the senators to disregard petitions for the recognition of the independence of Texas—a treatment they were not wont to accord to abolition petitions.[3] On the same day Shepley of Maine opposed the printing of the memorials. The sympathies that had been expressed for the Texan cause may have been raised, he said, "entirely by the perusal of the cruelties perpetrated in Texas. He hoped it was so. But it was possible there were other matters and motives which had their influence in operating on the feelings of a great number; and if so, any sympathies arising from such a source were unworthy of respect and consideration."[4]

[1]*Debates in Cong.*, 24 Cong., 1 Sess., 1534.
[2]*Ibid.*, 3519-3522.
[3]*Ibid.*, 1421.
[4]*Ibid.*, 1425.

May 16, Senator Walker of Mississippi referred to the treaty of 1819 by which five or six prospective states were torn from the Union, thus destroying the balance of power between the North and the South.[1] May 23, Morris of Ohio, who, on April 26, had presented the first memorial asking for the recognition of Texas, now said that he was not ready to take up the matter—that it involved a question which did not 'meet the eye, which was beyond the mere recognition of independence, a question that would convulse the Union from one end to the other.'[2] Calhoun of South Carolina spoke of the advantage of annexing Texas, thus preventing the possibility of annoyance to the slaveholding states from that section of the country. Rives of Virginia said Calhoun had given opinions as a southern man.[3]

On the same day Niles of Connecticut, on presenting resolutions from the legislature of his state, praying the recognition of Texas, called attention to the fact that the first state[4] to take such a step was in a remote part of the Union where no interested motives would be supposed to operate, and from whence there had been no emigrants to that country.[5] This, he went on to say, should prove that there was really little foundation for all that was being said concerning local jealousy in different sections of the Union. He was aware that there were ulterior questions of a most momentous character connected with the independence of Texas. Some of these were very delicate, involving the balance of political power in regard to a particular interest, to which he would not at that time allude. If these questions had been considered by his state they had not influenced her actions which had sprung from a sense of justice and a love of liberty.'[6]

The extreme caution with which it was necessary to approach such a question would naturally have prevented any free expres-

[1]*Debates in Cong.*, 24 Cong., 1 Sess., 1456-7.
[2]*Ib'd.*, 1525.
[3]*Ibid.*, 1531.
[4]Connecticut seems to have been the only state that sent in such a petition.
[5]In this statement Niles was perhaps substantially correct. A part of the interest taken by Connecticut in Texas, however, may have been due to the fact that Moses Austin, the father of Stephen F. Austin, and the first to conceive the idea of introducing into Texas Anglo-American colonists, was a native of Durham, in that state.
[6]*Debates in Cong.*, 24 Cong., 1 Sess., 1531.

sion of opinion; at the same time, there is sufficient evidence to show that as yet the significance of the slavery question in regard to Texas was not fully appreciated. One circumstance will help illustrate this. It will be remembered that Morris of Ohio, on April 26, presented to Congress the first petition—that from Cincinnati—asking for recognition of the independence of Texas. It was he, also, who nearly four months earlier had presented the two first abolition petitions that had reached the present Congress—and these, too, had come from Ohio. In each instance one of his most bitter opponents was Porter of Louisiana. Porter's attitude toward the abolition petitions was natural; toward the petition for recognition it was determined largely by the trade interests Louisiana had with Mexico. During the last twenty months, Porter claimed, the trade between New Orleans and the Mexican ports had amounted to nearly fifteen million dollars. Was this to be thrown away, asked the senator from Louisiana, simply because the country adjoining them had no free institutions? Another consideration, he said, which it behooved Louisiana to take into account was the fact that in case of war between the United States and Mexico the western portions of Louisiana would be exposed perhaps for years to inroads of the Mexicans and their Indian allies. Her property, especially her slaves, would thus be endangered. 'It was all very well,' he said, 'for gentlemen who came from states where peace and security could not be disturbed by hostilities to indulge in aspirations after the happiness of the human race. But he protested against their doing so at Louisiana's expense.'[1]

It would be necessary to examine into the local politics of Louisiana to understand fully her attitude in regard to Texas. As has been noted,[2] a memorial from Opelousas, Louisiana, praying the government to recognize Texas at the earliest period possible was presented by Senator Preston of South Carolina, June 24. But the fact that a Louisiana senator opposed recognition so vigorously at least tends to show that the importance of Texas to the slaveholding states was not generally realized.[3]

[1]*Debates in Cong.*, 24 Cong., 1 Sess., 73-78, 1286, 1418-9.
[2]See above, p. 213, note 2.
[3]It must be admitted that the attitude of Louisiana as expressed in the Senate was consistent throughout. When, on March 1, 1837, the

One other incident in this connection deserves mention. On his retirement from office in 1836, Governor McDuffie of South Carolina, after speaking in harshest terms of the Texans and their struggle for independence, said: "You are doubtless aware that the people of Texas, by an almost unanimous vote, have expressed their desire to be admitted into our confederacy, and application will probably be made to congress for that purpose. In my opinion, congress ought not .even to entertain such a proposition, in the present state of the controversy."[1]

These expressions from the governor of a slaveholding state, together with the preceding evidence from the congressional debates, show that the issue as regards the Texas question and slavery was by no means clearly drawn. Other interests called forth some opposition to congressional action concerning recognition. Louisiana's attitude has already been noted. Many undoubtedly were sincerely opposed to any violation of the neutrality which had been proclaimed. Some urged the preservation of the recent treaty with Mexico. Others were reluctant to provoke war with Mexico. Others still claimed to be restrained by the principles laid down in the Monroe Doctrine. Some hesitated to urge immediate recognition, because of the suspicion that would be cast on the motives of the United States should annexation follow. A few still clung to the hope of a cession of Texas by Mexico.

But the one insurmountable barrier to immediate action was the lack of authentic information upon which to base such a step. The expressions of sympathy for Texas were almost unanimous, especially in the Senate. All alike deplored the absence of any save newspaper accounts. The debates, as reported, are full of expressions such as these: "If the accounts . . . received from Texas were official, . . . he [Walker of Mississippi] would have moved a resolution for the immediate recognition of the independence of Texas";[2] "If the people of Texas had established a

question of recognition was before the Senate, Nicolas, then Senator from Louisiana voted in the negative. Morris, be it noted, also voted against the motion, but he voted at the same time in favor of recognition whenever information was received that Texas was capable of fulfilling the obligations of an independent power (*Debates in Cong.*, 24 Cong., 2 Sess., 1012-3).

[1]*Niles' Register*, LI, 229-230.
[2]*Debates in Cong.*, 24 Cong., 1 Sess., 1527; cf. 1526, 1529.

Government *de facto,* it was undoubtedly the duty of this Government to acknowledge their independence";[1] "The sole question is, has a revolution been effected in Texas? Has the Mexican Government been overthrown there? . . . [If so] then we shall violate the fundamental principle of the law of nations, if we continue to recognize the existence of the Mexican authority in a country from which it has been expelled."[2] Calhoun was ready to vote for annexation as well as recognition as soon as it became evident that Texas had established a government.[3]

Finally, in order to get all the light possible on the subject as well as for the moment to dispose of a question that was uselessly consuming time, it was decided both in the House[4] and the Senate to refer all memorials and petitions to committees of foreign affairs. June 18, five days after the reference, the Senate committee, of which Clay was chairman, was ready with its report. This report begins by discussing the former policy of the United States toward the recognition of a new or modified form of government, and concludes thus:

> The committee has no information respecting the recent movements in Texas, except such as is derived from the public prints. . . . No means of ascertaining accurately the exact amount of the population of Texas are at the command of the committee. . . . Nor are the precise limits of the country which passes under the denomination of Texas known. . . . [Therefore]
> *Resolved,* That the independence of Texas ought to be acknowledged by the United States whenever satisfactory information has been received that it has in successful operation a civil Government, capable of performing the duties and fulfilling the obligations of an independent Power."[5]

---

[1] Webster in *Debates in Cong.,* 24 Cong., 1 Sess., 1527.
[2] Walker in *ibid.,* 1534.
[3] *Ibid.,* 1531.
[4] The only record given in the *Globe* of a reference of memorials to the House committee on foreign affairs was on June 6 when memorials from the District of Columbia were referred (*Cong. Globe,* 24 Cong., 1 Sess., 533). But the opening words of the report of July 4 (*Reports of Committees,* 24 Cong., 1 Sess., III, No. 854) are as follows: "The Committee on Foreign Affairs, to which were referred certain resolutions of the Legislature of the State of Connecticut, and the petitions of many citizens of the United States, asking the recognition of the independence of Texas," etc.
[5] *Reports of Committees,* 24 Cong., 1 Sess., 1847.

This resolution, however, while gratifying as evidence of the friendly interest felt by Congress, left the question of recognition practically untouched. But even the most ardent friends of Texas realized that, under the circumstances, it was all that could˙ have been expected. In order, therefore, to help meet the condition named in the resolution, a motion was at once passed that the president be requested

to communicate to the Senate any information in his possession, not inconsistent with the public interest, touching the political condition of Texas—the organization of its Government, and its capacity to maintain its independence; and, also, any correspondence which may have taken place between the Executive of the United States and the Government of Texas or its agents.[1]

In compliance with this motion Secretary of State Forsyth, on June 23, wrote to the president:

The Secretary of State to whom was referred a resolution of the Senate of the 18th instant . . . has the honor to lay before the President the accompanying copies of papers addressed to and left at, the Department of State, by persons claiming to be agents of the republic of Texas; being all the information and correspondence called for by the resolution. No answers having been returned to any of these communications, they remain for further consideration, and such direction as the President shall hereafter give.[2]

Thus, unconsciously, Forsyth gives a terse and accurate summary of all that had been accomplished with the executive authorities by the combined efforts of the six commissioners who up to this time had labored in Washington.

In communicating these documents to the Senate on the same day Jackson said:

Not having accurate and detailed information of the civil, military, and political condition of Texas, I have deemed it inexpedient to take the necessary measures, now in progress, to procure it, before deciding upon the course to be pursued in relation to the newly declared Government.[3]

[1]*Debates in Cong.*, 24 Cong., 1 Sess., 1871.
[2]*Ibid.* None of this correspondence has been found.
[3]*Debates in Cong.*, 24 Cong., 1 Sess., 1871.

The "necessary measures" to which the president undoubtedly referred were those taken in dispatching to Texas a secret agent to
learn the true state of affairs. Two days after Jackson's communication to the Senate, Forsyth addressed to Burnet the following
letter :

I have the honor to introduce to you Henry M. Morfit, Esquire,
of this city, who has been chosen to endeavor to procure more accurate and detailed information than that now in possession of the
United States, relative to the civil, military and political condition
of Texas. I will thank you to facilitate Mr. Morfit's inquiries in
any way you can.[1]

Upon the strength of this measure another article, expressing
satisfaction at the president's course, was added to the resolution
reported by the Senate committee, June 18, and in this form the
resolution was unanimously adopted, July 1.[2] The House resolution, which was identical with the amended resolution of the Senate, was reported and adopted July 4[3]— the day Congress adjourned.

The status of affairs, therefore, when Congress adjourned for the
summer was this. Two sets of commissioners had worn themselves
out waiting in Washington for something definite upon which to
work. At the same time, independently of any effort on their part,
Congress had expressed itself almost unanimously in favor of recognition whenever circumstances would at all justify that step. Jackson, too, as the commissioners believed, was not unfriendly to the
objects they had in view. A secret agent had been sent out to
Texas, and, if his report were at all favorable, everything apparently pointed to the speedy consummation of both objects sought

---

[1]Forsyth to Burnet, June 25, 1836, Garrison, *Dip. Cor. Tex.*, I, 100.
[2]*Debates in Cong.*, 24 Cong., 1 Sess., 1915, 1928; see above, p. 218.
[3]*Ibid.*, 4621; *Reports of Committees*, 295, 24 Cong., 1 Sess., III, No.
854. In the former reference the vote on the resolution is given as yeas
128, nays 20, on the first article; yeas 113, nays 22, on the second. In
the latter reference the vote on these articles respectively is yeas 126,
nays 20; and yeas 113, nays 22.
  The second article as given in the House report was as follows:
  "*Resolved*, That the House of Representatives perceive with satisfaction that the President of the United States has adopted measures to
ascertain the political, military, and civil condition of Texas" (*Reports
of Committees*, 295, 24 Cong., 1 Sess., III, No. 854).

by Texas.[1] Collinsworth and Grayson, though naturally unable to effect anything themselves during the summer, believed that this was the situation. It was with confidence of success that the permanent government in the fall of 1836 took up the work which in the hands of the provisional government and the government *ad interim* had been carried on in so lax a fashion. And the prospects seemed not less bright from the fact that the permanent government was in a position to correct the mistakes of its predecessors, and to push forward with energy the two measures so much desired.

5. *The work of Wharton and Hunt.*

In September, 1836, a general election was held in Texas to ratify the constitution and to select the officials for the new government. The constitution was unanimously adopted. The officers chosen were Sam Houston for president and M. B. Lamar for vice-president; Stephen F. Austin was appointed secretary of state, and Henry Smith secretary of the treasury. At the same time the question of annexation was submitted to the people, and decided in the affirmative by an overwhelming majority.

October 22, Houston was duly installed as president. November 16, he approved the following joint resolution of Congress:

Whereas, the good people of Texas, in accordance with a proclamation of his Excellency David G. Burnet, president ad interim of the republic, did, on the first Monday of September last past, at an election held for president, vice-president, senators, and representatives of congress, vote to be annexed to the United States of America, with an unanimity unparalled in the annals of the elective franchise, only ninety-three of the whole population voting against it:

[1]It is true that during the summer of 1836 the credit of Texas fell rather low. Burnet was extremely unpopular. Moreover the failure of the government to ratify the New Orleans loans, and the sudden change of the Texan agency in New Orleans had done much to destroy confidence throughout the United States in the Texan government. Texas was no longer in immediate danger from Mexico, so all voluntary contributions had ceased. Until the establishment of the new government the treasury department was not placed upon a permanent basis. The sale of scrip, especially in New York, by different companies had reduced Texan lands to a nominal value. Equitable titles could be had at auction at less than one cent an acre, and legal titles at about ten cents (Samuel Ellis to Austin, August 23, 1836, Austin Papers).

Be it therefore resolved by the senate and house of representatives of the republic of Texas, in congress assembled, That the president be, and he is hereby authorized and requested to despatch forthwith to the government of the United States of America, a minister, vested with ample and plenary powers to enter into negotiations and treaties with the United States government for the recognition of the independence of Texas, and for an immediate annexation to the United States; a measure required by the almost unanimous voice of the people of Texas and fully concurred in by the present Congress.[1]

The choice for this important mission fell first upon Austin; but, owing to ill health and the necessity of closing out other business at home, he declined.[2] Houston then selected Wharton. Under ordinary circumstances Austin was much the better man to send upon an errand of diplomacy. He was cautious, discerning, conciliatory. Wharton, on the other hand, was impetuous and outspoken. But he possessed the energy, enthusiasm, and persistence, which in the present case were perhaps of greater value than the more characteristic qualities of a diplomat. Moreover of all the Texan agents with the exception of Grayson, whose work had counted for little, he had spent most time in Washington in a purely diplomatic capacity.[3] When Austin and Archer had left Washington to visit other cities for the purpose of raising money and volunteers for Texas, Wharton had remained to keep in touch with the government. He was there when Childress and Hamilton arrived, and, in spite of his haste to return to Texas,[4] he no doubt coöperated with them for a while.

A comparison of Wharton's credentials and instructions issued on this occasion and those with which he and his colleagues, Austin and Archer, had been furnished just a year earlier will show that during the interval the young republic had garnered much useful information in the realm of diplomacy.[5] To Austin, as secretary

[1]Gammel, *Laws of Texas*, I, 1089, 1090.
[2]Austin to Perry, July [undoubtedly intended for September] 25, 1836, Austin Papers.
[3]Wharton was in Washington more than two months; Grayson was there about three.
[4]See above, p. 212.
[5]Upon their receipt Wharton writes Austin, November 22 that he had not had time to read them, but "so far as their exterior appearance is concerned, they do credit to those who have prepared them and to our

of state, fell the important duty of drawing up the necessary papers, and for such a task no one was more capable. Several rough drafts of instruction in his own handwriting are still in existence[1] testifying to the effort expended in making these documents conform to required rules. When complete, Wharton's equipment as minister plenipotentiary consisted of: (1) his commission as minister; (2) general instructions; (3) private and special instructions; (4) copies of the declaration of independence, of the constitution, and of such acts and proceedings of the newly established authorities as would go to show that Texas had in operation a *de facto* government; and (5) a file of the *Telegraph and Texas Register,* the most important newspaper then published in Texas.[2] Finally, lest the authorities at Washington should refuse to receive Wharton as minister previous to recognition, it was decided to furnish him also with a commission as agent.[3] Through inadvertence, however, this document was omitted, and was not forwarded to him until a month later.[4]

The general instructions began by saying that, although the only fact to be established in order to base thereon a claim for recognition was that Texas was independent *de facto,* still it would add moral force to her plea to show that she was also independent *de jure.* This was evident when it was considered that Santa Anna

infant government" (Garrison, *Dip. Cor. Tex.,* I, 142). When Wharton presented his general instructions to Jackson and Forsyth he said that they "appeared well satisfied with them. I asked the President if there was anything unreasonable or objectionable in my instructions. He answered No" (*Ibid.,* 175).

[1]Austin Papers.

[2]Austin to Wharton, November 18, 1836, Garrison, *Dip. Cor. Tex.,* I, 127; Austin to Wharton, November 22, 1836, *ibid.,* 141-142. Austin drafted a letter of credence November 18, the same day on which the other papers were issued. For some reason, however, it apparently was not sent until April of the next year, after recognition was secured. The letter which was then sent is an exact copy of the letter first drawn up by Austin, except that it is signed by Henderson, then secretary of state, and sealed with the official seal. Both letters are in Dip. Cor. Tex. with U. S. (MSS.). See also Garrison, *Dip Cor. Tex.,* I., 135, 203.

[3]Austin to Wharton, November 18, 1836, *ibid.,* 127.

[4]In a letter to Austin, December 2, 1836, written on board the *General Gaines* when near Natchez on his way to Washington, Wharton said his commission as agent was not among his papers, and urged that it be forwarded forthwith (Garrison, *Dip. Cor. Tex.,* I, 149). In reply, this commission was made out and carried to Wharton by Hunt. (Henderson to Wharton, December 31, Garrison, *Dip. Cor. Tex.,* I, 160; see also below p. 225.)

himself had destroyed the federal compact, by which alone Texas was bound to the other states of the Mexican union. It was by no act of her own, therefore, that Texas was released from all allegiance to this union. But aside from this, the law of self-preservation had given Texas the right to provide a government for herself—that to which she had formerly been united was torn by revolution and wholly inadequate to furnish protection. So much for the right to declare independence. As for the fact that Texas was actually independent, the documents accompanying the instructions would amply testify. In regard to the physical capacity of Texas, the defeat of the Mexicans at San Jacinto should afford sufficient proof. Mexico at that time had been united under a popular leader, who had under his command eight thousand well disciplined men. Texas was disorganized and without an army. The situation was now reversed. Mexico was in revolution, her army scattered, and Santa Anna, the president and commander-in-chief of the army, a prisoner. Texas was now in possession of an army, a navy, and a government in good working order. Under these circumstances, the precedents of the United States in dealing with newly established governments demanded the recognition of Texas. Furthermore policy dictated the interposition of the United States to restore tranquillity on her southwestern frontier.[1]

The private instructions seemed intended primarily to prevent Wharton's making too great sacrifices in order to secure annexation. A treaty with Mexico and friendly manifestations on the part of England and France, he was told, might make independence more desirable than annexation. Should recognition and annexation both be denied, Wharton was to cultivate, with all due caution, the support and good will of the foreign ministers at Washington. Should recognition alone be secured, he was empowered to form with the United States a treaty of amity, limits, and commerce on the basis of a just reciprocity, and to make, also, if possible, a treaty of alliance.[2]

Before the end of the year two other persons were dispatched to Washington in a diplomatic capacity. One of these was Fairfax

---

[1]The remainder of the instructions relates to annexation. For the entire document see Garrison, *Dip. Cor. Tex.*, I, 127-135.

[2]*Ibid.*, 135-140.

Catlett, appointed, December 13, as secretary of legation, with authority to act as *chargé d'affaires* for Texas in case of the death or removal of Wharton.[1] The other was Memucan Hunt, commissioned, December 31, as minister extraordinary, with instructions to act in conjunction with Wharton in the effort to secure recognition and annexation. In addition to the evidence with which Wharton had already been furnished to prove that Texas was a *de facto* government, Hunt was to testify to the fact that, since Wharton's departure, the judiciary had been regularly organized. He was also given additional instructions concerning annexation.[2] Furthermore, he carried another commission for himself and Wharton, empowering them, in case they were not received as ministers, to act as agents,[3] "with full powers as such to negotiate for the recognition of the Independence of this Republic with the authorities of that Government and to do all necessary acts and things for the purpose of effecting the object of their agency."[4]

Besides these diplomatic agents there was one other individual who went on a similar errand from Texas to Washington in the winter of 1836-7. This was Santa Anna. Confessedly his object was to urge the mediation of the United States in bringing about a settlement of the Texan question. His chief desire no doubt was to get out of Texas.

The plan of using Santa Anna in the negotiations with the Washington authorities had originated shortly after Austin's return to Texas in the summer of 1836. It was intended at first that this should be done simply by correspondence. July 2, Austin went to Columbia to interview Santa Anna, who was imprisoned there. During his stay at this place, both he and Santa Anna wrote to Jackson, July 4, giving him a full account of the state of affairs, and enclosing copies of the public and private treaties of May 14.[5]

---

[1] For Catlett's commission, which is dated December 13, 1836, see Dip. Cor. Tex. with U. S. (MSS.); Austin to Catlett, December 14, 1836, Garrison, *Dip. Cor. Tex.*, I, 154-155.

[2] *Ibid.*, 161-165.

[3] See above, p. 223.

[4] Dip. Cor. Tex. with U. S. (MSS.); also see Garrison, *Dip. Cor. Tex.*, I, 166.

[5] It is difficult to say whether this was the plan of Santa Anna or of Austin. A letter from Burnet to Collinsworth and Grayson, July 8, 1836 (Garrison, *Dip. Cor. Tex.*, I, 104), says:

"Genl Austin arrived here a few days ago. He visited the President

Santa Anna, Jackson was told, was fully convinced that the interest of Mexico demanded the immediate termination of the war on the basis of a recognition by Mexico of the independence of Texas. The only means of accomplishing this end was through Santa Anna's immediate release and return to Mexico. The intimate knowledge of Texas which he had acquired during the past four months had convinced him of the futility of attempting to re-conquer Texas. Mexico as a whole was ignorant of the situation. Furthermore, it was important for Santa Anna to return to Mexico before the September elections, in order to prevent, if possible, the election to the presidency of his political opponent, Bravo—a contingency which would naturally result in the continuation of the war. The former attempt to release Santa Anna was touched upon, and its failure ascribed to the want of confidence on the part of the people of Texas in Santa Anna's sincerity relative to the treaties of May 14. Nothing but the guarantee of the United States, Austin said, would

Santa Anna at Columbia and another effort towards the adjustment of our difficulties with Mexico, was suggested by the distinguished Prisoner. He proposes to procure the friendly mediation of the government of the United States between Texas and Mexico and has addressed a letter to President Jackson, a certified copy of which I enclose to you, in furtherance of this object."

The following is Austin's account: "If the principle was adopted at all of using Santa Anna for the public good of Texas, on the basis of saving his life, the only use that could or ought to have been made of him in my opinion was with the U. S. Govt. and not by an armistice or a treaty. . . . I expressed this opinion to Mr. Barnett and other members of the Govt. and asked whether Santa Anna had written to the U. S. Govt. The answer was that he had not. I was at Columbia a few days afterwards and saw Santa Anna—he said much about his desire to procure the mediation of the U. S. I told him that no mediation would be accepted by Texas, except on the basis of a recognition of our independence . . . he said that was the basis on which he acted and proposed to write to Gen. Jackson. I replyed that he ought to do so, and to state in his letter his firm and full conviction that Mexico could not continue the war with Texas etc." (Austin's Letter and Memorandum Album, 1836, p. 36, Austin Papers).

The plan of having the United States guarantee the treaty with Santa Anna had probably originated with Houston. It was he who first drafted a rough sketch of the proposed treaty, which he sent in a letter to Rusk, dated, Headquarters of the Army, Camp San Jacinto, May 3, 1836. Among various stipulations suggested are the following:

"The guarantee to be obtained from the United States for the fulfilment of the stipulation on the part of the contracting parties. . . .

"Agents to be sent to the United States, to obtain the mediation of that government in the affairs of Mexico and Texas—*New Orleans Bulletin*, July 12, 1836" (Yoakum, *History of Texas*, II, 154, note).

satisfy public c‚inion in Texas on that point. "Your guarantee to the people of Texas," he wrote to Jackson, "for the fulfillment of the offers made by Gen'l Santa Anna would produce his *immediate release,* and he says this 'would end the war."[1] "The duration of the war and its disasters," wrote Santa Anna, "are . . . inevitable, unless a powerful hand interpose to cause the voice of reason to be opportunely listened to. It appears to me, then, that it is you who can render so great a service to humanity, by using your high influence to have the aforesaid Agreements carried into effect; which, on my part, shall be punctually fulfilled.

" . . . Let us establish mutual relations to the end that your Nation and the Mexican may strengthen their friendly ties and both engage amicably in giving existence and stability to a people that wish to figure in the political world; in which they will succeed within a few years, with the protection of the two Nations."[2]

September 4, Jackson who was still at the Hermitage replied to Santa Anna as follows:

The Government of the United States is ever anxious to cultivate peace and friendship with all nations; but it proceeds on the principle that all nations have the right to alter, amend, or change their own government as the sovereign power—the people—may direct. In this respect it never interferes with the policy of other powers, nor can it permit any on the part of others with its internal policy. Consistently with this principle, whatever we can do to restore peace between contending nations . . . is cheerfully at the service of those who are willing at rely upon our good offices as a friend or mediator.

In reference, however, to the agreement which you, as the representative of Mexico, have made with Texas, and which invites the interposition of the United States, you will at once see that we are forbidden by the character of the communications made to us through the Mexican minister from considering it. That government has notified us that as long as you are a prisoner no act of yours will be regarded as binding by the Mexican authorities.

[1]Austin to Jackson, July 4, 1836, in Austin's Letter and Memorandum Album (1836), pp. 1-9, Austin Papers. Austin also wrote to Gaines on this day asking him to guarantee the treaty (see above, p. 211).
[2]Santa Anna to Jackson, July 4, 1836, copy of the original in *ibid.,* pp. 13-16; translation in Garrison, *Dip. Cor. Tex.,* I, 106-107. A freer translation is to be found in Richardson, *Messages and Papers,* III, 274-275.

Under these circumstances good faith to Mexico, as well as the general principle to which I have adverted as forming the basis of our intercourse with all foreign powers, make it impossible for me to take any step like that you have anticipated. If, however, Mexico should signify her willingness to avail herself of our good offices in bringing about the desirable result you have described, nothing could give me more pleasure than to devote my best services to it. . . .

Your letter, and that of General Houston, commander in chief of the Texan army, will be made the basis of an early interview with the Mexican minister at Washington. They will hasten my return to Washington, to which place I will set out in a few days, expecting to reach it by the 1st of October.[1]

To Houston, who had also written to Jackson on the subject, August 9, the president replied at the same time and substantially to the same effect.[2]

Thus nothing was accomplished by this method, and, when the permanent government was installed, Santa Anna was still a prisoner. Finally he decided that he would attempt to secure permission to go to Washington and in person present the case to Jackson. November 2, he had a conversation with President Houston on the subject. Three days later he wrote to Houston urging him to grant this request. The treaty of May 14, he said, had contemplated the establishment of Texas as an independent nation, which should acquire its legal existence through a recognition by Mexico. This basis had been changed by the recent vote of the people of Texas for annexation to the United States. The situation, according to Santa Anna, was now much simplified. Indeed it reduced itself to the single question of fixing the boundary between the United States and Mexico—a question which had been pending many years. By his conversations with the cabinet at Washington, he hoped, without loss of time, to determine the extent of the United States, which, he said, "may be fixed at the Nueces, at the Bravo del Norte[3] or any other boundary as may be decided on at Washington—thus avoiding disagreeable discussions, which might delay the definite termination of this question, or cause a difficulty between two friendly nations. This in substance," he went

[1]Richardson, *Messages and Papers*, III, 276.
[2]Jackson to Houston, September 4, 1836, Jackson MSS.
[3]The Rio Grande.

on to say, "is a plain safe and speedy mode of terminating this important matter and as all are interested it becomes necessary that you facilitate my journey to Washington with the least possible delay."[1]

It is probable that neither Houston nor Austin had any great confidence in the disinterestedness of Santa Anna's motives, but they both, no doubt, felt that such admissions from the arch enemy of Texas would carry due moral weight. whether Santa Anna were sincere or not. Besides there was nothing to gain by retaining him in Texas as prisoner; while, on the other hand, his influence in Mexico would naturally decrease the longer he remained away.[2]

Accordingly, it was decided to allow him to make this journey. November 26 was the day set for his departure.[3] He was accompanied, at his own request, by Colonels Hockley and Bee and Captain Patton;[4] Colonel Almonte, his aide-de-camp and fellow prisoner, was also of the party.[5] He carried a letter of introduction from Houston to Jackson,[6] and for their guidance upon reaching Washington, Austin gave Hockley and Bee an informal "memorandum," as follows:

On your arrival in Washington City, Gen Santa Anna will, of course, request an interview with President Jackson—I recommend that this request should be made in writing, and that the outlines of his object in wishing the interview be stated—for example, after stating that he wishes to pay his respects etc to the President of the U. S. etc, etc, to go on and say that, "being fully convinced by personal observation that the true interests of Mexico, of the U. S. and of Texas, require a termination of the war between the latter and Mexico, on the basis of the separation of Texas from Mexico either as an independent nation or its annexation [that is, as annexed] to the U. S. he desires to have a conversation with Gen Jackson on that subject, with the view of endeavoring to promote the general good of all concerned" . . . or something to that ammount, that will be confirmatory of what he said to Jackson in

[1]Santa Anna to [Houston] November 5 [5 written in pencil and in an other hand over 6 (?)], Austin Papers.

[2]Austin to Henry Meigs, November 7, 1836, Austin Papers.

[3]Austin to Wharton, November 25, 1835, Garrison, *Dip. Cor. Tex.*, I, 143.

[4]Santa Anna to Houston, November 5 (see above, note 1), 1836, Austin Papers.

[5]Wharton to Austin, January 15, 1836, Garrison, *Dip. Cor. Tex.*, I, 176-177.

[6]Houston to Jackson, November 20, 1836, Jackson MSS.

his letter of 4th July last—I think that this course would open the way for a cordial reception, as it will be repeating at Washington where he is free, what he said to Jackson from this place on the 4 July last when he was a prisoner—and thus afford the strongest evidence of his good faith.[1]

Practically nothing came of it all. Santa Anna reached Washington, after much delay,[2] about the middle of January, 1837;[3] but he found nobody else in quite so accommodating a frame of mind as he apparently had been when he proposed the scheme to Houston. He discussed with Jackson and Wharton, who was then in Washington, the possibility of a treaty with Mexico, by which the United States was to have Texas, and, in return, as part payment, was to relinquish all claims held against Mexico by citizens of the United States. But against any treaty of cession between the United States and Mexico before recognition was extended to Texas by the former, Wharton made formal and vigorous protest.[4] Moreover, the Mexican *chargé d'affaires* at Philadelphia refused to coöperate with Santa Anna,[5] and thus made it impossible for the latter to fulfil any of his fair promises, even had he been so disposed. He had obtained, for himself, however, what he most desired, namely, freedom from his hated imprisonment; and after a stay of about a week in Washington he set sail from Norfolk for Vera Cruz in a government vessel provided for him by President Jackson.[6]

In the meantime Wharton had started upon his mission with characteristic energy. November 22, he acknowledged the receipt of his credentials and instructions. "You may rely," he wrote Austin, "upon my not delaying a moment in getting to Washington." On the 28th he reached New Orleans "in bad plight," as

[1]Memorandum for Colonels Hockley and Bee, November 25, 1836, Austin Papers.
[2]Bee to Austin, January 1, 1837, Austin Papers.
[3]Wharton to Austin, January 15, 1837, Garrison, *Dip. Cor. Tex.*, I, 176-177. Wooten (*A Comprehensive History of Texas*, I, 312) says he arrived on the 17th.
[4]Wharton to Rusk, February 16, 1837, Garrison, *Dip. Cor. Tex.* I, 187-192.
[5]*Ibid.*, 193.
[6]Santa Anna to Jackson, January 24, 1837, Jackson MSS. In this letter Santa Anna asks for a war vessel on which to sail from Norfolk on the 27th. See also Wooten, *A Comprehensive History of Texas*, I, 312, which says Santa Anna remained in Washington until the 26th and then sailed from Norfolk on the *Pioneer.*

he says, owing to the necessity of having no sleep on the deck all the way, unprotected from the weather—but still enthusiastic. "I feel every moment," he writes Austin, "more and more the vital importance of my being at Washington and nothing that human energy can surmount shall retard my progress."[1] He remained in New Orleans two days—just long enough to raise the necessary amount of money to defray his expenses and to interview some of the parties to the original loan secured in New Orleans the winter previous.[2] December 1, he again set forth upon his journey, and on the 19th, in less than a month after he left Velasco, he arrived in Washington City.[3]

One incident connected with Wharton's stay in New Orleans deserves notice, because the light it throws upon the growing significance of slavery in connection with the Texas question. It seems that attempts were being made to land African slaves on the coast east of the Sabine River within the territory of the United States for the purpose of transporting them into Texas, thus eluding that article of the Texas constitution which forbade the introduction of slaves except from the United States.[4] In a letter to Austin, November 30, on the eve of his departure from New Orleans, Wharton calls attention to this in his own vigorous style, as follows: "Crush for Gods sake and for our countrys sake crush these new projects for introducing Africans and put to death all concerned. Instruct me to complain formally to this govment that the Traffic is attempted by U. S. Citizens under the United States flag."[5]

Evidently in response to this request, but as if upon his own initiative, Austin sent to Wharton an official letter, dated December 16, as follows:

It has come to the knowledge of this Govt. through the channel of common rumor sustained by the statements of several persons of known verasity, that extensive projects are in contemplation to introduce African negro slaves into this country by citizens of the U. S. in a manner that will equally violate the laws of the U. S.

[1]Wharton to Austin, November 28, 1836, Garrison, *Dip. Cor. Tex.*, I, 144.
[2]See above, p. 175.
[3]Wharton to Austin, December 22, 1836, Garrison, *Dip. Cor. Tex.*, I, 157.
[4]Austin to Wharton, December 16, 1836, *ibid.*, 155.
[5]Wharton to Austin, November 30, 1836, *ibid.*, 148.

and the constitutional provision of this Republic on the subject. . . .

This attempt to evade the prohibition of the African slave trade,
contained in our constitution certainly will not be sustained by the
tribunals of this Republic, but it is also desireable that the Govt.
of the U. S. should be apprised of such attempts to carry on a
piratical commerce by her own citizens through her territory and
in American vessels. I am therefore directed by the president to
instruct you, to lay this subject before the Govt. of the U. S. and
to request its co-operation on the Sabine frontier and in the gulf
of Mexico to enforce the laws for the suppression of the African
slave trade.[1]

January 6, 1837, Wharton reported: "The complaint it is said
we are about making to this Government in regard to the African
Slave trade, has already silenced our traducers and rendered us
great service."[2] What persons were involved in this illegal traffic
there is no record to show. It was important, however, that the
Texan government should disclaim all responsibility in the matter,
because of the conciliatory effect it might have upon the non-slave-
holding sections of the country. Apparently the scheme was effective.

In his report from Maysville, Kentucky, December 11, Wharton
gave still further evidence of the fact that by this time the issue
between the free and slave states in regard to Texas was beginning
to be fairly well drawn. In striking contrast to the glowing accounts that the former commissioners had given of the universal
enthusiasm for the Texan cause, Wharton now spoke definitely of
the friends and the foes of Texas. He said:

Our foes namely the leading prints of the North and East and
the abolitionists everywhere oppose . . . [annexation] on the
old grounds of an opposition to the extension of slavery and of a
fear of southern preponderance in councils of the nation. Our
friends by which term I now mean those of Louisiana Mississippi
Kentucky etc (for I have seen and conversed with no others as yet)
oppose our annexation, on the grounds that a brighter destiny
awaits Texas. That she would be more happy and prosperous and
glorious as an independent nation than as a portion or tributary of

---

[1]Austin to Wharton, December 16, 1836, Garrison, *Dip. Cor. Tex.*, I, 155-
156.
[2]Wharton to Austin, January 6, 1836, *ibid.*, 172.

this. That in such situation she would soon complain, of and be oppressed by high Tariffs and other Northern measures. That we would be driven to nullification, secession, etc and be involved in a worse revolution than we are now engaged in. That we should go on as we have commenced conquering and to conquer and never pause until we had annexed all or the best portion of Mexico to Texas, thereby establishing an independent government that would rival this in extent, resources, and population.[1]

Thus through the "leading prints" Wharton had correctly divined the sentiments of the "foes of Texas." But the expressions of the "friends" with whom he had conversed were too altruistic and impracticable to have been representative. They are interesting, however, as showing that even yet many of the slaveholders did not understand the importance to the South of the annexation of Texas.

As for Wharton himself, he was keenly alive to the situation. "To be plain and candid," he said, "I believe the recognition of our independence will certainly take place,"—both friends and foes alike, he reported, agreed that simple justice demanded this much. "But," he continued, "I have not at present much hope of our being annexed. That question when proposed will agitate this union more than did the attempt to restrict Missouri, nullification, and abolitionism, all combined. Already has the war commenced violently commenced even on the prospect of our annexation. The Southern papers those in favor of the measure are acting most independently. . . . Language such as the following is uttered by the most respectable journals such as the Richmond Whig Charleston Mercury etc. The North must choose between the Union with Texas added—or no Union. Texas will be added and then forever farewell abolitionism and northern influence. Threats and denunciations like these will goad the North into a determined opposition and if Texas is annexed at all it will not be until after the question has convulsed this nation for several sessions of Congress."[2]

In the meantime, on December 5, two weeks before Wharton's arrival in Washington, Congress had re-assembled for its second session. The president's opening message touched upon the Texan questions, but was wholly non-committal. He referred to the

[1]Wharton to Austin, December 11, 1836, *ibid.*, 152.
[2]*Ibid.* 152-153.

natural sympathy felt by the citizens of the United States for the Texan cause, but urged all the more caution for that reason

lest it lead . . . into the great error of suffering public policy to be regulated by partiality or prejudice. There are considerations connected with the possible result of this contest between the two parties of so much delicacy and importance to the United States that our character requires that we should neither anticipate events nor attempt to control them. The known desire of the Texans to become a part of our system, although its gratification depends upon the reconcilement of various and conflicting interests, necessarily a work of time and uncertain in itself, is calculated to expose our conduct to misconception in the eyes of the world. There are already those who, indifferent to principle themselves and prone to suspect the want of it in others, charge us with ambitious designs and insidious policy.

In this connection Jackson referred to the departure of Gorostiza from Washington, adding, "It is hoped and believed that his Government will take a more dispassionate and just view of this subject, and not be disposed to construe a measure of justifiable precaution, made necessary by its known inability in execution of the stipulations of our treaty to act upon the frontier, into an encroachment upon its rights or a stain upon its honor." In dismissing the Texas question, Jackson promised that the "result of the confidential inquiries made into the condition and prospects of the newly declared Texan Government" would be communicated in the course of the session.[1]

Immediately upon Wharton's arrival in Washington, a fortnight later, he addressed Secretary of State Forsyth, asking for an interview.[2] The request was granted,[3] but the only information Forsyth would vouchsafe was that the president in a few days would transmit to Congress a special message concerning Texas.[4] Wharton seems to have felt at once conscious of a changed attitude toward the Texan question. In his first dispatch home he said he was convinced that Morfit's report was very favorable.[5]

[1]Richardson, *Messages and Papers*, III, 237-238.
[2]Wharton to Forsyth, December 19, 1836, Garrison, *Dip. Cor. Tex.*, I, 157. Wharton reached Washington on the 19th.
[3]Dayton to Wolfe, December 20, *Ibid.*
[4]Wharton to Austin, December 22, *ibid.*
[5]*Ibid.*, 158.

Three days after Wharton reached Washington, Jackson's message, dated December 21, together with the promised extracts from Morfit's report, was presented to Congress. The message astonished everybody. Wharton reported that it had pleased no party *en masse,* except perhaps the abolitionists.[1] Catlett on his way to Washington, wrote, from Mobile, "I cannot express the regret, with which I gradually awoke to the unwelcome truth, that he [Jackson] is opposed to the immediate recognition of Texan Independence. I did not anticipate so cold blooded a policy from him "[2]

The substance of the message was that, in submitting to Congress Morfit's report, Jackson advised delay in the recognition of Texas. He said that he would have considered no comment from himself on this occasion necessary, except for the resolutions concerning recognition passed during the last session of Congress by both houses acting separately. Such interest, he felt, called for a rather detailed presentation of the considerations which had led him to continue his original policy of neutrality. The policy of the United States, he said, had always been to treat such questions

as questions of fact only, and our predecessors have cautiously abstained from deciding upon them until the clearest evidence was in their possession to enable them not only to decide correctly, but to shield their decisions from every unworthy imputation. . . . Public opinion here is so firmly established and well understood in favor of this policy that no serious disagreement has ever arisen among ourselves in relation to it, although brought under review in a variety of forms and at periods when the minds of the people were greatly excited by the agitation of topics purely domestic in their character. Nor has any deliberate inquiry ever been instituted in Congress or in any of our legislative bodies as to whom belonged the power of originally recognizing a new State—a power the exercise of which is equivalent under some circumstances to a declara-

[1] Wharton to Austin, December 25, *ibid.* · This letter is dated "Sunday December 28"; the postscript is dated "Monday December 26." The first date should be the 25th. Austin died December 27, two days after the letter was written.

[2] Catlett to Austin, January 11, 1837 [written 1836 through inadvertence], *ibid.*, 173. An interesting comment upon the message is found in a letter from Andrew Stevenson, the United States minister to England, to Van Buren, January 30, 1837. He says, "The President's message about Texas has just been received. It has produced quite a sensation here. . . . I sent it in a private note to Ld Palmer[ston] . . . and he spoke of it as a most able and statesmanlike paper. . . . I presume the course of Gen Jackson met your approbation!" (Van Buren MSS.).

tion of war; a power nowhere expressly delegated, and only granted in the Constitution as it is necessarily involved in some of the great powers given to Congress, in that given to the President and Senate to form treaties with foreign powers and to appoint ambassadors and other public ministers, and in that conferred upon the President to receive ministers from foreign nations.

In the preamble to the resolution of the House of Representatives it is distinctly intimated that the expediency of recognizing the independence of Texas should be left to the decision of Congress. In this view, on the ground of expediency, I am disposed to concur, and do not, therefore, consider it necessary to express any opinion as to the strict constitutional right of the Executive, either apart from or in conjunction with the senate, over the subject. . . .

In making these suggestions it is not my purpose to relieve myself from the responsibility of expressing my own opinions of the course the interests of our country prescribe and its honor permits us to follow.

It is scarcely to be imagined that a question of this character could be presented in relation to which it would be more difficult for the United States to avoid exciting the suspicion and jealousy of other powers, and maintain their established character for fair and impartial dealing. But on this, as on every trying occasion, safety is to be found in a rigid adherence to principle.

Jackson then went on to call attention to the conservatism of the United States in recognizing Mexico and the South American republics.[1] In contrast with their condition when recognition was tendered, he refers to the fact that Texas was at this moment threatened by another invasion. He continued:

Upon the issue of this threatened invasion the independence of Texas may be considered as suspended, and were there nothing peculiar in the relative situation of the United States and Texas our acknowledgment of its independence at such a crisis could scarcely be regarded as consistent with that prudent reserve with which we have heretofore held ourselves bound to treat all similar questions. But there are circumstances in the relations of the two countries which require us to act on this occasion with even more than our wonted caution. Texas was once claimed as a part of our property . . . A large proportion of its civilized inhabitants are emigrants from the United States . . . ; and, more than all, . . . [they] have instituted the same form of government

[1]It is doubtful whether all will agree with Jackson in characterizing as conservative the policy of the United States in regard to the revolted Spanish provinces.

with our own, and have since the close of your last session openly resolved, on the acknowledgment by us of their independence to seek admission into the Union as one of the Federal States. This last circumstance is a matter of peculiar delicacy, and forces upon us considerations of the gravest character. The title of Texas to the territory she claims is identified with her independence. She asks us to acknowledge that title to the territory, with an avowed design to treat immediately of its transfer to the United States. It becomes us to beware of a too early movement, as it might subject us, however unjustly, to the imputation of seeking to establish the claim of our neighbors to a territory with a view to its subsequent acquisition by ourselves. Prudence, therefore, seems to dictate that we should still stand aloof and maintain our present attitude, if not until Mexico itself or one of the great foreign powers shall recognize the independence of the new Government, at least until the lapse of time or the course of events shall have proved beyond cavil or dispute the ability of the people of that country to maintain their separate sovereignty and to uphold the Government constituted by them. . . .

. . . I have only to add the expression of my confidence that if Congress shall differ with me . . . their judgment will be the result of dispassionate, prudent, and wise deliberation, with the assurance that during the short time I shall continue connected with the Government I shall promptly and cordially unite with you in such measures as may be deemed best fitted to increase the prosperity and perpetuate the peace of our favored country.[1]

When the message was communicated to the Senate, it was referred to the committee on foreign relations, and, without discussion, fifteen hundred extra copies were ordered printed.[2] The House also referred the message to its committee on foreign affairs. In the debate that followed the representatives of the slave and the free states seem to have been fairly well arrayed on opposite sides. Briggs of Massachusetts wanted ten thousand extra copies of the president's message printed for distribution. Pierce of Rhode Island increased the number to twenty thousand, which was finally agreed upon. Thompson of South Carolina was not sur-

[1]Richardson, *Messages and Papers*, III, 265-269. A rough draft of this message is among the Jackson MSS. The larger portion of it is in the handwriting of Amos Kendall, postmaster general and friend and advisor of Jackson. Another part, a partial copy of the first, is in Jackson's handwriting; while a third is apparently copied by a scribe.
[2]*Debates in Cong.*, 24 Cong., 2 Sess., 104.

prised, he said, at the number proposed. "He should not have been surprised at a proposal to print one hundred thousand . . . nor was he surprised at the hosannahs with which this message had been received, the joy and exultation which he had seen manifested, by gentlemen from a certain section, the rapturous plaudits, the enthusiastic exclamations, 'Oh! righteous judge, a second Daniel come to judgment', ... It was to be expected, sir, from that strange, unnatural, and disastrous (at least to the South and West) conjunction upon this occasion of hitherto most antagonistic elements . . . He had only risen today to say, that with the united power of sectional feelings, and the influence of the name and popularity of the President upon their side, that it seemed to him nothing more than fair to ask of gentlemen not to seek occasion on a proposition to print, which no one opposed, further to forestall public opinion on this subject."[1]

Pierce of Rhode Island summed up the situation when he spoke of it as a subject "in relation to which, whatever might have been the notions of the members of that House at the last session of Congress, whatever might have been the feelings of gentlemen representing certain portions of the Union, there had been a change of opinion, an alteration of sentiment. And whatever might have been the surmises and conjectures as to what would be the course of the distinguished individual who now filled the executive chair, he (Mr. P.) presumed that those surmises and conjectures would now be found to have been without foundation."[2]

An examination of Morfit's report will show that the president's message was substantially in accord with the course recommended there. In the form in which it was communicated the report consisted of ten letters, ranging in date from August 13 to September 14.[3] The information contained therein was explicit, fairly accurate, and on the whole favorable to Texas. Details were given concerning the organization of the government, the military situation, the history of events leading up to the revolution, and the attempt to enter into negotiations with Mexico through Santa Anna.

[1]*Debates in Cong.*, 24 Cong., 2 Sess., 1143.
[2]*Ibid.*, 1141-1142.
[3]Five of these letters were written from Velasco; the other five from places in the immediate neighborhood. The whole report is given in *Senate Docs.*, 24 Cong., 2 Sess., I, No. 20, pp. 5-36.

Texas herself was described, and details given as to her population—including the Indian tribes, the extent of her territory, her debts, and her resources.   Finally, after enumerating certain requisites of an independent nation—all of which, according to the report, Texas possessed—Morfit said:

The reasons I should urge against the present declaration of this opinion [that is, that Texas was capable of becoming an independent power] are these:

First.   The Mexicans, it is said, are preparing to invade Texas during the winter, and already there are 4,000 at Matamoras.

Secondly.   The increase of emigrants from the United States is contingent, and may be prevented by various causes—some of which have already operated.

Thirdly.   The ordinance of the 16th of March diminishes the quantity of bounty lands to soldiers who shall enter between that time and the 1st of July, and leaves the quantity for those after that period undefined and to be determined by Congress.   This has lessened the zeal of many already in the service, and has taken away a strong motive for the services of others.

Fourthly.   Enlistments are expiring every week, and there may not be one thousand in the main army in one month.

Fifthly.   The troops expected in a body from the South are to be furnished by contract, so that, without any imputation against the motives or chivalry of the individuals, the obligations may fail when the hope of profit is destroyed.

Sixthly.   The great majority of the emigrants, no matter by what good feelings actuated in the commencement of service, always manifest a reversionary desire for home, and return to the United States as soon as their duty is over, so that the population of the country is never actually augmented.

Seventhly.   The old colonists would not by themselves be able to sustain an invasion, and, at the same time, supply the means for the war.

And, finally, independent of any other objections, the ardor of the volunteers and the interest which the fate of the brave in the late battles produced, have greatly abated by the suggestions and arguments that this whole enterprise of independence is a mere speculative scheme, concocted and encouraged for the aggrandizement of a few.[1]

---

[1]*Ibid.*, 23-25. Another piece of evidence to the same effect may have reached Jackson in time to help determine the decision he gave in his message that Texas was not yet a *de facto* government. This was a letter from Houston, November 20, as follows: "My great desire is that our country Texas shall be annexed to the U. States and on a footing of Jus-

Thus, according to Morfit's report, the whole situation resolved itself into this,—that without foreign aid the success of Texas depended more upon the "weakness and imbecility of her enemy than upon her own strength."[1]   Nevertheless if the future of Texas under Mexican dominion were compared with her future as a part of the United States, Morfit believed that "humanity would speedily dictate her redemption, and the philanthropy of nations give a sanction to the act."[2]

The report concludes thus:

The rigid course of duty, which requires a candid statement from facts, prevails over partialities that prompt a different picture; and though a regard for truth, a sense of national integrity, and a desire to manifest their strict exercise by the United States, may justly delay the period for enrolling Texas in the list of nations, her citizens, and those who participate in the principles of her cause, may be consoled by the certainty that, without the aid of any government, the career of political freedom which is extending throughout the world will of its own speed accomplish what caution now withholds.

Foreign policy, the conventional faith of nations, or the efforts of Mexico, may detain Texas lingering in her embryo state for many years, but the fertility of her soil, the remoteness of her situation, which affords an asylum from the angry subjects that often agitate the Northern and Southern parts of our country, and, above all, the current of emigration, which through the whole West looks like the advent of the oppressed of all nations seeking to build up free altars in a new hemisphere, must disenthral her by a moral force which no power nor potentates can resist.[3]

But in spite of the fact that the president's message of December 21 had recommended the only course that would have been justified by this report—which, presumably, was the most unbiased and reliable information at the disposal of the government—there were

___

tice and reciprocity to the parties. It is policy to hold out the idea (and few there are who know the contrary) that we are very able to sustain ourselves against any power, who are not impotent [omnipotent?] yet I am free to say *to you* that we cannot do it. . . . I look to you, as the friend and patron of my youth and the benefactor of mankind to interpose in our behalf and save us" (Houston to Jackson, November 20, 1836, in Austin's Letter and Memorandum Album, 1836, pp. 51-52, Austin Papers).

[1]*Senate Docs.*, 24 Cong., 2 Sess., I, No. 20, p. 26.

[2]*Ibid.*, 28-9.

[3]*Ibid.*, 35-36.

many people at the time who felt that it had been called forth also by other ulterior motives. The sensation it created warrants the assumption that, when it had become known that Jackson would send a special Texas message to Congress, a recommendation of recognition was anticipated, with varying emotions, by all parties. In the message Jackson assigns three reasons why this recommendation had not been made: (1) doubt as to the ability of Texas to maintain her independence, especially in view of the threatened invasion; (2) unwillingness to extend premature recognition, which, if not a justifiable cause for a declaration of war by Mexico, was at least a proof of partiality toward one of the contending parties; (3) desire to avoid suspicion on the part of other nations, which the delicacy of the situation—involving a combination of the two questions, recognition and annexation—might easily arouse.

These difficulties, however, had been known from the first to exist. There was, to be sure, no reason to doubt that, at any stage of the negotiations, they would have influenced the president as they now did, had he been forced to assume the responsibility of a decision. And yet the impression had been rather general that recognition would not long be delayed. Many, therefore, went further in seeking an explanation. At least two other motives—more private in their nature than those proclaimed in the December message —were suggested as accounting for Jackson's present attitude. These were, first, the hope of acquiring Texas, even yet, by treaty with Mexico, through Santa Anna's agency: second. the Van Buren politics.[1]

Wharton, who was on the alert for all such expression of public opinion seemed also inclined to look below the surface for the real explanation. So far as the threatened invasion of Texas by Mexico was concerned, he felt fully convinced that it was used merely as an excuse for delaying recognition—the only "earthly pretext," he says, ". . . that can be given to the World for the step."[1] Indeed, not later than two weeks after the message, Jackson asserted,

---

[1]Wharton to Austin, December 28, 1836, Garrison, *Dip. Cor. Tex.*, I, 158-159.
Ibid.; Wharton to Austin, December 31, 1836, *ibid.*, 167.

according to Wharton, that he no longer doubted the ability of Texas to maintain her independence.[1]   Moreover, Ellis, the late *chargé* to Mexico,[2] returned about the end of January and pictured Mexico in a most deplorable state of "anarchy, revolution and bankruptcy."[3]   Since the delay recommended by Jackson was "predicated upon the impending invasion . . . we would naturally suppose," Wharton commented, "that cessante causa, cessat effectus, and that there was nothing to prevent an immediate recognition at this moment."[4]

As for the fear of exciting the suspicion of other nations, Wharton soon reassured himself, if no one else, on that point.   On January 6, he reported to his government a conversation with Forsyth, in which the latter volunteered the information that both Fox, the English minister to the United States, and Lord Palmerston had pronounced themselves satisfied with the neutral course pursued by the United States.   Wharton added that it was generally believed that England expected the United States to annex Texas.   Moreover, he also asserted that the French minister, the summer past, had said "that his Government had no more right to interfere in regard to Texas than had the government of the United States to interfere in the affairs of Belgium or any other country bordering on France."   "So it seems," Wharton concluded, "that the fear of offending foreign powers need no longer prevent this government from recognizing or indeed annexing Texas."[5]

In regard to the proposed treaty with Santa Anna, Wharton correctly divined that it did have some influence with Jackson. "As yet I am fully aware," he wrote to his government, "that à strong but secret reason for delay is the expected arrival of Santa Anna and the prospect of a treaty with him which will satisfy Texas and Mexico and at the same time save the United States Government in the eyes of the world from all imputation of having aided in our revolution or of having recognized us too promptly. This reason of course will soon be productive of the desired result,

[1]Wharton to Austin, January 6, 1837, Garrison, *Dip. Cor. Tex.*, I, 170.
[2]See above, p. 209.
[3]Wharton to Houston, February 2, 1837, Garrison, *Dip. Cor. Tex.*, I, 179.
[4]*Ibid.*
[5]Wharton to Austin, January 6, 1837, *ibid.*, 168-169.

namely recognition or will cease to exist."[1] As has already been pointed out, Santa Anna's visit to Washington was altogether fruit-less.[2]

The only other consideration that had been suggested as having influenced Jackson in delaying recognition was the political situa-dent's message Wharton had said, "Some say it was the work of Mr. Van Buren for the purpose of transferring the responsibility tion of the time. In his first report home concerning the presi-from the Administration to Congress and that the President will recognize immediately if Congress recommends it by a majority of even one."[3] With a view to having Jackson consent to such a recommendation by Congress, Wharton used his influence to have some of the president's friends, who were also friendly to Texas, approach Jackson on the subject. Finally Wharton himself called, at Jackson's request. The interview that followed was strictly confidential. In reporting it to the Texan government Wharton said, "I repeat it again and again, that Genl. Jackson impressed upon me the importance of the most sacred confidence in regard to our interview which I hereby wish to reimpress upon you." Jack-son then confessed, Wharton said, "that the object of his message was to obtain the concurrent action of Congress on the subject. I answered," he continued, "[that] a majority of Congress were in favor of immediate recognition, but that many of the administra-tion party forbore acting for fear of its being considered (*after his message*) as an attack on the administration. He said that was all foolishness, he doubted the power of the President to recognize of himself he wished the sense of Congress on the subject and would immediately concur if a majority recommended it."

Accordingly Wharton bent all his energies toward having Con-gress take up the matter. He met with the House committee on foreign affairs, before whom he discoursed at length in answer to the "thousand interrogatories" which he said they propounded to him. Moreover, for the edification of the other members of Con-gress and also to counteract the influence of "pamphlets written

[1]Wharton to Austin, December 31, 1836, *ibid.*, 167.
[2]See above, p. 230.
[3]Wharton to Austin, December 18, 1836, Garrison, *Dip. Cor. Tex.*, I, 158.

by the abolitionists for the purpose of injuring and calumniating Texas," he published, besides many "small essays," a pamphlet signed "Jefferson," which, he says, "puts the matter in a proper light and which has done great good."[1]

Partly, no doubt, as a result of Wharton's activity, Walker of Mississippi submitted, January 11, the following joint resolution:

Resolved, that the state of Texas having established and maintained an independent Government, capable of performing those duties, foreign and domestic, which appertain to independent Governments, and it appearing that there is no longer any reasonable prospect of the successful prosecution of the war by Mexico against said State, it is expedient and proper, and in perfect conformity with the laws of nations, and the practice of this Government in like cases, that the independent political existence of said state be acknowledged by the Government of the United States.[2]

There, however, the matter stopped, and Wharton feared that Congress, too, as well as the president, would refuse to take the initiative. Jackson, to be sure, seemed thoroughly convinced that Texas was able to maintain her independence, and, in order to further matters, he suggested that Ellis, the late *chargé*, be interviewed by the committee on foreign relations, declaring that he "would convince them in five minutes of the utter impossibility of a new invasion."[3] But Congress refused to act without another message from the president, and this, according to Wharton, Jackson was not disposed to give, 1st. because he deems it unnecessary, 2dly. he says that the call for it by Congress is with a view to screen themselves from proper responsibility, and he is unwilling to gratify them." "Although the question has been frequently and warmly urged by our friends," Wharton wrote "the committee on foreign affairs have refused to report, and Congress of course has not acted up to this period, for they will not act without a report from the committee."[4] There was a stumbling-block somewhere—some influence in Congress that was successfully preventing all discussion of the Texas question.

[1]Wharton to Austin, January 15, 1837, Garrison, *Dip. Cor. Tex.*, I, 176.
[2]*Debates in Cong.*, 24 Cong., 2 Sess., 360; Wharton to Austin, January 15, 1837, Garrison, *Dip. Cor. Tex.*, I, 176.
[3]Wharton to Houston, February 2, 1837, *ibid.*, 179.
[4]*Ibid.*

At last, on February 2, Wharton wrote home:

I will now tell you the whole secret of the reluctance of Congress to act on this matter. I have made it my business to unravel the mystery, and I know that I have succeeded. Some of the members have openly avowed to me their reasons for wishing to postpone our recognition until the next Congress. It all proceeds from the Van Buren party. They are afraid that the subject of annexation will be pressed immediately after recognition; that annexation or no annexation will be made the test of the elections for Congress during the ensuing summer; that the North will be opposed to the South in favor of annexation, and that Mr. Van Buren will of course have the support of either the South or North in mass accordingly as he favors or opposes annexation. The fear then of throwing Mr. Van Buren into a minority in the next Congress induces his friends to desire a postponement of recognition at present, thereby keeping down the exciting question of annexation at the next elections and giving Mr. Van Buren more time to manage his cards and consolidate his strength. All of Mr. Van Buren's friends are not operated upon in this way, but a sufficient number are to prevent the favourable action of Congress at this session, without a new message or other impulse is given by the President. Be it understood also that many of those same individuals are in favor both of annexation and recognition, but they wish Mr. Van Buren to have his own time and select his own mode of bringing them about, and in their devotion to him they prefer that Texas should in the mean time suffer by the delay of her recognition, rather than jeopardise his popularity. There can be no mistake in regard to the correctness of the above news. All that remains for me is to operate with the President, and to get him to quicken the action of Congress by another message. This I shall night and day endeavor to effect by using every argument that can operate upon his pride and his sense of justice. At an interview last evening, he told me to feel easy on the subject, that all would go right. He told me moreover that he was preparing a message to Congress, in which he intended to recommend the granting of letters of marque against Mexico and that his government would not longer submit to her injustice and outrages.[1]

[1]Wharton to Houston, February 2, 1837, Garrison, *Dip. Cor. Tex.*, I, 179-180. February 6, Jackson sent this message to Congress, recommending the passing of an act authorizing reprisals, "and the use of the naval force of the United States by the Executive against Mexico to enforce them, in the event of a refusal by the Mexican Government to come to an amicable adjustment of the matters in controversy between us upon another demand thereof made from on board one of our vessels of war on the coast of Mexico" (Richardson, *Messages and Papers*, III, 278.)

Three days later Wharton wrote:

The reasons, assigned in my last, as inducing Mr. Van Buren's friends to desire postponement, cannot be urged in debate, and I am of the opinion, that, when the subject is agitated, they will not oppose our recognition, for that would be to proclaim their leader the enemy of Texas, in which light he is not willing to be viewed, especially as the friends of our much mistreated country are so numerous and respectable and zealous in all parts of the United States. . . . Moreover, there is one consolation which I fondly clasp to my bosom as the pillar of my hope and support amid all the coldness, illiberality and injustice, with which we have been treated, which is that if Genl. Jackson finds that Congress will not act without another message from him, I am more deceived in him than I ever was in mortal man, if he does not under these circumstances send another message to Congress and have us formally recognized before he quits the Presidential Chair.[1]

Such, then, was Wharton's solution of the Texas situation in the winter of 1836-7, and certainly no one was in a better position than he to learn the facts.

So far as one may judge from the evidence at hand, Jackson's own personal attitude toward Texas was consistent throughout. He had never attempted to disguise his desire to obtain Texas—his negotiations to that end before the Texan revolution were widely and generally known, and, from the first effort on the part of the revolutionists to establish relations with the United States, the commissioners invariably report the president a friend, both to recognition and annexation. Further than this we have no direct evidence as to his attitude previous to the December message. But, as he tells us there, a question more difficult to deal with could scarcely arise, owing to the peculiar relations between Texas and the United States —the well-known desire of the latter to regain the territory she had once possessed; the active sympathy of the citizens of the United States toward the revolutionists, who were their own kinsmen; and the recent vote of Texas for admission into the Union as one of the Federal states. Since the revolution offered strong temptations both to the government and to the people of the United States to interfere in behalf of Texas, there was all the more reason for

[1]Wharton to Houston, February 5, 1837, Garrison, *Dip. Cor. Tex.*, I, 182.

greater caution. This he continually urged in attempting to enforce neutrality, and this we may well believe would have governed his own position had he been called upon earlier to take a positive stand. Whatever other considerations may have been influencing him when he sent his message to Congress, on these grounds alone Jackson undoubtedly adopted the wisest course. Tardiness in extending recognition to the republics that have arisen on American soil is certainly not an accusation that can be urged against the United States government.

Granting, however, that it was best for the present to withhold recognition by his own government, Jackson still saw three possibilities by which the same end might be reached: (1) Recognition might first be extended by some other power—Forsyth even approached Wharton on the subject, asking him if he were not authorized to treat also with England, explaining that the president would like to see Texas recognized elsewhere first, as the Texan "vote for annexation embarassed the matter";[1] (2) A treaty might be arranged between Texas and Mexico by Wharton and Santa Anna, acting through the Mexican *chargé d'affaires* at Philadelphia, which Jackson assured Wharton would be valid;[2] (3) It was still hoped that, through the agency of Santa Anna, a treaty of cession might take place between the United States and Mexico, and the subject was discussed in detail by Jackson with both Santa Anna and Wharton.[3] From some personal notes of his we learn that he then contemplated offering Mexico three and a half million dollars for territory, the southern boundary of which was to be the Rio Grande up to thirty-eight degrees north latitude, thence west to the Pacific—including all north California. "But it must be understood," he wrote, "that this proposition is made to meet the views of the Genl [Santa Anna], and not by the U. States to acquire Territory or take advantage of the disturbed state of Mexico."[4] Nothing, however, came of any of these plans.

[1] Wharton to Austin, December 22, 1836, *ibid.*, 157-158.
[2] Wharton to Austin, January 6, 1837, *ibid.*, 171-172.
[3] Wharton to Rusk, February 16, 1837, *ibid.*, 190.
[4] Memorandum, undated, Jackson MSS. Jackson seems to have wanted California partly for political reasons. In one of his reports home Wharton wrote: "Genl. Jackson says that Texas must claim the Californias on the Pacific in order to paralyze the opposition of the North and East to Annexation. That the fishing interests of the North and East wish

In the meantime Jackson had been trying earnestly to decide whether the situation in Texas would really justify a recognition of independence by the United States. The careful attention that he gave to this question alone, unhampered by further considerations of a more selfish or diplomatic nature, is in part revealed by the following fragmentary note in his handwriting, preserved in the Van Buren Papers:

The great and delicate question of, shall we acknowledge the Independence of Texas,—is the evidence contained in the roport of our confidential agent, Mr. Moffet, sufficient to show that Texas has a de facto Govt. and the means to support it. See the Resolutions of Congress and compare the facts contained in the report with it—see report on which the Independence of So. America was acknowledged.[1]

The solution of the situation, however, did not depend upon the answer to this question alone. For, along with the agitation of the Texas problem, political complications within the United States had arisen, which, regardless of considerations as to foreign policy, made it expedient for the president to refrain from committing the administration too definitely on the subject of recognition. However friendly Jackson's personal attitude toward that measure may have been, that of a certain element in Congress and throughout the country generally had undergone, during the year, considerable change. The states were beginning to divide on the subject of slavery—party ties were giving way. Recognition of Texas would precipitate the question of annexation, and annexation meant the addition to the United States of a vast slave-holding territory. The Van Buren party felt that in order to insure the success of their leader the question must be kept out of the party platform. The chief concern of Jackson, also, during the latter part of his administration, was the political triumph of Van Buren; there-

a harbour on the Pacific; that this claim of the Californias will give it to them and will diminish their opposition to annexation. He is very earnest and anxious on this point of claiming the Californias and says we must not consent to less. This in strict confidence" (Wharton to Rusk, [February 18, 1837] Garrison, *Dip. Cor. Tex.*, I, 193-194).

[1] Memorandum dated in pencil and in another hand, "December, 1836, or January, 1837," Van Buren MSS.   •

fore, had there been no other reasons, he no doubt would have hesitated to extend recognition too promptly as an executive act, lest, by arraying the abolition faction in the opposition, he should embarrass the incoming administration of Van Buren, who was committed to a continuance of the Jackson policy.

If, however, the friends of recognition were strong enough to carry the measure in Congress all objection on this score would be removed. And it was doubtless partly with this idea in mind that he had suggested in his message that Congress was at liberty to take up the matter. "If Congress shall differ with me," he had said "I shall promptly and cordially unite . . . in such measures as may be deemed best fitted to increase the prosperity and perpetuate the peace of our favored country."[1] The objections he had openly urged in his message against immediate recognition would naturally disappear in the course of time, but meanwhile, on their account, as well as for political reasons, if recognition was to be granted, it would be better to have the representatives of the people shoulder the responsibility.

But the Van Buren party in Congress was strong, and for weeks the question was successfully kept out of the discussions. Finally, on February 8, believing that another message from the president was necessary, Wharton and Hunt, the latter of whom had just reached Washington,[2] addressed to Jackson the following earnest appeal:

The impossibility of holding any intercourse with the Department of State, in consequence of the refusal of the honorable Secretary to receive our communications, and the fear of interrupting you by a visit when you might be engaged, has induced us to address you this communication, which you can read at your leisure. Our zeal for the honour and the welfare of our adopted country is our only apology. . . . By this delay [of Congress to extend recognition] Texas is suffering at every pore. Public confidence in our government is to a great extent destroyed. Immigration is partially suspended. Our financial resources cannot be properly developed, and our credit is immensely injured. Had our independence been recognized at the first of this session, fifty families would have gone

[1] See above, p. 237.
[2] Wharton to Rusk, February 12, 1837, Garrison, *Dip. Cor. Tex.*, I, 185.

into Texas this winter, where one has gone. Instead of begging off
our lands with difficulty at 50 cents the acre, they would readily
command one dollar, and our Govt would have been in possession
of means to discharge all its pecuniary obligations and to establish
its credit for the future on a firm foundation. We feel that in
asking a recognition of the Independence of Texas, we are not sup-
plicating a favour, but are respectfully imploring the extension to
us of that act of justice which this Government has properly and
nobly extended to other rising Republics under far worse circumstances. We know that the claims of Texas to an immediate recognition are a hundred fold stronger than were those of Mexico or of
the South American States at the period of their recognition. We
present a perfectly organized government in all its departments,
in undisturbed possession of all the country we claim or contend for,
and with ample physical ability to repel any invasion of our im-
beeile and bankrupt enemies. Indeed, what mortifies and aston-
ishes us most is, that those, who refuse to recognize our Independence, at the same time, admit the truth of the only facts necessary
to be enquired into before recognition;—that we are a de facto government, with ability to maintain our national existence. From
sad experience we perceive that Congress will not act without you
give another impulse to the matter. To you then we appeal most
confidently, not to your sympathies but to your stern sense of justice. The eyes, the hearts and the hopes of our whole country are
directed to you more than to all the people of the United States,
put together. We have sincerely thought that we could not be
treated with coolness, illiberality and injustice, while you were at
the head of the Government. . . . It is not difficult to perceive
that Texas, once independent by the recognition of England or
France, with the superaddition of a favourable commercial treaty,
is forever lost to the United States, so far as annexation is concerned. Considering the shortness of the present session, there is
certainly not a moment for delay. For in such case, the Senate
will not have time to act upon a treaty of amity, commerce etc. at
this session. . . . We do not wish the question of Independence
to be connected with or embarrassed with annexation, nor with
Mexico or anything else. We write this letter for your own eye
alone.[1]

But Jackson still preferred to remain in the background, submitting from time to time to the committee on foreign relations such
additional evidence as might prove useful to them. They had been

[1]Wharton and Hunt to Jackson, February 8, 1837, Garrison, *Dip. Cor.
Tex.*, I, 196-197.

recommended to consult Ellis as to the situation in Mexico.[1] About the same time a long and detailed account of conditions in Texas written by Austin, just two weeks before his death, to Donelson, Jackson's former private secretary, was sent to the chairman of the House committee, with the following comment from Jackson: "The Col [that is, Howard, the chairman] will find the idea held forth by Mr. Austin in his letter 'that if the U. S. *does not now accept the proposition, it may be forever lost to her'*—this the P. has heard from other sources, and there is no doubt, if the Independence of Texas be not acknowledged by the U. States, an effort will be made by Texas to great Britain to have the Independence of Texas acknowledged by her, giving and securing to great Britain as a consideration, enclosure commercial benefits."[2]

On February 12, Wharton wrote: "There are three chances of reaching the consideration of our Independence at present [that is, before Congress adjourns]—1st. A report from the Committee on Foreign Affairs, which is very slow in coming and rather doubtful if it ever will come. 2dly. Resolutions to recognize, which have been introduced by our friends in both Houses, and the mass of business has heretofore kept off these resolutions:—3d. Our friends will endeavor to discuss the merits of our question, when the appropriation bill comes up, by inserting an appropriation to defray the expenses of a diplomatic intercourse with Texas. In addition to these," he said, "I am now endeavoring to add another string to our bow, by getting up a memorial to Congress from the inhabitants of this District. . . . In this way our case may be reached, and I am satisfied that it will pass, if ever discussed."[3] This memorial was presented the next day.[1]

At last, on February 18, the House committee on foreign affairs reported resolutions as follows:

Resolved by the House of Representatives of the United States, That the independence of the Government of Texas ought to be recognized.

Resolved, That the Committee on Ways and Means be directed

[1]See above, p. 244.
[2]Jackson to Howard, February 2, 1837, Jackson MSS.
[3]Wharton to Rusk, February 12, 1837, Garrison, *Dip. Cor. Tex.*, I, 185.
[4]*Ibid.* For resolutions see *Senate Docs.*, 25 Cong., 2 Sess., II, No. 172.

to provide, in the bill for the civil and diplomatic expenses of the Government, a salary and outfit for such public agent as the President may determine to send to Texas.[1]

These resolutions were adopted February 28.[2] On March 1, the Senate, by a vote of twenty-three to nineteen, passed the resolution presented by Walker, January 11, recommending recognition.[3] Two days later Wharton and Hunt appealed to the president thus:

Believing that the late votes in Congress have sufficiently indicated that, in the opinion of that body, the time has now arrived, when the Independence of Texas should be formally recognized, we again take the liberty of appearing before you, to implore you, in the name of our country and by the friendship of our President and our whole population for you, to close your brilliant career by admitting Texas, at once, by some executive act, into the family of nations. The people of Texas feel that they have claims of the strongest nature upon you, individually. Many of them are from your own State and were induced to emigrate to Texas by the confidence they entertained, that they would be again received under the flag of their native land by the acquisition of Texas during your administration. Moreover, a large number of those, who won the battle of [San] Jacinto, sprang from the same noble State, and were taught the way to victory and to fame by your own practice and precepts. In addition to this, we feel assured, that in making the recognition which we here so ardently implore you will only be fulfilling what has been long expected from you by the whole people of the United States, and that you will also embalm your name forever in the gratitude of a rising Republic, which has proved herself so worthy to be free, alike by her wisdom and moderation in the Cabinet and by her valour and success on the field.[4]

To this request Jackson responded, as one of his last executive acts. Wharton, in his dispatch to the Texas government, relates the circumstance thus:

I have at length the happiness to inform you that President Jackson has closed his political career by admitting our country into the great family of nations. On Friday night last, [March 3],

[1]*Debates in Cong.*, 24 Cong., 2 Sess., 1880.
[2]*Ibid.*, 2066.
[3]*Ibid.*, 1013, 1019; Walker to Jackson, March 1, 1837, Jackson MSS. For contents of this resolution see above p. 244.
[4]Wharton and Hunt to Jackson, March 3, 1837, Garrison, *Dip. Cor. Tex.*, I, 201-202.

at near 12 o'clock, he consummated the recognition of the Senate and the diplomatic appropriation bill of the lower House, by nominating a Mr. Labranche of Louisiana, charge d-affaires near the Republic of Texas. He also sent for Gen. Hunt and myself and requested the pleasure of a glass of wine, and stated that Mr. Forsyth would see us officially on Monday.[1]

Thus the long negotiations closed. To the Texans it had seemed a weary struggle; but the United States had exercised no more than the proper precaution before assuming the responsibility of extending to Texas her first recognition. France did not take the same step until September, 1839, and recognition from England was not secured until November, 1840.[2] But if, after independence was declared, Texas had been in a position properly to urge her claims, it seems probable, unless conservatism alone had prevented, that the first session of the twenty-fourth Congress would have been inclined to recommend not only recognition, but perhaps annexation as well. The opportunity was allowed to pass; and before Texas finally learned the necessary lessons in diplomacy there had grown up, along with the question of the abolition of slavery and the right of petition, a sentiment of opposition to annexation, which hitherto had not existed. It is, of course, only by a study of the annexation movement that one comes to realize the great significance of this circumstance—the decade of political strife contingent thereon, the Mexican war, and the acquisition by the United States of the whole Southwest, from the Rio Grande to the Pacific. But its importance in connection with the subject under discussion lay in the fact that in order to control the political situation the Van Buren party conceived it to be essential to assume, as far as possible, a neutral attitude concerning the whole question of annexation. Jackson's method in dealing with recognition was, to a certain extent, at least, a part of this general policy. By this means, he did succeed in preventing, in some degree, the agitation of the question of annexation during his administration, and in deferring recognition in a cautious and conservative way until it was more fully justified. But by so doing he undoubtedly delayed annexation far longer than he had anticipated or desired.

[1]Wharton to Henderson, March 5, 1837, Garrison, *Dip. Cor. Tex.*, I, 201.
[2]Worley, "The Diplomatic Relations of England and the Republic of Texas," in THE QUARTERLY, IX, 11.

BIBLIOGRAPHY.

I. MANUSCRIPT SOURCES.

Archives of the office of secretary of state. Books 3, 34, 41-45, 49 contain attested copies of the diplomatic correspondence. Since these copies were made many of the originals have been lost. The collection is, therefore, a valuable supplement to the diplomatic correspondence (see below).

Austin Papers (in the possession of the University of Texas). This collection is especially rich in materials for a study of the movement with which this paper deals. Austin, as one of the set of commissioners first sent out by Texas to treat for recognition and as the first secretary of state of the permanent government of the republic of Texas, naturally gathered a mass of documents highly valuable for this period. Many letters and papers missing from the diplomatic correspondence may be found here either in the original or in duplicate. It is probable, indeed, that several documents which were prepared for preservation in the archives found their way by some inadvertence into this collection.

Diplomatic correspondence of the Republic of Texas with the United States (in the Texas State Library).[1] It is upon material found in this collection that the foregoing study is chiefly based.

Jackson Manuscripts (in the Library of Congress).

Van Buren Manuscripts (in the Library of Congress).

II. PRINTED SOURCES.

Congressional Globe, 24 Cong.

Debates in Congress, 24 Cong. 4 Vols.

Gammel, H. P. N., *Laws of Texas,* Vol. 1 (1898) contains, as reprints, the following records and compilations which have been used in the preparation of this paper:

Journals of the Consultation (1838).

Journals of the Convention (1838).

[1]The diplomatic correspondence of the Republic of Texas with the United States is only a part of a larger collection known as the Diplomatic Correspondence of the Republic of Texas, the editing of which has been assigned by the Historical Manuscripts Commission to Professor George P. Garrison, of the University of Texas. Since the preparation of this paper Professor Garrison's edition of the correspondence with the United States, 1835-1842, has appeared as the *Annual Report of the American Historical Association for the Year 1907,* Vol. II (see below under "Printed Sources"). The manuscript collection, however, contains much material which is not strictly diplomatic in character, and which, therefore, has been excluded from the published edition. Such documents I have cited, Dip. Cor. Tex. with U. S. (MSS); reference to the printed collection is made, Garrison, *Dip. Cor. Tex.,* I.

Journal of the Proceedings of the General Council (1839). Laws of the Republic of Texas.

Ordinances and Decrees of the Consultation, Provisional Government of Texas and the Convention (1838).

Garrison, George P., *Diplomatic Correspondence of the Republic of Texas*, Part I (published as the *Annual Report of the American Historical Association for the Year 1907*, Vol. II).

House Reports of Committees, 24 Cong., 1 Sess. III, (Serial No. 295) No. 854.

Niles' Register, XLIX-LI.

Richardson, J. H., *Messages and Papers of the Presidents* (1896), Vol. III.

Senate Documents, 24 Cong., 2 Sess., Vols. I and II (Serial Nos. 297, 298).

Telegraph and Texas Register, 1835-6.

Texas. Address of the Honorable Wm. H. Wharton delivered in New York, on Tuesday, April 26, 1836. Also Address of the Honorable Stephen F. Austin delivered in Louisville, Kentucky, on the 7th of March, 1836, Austin Papers.

Texas Republican (clippings in Austin Papers).

Various letters and documents printed in the following secondary works:

Brown, John Henry, *History of Texas*, 2 Vols. (1892).

Brown, John Henry, *Life and Times of Henry Smith* (1887).

Holley, Mrs. Mary Austin, *Texas* (1836).

Wooten, Dudley G. (editor), *A Comprehensive History of Texas*, 1685, 1897, 2 Vols. (1898).

Yoakum, H., *History of Texas*, 2 Vols. (1856).

III. AUTHORITIES.

Barker, Eugene C., "The Finances of the Texas Revolution," in *Political Science Quarterly*, XIX, 612-635.

Barker, Eugene C., "Land Speculation as a Cause of the Texas Revolution," in *The Quarterly of the Texas State Historical Association*, X, 79-95.

Barker, Eugene C., "President Jackson and the Texas Revolution," in *The American Historical Review*, XII, No. 4, July 1907.

Garrison, George P., *Texas* (1903).

Garrison, George P., *Westward Extension* (1906).

Garrison, George P., "The First Stage of the Movement for the Annexation of Texas," in *The American Historical Review*, X, 72-96.

Garrison, George P., *"Another Texas Flag,"* in *The Quarterly of The Texas State Historical Association*, III, 170-176.

Gouge, William M., *The Fiscal History of Texas* (1852).

MacDonald, William, *Jacksonian* Democracy (1906).

Mayo, Robert, *Political Sketches of Eight Years in Washington.*

Reeves, Jesse S., *American Diplomacy under Tyler and Polk* (1907).

Schouler, James, *History of the United States* (1899).

Smith, W. Roy, "The Quarrel Between Governor Smith and the Provisional Government of the Republic," in *The Quarterly of the Texas State Historical Association,* V, 269-346.

Sumner, William Graham, *Andrew Jackson* (1899).

Tornel, *Tejas y los Estados-Unidos de América en sus Relaciones con la República Mexicana* (1837).

Von Holst, H., *The Constitutional and Political History of the United States,* 1828-1846 (1888).

THE QUARTERLY

OF THE

TEXAS STATE HISTORICAL ASSOCIATION

Vol. XIII.   APRIL, 1910.   No. 4.

*The publication committee and the editors disclaim responsibility for views
expressed by contributors to* The Quarterly.

STEPHEN F. AUSTIN AND THE INDEPENDENCE OF TEXAS

EUGENE C. BARKER

The personality of Stephen F. Austin looms large in the history
of Anglo-American Texas. During the first decade, while on the
one side he smoothed out the real or fancied grievances of the colonists and on the other persuaded the Mexican government against
its better judgment to hope for the abiding loyalty of its adoptive
citizens, he held the fate of the colonies in the hollow of his hand.
And one who studies his carefully preserved correspondence cannot
doubt that he fully realized and keenly felt the responsibility, or
that his polar star, to use a metaphor of which the men of his day
were fond, was always the ultimate good of the colonists. Although he may at times have erred in the means for attaining his
end, there is a fine consistency in his aim to subserve, as he understood them, the best interests of the people whom in a peculiar
sense he felt to be his own. It is the purpose of this paper to examine his attitude toward the most vital question that Texas ever
faced—that, namely, of independence. And from the view point
just stated it is not difficult to forecast his position at any given
moment.

For the purpose of this examination Austin's career falls into
three periods. In the first, which may extend from 1821 to 1832
he perceived the best interest of Texas in unswerving allegiance to
Mexico. This happened to be the period in which he was laying

deep the foundation of his colonies, and it was also the time when for various reasons Texas suffered least interference from the general government. The second extends from the middle of 1832 to perhaps the end of 1834; during these years Texas came more into the current of national politics, and loyalty in his mind became conditional upon the organization of Texas as a separate state of the confederation in order to correct in a measure the evils of the federal administration. The third covers the fifteen months or so preceding March 2, 1836, when Santa Anna was destroying the federal system and establishing a centralized government somewhat like that of the consular government of France under Napoleon Bonaparte; Austin now realized that even separate statehood would not protect Texas and mentally advanced to the last step—the declaration of independence.

Passing from generalities to particulars, Austin in the first period showed his loyalty to Mexico and his protective relation to the colonists by his attitude toward the Fredonian Rebellion, Guerrero's emancipation decree of 1829, the law of April 6, 1830, and the troubles of 1832. It will suffice to review these episodes very briefly. In 1825 Hayden Edwards entered into a contract with the government to settle eight hundred families in the district around and including Nacogdoches. There was already there a considerable population, mostly Mexican, and Edwards early incurred the resentment of the old settlers by questioning their land titles; later he had trouble with some of his own colonists who objected to paying the small fee that he charged them for land; finally he became involved in an election dispute at Nacogdoches which the political chief at Bexar decided against him. By October, 1826, feeling against him, and especially against his brother, B. W. Edwards, was so high that the political chief somewhat arbitrarily issued a decree banishing him from the country. He determined to resist, and with a handful of followers declared Texas independent; made an alliance with the Cherokees; and tried to incite Austin's colonists to a race war against the Mexicans. In this last, however, he failed, for Austin not only prevented his colonists from responding but actually caused them to join the Mexican troops in putting down the rebels. Austin then detached the Indians from their alliance and exerted his influence to secure an amnesty for all who laid down their arms, so that by the last of January, 1827, Edwards fled across the border and the Fredonian Rebellion, as it was called, was over.[1] Austin's part was an important one. He gave Edwards sage advice which, if he had followed it, would have enabled him to avoid most of his trouble; and in the end took the only possible course to preserve the confidence of the government and the interests of the colonists.

On September 15, 1829, President Guerrero issued a decree emancipating all the slaves in the Mexican Republic, and it fell with the presage of ruin upon the Texans who, with no free labor to be obtained, felt that slaves were absolutely essential to the opening up of their new-land farms. Through Austin's influence the political chief at Bexar suspended the official publication of the proclamation until a memorial could be forwarded to Mexico praying for relief. In this petition the political chief and the governor of the state both joined, and on December 2, 1829, the general government was pleased to issue a second decree exempting Texas from the operation of the first. Austin's steadiness had prevented the colonists from hurrying into precipitate action; but he realized as clearly as they the effect that the September decree would have in retarding the development of the country, and the late Lester G. Bugbee who carefully investigated this subject in 1898 could not determine what would have been his procedure if the withdrawal of the law had been refused. Fortunately that issue did not arise. What is certain is that it was due to Austin alone that the incident closed without a greater mutual loss of confidence between the colonists and the government.[2]

On April 6, 1830, the Mexican Congress passed at the instigation of Lucas Alamán, the Secretary of Foreign Relations, a law regulating colonization. Though in form a general law, it was in fact directed especially at Texas and the United States. The famous eleventh article prevented the settlement of immigrants in any province of the Mexican Republic contiguous to their native land. The efforts that the United States had been making since

[1]This affair can best be studied from the documents in *A Comprehensive History of Texas*, I, 518-532; and Foote, *Texas and the Texans*, I, 260-268.

[2]See Bugbee, "Slavery in Early Texas," in *Political Science Quarterly*, XIII, particularly pp. 649-655.

1825 to purchase Texas caused Mexico to fear its forcible seizure as soon as there were enough Americans in the country to make the venture a success, and it was against this contingency that Alamán was seeking to guard. Its effect on the Texans who saw themselves cut off from their friends and families in the United States may well be imagined. They appealed to Austin to protect them from the "violent and fatal measures" of the government,[1] and he forthwith applied himself to this task. The law was not repealed until 1834, but the excitement gradually subsided—partly no doubt because the government could never enforce the law.

The government did, however, attempt to enforce the decree, and for that purpose ordered General Terán to establish garrisons in Texas. At the same time the seven years expired for which, according to the colonization laws, the settlers were exempt from the payment of custom duties, and the custom houses were put in operation. George Fisher, the collector at Galveston, or rather Anahuac, and Colonel John Davis Bradburn, the commander of the garrison there, soon had the colonists greatly irritated by their arbitrary proceedings. In the spring of 1832 the colonists were driven to an insurrection which ended in the expulsion of both soldiers and collectors from the country. Austin had all along held a firm tone against the methods of Fisher and Bradburn, and was accused by Terán therefor of being responsible for the opposition to those officials.[2] He was at Saltillo, attending the legislature, when the conflict occurred. Whether he could have prevented it is uncertain, but certainly it was largely through his influence that Colonel Mexia, whom Santa Anna sent to investigate the trouble, was convinced that the Texans were not to blame.[3]

This ends the review of the first period. While never deviating from his declared motto of "fidelity and gratitude to Mexico,"[4] Austin stood always ready to guard the interests of the colonists. Thus we find him at the same time boldy writing to one Mexican official that the only way to remedy the affairs of Texas was to re-

[1]Chambers to Austin, May 12, 1830. Austin Papers.
[2]Terán to Austin, January 27, 1832. Austin Papers.
[3]See Rowe, "The Disturbances at Anahuac in 1832, in THE QUARTERLY, VI, 265-299; Turner, "The Mejía Expedition," in *ibid.*, VII, 1-28.
[4]Austin to Muldoon, November 15, 1831. Austin Papers.

store the constitution and authority of the state, assuring another that the colonists had no desire for independence or union with the United States, and complaining to Santa Anna himself of the injustice of the law of April 6, 1830, and of the military tyranny to which the people had been subjected.[1]

Since 1824 Texas had been united with Coahuila, and the movement to secure a separate state organization began in August, 1832, when the *alcalde* of San Felipe issued a call for a convention to meet October 1. One reason that he gave for the convention was the necessity of explaining officially that the recent rising against the troops did not have for its object the separation of Texas from Mexico. The meeting was in session six days (October 1-6), and passed, among other things, a resolution for the administration of the custom houses until the government could send new collectors, and adopted reports praying for the reform of the tariff, the appointment of land commissioners, a grant of land for the support of primary education, and for permission to organize the local government. Some of the delegates were in favor of drafting a provisional constitution at once and asking the general government to approve it, but Austin, who was president of the convention, thought it more prudent to petition first for the privilege of doing so, and his opinion prevailed. William H. Wharton was elected to carry the various memorials to Mexico, but for reasons unknown he did not go.[2]

The Mexican authorities undoubtedly believed that the colonists were planning separation not only from Coahuila, but also from the Republic;[3] and it is true that the subject of independence had been discussed among them, but the evidence seems to show a decided sentiment against it. This evidence is as follows: (1) previous to the convention Austin had, in the letter mentioned above, disclaimed for the colonists any idea of secession; (2) the

[1]Austin to Músquiz, June 29, 1832; to Ugartechea, June 29; to Santa Anna, July 6. Austin Papers.

[2]See in general the Proceedings of the Convention in Gammel, *Laws of Texas*, I, 475-503; and *A Comprehensive History of Texas*, I, 499.

[3]See extracts from letters of Garza, Ramón Músquiz, Angel Navarro, Eca y Musquiz, Santa Anna, and others in Brown, *History of Texas*, I, 215-221.

ayuntamiento of Gonzales had refused to participate in the convention for fear that this very motive would be attributed to it;[1] (3) letters to Austin from a correspondent in the district of Teneha declared that everybody in that neighborhood was opposed to independence, while not one in ten favored union with the United States;[2] and finally (4) the tone of the convention itself, so far as one can judge from its journal, was very respectful.

The disorders in Mexico were causing Austin, however, to think of the future. To a friend in the United States he wrote that the Mexican confederation might break up and leave Texas to itself; but it would be better for Texas to remain a Mexican state, "unless we could float into the Northern Republic with the consent of all parties."[3] And an outspoken letter to the political chief reveals his firm conviction of the necessity of separating from Coahuila: "There is little probability," it declares,

that we shall soon have a stable and peaceable order of public affairs; and I give it as my deliberate judgement that Texas is lost if she take no measure of her own for her welfare. I incline to the opinion that it is your duty as Chief Magistrate, to call a general convention to take into consideration the condition of the country. I do not know how the State or General Government can presume to say that the people of Texas have violated the constitution, when the acts of both governments have long since killed the constitution, and when the confederation itself has hardly any life left. I cannot approve the assertion that the people have not the right to assemble peaceably, and calmly and respectfully represent their wants. In short, the condition of Texas is bad, but we may fear to see it still worse.[4]

Conditions did not improve during the winter of 1832-3, and in the spring another convention met at San Felipe. The journal of this meeting, if any was kept, has disappeared, but we know that it adopted resolutions condemning the African slave trade, petitioned for the establishment of regular mail service, modifica-

[1]Brown, *History of Texas*, I, 216; Rather, "DeWitt's Colony," in THE QUARTERLY, VIII, 146-147.

[2]Harrison to Austin, November 30, December 8, 1832. Austin Papers.

[3]Austin to Ashby, October 10, 1832. Austin Papers.

[4]Austin to Ramón Músquiz, November 15, 1832, in Brown, *History of Texas*, I, 219.

tion of the tariff, and repeal of the law of April 6, 1830, and that it went beyond the action of the previous convention and drew up a provisional state constitution with a long memorial to the government praying for its approval.[1] Austin and two other commissioners[2] were elected to lay these documents before the government, but Austin alone served. He reached the capital July 18. Generals Arista and Durán had just begun an insurrection, and Santa Anna was leading a campaign against them, while Vice-President Farias was carrying on the government. Farias received him courteously and referred his petition to a committee of Congress, but gave him little enough real encouragement. Austin, when he left home, claimed to be sanguine of obtaining the repeal of the law of April 6, 1830, and permission for the Texans to hold a convention and adopt a constitution. [3] Conditions in Mexico disappointed him, and for the first time he seemed clearly to recognize the possibility of Mexico's being unwilling or unable to administer Texas in a manner consistent with its highest development. While still declaring himself hopeful of success, he wrote: "But if our application is refused, I shall be in favor of organizing *without it*—I see no other way of saving the country from total anarchy and ruin—I am totally done with conciliatory measures, and for the future shall be uncompromising as [to] Texas matters."[4]

As August and September wore along the issue of the civil war in Mexico appeared doubtful, and Austin became more and more impatient. If a change of administration occurred, his object might be indefinitely delayed. On the first of October therefore he called on Farias and told him plainly that if some attention were not paid to the wishes of the Texans he feared that they

[1]Edward, *History of Texas*, 196-205; Yoakum, *History of Texas*, I, 467-482; THE QUARTERLY, VI, 151, VIII, 240-246.

[2]There is some difference of opinion as to who the others were. Yoakum (I, 312), Bancroft (*North Mexican States and Texas*, II, 134), and Bryan (*A Comprehensive History of Texas*, I, 499) say W. H. Wharton and J. B. Miller; Kennedy (*Texas,* II, 23) and Garrison (*Texas*, 185) say J. B. Miller and Erasmo Seguin. Thrall (*History of Texas*, 189, note) calls attention to the difference between Yoakum and Kennedy, but follows Yoakum.

[3]Austin to Perry, April 22, 1833. Austin Papers.

[4]Austin to Perry, July 30, 1833. Austin Papers.

would take the remedy into their own hands. The vice-president interpreted this as a threat and was greatly offended, and Austin left the conference with the conviction that nothing was to be expected from the government. The next day he wrote: "I am tired of the govt. Texas must take care of herself without paying any attention to these people or to this govt.—They a[lways have been in?] revolution and I believe always will be. I have had much more respect for them than they deserve—but I am [done with?] all that."[1] The same day he wrote to the *ayuntamiento* of Bexar stating his belief that no reforms were to be gained from the government, and urging it to take the lead in declaring Texas a separate state. He appears to have thought on the one hand that the Texans, if left to themselves, might go even further than that, and on the other that a movement begun by the Mexican population of Bexar would encounter less resistance from the government.[2] The *ayuntamiento* had adopted a vigorous protest in December, 1832, against the same evils of which the convention complained,[3] and it was not unreasonable to hope that it might now inaugurate the local organization. Later Austin made his peace with Farias and became slightly more hopeful, though on the 23d he wrote his brother-in-law, "the fact is this govt. ought to make a state of Texas, or transfer her to the U. S.—without delay, and there is some probability at this time that one or the other will be done. A short time will now determine this matter in some way."[4]

Early in November Santa Anna returned to the capital, after winning a decisive victory over the insurgents at Guanajuato, and promised favorable action on all of the petitions presented by Austin except that for separate statehood; and even that should be granted, he said, as soon as the country was prepared for it. Austin remained in the city until December 10 and then started home very well satisfied. At Saltillo on January 3, 1834, he was arrested by order of the vice-president, on account of the letter

[1]Austin to Perry, October 2, 1833. Austin Papers.

[2]Austin's "Explanation to the Public," etc., translation by Ethel Zivley Rather in THE QUARTERLY, VIII, 247, 248, 249.

[3]The document is printed in Filisola, *Memorias para la historia de la guerra de Tejas*, I, 272-293.

[4]Austin to Perry, October 23, 1833. Austin Papers.

that he had written to the *ayuntamiento* of Bexar, and taken back to the City of Mexico. The next eleven months, from February to December, he spent in various prisons of the capital, while court after court disclaimed jurisdiction over his case. Christmas day he was liberated on bail, but was not allowed to leave the city. Finally, under the operation of a general amnesty law, he started again for Texas in July, 1835.

Austin's letters from prison are not always ingenuous. His first aim was to obtain his release, and to do this it was necessary to keep the colonists from making any hasty demonstrations and to convince the government of his loyalty. He wrote, therefore, for two sets of readers—for he doubtless expected his letters to be intercepted and read by the government before they reached Texas. He tried to soothe the colonists by reminding them that their most serious grievances had been removed by the state legislation of 1834—and this was literally true,[1] though perhaps neither he nor they believed the prospect to be as fair as he represented it;— while upon the government he sought to create a double impression of his satisfaction with the reforms and of his pacific influence over the colonists. At the same time it is not necessary to believe that as yet Austin's words did real violence to his convictions. Though beginning to doubt, he was still loyal to Mexico, and he did believe it to the best interest of the colonists to remain tranquil. Such deception as he may have practiced may certainly be forgiven to a man in his position, for in his own mind he had committed no wrong.

Some extracts from Austin's letters will illustrate his double motive. Announcing his arrest to his brother-in-law, James F. Perry, he wrote:

All I can be accused of is that I have labored most diligently and indefatigably to get Texas made a state separate from Coahuila, and that is no crime, nor no dishonor—it is quite the reverse. . . I hope there will be no excitement about my arrest—it

[1]Several new municipalities were created; the province was divided for administrative purposes into three departments, two of the three being Anglo-American in population; the use of both English and Spanish in public documents was permitted; and a judicial system was organized, granting trial by jury. See Gammel, *Laws of Texas*, I, 352, 355-356, 364-380, 384.

will do me harm and no good to Texas, that is, unless I should be unjustly dealt by, in that case there will be cause for excitement.
. . . A little time will put all right—there will be toleration of religion—Texas will be a state, and all will go right. . . .
There is no sort of doubt of the *right* of the people of Texas to take care of themselves, if there be no other remedy—this is more than a right—it is a duty—but evil may be done by precipitation.[1]

Two days later he wrote again to Perry: "My advice to Texas is what it has always been—remain quiet—populate the country—improve your farms—and discountenance all revolutionary men or principles." To S. M. Williams he wrote May 3, 1834,[2] suggesting that the people publish an address of thanks to the state government for the recent laws in favor of Texas; the evils were now· removed and a public acknowledgment should be made to place Texas in a true light both in Mexico and in the United States, where the object of the Texans was misunderstood. On May 10 he wrote Perry that his own principles had always been "peace, quietness, patience, and submission to the laws, no revolutions"; if he had ever wandered from those principles it had been to prevent the increase of the evils by party divisions; it was "very certain that Texas must become a state at some future and not very distant day," but he had made a mistake in agreeing to the convention of 1833 which was called during his absence; however, he concluded, "the only substantial matter in this business that is worthy of consideration is that *much substantial good will result to Texas from my sufferings, and I am content.*" Again, August 25, "S. F. Austin's motto always has been Fidelity to Mexico, opposition to violent men or measures"; and finally, November 10, "I have done my duty to the people of Texas so far as it was in my power to do it, and I have not in anything departed from my duty as a good and faithful Mexican citizen."[3] One thing at least these quotations show, and that is an unvarying regard for the welfare of Texas.

Austin believed that his imprisonment was prolonged by the

[1]Austin to Perry, January 14, 1834. Austin Papers. Of the same tenor is ·his letter to George Fisher, January 15.

[2]Austin Papers.

[3]All these letters are from Austin to Perry. Austin Papers.

machinations of his personal enemies in Texas and Mexico,[1] and there are some indications that he was right. A man whose name a Mexican copyist makes out to be Alexandro Calecik wrote from Texas to J. A. Mexia, August 29, 1833, that Austin had acquired land and property to the value of a million and a half *pesos* and asked the unsuccessful native's universal question concerning the enterprising foreigner, "why should the government allow such a person so much money that ought to go to its own support." Austin was obnoxious *(nocino)* to Texas as well as to the general government, he said, and he expressed the hope that Mexia would detain him in Mexico five years. The personal motive is disclosed by the intimation that Austin's presence in Texas might interfere with the writer's plan to obtain a grant of land in the profits of which Mexia was to share.[2] Pointing in the same direction is a strange letter written from New York by J. Gutierrez, of whom I know nothing, to President Van Buren, May 29, 1834. He declared that he had it on the best authority that a number of Mexican officials, particularly Mexia and Zavala, wanted to make Texas independent of Mexico, and

to secure there a safe retreat or property, should there be a fresh revolution in Mexico. There was but one man in the whole Colony Who *leur portait ombrage* and migh[t] have opposed their schem[e], or neutralized their views to sway the projected state, and this was the enterprizing Colonel Austin, of whom they were on the point of getting rid when on the 24th of April Santa Anna the President informed of this mismanagement of affairs returned to the capital and took charge of the Government.[3]

Finally H. Meigs wrote Austin from New York, September 29, 1835, congratulating him on regaining his liberty and declaring

[1] He wrote to Perry, March 4, 1835 (Austin Papers), that Anthony Butler, John T. Mason, and J. A. Mexía would have kept him in a dungeon for years if they could, because he had opposed the plan of organizing Texas as a territory, and so had interfered with some of their land speculation schemes.

[2] Fomento Sección de Archivo Colonización, Exp. Num. 5, Legajo 2.

[3] Van Buren MSS. in the Library of Congress. The writer goes on to say that Santa Anna instituted an impartial inquiry into the proceedings against Austin and that it was expected that he would soon be at liberty. It was in fact about this time that Santa Anna revoked the order that had kept Austin *incommunicado* since his imprisonment.

that a great interest had been exerted to destroy him and his property. "Truly your escape is most fortunate."[1]

His observation of Mexican politics at close range, and perhaps to some extent his personal experience, led Austin to his third position—the decision that the ultimate welfare of Texas demanded its separation from Mexico. And the disorganization of the national government during the past decade had been enough, in all reason, to shake the confidence of the most pronounced optimist. President Victoria's administration from 1824 to 1828 had been filled with plots and counter-plots of rival factions; Pedraza had won the presidency in the exciting election of 1828 only to be forced after a month's tenure to resign in favor of his opponent, General Guerrero; Guerrero held the office some nine months, and was overthrown by Bustamante; in 1832 Santa Anna overthrew Bustamante, and restored Pedraza to power for a fleeting three months; and then was elected himself; the first two years of his term were filled with schemes that historians have not yet fathomed, there were some pretended rebellions and at least one real insurrection; and by the beginning of 1835 the clanking of tho machinery that was to transform the government into an absolutism was plainly to be heard.

Austin probably came around to the idea of separation slowly. His letter to Ashby, referred to above,[2] might indicate that he was thinking of the contingency in 1832, but as late as July, 1834, he excited the contempt of Anthony Butler by refusing to further the latter's efforts to purchase Texas for the United States. Secretary of State McLane had written Butler to intercede for the amelioration of Austin's confinement, and Butler replied that he was already faring far better than his deserts; that he did not merit either the sympathy or the assistance of the United States government. "He is unquestionably one of the bitterest foes to our Government and people that is to be found in Mexico, and has done more to embarrass our Negotiations upon a certain subject than all the rest of the opposition together: and I am very sure that he was the principal cause of my being defeated

[1]Austin Papers.
[2]See page 262.

in the last effort made to obtain a cession of Texas." . . .[1]
The assumption that Butler was telling the truth is perhaps not
too hazardous; though Austin gives one the impression that he incurred at least a part of Butler's enmity by opposing a territorial
government for Texas.[2]

There are in the Austin Papers nine letters from H. Meigs to
Austin which give one side of an interesting correspondence from
which we can guess only too vaguely at the other, but they plainly
suggest on Austin's part a reconnoisance to learn how far the
United States could be depended on for help in case of a breach
between Texas and Mexico. In the first one Meigs merely an-
nounces that the United States government has interceded for
Austin, and remarks that he wrote to him several months ago and
hopes for a favorable reply. In the second he repeats that the
government is interested in Austin's case and adds the information
that he himself stimulated the interest through his friend Louis
McLane and his brother-in-law John Forsyth. These letters were
dated May 30 and September 27, 1834. The remaining seven
were written in 1835—May 2, September 1, September 29, November 15 (two letters of this date), November 22, November 27.
In the earlier ones he says that he conceals what Austin writes
from everybody except Forsyth, who promises to give him all proper
aid; assures Austin that sympathy for himself and his colony is
almost universal; and exhorts him to maintain his "accustomed
prudence and fortitude." Later he refers to Austin's "philan-
thropic and just designs in favor of Texas." November 15, after
the revolution had begun, he writes: "Public sentiment is aroused
for your cause. We know that you are Bone of our Bone! and
Flesh of our Flesh! That none but a Republican Government can
exist over you! . . . Tens of thousands will join you, and
with you, lay the firm foundations of your Republic." But as yet
the law of nations and treaty with Mexico prevented the United

[1]McLane to Butler, May 26, 1834, MSS. Department of State, Instruc-
tions to Agents to Mexico, 1835, p. 25; Butler to McLane, July 13, 1834,
MSS. Department of State, Despatches from Agents to Mexico, Vol. 6.
The attention of the government seems to have been called to Austin's
plight by H. Meigs, the brother-in-law of John Forsyth (see Meigs to
Austin, May 30, September 27, 1834. Austin Papers).

[2]Austin to Perry, March 4, 1835. Austin Papers.

States from interfering.   The letter ends with a significant prayer, "May the Almighty protect you and your Republican Brethren in your progress to that glorious Independence which is in my mind's eye not only Before you but very near to you."   A second letter of the same date acknowledges receipt of one from Austin dated October 6, and adds, "the package relative to the Indians I have already sent to Washington (confidentially)."   Finally on November 27 he quotes from Forsyth who wrote him that the government had warned the Indians on the western frontier of the United States to remain quiet and take no part in the troubles which were involving Texas.   The significance of this correspondence can be appreciated only by considering the earlier letters in connection with the later ones, and for that reason the course of events has been somewhat anticipated.

Having determined in his own mind that a breach must come, Austin believed that the essential thing was to make Texas so strong that Mexico could not resist.   A letter to Perry of March 3, 1835,[1] gives one a glimpse of his mental process.   After saying that a friendly feeling prevailed in Mexico toward Texas, and that Congress would do something for it, if it were not so distracted by national affairs, he continues, "However, it is really not so *very* important whether anything is done or not if a dead calm and union can be preserved in that country—emigration—good crops—no party divisions—no excitement—no personalities should be the political creed of every one in Texas."   March 31 S. M. Williams wrote him[2] that during January and February two thousand immigrants had landed at the mouth of the Brazos alone, and from this he say that the goal was nearer than he had expected.

As has been said, Austin finally left the City of Mexico about the middle of July and reached Texas September 1, by way of Vera Cruz and New Orleans.   Filisola declares[3] that he went to New Orleans to buy arms and munitions of war, but it is more likely that he could not get passage directly home from Vera

[1]Austin Papers.
[2]Austin Papers.
[3]*Memorias para la historia de la guerra de Tejas*, II, 141.

Cruz.[1] Whatever may have been his reason for going, while there he unbosomed himself as to his plans for Texas in a very candid letter to his cousin Mrs. Holley. Long as it is, it is worth quoting in full:[2]

NEW ORLEANS, August 21, 1835.

My dear Cousin,

I am, as you will see by my date, once more in the land of my birth, and of *freedom*—a word I can well appreciate. I shall leave here in a day or two for Texas. I wished to have taken a trip up the river, and thence to the North, but shall have to defer it until spring. I have been so long absent from home, that my affairs there are behind hand, and require my attention.

The situation of Texas is daily becoming more and more interesting, so much so that I doubt whether the Government of the United States or that of Mexico can much longer look on with indifference, or inaction. It is very evident that Texas should be effectually, and fully, *Americanized,*—that is—settled by a population that will harmonize with their neighbors on the *East,* in language, political principles, common origin, sympathy, and even interest. *Texas must be a slave country. It is no longer a matter of doubt.* The interest of Louisiana requires that it should be. A population of fanatical abolitionists in Texas would have a very dangerous and pernicious influence on the overgrown slave population of that state. Texas must and ought to become an outwork on the west, as Alabama and Florida are on the east, to defend the key of the western world—the mouths of the Mississippi. Being fully Americanized under the Mexican flag would be the same thing in effect and ultimate result as coming under the United States flag. A gentle breeze shakes off a ripe peach. Can it be supposed that the violent political convulsions of Mexico will not shake off Texas as soon as it is ripe enough to fall? All that is now wanting is a great immigration of good and efficient families this fall and winter. Should we get such an immigration, especially from the Western States—all is done; the peach will be ripe. Under this view, and it is the correct one, every man of influence in the Western States, who has the true interests of his country at heart ought to use every possible exertion to induce such an immigration. They can get lands; *now is the accepted time,* and none too soon. The door is still open for them to come in legally. The

---

[1] I have the greater confidence in this hypothesis because in one of his letters to Perry (January 14, 1834—Austin Papers) Austin gives instructions for forwarding his mail by Tampico or Vera Cruz, and tells Perry if no other opportunity offers to send it by New Orleans.

[2] From a copy by Mrs. M. A. Holley in the Austin Papers.

government of Mexico cannot complain—it has invited immigration.

General Santa Anna told me he should visit Texas next March—as a friend. His visit is uncertain—his friendship more so. We must rely on ourselves, and prepare for the worst. A large immigration will prepare us, give us strength, resources, everything. I do not know the state of public feeling in Texas, but presume they mean to avoid all collision with Mexico if possible to do so, and be also ready to repel attacks should they come. This is my opinion. A great emigration from Kentucky, Tennessee, etc, each man with his rifle or musket, would be of great use to us—very great indeed. If they go by sea, they must take passports from the Mexican consul, comply with all the requirements of the law, and get *legally* into the country, so long as the door is legally open. Should it be closed it will then be time enough to force it open—if necessary. *Prudence and an observance of appearances* must therefore be strictly attended to for the present. Here, I figure to my self, you start and exclaim "Dios mio," my cousin Stephen has become a very Mexican politician in hypocrisy. Not so; there is no hypocrisy about it. It is well known that my object has always been to fill up Texas with a North American population; and, besides, it may become a question of *to be, or not to be.* And in that event, the great law of nature—self preservation —operates and supersedes all other laws. The cause of philanthropy and liberty, also, will be promoted by Americanizing Texas. I am morally right, therefore, to do so by all possible, honorable, means.

In all countries, one way or another, a few men rule society. If those few were convinced of the great benefits that would result to the Western world by *Amercanizing* Texas, they would exert their influence to promote that object, and in so doing use such arguments as would best effect it, without letting anything transpire in the public prints to alarm the Mexican government, or place that of the United States in the awkward necessity of taking any steps, as a friend of Mexico under the treaty etc.

If there were any way of getting at it, I should like to know what the *wise* men of the United States think the people of Texas ought to do. The fact, is, we must and ought to become a part of the United States. Money should be no consideration. The political importance of Texas to the great western world, from the influence it may one day have on Louisiana, is so great that it cannot fail to have due weight on all reflecting men, and on Gen. Jackson and the Senate in particular. The more the American population of Texas is increased the more readily will the Mexican Government give it up. Also, the more the people of Texas seem to oppose a separation from Mexico, the less tenacious will they be to hold it. This seems paradoxical, but it will cease to appear so when you consider that strange compound the Mexican character. If Texas insisted on separating, and it should be given up in consequence, it would appear as if they had yielded to force, or fear, and their national pride would be roused. They are a strange people, and must be studied to be managed. They have high ideas of National dignity should it be openly attacked, but will sacrifice national dignity, and national interest too, if it can be done in a *still* way, or so as not to arrest public attention. "Dios castiga el ascandolo mas que el crimen" (God punishes the exposure more than the crime) is their motto. The maxim influences their morals and their politics. I learned it when I was there in 1822, and I now believe that if I had not always kept it in view, and known the power which *appearances* have on them, even when they know they are deceived, I should never have succeeded to the extent I have done, in Americanizing Texas.

To conclude, I wish a great immigration this fall and winter from Kentucky, Tennessee, *every where;* passports or no passports, *anyhow.* For fourteen years I have had a hard time of it, but nothing shall daunt my courage or abate my exertions to complete the main object of my labors—to *Americanize Texas.* This fall and winter will fix our fate—a great immigration will settle the question.

Truly yours,

S. F. Austin.

Arrived in Texas, Austin found conditions more critical than he expected. The country was divided between those who believed that resistance to Santa Anna's measures was the only course left and the moderates who favored submission, or at least continued patience. A consultation had been called to meet on October 15 to settle upon a definite policy, and Austin from the beginning devoted himself to making this a completely representative body. He feared that Texas was not yet strong enough to cope with Mexico, but could not give the peace-party any encouragement. On September 8 he spoke at a public dinner at Brazoria. He deplored the existing confusion, which he attributed to the "total want of a local government in Texas"; he declared that the revolution in Mexico was for the purpose of destroying the federal constitution of 1824 and setting up a centralized government; that the people had a right to say whether they were willing to surrender their vested constitutional rights, which such a change involved; and that a consultation would enable them to answer the question with calmness and deliberation. While Santa Anna had repeatedly called himself the friend of the Texans and promised to use his influence to secure for them in the new constitution "a special organization suited to their education, habits, and situation," Austin plainly put little faith in his promise. He closed his speech with these words:

My friends, I can truely say that no one has been, or now is more anxious than myself to keep trouble away from this country, no one has been or now is more faithful to his duty as a Mexican citizen, and no one has personally sacrificed or suffered more to discharge this duty. I have uniformly opposed having anything to do with the family political quarrels of the Mexicans. Texas needs peace and a local Government; its inhabitants are farmers, they need a calm and quiet life. But . . . the crisis is certainly such as to bring it home to the judgement of every man that something must be done and that without delay. . . . Let all personalities, or divisions, or excitements, or passions, or violence be banished from among us. Let a general Consultation of the people of Texas be convened as speedily as possible, to be composed of the best, the most calm, and intelligent, and firm men in the country, and let them decide what representations ought to be made to the general government, and what ought to be done in the future.[1]

Four days later (September 12) Austin presided over a meeting at San Felipe which endorsed the consultation and elected him a member of the local committee of vigilance and correspondence.[2] Thereafter he was the recognized head of Texas, hearing reports, answering questions, offering suggestions, and even issuing orders that were obeyed He turned first to the task of ensuring the consultation, and a circular letter of September 13 shows that he interpreted the meaning of the word literally—the delegates were to *consult* and recommend measures for the definitive action of a subsequent convention. Measures advised by such a meeting would "carry with them the weight of being the *voice* of all Texas instead of the *opinion* of a few," and could not fail "to produce unanimity

---

[1] *The Texas Republican*, September 19, 1835. The speech may also be read in Foote, *Texas and the Texans*, II, 60-65.

[2] *The Texas Republican*, September 19, 1835.

at home, respect and confidence abroad."[1] Less than a week later.
however, he had received information which caused him to advise
that delegates be given plenary powers "to do whatever may be
necessary for the good of the country."[2]

Soon the march of events forced a war note into the correspondence which was not long in excluding everything else. Edward
Gritten wrote from Bexar that troops would march into the colonies and put things to rights whether the Texans submitted or
not,[3] and Austin made this letter the basis of a broadside of September 19,[4] in which he said that nothing was to be gained by
further conciliatory measures; that every district ought to organize its militia and report its strength in arms and ammunition to
the political chief. of the department, so that he could lay it before the consultation; and concluded "War is our only resource."
The next day he wrote W. D. C. Hall that Cos "lays down the
principle that the General Government have the right to force us
to submit to any reform or amendment or alterations that Congress may make in the Constitution etc. This is impossible; we
had better leave the country at once, for we should be, under Cos'
doctrine, without any rights or guaranties of any kind. I therefore think that war is inevitable; we must prepare."[5] In similar
vein on the same day he wrote to P. W. Grayson, and this letter
shows that the responsibility of his position was beginning to tell
upon him. He seemed uncertain whether the people would agree
with him. "Tell me," he begged, "what we can do except to
fight . . . Give me your opinion and that of the people of
that quarter. These things have come on us much sooner than I
expected, . . . but there is no remedy that I can see. Cos
has precipitated them."[6] But if he hesitated, it was not for long;
on the 21st he wrote the committee of Columbia, "There must now
be no half way measures—War in full. The sword is drawn and

[1]*The Texas Republican*, September 19, 1835.

[2]*The Texas Republican*, September 26, 1835.

[3]Gritten to Barrett, September 8, 1835. Austin Papers.

[4]Archives of Texas, D 267; *The Texas Republican*, September 26, 1835.
The circular is printed in full in Foote, *Texas and the Texans*, II, 67-68,
and in Brown, *History of Texas*, I, 355-356.

[5]*The Texas Republican*, September 26, 1835.

[6]Austin to Grayson, September 19, 1835. Austin Papers.

the scabbard must be put on one side until the military are all
driven out of Texas."[1]   And on the 22d a ringing call urged every
man in Texas to seize his weapons and defend his country and his
rights.[2]   A busy correspondence of this type was kept up[3] until
the first blow had been struck and it was no longer a question of
whether there should be war, but of how the war should be carried on.

A contemporary appreciation of Austin's influence by one who
did not always agree with him is afforded by a letter to him from
W. B. Travis.   The latter said:

War in defence of Texas and our dearest rights has infused itself
into the minds of the people, and I think it will require but little
exertion to get troops together for the promotion of any project
which you recommend.   All eyes are turned toward you; and the
. . . stand you have taken has given the *sovereigns* confidence
in themselves.   Texas can be wielded by you and *you alone;* and
her destiny is now completely in your hands.   I have every confidence that you will guide us safely through all our perils.[4]

Austin himself explained his position to his friend Thomas F. Mc-
Kinney thus:

I believe you know and understand the principles that have always
influenced me.   I was in times past opposed to mixing *war* measures with our affairs—we were then at peace and a calm was all
important to draw immigration to the country.   At that time no
important fundamental or permanent right or principle was attacked.   I was therefore for *peace in full,* no half way measures.
I acquiesced in some, but reluctantly as is well known . . .
Now our position is quite different—our *all* is at stake, it is even
a question of life or death . . . I now believe that our

[1]*The Texas Republican*, September 26, 1835.

[2]*Ibid.*

[3]To the committee of Matagorda, October 2, 1835, archives of Texas,
D 28; Circular, October 3, 1835, in *The Texas Republican*, October 10,
1835.   Brown, *History of Texas*, I, 358-363, Foote, *Texas and the Texans*,
II, 85-90; to Kerr and Alley, October 3, 1835.   Archives of Texas, D 27; to
the committee of Harrisburg, October 4, 1835, archives of Texas, D 25; to
the committee of Nacogdoches, October 4, 1835, in the *Telegraph and Texas
Register*, April 4, 1837, Brown, I, 353-354, and Foote, II, 84-85.

[4]Travis to Austin, September 22, 1835, Austin Papers; *Publications of
So. His. Assn.*, VI, 420-421.

rights are attacked and that war is our only remedy. I am therefore for *war in full, and* no half way measures.[1]

A letter of September 30 to Perry[2] shows that Austin realized that the present trouble might lead to independence: "The foundation of a govt. (perhaps of a nation) is to be sketched out—the dayly progress of events is to [be] watched over, and public sentiment kept from going too fast or too slow." But he did not yet believe that Texas was strong enough to stand alone. At the outbreak of hostilities (October 2) he was called to command the army, and from his camp at Salado, October 25, he wrote a memorandum to guide the action of the consultation which had been postponed to November 1. In his opinion it ought to issue a statement confirming the declaration of the recent municipal meetings in favor of the constitution of 1824; to declare Texas a state of the Mexican confederation, and organize a government with a provisional governor and lieutenant-governor; to retain provisionally the existing laws and constitution of Coahuila and Texas; to pledge the resources of the state for funds to maintain the war in defence of the federal system; to raise a small regular army and organize the militia; to make peace with the Indians, annul fraudulent land grants, and establish a messenger service. "Anything beyond this, like forming a new constitution &c would do harm, and possibly produce great confusion." He thought that if there had been "too much precipitation heretofore, it ought to be a lesson to avoid that error in future."[3] The substance of this was embodied by the consultation in the declaration of November 7.[4]

But Austin had no intention of sacrificing principle to expediency, and after seeing a copy of the decree of the Mexican Congress which on October 3 abolished the federal system he wrote a very strong letter to the provisional government. The volunteers at Bexar were fighting, he said, to sustain the constitution of 1824, but if the decree of October 3 were carried into effect "and a central and despotic government established where all authority is to

[1]Austin to McKinney, September 27, 1835. Austin Papers.
[2]Austin Papers.
[3]Archives of Texas, Records in Department of State, Vol. 3, pp. 24-25.
[4]For this declaration see *Journals* of the Consultation, 21-22; THE QUARTERLY, VI, 280-281.

be concentrated in one person or in a few persons in the City of Mexico, sustained by military and ecclesiastical power, the volunteer army will also in that event do their duty to their country—to the cause of Liberty and themselves, as honor, patriotism, and the first law of nature may require." Certainly a people have the right to change their government, but it must be done legally and constitutionally, otherwise they cannot force a portion of the people who oppose it to accept the change.

However necessary then the basis established by the decree of 3d· of October may be to prevent civil wars and anarchy in other parts of Mexico, it is attempted to be effected by force and unconstitutional means. However beneficial it may be to some parts of Mexico, it would be ruinous to Texas. . . . if carried into effect, [it] evidently leaves no remedy for Texas but resistance, secession from Mexico and a direct resort to natural right.

Concerning his own position he said:

I have labored for years to unite Texas permanently to the Mexican confederation by separating its local government and internal administration so far as practicable from every other part of Mexico, and placing it in the hands of the people of Texas, who are certainly best acquainted with their own local wants and could best harmonize in legislating for them. . . . This country must either be a state of the Mexican confederation or must separate in toto as an independent community or seek protection from some power that recognizes the principles of self government. I can see no remedy between one of these three positions and total ruin.[1]

On December 3 at the request of D. C. Barrett, a member of the provisional government, Austin prepared a lengthy opinion on the subject of a new and more completely representative convention. He thought that one should meet as soon as possible to adopt a more definite position than that defined by the declaration of November 7;[2] the Texans should declare unequivocally either for the constitution of 1824 or for absolute independence, so that

---

[1] Archives of Texas, Records Department of State, Vol. 3, pp. 159-164, *passim.*

[2] In a letter of December 22 he explained that his chief objection to the declaration of November 7 was that it did not in plain terms declare Texas a Mexican state.

no doubt could remain of their real intentions. He still favored the former of these positions in the hope of drawing the Mexican Liberals to their assistance;[1] and his opinion was strengthened and given great weight by the fact that Captain Julian Miracle was then at San Felipe asking the intentions of the Texans and promising cooperation by the Liberals of Tamaulipas and Nuevo León if their object was to uphold the constitution of 1824.[2] Austin helped to draft a statement giving the proper assurances to Miracle, and on the 11th wrote to the president of the general council urging the adoption of a constitution and the organization of a permanent government "in conformity with the Declaration of 7 November last, especially with the 5th article,[3] and without making any change in the principles of that declaration." This, he thought, could be done only by a new convention elected on the basis of equal representation.[4]

Immediately after writing this letter Austin left San Felipe for Velasco whence he was to embark as one of three commissioners to enlist sympathy and raise funds for Texas in the United States. On his way he met Colonel Mexia who was returning from his disastrous expedition to Tampico and who still had great plans for the overthrow of Santa Anna and the restoration of republi-- canism. He showed Austin a number of letters from important persons in Mexico who promised aid, and Austin became more confident that the November declaration outlined the proper policy for Texas. From Columbia he wrote to the provisional government on December 14,[5]

I am more and more convinced every day, and especially, on calm

[1]Archives of Texas, Records Department of State, Vol. 3, pp. 157-159. This copy is dated December 2, but Barrett's letter and the rough draft of Austin's reply, which are in Austin Papers, are dated the 3d.

[2]See report of information given by Miracle, December 5, 1835, Archives of Texas, State Library; THE QUARTERLY, V, 299-300.

[3]This article reads, "Fifth, That they hold it to be their right, during the disorganization of the federal system and reign of despotism, to withdraw from the Union, to establish an independent government, or to adopt such measures as they may deem best calculated to protect their rights and liberties; but that they will continue faithful to the Mexican government so long as that nation is governed by the constitution and laws that were formed for the government of the political association."

[4]Austin to General Council, December 11, 1835. MS., Texas State Library.

[5]MS., Texas State Library.

reflection during a solitary ride down here, that the political position of Texas should continue as established by the declaration of 7th Novr. last. This declaration secures to Texas *everything*, and without any hazard, for it satisfies the federal party, and is sufficient to secure their support and co-operation. Should the federal system fall, the 5th article is a declaration of independence as a matter of course.

A change to the basis of independence now might create an impression of indecision and unstableness abroad and would certainly forfeit the support of the Federalists. "Texas ought therefore to adhere rigidly and firmly to the declaration of 7 Novr. and the public acts should correspond with it, in *words* and in object." From Velasco, a week later, he wrote another extremely interesting letter which deserves quotation in full.

Velasco Deer. 22. 1835.

The best interest of Texas I think requires that the war should be kept out of this country and beyond the Rio Grande. On this principle I was in favor of fitting out Col Gonzales and did every thing I could to do so. I was, and am in favor of giving to Genl. Mexia and his men what aid we could, and generally of affording assistance to the federal party in the interior by such *auxiliary* forces as we could spare. I have been and am opposed to any measures that will give the general govt. in Mexico any foundation to say that the Texas war, is purely a national war against foreigners and foreign invaders—In short I have thought, and still think that Texas should rigidly adhere to the leading principles of the declaration of 7 Novr. last. By so doing we preserve our character for consistency and good faith.

I will here observe, that in my communication to the provisional govt. of 2d. instant recommending the convocation of a convention on the basis of equal representation, I objected to the declaration of 7 Novr. as being liable to [mis]construction. Perhaps I ought to state the extent and nature of my objection—it is this—The declaration does not declare Texas to be a state of the Mexican confederation, which I think it ought to have done, subject however to all the other provisions and principles established in it—- This would have given a fixed and definite character to the political position of Texas and concentrated public opinion, and at the same time left her the option of reuniting with Mexico or not hereafter, according as the federal constitution when reestablished conformed or not to the republican principles of the federal system, for it is to be remembered that the declaration of 7 Novr. does not adhere to all the anti-republican features and defects of the constitution of 1824, it only adheres to its *republican principles* and to the federal system.

It is well known that the object of the federal party of Mexico at this time is to reform the constitution of 1824 so as to expunge all its anti-republican principles. Our declaration of 7 Novr. in this respect is therefore in strict conformity with the basis on which the federal party are acting.

But it is objected that Texas cannot declare herself a "state of the Mexican confederation, unless she does so under the constitution of 1824 with all its defects &c. To this I answer, that, the disposition of the social compact and the present political situation of all Mexico, gives to Texas the right of declaring herself an independent community—This being the case she certainly has the right to do much less, that is, to say she will continue united with the Mexican confederation, provided the federal party succeed in reestablishing the federal system on truly republican principles, free from the defects of the constitution of 1824, at the same time offering her aid to that party to effect this object.

As to independence—I think it will strengthen the cause of Texas to show that we have *legal* and *equitable* and just grounds to declare independence, and under this view I touched upon this subject in my communication to the provisional Govt. of the 30th ultimo. But I also think that it will weaken Texas, and expose the old settlers and men of property in this country to much risk, to make such a declaration at this time, and under the present circumstances, for the reason that it will turn all parties in Mexico against us—bring back the war to our own doors, which is now removed from Texas by the fall of Bexar, and compel the people to seek aid at any sacrifice—I do not think it necessary to run any such risk, for the natural current of events will soon regulate everything. A large portion of the Mexicans are determined to be free, if they succeed, Texas will participate as a state in conformity with the declaration of 7 Novr.—if they fail, Texas can at any time resort to her natural rights.

[A paragraph here omitted speaks of the arrival of volunteers from the United States, and advises the formation of "a ·federal auxiliary army."]

I write this letter as a citizen of Texas, and not as a Commissioner—I give my opinions frankly and refer you to Col. Fannin for a farther explanation of them.   .   .   .

Respectfully
Your Obt. Servt.

S. F. Austin.

To the Provisional Government
   of Texas.[1]

---

[1]MS., Texas State Library.

This is Austin's final word before leaving Texas. It is certainly distinctly pronounced in favor of the November declaration; but notice carefully that adherence to Mexico is based on a very definite condition—namely, the maintenance of democratic government with considerable local power in the states, of which Texas must be one in its own right. The Mexican Liberals were, in fact, a broken reed, and when Austin wrote this letter most members of the provisional government were beginning to realize it. By the middle of January the hope of assistance from them had been abandoned.[1]

The first expression that I have found from Austin after his arrival in New Orleans is a letter of January 7, 1836, to General Sam Houston.[2] In this he said that he was now in favor of an immediate declaration of independence; he had felt when he left Texas that it was premature to stir that question because it would at once give the war a national, racial character, and he was not sure that the Texans would be sustained (presumably by the people of the United States). He now knew that they could get all the aid that was needed; moreover, he had not only not heard of any movement on the part of the Federalists to assist them, but rather that all parties were united against them. The provisional government might have some cause for encouragement of which he did not know, but in the face of such information as he had before him he was for a declaration of independence. If his position had hitherto been disingenuous the first two paragraphs of this letter afford an ample justification:

In all our Texas affairs, as you are well apprised, I have felt it to be my duty to be very cautious in involving the pioneers and actual settlers of that country, by any act of mine, until I was fully and clearly convinced of its necessity, and of the capabilities of our resources to·sustain it. Hence it is that I have been censured by some for being over cautious. Where the fate of a whole people is in question, it is difficult to be over cautious, or to be too prudent.

Besides these general considerations, there are others which ought to have weight with me individually. I have been, either directly or indirectly, the cause of drawing many families to Texas, also

[1]See THE QUARTERLY, IX, 246-247.
[2]Foote, *Texas and the Texans*, II, 194-196.

the situation and circumstances in which I have been placed have given considerable weight to my opinions. This has thrown a heavy responsibility upon me—so much so, that I have considered it to be my *duty* to be prudent, and even to control my own impulses and feelings: these have long been impatient under the state of things which has existed in Texas, and in favour of a speedy and *radical change.* But I have never approved of the course of forestalling public opinion, by party or partial meetings or by management of any kind. The true course is to lay *facts* before the people and let them judge for themselves. I have endeavoured to pursue this course. . . .

Henceforth, having finally laid his course, Austin looked not backward.[1] He did not escape contemporary criticism and charges of vacillation, for R. R. Royall wrote: "I must acknowledge he changes with great rapidity. If he could send us the men, money, and provisions with half as much rapidity we could Declare for any policy we pleased and maintain it."[2] While his old friend Thomas F. McKinney wrote him that they must at last part company in politics; "I am now fully convinced that you cannot be anything else but an injury to your country when you have influence."[3] But with the mass of the people his opinion carried weight, and did much to unite them in favor of that declaration of independence which the convention adopted on March 2, 1836.

Local students of Texas history have usually resented any imputation that Austin was disloyal to Mexico, but from the foregoing study it appears that his guiding motive was fidelity to Texas rather than to Mexico. For a long time he perceived in loyalty to Mexico the true interest of Texas—and it is pleasant to believe that he would have been glad to have it always so,[4]—but when few intelligent observers thought this longer possible, and Austin himself became convinced of it, he turned the whole weight

[1] See among others his letters of January 10, 14, 16, 18, 21, February 18, March 3, April 4, etc., etc., in Austin Papers and Texas State Library.

[2] Royall to President of General Council, January 27, 1836. MS., Texas State Library.

[3] McKinney to Austin, February 22, 1836. Austin Papers.

[4] Study his letter of December 22, 1835, to the provisional government: "A large portion of the Mexicans are determined to be free, if they succeed, Texas will participate as a state in conformity with the declaration of 7 Novr.—if they fail, Texas can at any time resort to her natural rights." See page 281 above.

of his influence to uniting the people in opposition to the government. He could not have prevented the Texas revolution if he had tried, because Santa Anna in 1835 was determined upon measures to which the Texans would not have submitted; he did not hasten it because the Mexican troops that precipitated the revolution were already in the country when he returned from his long detention in Mexico; what he did do was to prepare the people in some degree to meet the inevitable, approaching danger. The clash of arms necessitated the organization of a provisional government in Texas, and by Austin's influence it issued a declaration on November 7, 1835, in favor of the Mexican constitution of 1824. Probably loyalty to Mexico not less than expediency for Texas dictated this measure. There is grave doubt whether at that time the majority of the Texans would have acquiesced in a declaration of independence, and moreover, many Mexican Republicans were opposed to Santa Anna's centralization of the government and a declaration such as that of November 7 might draw their support to Texas; if they won, and succeeded in maintaining a republican government, the Texans would be content. During the winter, however, it became increasingly evident that help was not to be expected from the Mexican Liberals; the public tone hardened; and Austin, with William H. Wharton and Branch T. Archer, was sent to the United States to negotiate a loan and solicit assistance. At New Orleans he found capitalists unwilling to advance money unless Texas would declare independence. The declaration of November 7 had failed to bring Mexican support, and repelled the Americans. The time had clearly arrived to sever Texas in its own interest from the Mexican system, and from January, 1836, until March 2 Austin was one of the most outspoken advocates of independence.

REMINISCENCES OF THE TEXAS REVOLUTION[1]

ANDREW A. BOYLE

On the seventh day of January, 1836, at San Patricio de las Nueces, I enlisted in Captain Westover's battery (the first company of regular artillery in the Texas army). Our command was soon after ordered to Goliad, where it was incorporated with the forces commanded by Colonel Fannin. Colonels Bowie and Crockett,[2] then in command of the Alamo, sent a courier to Colonel Fannin in the latter part of February, asking him for reinforcements. A hundred men[3] were at once detailed, and had crossed the San Antonio river on their way to the assistance of the doomed garrison, when they were recalled on account of a report brought in by a scout named "Comanche," of the advance of the Mexican army under General Urrea, toward San Patricio. The main body of the enemy, under Santa Ana, had marched directly from Laredo upon San Antonio. Our commander, by the advice of "Comanche," determined to march to San Patricio, leaving one company in garrison at Goliad. The character of the scout was notoriously bad, and Colonel Fannin was informed of the fact, but gave no heed to the warning, although two of us volunteered to go to San Patricio and ascertain the truth of the report. Three days' rations were distributed, and everything was in readiness to commence the march the next morning, when an American named

[1]These recollections of the Texas revolution were dictated by Andrew A. Boyle in 1870, just before his death, to his daughter, Mrs. W. H. Workman. For the manuscript THE QUARTERLY is indebted to his granddaughter, Miss Gertrude Dardin Workman. Although Mr. Boyle's memory of details was inaccurate, the paper is important in two particulars: (1) it adds another witness to the list of Texan participants who have unanimously testified that Fannin did not surrender at discretion, as General Urrea claimed, and (2) it gives a first hand account of the execution of the wounded prisoners at Goliad.

[2]The regulars at the Alamo were commanded by Travis, the volunteers by Bowie. Crockett held no official position.

[3]Contemporary statements place this number between three and four hundred men. See letters of Captain John Sowers Brooks (THE QUARTERLY, IX, 179, 181, 183, 191) and Dr. Bernard's Journal in *A Comprehensive History of Texas*, 1, 616.

Ayres arrived from the Old Mission, some fifteen miles distant in the direction of San Patricio, and brought reliable news of the arrival of the Mexicans at that place, and of their maltreating all Americans there, bearing themselves with special insolence toward the women. Colonel Fannin immediately despatched Captain King with a party of twenty men to remove all American women and children to our fort. Captain King was surrounded by a superior force of the enemy, but cut his way through them and retreated to the Old Mission Church, from which point he sent a messenger to Colonel Fannin, stating his position and asking for reinforcements. Fannin sent Colonel Ward, with his Georgia Battalion, to King's assistance. On Ward's arrival at the Mission Church, a difference of opinion arose as to who should command the whole force. Not being able to come to any agreement, they separated; Ward retreating in a southeasterly direction for some distance, and then striking for the San Antonio river with the intention of joining us. King got out of the church, and after a skirmish with the Mexicans, retreated on the direct road to Goliad. He and his men were taken prisoners, tied together with rawhide, and shot immediately. We heard of the surrender and killing of King and his men, and the retreat of Colonel Ward in the direction above mentioned, and were in daily expectation of Ward's command arriving at Goliad. About the 8th or 9th of March we heard of the fall of the Alamo and the killing of Colonels Bowie and Crockett and all their men. Colonels Bowie and Crockett having refused all propositions for surrender or capitulation, the garrison held out until reduced to seven men, who asked for quarter and were refused.[1] On the 17th of March the enemy appeared on the opposite side of the river. We sent over a skirmishing party of one company (under Captain Shackelford's command, I think), who had an engagement with the enemy, we watching from the ramparts with the most intense anxiety.[2] They were recalled by Colonel Fannin, after the enemy's retreat to the Old Mission Church.

---

[1] Ramón Martinez Caro, Santa Anna's secretary, says (*Verdadera Idea de la primera Compaña de Tejas*, etc., 11) that after the Alamo was taken five men who had hidden themselves during the action surrendered to General Castrillon, but were shot by Santa Anna's order.

[2] Compare Bernard's account of this skirmish, which he dates March 18. *A Comprehensive History of Texas*, I, 619-620.

On the following day the enemy appeared in force at the same place, and orders were given by Colonel Fannin to bake bread sufficient for several days, and carry dried beef sufficient for the same length of time. The guns were taken down from the bastions, and orders were also given to be ready to march before daylight in the morning. From cause unknown to me, we did not evacuate the fort until between 8 and 9 o'clock next morning. We marched down the river and crossed at a ford below, which was effected without difficulty. Our object in crossing at the lower instead of the upper ford in front of the Old Mission, was to avoid, if possible, an action with the enemy (he outnumbering us at least six to one), and to get into the interior of Texas and join Houston's army. We continued our march until we crossed a creek called Manawee [Manahuilla], distant from the crossing about three miles. We traveled slowly, our cannon and baggage wagons being drawn by oxen. A halt was called and we ate some breakfast.

After breakfast, the march was continued; nothing new transpiring until about half past twelve o'clock; the Mexican army was then descried on our left and rear; their cavalry approached us rapidly, seemingly with the intention of cutting us off from the timber of the Colet creek; they fired a few shots at us, when Colonel Fannin exclaimed (I was standing close by him at the time), "that's the signal for battle; I won't retreat another foot." We then unlimbered our pieces, being six in number, formed ourselves into a hollow square, placing the baggage wagons, hospital wagon and magazine in the centre; we remained in this position five or ten minutes, when Colonel Fannin, seeing clearly the main object of the enemy was to cut us off from the timber, ordered us to limber up again and continue the march. We left the road, marching in an oblique direction to the left toward the nearest timber; when within as well as I can recollect, three-quarters or one mile of the timber, the enemy's infantry overtook us and we were obliged to halt. We formed as previously, our little force then not numbering more than 311 men, maintained an action from half past one o'clock, P. M., and fought until near dark, when the enemy retreated, leaving twenty-five of us killed and wounded. I had been shot in the right leg at about halt past three in the afternoon. Our real trouble commenced after the retreat of the enemy, and arose principally from the want of water, from which the wounded especially suffered severely. A few of our men dug for water while the rest were throwing up intrenchments, as we expected to renew the battle on the following day. In the fight just finished we had killed our oxen and used the carcasses for breastworks. I lay that night near Colonel Fannin, who had been slightly wounded in the thigh. I remember his good-naturedly offering me his "good leg for a pillow." In the morning the Mexicans again advanced, largely reinforced from General Santa Ana's division, and well supplied with artillery. After firing a few round shot, all of which passed over our heads, they hoisted a white flag, which we answered. A consultation of officers was held, at which it was concluded to capitulate, as preferable to attempting to prolong a hopeless struggle. Our wounded men were on our hands, and suffering; we had no means of caring for them, and Colonel Fannin strongly expressed his determination not to abandon them. Two officers from each army then met in parley and agreed upon articles of capitulation, guaranteeing our lives and personal property. We agreed to give up all government property in our possession, and to remain prisoners of war until honorably exchanged or sent to the United States, upon parole never to return to Texas. These articles were signed by both parties, and the surrender was completed. Those of our command able to march were at once taken to Goliad, the wounded waiting two or three days for Mexican carts. Our sufferings were intense, on account of the heat of the sun, thirst, and want of medical attendance. Upon our arrival at Goliad we—the wounded—were placed in the hospital; the rest of the command was guarded in the yard of the fort. Just one week after the surrender, all the wounded men were marched out of the fort in separate divisions and shot. Soon after, a Mexican officer came into the hospital, and ordered me to tell all those able to walk to go outside. I interpreted for him, and the men commenced gathering up their blankets. In the meantime, four Mexican soldiers came in and began to carry out those who were too severely wounded to walk. I was assisted by two comrades who were but slightly wounded. As we passed the door, an officer told me we were all to be shot. This I told the men. The wounded were placed in the corner of the yard upon which the church door fronts. A company of soldiers formed in front of us and loaded their pieces with ball cartridge. Then a file of men under a corporal took two of our number, marched them out toward the company, and after bandaging their eyes, made them lie with their faces to the ground, after which, placing the muzzles close to their heads, they shot them as they lay. At this time an officer, apparently of distinction, came into the yard and asked in a loud voice, in English, whether any one named Boyle was there or not. I was near him as he entered, and answered at once. He then ordered an officer to take me to the officers' hospital and have my wound attended to, saying that he would call upon me there. When I arrived at the hospital the Mexican officers seemed kindly disposed to me, and gave me a pair of "armas de pelo" to lie on. Mr. Brooks, Aid to Colonel Fannin, was there at the time, with his thigh badly shattered near the hip. I found him entirely ignorant of what had been going on. Upon being informed he said, "I suppose it will be our turn next." In less than five minutes four Mexicans carried him out, cot and all, placed him in the street not fifteen feet from the door, in a position in which I could not avoid seeing him, and there shot him.[1] His body was instantly rifled of his gold watch, stripped, and thrown into a pit at the side of the street. Colonel Ward and his command, who had been captured between the Lavaca and Navidad rivers a few days after our surrender, were also shot. The whole number of men thus barbarously executed was, according to Mexican report, four hundred and seventeen.[2]

A few hours after the murder of Mr. Brooks, the officer who had asked for me in the yard came into the hospital. Addressing me in English he said: "Make your mind easy, Sir; your life is spared." I asked if I might inquire the name of the person to whom I was indebted for my life. "Certainly," said he, "my name is General Francisco Garay, second in command of Urrea's division." He had taken my name and description from my sister,

[1] This account of Brooks's death agrees exactly with that of Doctors Shackleford and Field. THE QUARTERLY, IX, 196-198.

[2] The real number seems to have been between three hundred and twenty and three hundred and thirty. See Bancroft, *North Mexican States and Texas*, II, 235, note 70.

Mary, at whose house he had been quartered while his division occupied San Patricio, and by whom and my brother Roderick he
had been kindly treated. She and my brother had refused all re-
muneration from him, only asking that if I should ever fall into
his hands I should be kindly treated. The General informed me
that he himself was on the eve of departure to join General Urrea,
but that he had given orders to General Portillo, commandant of
the garrison, to furnish me a passport whenever I should call for it.
With this he took his leave. The passport was obtained without
difficulty in pursuance of the order given by General Garay, and I
secured passage in an ox-cart to the Mission and thence to San
Patricio, where I remained. We knew nothing of the battle of
San Jacinto until about the 28th of April, although we had noticed
Mexican troops traveling towards the Rio Grande. A dragoon
rode up one day and asked me to sell him two bits' worth of dried
meat; I offered to give him all the meat he might want if he would
answer a few questions. He consented, and I learned for the first
time that a battle had been fought on the 21st near San Jacinto
Creek, and that the result had been disastrous to the invading army;
that General Santa Ana had been taken prisoner, and that the
Americans had seemed inclined to give no quarter, charging with
the cry of "Alamo and Fannin." The remains of the Mexican
forces engaged, as well as General Urrea's division, which had been
stationed at Brazoria, were in full retreat. The effect of such glad
news upon my feelings may be imagined. General Garay arrived
a few days afterwards, and called to see us as he passed hastily
through town. At his request, I accompanied him to Matamoras.
Upon arriving there, he explained that stringent orders had been
given to the effect that no American, who had been at any time a
prisoner in Mexican hands, should be suffered to remain in Texas.
He also informed me that all prisoners were to be closely confined,
but that he would allow me the freedom of the city, upon my
giving my parole not to attempt to escape. About three weeks
afterward, the General invited me to accompany him to the City
of Mexico, stating that I should no longer be considered as a prisoner, in case I accepted his offer, which was accompanied with the
most profuse offers of friendship and assistance. Notwithstanding
the gratitude which I naturally felt toward the preserver of my

own life, I was compelled to decline, on account of my anxiety to see my relatives in the United States. At my urgent solicitation, General Garay then released me from my parole, and left me free to control my own movements. I concluded to start on foot for Brazos Santiago, but experienced great difficulty in procuring from the alcalde the necesary permit to leave the city. I was afraid to apply to him directly, and all the American and Irish residents strongly remonstrated against my doing so. I finally succeeded in passing myself as the son of an old Irishman who had obtained a passport for New Orleans, and had myself included in it; afterwards I had a separate document made out for myself. The next day I took passage on a brig at Brazos Santiago, and six days after, landed at New Orleans. I at once visited the Texas Consul in that city, Mr. Bryan,[1] but found that he could do for me nothing more than to furnish a free pass to Texas. Being out of money and in rags, I was compelled to seek employment. I engaged with a painter for two dollars and a half a day, and went to work painting St. Mary's Market, though I had never painted except in water colors. I worked eleven days, at the expiration of which time I drew my money, purchased some clothes, and accepted Mr. Bryan's offer. He procured me passage on a schooner for the mouth of the Brazos river, where I landed in a few days. General Burnet, the first President of the Republic of Texas, then living at Velasco, gave me a letter to General Rusk, at that time commanding the army on the Guadalupe River. I walked to General Rusk's camp, a distance of a hundred and fifty miles, in five days. He was in daily expectation of the advance of the Mexicans, but excused me, on account of my impaired health, from further service in the army. I had a severe attack of fever and ague in Victoria, where General Rusk's head-quarters were. As soon as I recovered, I went to Columbia, then the seat of government, and obtained a passport for New Orleans.

Los Angeles, December 15th, 1870.

---

[1]Bryan was not officially a consul, because at that time the United States had not recognized the independence of Texas, but he discharged many of the duties of a consul.

THE BEXAR AND DAWSON PRISONERS

EDITED BY E. W. WINKLER

The three accounts of the capture and imprisonment of the Bexar and Dawson prisoners presented below, it is believed, have not been printed before. They appear to have been written independently of each other. The earliest to be completed is Neill's, dated January 29, 1843. Hutchinson's Diary terminates July 10, 1843. William E. Jones wrote his narrative, it is supposed, at the request of Ex-President Lamar, on February 1, 1844. None of the accounts embraces the entire period of the captivity of these prisoners. Neill escaped December 14, 1842. Hutchinson and Jones were liberated March 29, 1843. The majority of the prisoners remained in capitivity at Perote until March 23, 1844. Some facts concerning them are narrated by Thomas J. Green (*Journal of the Texian Expedition against Mier*). Green was their fellow prisoner at Perote from March 25, 1843, until he effected his escape on July 2 following. Additional items may be gleaned from William Preston Stapp (*Prisoners of Perote*). Stapp was confined at Perote from September 21, 1843, until May 14, 1844. Two of the Dawson prisoners, Joseph C. Robinson and Milvern Harrell, have written brief accounts of their captivity. Robinson's account appeared in the *Texas Monument* (La Grange,) of August 27 and September 3 and 10, 1851, and should be distinguished from his account of Dawson's massacre, which has been frequently printed. Harrell's reminiscences were printed in the *Dallas News,* June 16, 1907.

The fate of the Bexar Prisoners was a peculiarly severe one. Among them were men of talent and high respectability. Many were heads of families, and away from home when made prisoners. None anticipated or had prepared for the captivity into which he was dragged. They have not received the attention in the past that their case merits. The Santa Fé expedition and the Mier expedition had each its chronicler; the sufferings of those who took part in them are well known. The Santa Fé prisoners were taken in December, 1841, and released in June, 1842; the

Mier prisoners surrendered December 26, 1842, and remained in confinement until September, 1844. The Bexar prisoners suffered the same hardships and endured a period of captivity only two months shorter than that undergone by the Mier prisoners. When they were relased it was upon their oath that they would not bear arms again in the contest between Texas and Mexico.

Their case is stated as follows by one of the Mier prisoners: "An unoffending and peaceable class of citizens, engaged in the prosecution of civil and domestic pursuits, they had been surprised in their distant homes by a cowardly and marauding banditti, and torn from their families and fireside-altars to grace the triumph or their craven captor. Since they have been detained by the dictator in his dungeons for sixteen months, without other warrant than his own love of tyranny and inhumanity. For every pound of fetters we wore, a Mexican soldier's life had already atoned. But no widow or orphan's wail appealed to the vengeance of their country against a solitary individual of this unfortunate corps. They had scarcely resisted when assailed, been submissive and subordinate on their march, and during their imprisonment, and yet had been made to endure enormities which the pen recoils from inditing." (Stapp, *Prisoners of Perote,* 122.)

The fact that some of Captain Dawson's men were made prisoners is almost forgotten. The news of the capture of San Antonio by General Woll was a call for the gathering of companies of frontiersmen in the valleys of the Guadalupe and the Colorado. They united under the leadership of Colonel Caldwell, "Old Paint," who had only recently returned from imprisonment in Mexico, having been a member of the Santa Fé expedition. He planned to punish the Mexican invader and to liberate the Texan prisoners at San Antonio. On Sunday, September 18, General Woll was led to attack the Texans in their position on the Salado, and was repulsed with severe loss. Unfortunately, about the time the Mexican force was withdrawing, Captain Dawson with his company from Fayette county came upon the Mexicans on the side farthest from Colonel Caldwell's position. The company was entrapped; two-thirds of their number were slain, fifteen made prisoners, and only two escaped. From what they saw of the enemy's vengeance those who escaped concluded that nearly if not quite all were killed.   Their reports were the first to be received, and have been followed by some of the later writers.

I.   HUTCHINSON'S DIARY.[1]

Monday Sep 5, 1842 Opened the District Court of Bexar   No invasion expected.   The third treaty between England and Texas having been ratified stipulating intervention for the recognition of Texas by Mexico; and the U. States government having requested that of Texas to suspend hostilities against Mexico with a view to its cooperation—peace was believed inevitable.

Friday 9.   Late at night Antonio Parez warned John W Smith in confidence of the approach of 1500 Mexicans

Saturday 10.   A public meeting—myself presiding—report discussed—and generally discredited.   The Mexican citizens—100 under Salvador Flores—and the Americans 75 under C. Johnson —formed and appointed Hays to command the whole.   Hays and six[2] others started as scouts, directing us to remain until some one or more returned.   The Mexicans sent out three[3] commissioners.

[1]Anderson Hutchinson was born April 7, 1798, in Greenbrier county, Virginia.   On attaining to manhood he removed to Knoxville, Tennessee, where he read law and obtained a license to practice.   He was located for some time at Huntsville, Alabama, and then removed to Mississippi and formed a partnership with H. S. Foote.   He followed his profession in Mississippi about ten years, and shortly before his removal published in association with Volney E. Howard, in 1840, a digest of the laws of Mississippi.   In the fall of 1840 he opened a law office in the City of Austin.   He was elected judge of the fourth judicial district in January, 1841.   By September, 1842, he had prepared a Texas code, which he purposed to submit to the seventh congress for approval, but the inroads of the Mexicans into Texas during this year frustrated his plan.   He had to flee from San Antonio in March, 1842, on account of Vasquez' raid, and his family lost their piano and most of their clothing.   His capture at San Antonio in September, 1842, by General Woll, and his seven months' captivity in Mexico is the subject of the Diary.   Judge Hutchinson died in Mississippi in 1853.
   The diary was kept in a small note book, 4¼ by 7¼ inches in size, and bound in limp leather, with flap and band for fastening.   The writing fills 43 pages.   The original Diary is in the Texas State Library; it was purchased in October, 1909.

[2]In a letter to the Secretary of War, dated Seguin, 12 Sept. 1842, Hays says he was accompanied by five men.—*Appendix to House Journal*, 7 Tex. Cong., 16.

[3]In a letter to the editor of the *Telegraph*, dated 14 Dec. 1842, A. Miskel gives the names of two of the Mexican commissioners, Don Domingo Bustillo and Don Ignacio Chavez.—*Telegraph and Texas Register*, 21 Dec., 1842.

Late in the evening one of the Mexican comrs reported 100 horses some distance north of the Presidio road. These were believed to be the whole force of a marrauding band.

Sunday 11th. at break of day and under a dense fog Gen Woll advanced into the military square firing a gun and with music in front, having surrounded the town with his cavalry and posted Cordova and his Cherokees at the passes to the alamo. Awakened by the gun I hastened from Callaghan's, where I slept on my arms, to Maverick's corner, the point where Johnson's company were stationed and which had been hastily fortified the day preceding. No object could be seen; but Johnson ordered his men to fire toward the music down the street to Callaghan's house. Flores' company also fired. At this moment Manshaca, who was the only Mexican in our company, cried out that our d—d Mexican friends had retreated. Woll's infantry and artillery opened a heavy discharge on Mavrick's corner—and he endeavored to enter the government square; but a destructive fire from our corner threw his column into disorder and it retired and took shelter behind the eastern line of the military square. Johnson ordered his son to open the back and front doors of his house on the north front of the government square with a view to charge through it upon the artillery—and had given the proposition to charge—when a white flag was seen followed by Corasco—who stated that Woll with 2000, the van of a large army, had invested the place and that he gave us an half hour to treat for surrender. Jones, Maverick, Van Ness and Peterson were sent to him as Comrs. They agreed to surrender as prisoners of war—our lives and property (arms excepted) to be spared and secured. Informed of the mistake under which we had resisted, he admitted he was satisfied of it, and but for the mischief done—(some 30 killed and wounded) he would permit us to disperse, but that we should be treated as gentlemen. Fifty-five surrendered. Callaghan, McClellan, Johnson's son and Manchaca were released before the 15th.[1] The Mexican company was not even taken as prisoners, but permitted to return to their houses. On the day previous a courier was dispatched to the Guadalupe

[1]Cf. with date under which this entry is made.

with a letter drawn by me and signed by some three others requesting 110 men to our aid.[1]

Sep. 12.   Miller's letter tendering dept of State—not recd.[2]

Sep 13.   An interview with Gen Woll of some two hours duration at his quarters.   He received me with much courtesy.   Spoke of his own personal history as connected with the campaign into Texas in '35-6—stated he had convinced Santa Anna of the fatal impropriety of the order to shoot Fannin and his men; but the order had departed and could not be recalled—that now, since the recognition of Texas by other nations, the war would be conducted in all things according to the usages of civilized warfare—that Houston had slandered him in his letter to Santa Anna etc—that in regard to the mistake alledged by us he was satisfied we did not expect an invading army, because he had rendered it impossible for us to discover his approach by opening for himself a road thro' the wilderness north of the Presidio road.   I claimed release as a civil officer.   He said he would write to Gen Reyes, recommending my discharge—and that on my way to San Fernando I should be treated with every attention and kindness suitable to my office. He said repeatedly he had no doubt of my release by Gen Reyes, whom he stated had full power to do so as the commander of the Northern Army of Operation.   He said he would write for my release to Gen Santa Anna also.

Sep 14th   W. D. Miller's 2d letter asking me to take the State Department.[3]

Sep 15.   Thursday.   Left San Antonio under a strong guard commanded by Cap Posas, an ignorant man who had risen from the ranks after near 30 years' service.   On passing the window occupied by Gen: Woll he called to me to ride up.   He, in English, before the crowd that filled the square, assured me he *had written*

[1]This letter is printed in *Appendix to House Journal,* 7 Tex. Cong., 18, 19.

[2]This entry is written with pen and ink different from that used in the body of the Diary. The entry appears to have been made at a later date.

[3]This entry is written in the margin opposite the one above. Cf. note 2 above.

W. D. Miller was President Houston's private secretary. Anson Jones was nominally secretary of state, but he had been absent from the office since April.

on my behalf as he had promised and that he had sent along a confidential officer to see that the prisoners should be well treated and myself in particular. Prior to leaving San Antonio I drew another letter, signed by myself and some three or four others, as a committee, addressed to the citizens on the Guadalupe and Colorado, informing them of our capture and the terms of surrender etc.[1] Camped 4 m. West of the town.

16th. Heard a salute fired at Bexar—[was] told it was to celebrate the battle of Tampico—marched 28 or 30 miles and camped on a hill on the right bank of the Modena.[2] A consultation:[3] but the proposition rejected; there being several of the company desirous to avail of the opportunity of being taken into Mexico— *there to remain!* Distrust prevailed—and multiplied its objects too unduly. If any ten had made the onset it would have been carried.

17th. Rested on the arroya Honda. Cap. Luis Vidal, the General's aid and the superintending officer, finding me exhausted, made a tent for me, gave me of his rice and assured me of his friendship. Reached the arroya Seco. 30 miles.

Sep 18. A few miles after starting, Cunningham fell from his horse. The fever contracted at Houston had assumed a congestive type. We insisted that Booker or McCay[4] should be left to attend him. Refused. He was buried on the Leona.[5] Camped this night on the right bank of the rio Frio. This day Woll attacked Caldwell on the Salado and was defeated. Bradley and 9 others captured in the afternoon.[6] 500 and artillery agt 53 in an open plain. all of the 53 killed except 13.[7] At San Antonio on the

[1]This letter is printed in *Appendix to House Journal*, 7 Tex. Cong., 20, 21, and in the *Telegraph and Texas Register*, 28 Sept. 1842. Cf. C. W. Peterson to Editor of *Telegraph*, 12 September, 1842, in *Telegraph and Texas Register*, 21 September, 1842.

[2]Medina.

[3]Apparently concerning a plan to escape.

[4]Physicians.

[5]Neill states that Cunningham died on September 19th. See page 320 below.

[6]Since Bradley's party did not join Hutchinson's party until October 9, it seems probable that the above entry was not made until that date or subsequently.

[7]Seventeen of Captain Dawson's company survived the battle. Alsey S. Miller and Henry G. Woods escaped, and fifteen were captured. For a list of the names of the captives, see page 319 below.

11th and in these affairs this day they lost in killed and wounded and otherwise near 400—as afterward ascertained. Camped on the rio Frio—right bank. 30 m

19th   At lake Espantosa. 25 m

20.   Crossed the Nueces. Camped in Chaperal plain 28 [miles]

21.   At Cueva creek. 25 m. Mrs. H. to Gen Terrell[1]

22.   Crossed Rio Bravo in two large canoes—probably those used by Woll in crossing at the same point. He was 9 days in crossing. We camped on the right bank in a coral! Lt. *Elihu Rodiriguez* assisted me in the passage—kind and generous—a warm hearted fellow that should be regarded and cherished by gentlemen all over the world.

Day clear—bathed in the river with Rodoriguez.

23.   Reached the Presidio Rio Grande—a town not so large as San Antonio about 6 m. below the crossing. It is built entirely of adobies.

On entering the village our ears were on each side pierced with the screams of the wives of the Presidiales whose husbands had fallen.

25th   Mrs H. left old Mrs. Jones'.[2]

27th.   We passed on to the village of Nava—going up the Rio Grande toward San Fernando—thro' a bountiful and rich plain, well watered. Supped with the alcalde Garcia.

28th.   About 12 oclock, noon, entered San Fernando—a town about the size of San Antonio de Bexar, but built of mud—the present head quarters of Major Genl Reyes. Here too we heard the cries of grief for husbands and friends slain in battle.

Octo 2.   Sunday.   Reyes came to our prison—received our verbal address—received also a statement of the facts of our resistance and surrender and thro Folac, his interpreter, promised to send the document to Santa Anna with his favorable recommendations. This Memorial was drawn by W. E. Jones and signed by him and Maverick, as the representatives of the crowd. Previously I had been taken to the house of Gen Cela, the Adjutant General (a Spaniard) to be entertained there during my (sojorn) at San

---

[1] Last five words in pen and ink that differ from those used in the body of the Diary. Cf. note 2, page 296.

[2] In regard to this entry, see note 2, page 296.

Fernando; but I became satisfied that the Memorial contained an able and clear statement—such as ought to have been prepared and given.

Oct 3   Letter of Terrell and Houston to Mrs. Hutchinson[1]

Oct 7.[2]   (Friday)   Being joined by Bradley and the nine[3]

[1]In regard to this entry, see note 2, page 296.

[2]A letter, unsigned, written by one of the prisoners at San Fernando on this date, is printed in the *Telegraph and Texas Register*, 23 Nov. 1842.

[3]For a list of the ten Dawson prisoners, see page 319 below. This number does not include the wounded of Captain Dawson's company who were too ill to travel and were with General Woll's army at this time. These wounded prisoners have been lost sight of by nearly all who have essayed to write of this period. In a letter, dated at Camp Leon [24] Nov. 1842, Memucan Hunt informed the Editor of the *Telegraph* that "four men who left here wounded attempted to make their escape on the 2nd instant, from the hospital at Presidio; two were retaken, and nothing as yet has been heard of the others. . . . Those who communicated this information left Presidio on the 7th." (*Telegraph and Texas Register*, 21 Dec. 1842.) One of the two recaptured prisoners, Milvern Harrell, gives the following account of events: "As we were still suffering from our wounds, we were placed in a house at the Presidio del Rio Grande, just across the river on the Mexican side. Here we were guarded and kept confined for two months. Finally we planned to make our escape, but gave it up, as we concluded that we could not cross the river. A Frenchman came in soon after, and telling him of the plans we had entertained, he said that crossing the river would be easy, as it was low at that season. Encouraged by this, we again determined upon escaping.

"Having noticed that the soldiers played cards a good deal, and satisfying ourselves that their guns were unloaded, one bright moonlight night, after the guard had passed the door, we slipped out and ran around the house toward the river. The ground was covered with rocks, and we fell several times. My uncle, Norman Woods, as he had not recovered from his wound, was easily retaken, but a man named Pattison, myself and McReady ran on. We did not go directly to the river, which was only a mile or two distant, but ran up stream for ten or twelve miles, reaching it about daylight. We looked for a shoally place to cross, as we thought there the water would be shallow. As Pattison was the eldest of the three, we followed his advice. He selected a place where the river was narrow, and bent in toward the Texas side. A sandbar lay out in the water a little distance, and a high bluff arose on the opposite side. After wading past the sandbar, Pattison suddenly stepped into deep water, and swimming forward called us to come on, that we could swim over. The water was icy cold, and we had been confined until we were weak. We had gone only a little distance when McReady called to us that he could go no further, and sank. Pattison and myself swam on. A jeans coat that Pattison had tied around him had slipped off, and he asked me to get it for him. I turned back for the coat, and taking it in my teeth, swam after him. On nearing the Texas bank we got into a swift current and were washed rapidly down stream. Pattison called out to me that he could go no further, but must drown, and sank almost immediately. By this time I was completely exhausted, and was helpless in the current. Thinking every second would be the last, I was suddenly washed upon a rock in the taken on the 18th Sep. we departed upon an official Diary for the city of Mexico. Gen Reyes embraced me saying he had written to S. A. for my release. Gen Cela the same etc. Cap: Vidal shed tears at leaving me.

☞On the day prior Van Ness, Fitzgerald and Hancock[1] were separated. Alas! the Santa Fé expedition.

river, and carried high upon it, the water being only about six inches over its surface. I stood up and stretched myself. It was sleeting now, and I was almost frozen. I decided that I could not reach the Texas side, and knowing that I would freeze where I was, I went back to the Mexican side of the river. There was a long smooth beach where I reached the bank, and I ran up and down it for some time to warm myself and to loosen my joints, which had become stiff from being in the water so long.

"Then leaving the river and going upon a hill to get my location, I saw a house in the distance, and went toward it. A Mexican, seeing me approaching, came down to meet me. When he drew nearer, I recognized him as a Mexican I had known at San Antonio, and with whom we had traded. He came up and taking off his overcoat threw it around me. I went up to the house with him, where he had a big, bright fire burning in the chimney. He would not let me go near it, but had me to sit down across the room from it, and would have me move up a little at a time. His wife brought in some hot coffee for me, and I thought it was the best I had ever tasted. After getting warm, I told them that I desired to lay down, as I was sleepy. A bed was prepared, and I slept from about 7 o'clock in the morning until 2 or 3 o'clock in the afternoon, and on awaking I saw four Mexican soldiers in the room.

"They had been scouring the country in search of us, and came to the house where I was. Of course they carried me back with them.

"Soon after this we left the Presidio for the City of Mexico. At Saltillo we were joined with the Mier prisoners and kept with them until we were liberated."—*Dallas Morning News,* June 16, 1907.

While the last sentence of Mr. Harrell's statement is true, it must not be forgotten that the principal officers of the Mier Expedition marched from Saltillo in a separate body a short distance in advance of the men. This circumstance prevented the participation of the officers in the attack on the guard at Salado, 11 February 1843. After the Mexican guard had been put to flight, about twenty Texans refused to join in the march homeward (Stapp, *Prisoners of Perote,* 59). Harrell was of this number because his uncle Norman Woods was too ill to undertake the journey and needed attention. The wounded Texans were left in the care of these "eccentric knights." The latter were marched toward the City of Mexico. They came up with the party of Texan officers at San Luis Potosi (Green. *Journal of the Texian Expedition against Mier,* 177). Some of the sick were left behind at this place (Stapp, 78), but Harrell proceeded with those accompanying the officers.

[1]George Van Ness, Archibald Fitzgerald, and Thomas Hancock were residents of San Antonio in 1841. They joined the Santa Fé expedition and were made prisoners. Van Ness was released 3 February 1842, "entirely through the influence of the Mexican Secretary of War and Marine, General Tornel." (Kendall, *Narrative of the Santa Fé Expedition,* I, 200.) Fitzgerald and Hancock were probably among those released in June, 1842. In that case, their release was conditioned on their signing

Wrote to Mrs. H. and Gen Foote etc.[1]

Gen Cela gave me a letter of favor to his female friend Dona Catalina Canal de Semarriego at San Miguel Ayenda of the 6th recommending me.

Lodged with the alcalde (Trevinio) at San Juan de Matas a hamlet in a rich irrigable plain. Rumors of a revolution—more rumor. Consulted.

8th. After a long day's march—slept in a bed of rocks—a severe norther. (A)

(A) About half of this days march was thro small hills perfectly barren. 25 miles.[2]

9th. After marching some 30 miles we found ourselves in a coral on the bank of the Sabinas—a stream nearly as large as the rio Brazos. Revolted agt the coral. attempts!

10. Crossed the river. This river is fabled for its pearls. It is a deep rapid stream; and, of course, no opportunities of accurate observation were allowed.

11. Lodged at the hacienda de Alamos—a most miserable hamlet. (B)

a document on oath stating that they would not again take up arms against the Republic of Mexico until they had been regularly exchanged. (R. D. Phillips, one of the Santa Fé prisoners, to his father, Dr. M. Phillips, 19 June 1842. MS. letter in King Texas Collection, Texas State Library.) They had returned to San Antonio and were among those captured on 11 September 1842. They were included in the terms of surrender granted by General Woll. Santa Anna, however, ordered these three men to be shot (Neill's Narrative, page 315 below), alleging that they had broken their parole (Thompson, *Recollections of Mexico*, 76, 78). Through the intercession of General Woll their sentence was modified to ten years imprisonment in San Juan de Ulloa. (Neill's Narrative, page 315 below.)

When Green and his companions arrived at Saltillo, 30 January 1843, they found there in prison Van Ness, Fitzgerald, Hancock and three of the wounded prisoners of Dawson's company. At the request of Green, Van Ness was permitted to accompany the Texan officers. Fitzgerald and Hancock and the Dawson prisoners were joined to the Mier Prisoners when the latter arrived at Saltillo February 5. A few days later Fitzgerald was fatally wounded during the attack on the guard at the Hacienda de Salado, 11 February 1843. Hancock also was wounded, but recovered and survived the period of imprisonment at Perote. He was released with the Bexar Prisoners, 23 March 1844. Van Ness was liberated about a fortnight later. (Stapp, *Prisoners of Perote*, 123.)

[1]In regard to this sentence, see note 2, page 296.

[2]This note is in same hand and ink, but inserted with other notes, marked A to M, near the back of the booklet in which the Diary is kept.

(B). Where the palmeto tree was at the corner of the alcalde's house and where I urged escape. a rich well watered plain. a view of the Candela and Monclova mountains 30 m[1]

12. Crossed a small deep rapid stream called the rio Salado and bore westward to the Gap of the Hermanas mountains—being the eastern verge of the grand Siera Madre Nighted at hacienda *Enceros,* remarkable for its 20,000 sheep. 20 m. (C)

(C) Altercation between Posas and the alcalde. beautiful fountain in which we bathed. Neill wrote to Santa Rosa.[1]

13. At Hacienda las Hermanas—a large stone establishment belonging to Sanchez—among the mountains. This is indeed a large, strong and formidable square of massive stone apartments and towers, of recent erection—and forms a singular contrast to the dilapidations at every point we had previously passed (D) 18 m

(D) Next morning passed the hot spring about a mile beyond the place.[1]

14. Hac[iend]a las Ajuntas. 15 m (E)

(E) A small town—a miserable place.[2]

15th. Monclova—on the west foot of the largest mountain we had seen. Beautiful town! Full of friends. Musquis with whom I dined. Victor Blanco—his son Miguel Blanco. Baker etc etc etc!!!

Oct 17. village Castaño. 10 m

18. rancho Bajan, where Hidalgo was taken. 25 m

19. Tank San Felipe. In reaching it the long low mountain on our left always terminating and never ending. 30 m.

20. Rancho Anela. 20 m

21. Mesias—the robbers' ranch. a severe hail-storm 20 m

22. Passed thro the mountains to village capellanilla F.

(F) On this day's march crossed a creek repeatedly and passed thro a gorge of the mountains. 25 m reached the valley of Saltillo[1]

23. Arrived at Saltillo. Here we remained until the 7th Nov. None of the Mexican inhabitants visited us or showed the least

feeling for us. Dr Jas Hewitson and Dr Knight called every day. Dr H. advanced me $25—and promised me funds at Mexico.

News of the 3 at San Fernado being shot—contradicted. Wrote to Mrs. H and to Fearn & Donegan and Generals Foote and Terrell

Mrs H. at Mrs Woolridge's in Washington. Her letter to Mrs. Hadley of the 3rd.[1]

Nov 7· Monday. Went to rancho Buenavista   10 m

Mrs. H drew. $437.50 Exchequer[1]

8. Hac[iend]a Aguaneuva—where Dimit died.[2]   15 m

9. Crossed mountains to hac[iend]a Encarnacion   30 m

Gen Houston to Mrs. H.[1]

10. hac[iend]a San Salvador. consulted again.   30 m

Kavanaugh—Mrs H' removal to Dr Perry's[1]

11. [Hacienda] Salado. 15 m   (G)

(G) The first place where we quartered at a meson.[3] Invited out to sup with the Capn

Where the Mier prisoners' ecaped.[4]

12. rancho Las Anemas. 15 m.

13. Village San Juan de Vanegas—mining establishment. Near the mines of Catorce   25 m

15. Cedral—a large town. 12 m

16. Matehuala—large town—10,000.   20 m

17. Repusedaro—village—(guitar)   25 m

18. Hac[iend]a Lahuna Saca. 20 m

19. Benado—large town. 30 m

Nov. 20. Hac[iend]a Las Bocas—cold night   30 m

21. [Hacienda] Peñasco. 20 m

22. San Luis Potosi. Reached at noon this day (Tuesday). city of 30,000. Antonio de Soberon.   10 m

---

[1]See note 2, page 296, in regard to this paragraph.

[2]For an account of Captain Philip Dimit's capture and the circumstances attending his death, July, 1841, see Yoakum, *History of Texas*, II, 319, 320.

[3]An inn.

[4]See note 2, page 301. The last sentence of this note appears to be a part of the original entry. The date when these notes were written would then be fixed at some time after 9 April 1843. See second paragraph of entry under April 9, 1843.

25. Hac[iend]a de la Pela. 15 m
26. [Hacienda] de Jaral. 30 m (H)

(H) Residence of the Conde de Jaral. fine church being erected. Corn kept 10 years in sealed houses. Mina taken near this place.[1]

27 [Hacienda] de Cubo. 20 m. (I)

(I) Slept in the upper rooms of one of the Count's palaces.[1]

28 Dolores—the Lexington of Mexico. 30 m (K)

(K) On this day's march passed the battle ground of Gallineras where Gen Montezuma was defeated.[1]

29. San Miguel Ayenda—passing the ancient church Atotonilco. 20 m (L)

(L) Fine church. water carried to third stories. monument to Morelos.[1]

Gen Terrell recd my law library.[2]

30. Hac[iend]a Santa Rosa. 30 m

Dec 1. Queretero—40,000. called on Doña Catalina whose correspondent is Don Jose Maria Pazguel, Vera Cruz. 12 m Major Quixana, nephew of Tornell.

3. Hac[iend]a Colorado 15 m (M)

(M) This is where the natives came up to receive their week's pay—and rations—pay a bit a day and rations an almud and a half or an almud.[1]

4. San Juan del Rio—large town. 28 m

5. Rancho at arroyo Saco. (Jones) 30 m

6. Passed thro the mountains to Tula in the valley of Mexico and 18 leagues from the city. Rodoriguez, Duran, Gonzales, Posas superseded by Madrid. 30 m

10. Memorial to Bravo.[3]

11. Town Huevatoca 20 m

12. Town Cuatitlan—first view of the snow mountains 18 m

13. San Cristobal. Ruins of the Viceroy's palace 15 m

14. Village San Juan de Teihuacan—where Neill escaped. 15 m

---

[1]See note 2, page 301.

[2]See note 2, page 296. G. W. Terrell was attorney general of the Republic of Texas at this time.

[3]See note 2, page 296. Bravo was acting president of Mexico at this time.

15. Village Calpulalpan. 25 m.

16. Town of San Martin in the great road from Mexico to Vera Cruz. 30 m.

17. Puebla—70,000—Brindley, etc. 24 m

18th Wrote to Hewetson to Foote and my wife.[1]

19. Village Acajete—(Mexia killed)[2] 18 m

20. [Village] Cuapesela. 24 m

21. [Village] Tepiohualela. 18 m

22 (Thursday) under a fierce norther reached the castle of Perote. 17 miles.

25. Mrs. H. left Perry's on the Mustang steamer[1]

28. Put in chains.

30. My chain with Gray severed.

31st wrote to my wife by Lt. Hartstane of the U. S. Navy.[1]

1843. Jan 1. Sunday—sad day—cold—clear.

6. Part of us put to work.

7. I was sent out in charge of 10 of my fellow prisoners— to carry out manure and to bring in sand. Offered to assist them but they declined. Treated them on their return.

Mrs. H. at Galveston[1]

8. (Sunday) Victory of the Mexicans at Mier celebrated here by the firing of artillery. The reports are that 250 surrendered (including 2 generals) on the 25th Decr.

10. A Memorial to Santa Anna, drawn by Jones and myself, and signed by all of us (55) except Colquohoun, O'Phelan, W. Riddle, Ogden, Trapnell, Davis, and Twohig (7) and sent by mail

11. Six of us compelled to work as oxen in a tumbrel, carrying out dung and bringing in sand and rock.

Jan 19 Mr Southall, bearer of despatches from the U. S. to Mexico called upon us.

Feb 2. He revisited out prison, giving assurances of our discharge within three or four weeks. Wrote of this date to Gen Foote and Mrs. H. Did not send a letter I had prepared to Gen

[1]See note 2, page 296.

[2]General Mexia was shot, by order of Santa Anna, in 1839.

Terrell, on the advice of W. E. Jones, on account of a special interposition in my favor at Mexico. *Norville.*[1]

Mrs H to Judge Franklin.[2]

5. The Mayor of the plaza caused Santa Annas letter to the Govr of the 1st instant to be read to us—stating his reception of the Memorial and of the letters of Booker Davis and Robinson;[3] that he not being the Head of the˙ nation c[oul]d not act on the three first; and that the latter being on matters of grave national concern w[oul]d be transmitted to the government.

13. Robinson left on an order to visit Santa Anna at Manga de Clavo. This night recd N. Orleans papers stating Hartstane's return—Neill's arrival in U. S.—the refusal of the Texan Congress to remove the archives from Austin—Somerville on the west of the Rio Grande on the 10th Deer with some 800 etc.

Mar 1. Santa Anna came to Perote on his way to the city—was recd at 7 p m—and left at 10 a m next day. We were kept locked up.

2. The comet appeared.

Mar 11. L Dobbins, com[missio]n Mer[chant] N O wrote to Mr. Toohig of the 13th and to W. Riddle of the 14 Jany—reed this day—stating that Mrs H had brot to him a letter from Mrs Riddle—that she [Mrs. H.] on the 13th departed in good boat to Alabama under protection of Judge Franklin and w[oul]d in a few days be with her friends in Georgia By Dr Chalmers' letter to the Hon W Thompson of Dec 18th she was in Washinton Cy.

☞T'—letter to M. naming me dated Feb 16th recd the 19th. my note to T. of the 22d—enclosed in one to him from M.

☞On the 4th Mr Cozens called to see me and gave inform[atio]n of the application of Messrs Walker and Thompson[4] to Mr Webster for my release etc

18th Saturday. Gen Thompson's letter to Mavrick recd informing [us] that the order for the liberation of himself, of Jones and

---

[1]Perhaps a reference to S. G. Norvell; see note 1, page 320, below.

[2]This last sentence is written in the margin; see note 2, page 296.

[3]The memorial and the letters were written while the Texans were at Tula, December 7-10.

[4]Perhaps, the reference is to Robert J. Walker, senator, and Jacob Thompson, congressman, from Mississippi.

me had been given but that we had to go to Mexico. Booker's accident.[1]

19th We three called to the Governor's office where was read to us the order for the removal of our chains and for our being conducted to Mexico.

21. Gen Victoria and Dr Booker died at the castle. wrote to Mrs Hutchinson at Covington Georgia.

22. Wednesday. at 3 p m left Perote with Jones and Maverick under military guard. lodged at Tepiohualela—scene at the Cocena.[2]

23. Ha[cienda] Floreta. robbed here of some clothing. 13 *l.*[3]

24. Amasoke. 6 *l.* 16 m.[4]

25· Puebla. 10 m. 78 m from Perote. put in the Prison containing about 400 convicts.[4]

Capt Eastland and 16 others shot at Salado !·[5]

26. San Martin 21 m[4]

27. Rio Frio. 21 m French house.[4]

28—Ayotla. 20 m.[4]

29. Mexico 16m. 156 m from Perote. visited at quartel by Mr. John Black Am Consul and carried to Gen Thompson's room at Mrs Wyly's meson.[4]

30. Cathedral—Chepultepec.[4]

31. Recd our passports—Alemeda[4]

Ap 2 Set out in the Diligencia for Vera Cruz having on the evening before drawn on L Dobbin N O in duplicate fav[o]r Gen W Thompson for $100. Our friends in Mexico Togño, West, Oury,

---

[1]"Dr. Booker, one of the San Antonio prisoners and a brave and meritorious man, was accidentally killed, . . . by a drunken Mexican soldier. The latter pointed his gun with the intention of shooting one of his own officers, but unfortunately the ball lodged in the breast of Dr. B., who survived but a few days."—*Telegraph and Texas Register*, 3 May 1843.

[2]The entry for this date, and those for the dates following to and including April 7, appear to have been written originally with pencil and subsequently traced with pen and ink.

[3]See note 2 above. During the night Hutchinson, Maverick, and Jones, on their way to the City of Mexico, must have lodged in close proximity to Fisher, Green and the other officers of the Mier Expedition, who were on their way to the **Castle of Perote.**

[4]See note 2 above.

[5]This entry was interlined with pen and ink, and not traced like the original entry for this day. Cf. note 2, page 296.

Officer Seeger, Dr. Gardiner, ———Curson, ———Bull, ———
Voss. reached Puebla.[1]

3. To Perote. 78 m.[2]

Ap 4. Las Vigas. 4 *l.* San Miguel 4 *l.* Rio Alopan 3 *l.*
Xalapa 1 *l.* Dos Rias 4 *l.* Coral Falsa 2 *l.* Plan del Rio 3 *l.*
Calera. Santa Fé a league and a half from Manga de Clavo and
that 4 *l.* from Vera Cruz— on the north of the road—whole distance from Perote 40 *l*—105 m—260 m to Mexico. About 6 in
the morning of the 5th (Wednesday) reached Vera Cruz. break-
fasted at the stage hotel where we met Mr F M Dimond Am Consul. Invited to the house of L S Hargous Esq—where we found
the two Messrs Youngs.[1]

6th Thursday. norther preventing the Vincennes and Chatahooche from sailing.[3]

7th Norther continues.[4]

8th Norther continues[5]

April 9th. Sunday. Went aboard the U S Sloop of War [Vin-
cennes] 22 guns (24 pounders) commanded by Cap. F. Buchanon.
I was conducted to his cabin to lodge with him. Messrs. Jones and
Maverick were taken to the wardroom to lodge with the lieutenants.
Here I met with Lt Ro E Hoe, son of Seymore Hoe, midshipman
W. P. Harrison son of Dr D. P Harrison and midshipman Doug-
lass from Canton (Mis). Treated with many kind attentions by
officers and crew.[6]

[1]See note 2, page 307.

[2]See note 2, page 307. They called upon their fellow citizens imprisoned
in the Castle, and carried away with them many messages for friends at
home. (Green, *Journal of the Texian Expedition against Mier*, 256.)

[3]See note 2, page 307. The following words, after the word Chatahooche,
were not traced: "on which are the Riddles and O'Phelan."
"John and Wilson Riddle and Capt. O'Phelan, all of them taken at San
Antonio, have been released through the intercession of the British Minister." (*Telegraph and Texas Register*, 3 May 1843.)

[4]See note 2, page 307. The following sentence, however, was not traced
in ink: "This is my forty-fifth birthday."

[5]Beginning with the entry for this day the original entries in the Diary
are again written in ink.

[6]The following list of officers of the Vincennes is recorded near the end
of the booklet containing the Diary:
Cap: Franklin Buchanan, Phila.
Lt John K Mitchell—N. Car.
  " Ro Emmet Hooe, King George Cy—Va

Sailed from the island Sacrificios off Vera Cruz at 2 o'clock p. m this day. passed Tampico 19 m—(weather hazy)—tacked and cast anchor off the bar on the evening of the 12th. Lt Lewis sent in a boat to the town for Crittenden[1] and on the next evening he returned without him: he having been sent to Mexico.[2] Lt Lewis was informed that the British consul had recd a letter from the interior stating that the prisoners who had been retaken were decimated; 16 being selected who were shot, one of whom was not killed and had escaped.[3] Sailed again that evening and on the 17th—got off the Bellise having on the evening preceding passed a skooner.

At 5 p. m. spoke the New Zealand, last from Richmond bound for N. Orleans—and after dusk passed two other ships going in the same course. Tomorrow we expect to reach Pensacola, which is about 1000 miles direct from Vera Cruz.

18th (Tuesday) reached Pensacola harbor—saluted passed between the Independence—Commodore Stewart and the Vincennes. got to the Florida house, Capt Carone, at 10 p. m.

Lt Montgy Lewis—Phila
" Rd Wainwright
" Woodhull S Schenck—Ohio
Surgeon John A Lockwood—Delaware
Sailing Master Jo: N. Barney—Md.
Purser Jo: Bryan—Geo.
Asst Surgeon—A A Henderson
Lt of Marines M. R. Kintzing
Captain's Clerk Jo: Gideon
Midshipmen—Ch. R Smith, Sam Edwards, N. W Bassett, Walter P. Harrison, Jona: Young, Jo Parish, Geo B Douglass, Ch Gray, C H Hopkins, Jo L Byers.

[1]Lieutenant George B. Crittenden was one of the Mier prisoners. He was left behind with others at Matamoros in January, 1843, being too sick to travel. (Stapp, *Prisoners of Perote*, 45.) In a letter dated Monterey, 24 March 1843, the writer says "The sick and wounded, together with the three boys who were left at Matamoros, were secretly marched out of town on the 4th instant, and sent on foot to Tampico." (*Telegraph and Texas Register*, 3 May 1843.) Through the efforts of General Waddy Thompson Lt. Crittenden was released about the same time that Judge Hutchinson, Wm. E. Jones, and S. A. Maverick were released. Perhaps, they had heard of his having been sent to Tampico, and of the subsequent order for his release, while they were in the City of Mexico.

[2]Lt. Crittenden had left three days before for the City of Mexico. (*Telegraph and Texas Register*, 3 May 1843.)

[3]This reference is to James L. Sheperd. He was recaptured and shot to death. (Stapp, *Prisoners of Perote*, 74.)

19.   Took the stage for Mobile and arrived at 10 a m next day.

20th.   Met with D M Riggs and Mr Case

21.   Wrote to Mrs. H.   met with Wm P Aubry and Mr Bullard from Matagorda.   Aubry lent me $20 to be sent him from N. O. or paid to Thomas F McKinney, Galveston.

23.   Went on the steamer Fashion to N. Orleans—arrived next morning—18 hours passage.

24.   Recd Mrs H's letter of the 16th.

25.   Answered her letter.

26.   Sick all day

27.   Drew on Gen H. S. Foote, single bill, this date, 20 days date, favor McMahan Trotter & Pearsall, endorsers—cashed by Mr Ricks for $300.   left $100 with Dobbin, to meet my draft from Mexico.   refunded $5 to John Riddle.   Wrote to Mrs H.   Bill at Verandah $11.25[1]

28.   left for Vicksburg on Steamer Buckeye

May 1.   Monday arrived at Vicksburg and went with Gen Foote to his house in Raymond where I met Ellen.

3.   Went to Jackson.

6.   Back to Raymond

8.   To Jackson

16.   Recd Mrs H's letter of the 9th requesting me to go for her to Montgomery.   started next day via New Orleans.   Went in the Luda

23rd   Met Mrs H.—her mother and Mr Graves of Montgomery.

24.   Descended on the Canebrake.   Due Cap Th: Adams, Mobile, nine dollars.

June 1.   Reached Jackson

8.   (Thursday) moved to Mr Moore's house—rent $16.66⅔ pr month for three months with preference.   hired Maria from Mrs Stamps at $10 pr Month.[2]

[1]Last sentence is placed in the margin and written in ink of different color.

[2]Although not a part of the Diary, the following extract from a letter written by Judge Hutchinson at Jackson, Mississippi, June 10, 1843, to W. D. Miller, the private secretary of President Houston, is so intimately connected with the events covered by the Diary that it may with propriety be introduced here:

"My Dear Friend:—On the 18th April I arrived at Pensacola.   On the 23rd recd Mrs. Hutchinson's letter of the 16th requesting me to meet her

14 Partnership with Foote & Russell—to begin the 19th.

17. Wrote my letter of resignation of thanks and of business to Texas

19. At Raymond

24 Saturday to Vicksburg saw Russell who left this day—to Jackson

25. To Ben Ricks—returned Tuesday

28 To Raymond

July 1. Brot Ellen to Jackson

3. Sent her to school to Mrs Robinson

10. Spl session of legislature—Demo Convention[1]

TEGANOS.

[Some pages of notes intervene, and then, on next to the last page of the Diary, appears the following list of names. Apparently the list was prepared after their arrival at Perote as no

at Jackson. On May 1st reached Raymond and on the 3rd Jackson. On the 16th got another letter from Mrs. H. desiring me to meet her at Montgomery. On the 23rd she with her mother and Mr. Graves, my brother-in-law, met me at that place, and on the 1st instant we reached this place. I am engaged in locating my family here and expect in about a week to leave on a visit to Texas, where I trust I shall meet you and be enabled to express my grateful acknowledgments for your kind attention to Mrs. H. when she was on her way from the land of privations and difficulties, and also for your letters of Sep 12 and 14th 1842.

"But for the necessity of collecting my family I should have been enabled to have got to Washington by the 5th instant, the day for the session of the Supreme Court: I shall therefore, with the tender of my resignation as Judge of the fourth district, declare my salary as terminating on the 5th instant. I learned in N. Orleans that my district had been reduced to Goliad, Refugio and San Patricio, so that no circuit duties have been needed. In a word it is impossible for me to sustain in safety my family in any part of the 4th district, and being unwilling to reside in middle or eastern Texas, I am compelled to resume professional practice in Mississippi.

"My Code of Texas is here as complete as I left it. Two weeks labor will enable me to engraft the legislation of the last Congress. . . .

"Oblige me by expressing to Generals Houston and Terrell and Col Hockley my gratitude for the kindnesses to Mrs. H. during my captivity. . . .

"I go to Texas to exchange my negroes with Gen. Henderson for others in Mississippi—to get my salary—to sell my Code—and to bring away my library. . . . Any aid you can afford in the accomplishment of any of those objects will be a great favor." (MS. letter in Miller Papers, Texas State Library.)

[1]This is the end of the Diary.

mention is made of those who dropped out of the **ranks** between San Antonio and Perote.]

Alex: Allsbury—medico, physician.[1]

Isaac Allen— sastre, tailor.

Edw: Brown—labrador, laborer.

James H Brown—albeites, farrier.

Freeman B. Beck—labrador, laborer.

Shields Booker—medico, physician.

Wm. Bugg—labrador, laborer.

John Bradley ———

Rd A Barclay—sillero, saddler.

Jo A Crews   comerciante, merchant.

Ludovic Colquohoun ———

Wm Colton—pintor, painter.

Dav: J Davis—labrador, laborer.

John Dalrymple—escribano, clerk.

Augustin Elly—minero, miner.

John Forester—labrador, laborer.

Nathl W Faison—comerciante, merchant.

French S. Gray—abogado, lawyer, assistant district attorney in a number of cases.[2]

A. Hutchinson—juez, judge, district judge.[2]

Geo. C. Hatch—labrador, laborer.

N. Herbert—carpintero, carpenter.

Chauncey Johnson, relojero, watch-maker.

Wm E Jones—abogado, lawyer, member of congress.

Dav: S Kornegay—labrador, laborer.

John Lehman, escribano, clerk.

John Lee—labrador, laborer.

A. J. Lesslie ———

Riley Jackson—labrador, laborer.

Jo. C. Morgan—carpintero, carpenter.

Sam A. Maverick—abogado, lawyer, member of congress.

Dav: Morgan—comerciante, merchant, sworn interpreter to the district court.[2]

Francis Macay—medico, physician.

[1]The translations and notes have been added by the editor.

[2]Minutes of the District Court, September term, 1842, in District Clerk's Office, San Antonio.

Edw Manton—labrador, laborer.
Allen H Morrell, a youth, son of Rev. Z. N. Morrell.
S. Nobles ———
Ro S. Neighbors ———
Wm H O'Phelan—viandante, traveler.
Duncan C Ogden   comerciante, merchant.
C. W. Peterson—abogado, lawyer, district attorney.[1]
J. W. Robinson ———
John Riddle—comerciante, merchant.
Marcus L B Raper   carpintero, carpenter.
John Perry—labrador, laborer.
Wilson J Riddle   comerciante, merchant.
Jo C Robinson—labrador, laborer.
Geo Schaffer ———
Sam Stone   combrerero, hatter.
John Smith   albañil, mason.
Jo Shaw—labrador, laborer.
J. L. Trueheart   escribano, cleck, district court.[1]
Jno Twohig—comerciante, merchant.
Wm Trimble   labrador laborer.
John G. Andres Voss   comerciante, merchant.
John Trapnell ———
John Young—carpintero, carpenter.

II.   NEILL'S NARRATIVE.[2]

Washington Texas Jany 29th. 1843

Hon: Anson Jones
    Sec: of State etc.

The undersigned citizen of Texas has the honor to make known to you and through your Department to his Excellency the President of the Republic that he effected his escape on the 14th. ultimo from the guard having him in charge near the City of Mexico and has arrived in safety in Texas a few days ago.

It of course is known to your Department the manner of the surprise and capture of fifty two citizens at San Antonio de Bexar on the 11th. day of September last but in order that you may be more fully advised of the circumstances attending that

[1]See note 2, page 312.
[2]D. S. in the collection of papers presented to the State Library by Mr. L. K. Miller.

event and the situation and treatment of the prisoners then taken
the undersigned begs leave respectfully to represent That he in
company with the Hon Judge of the fourth Judicial District and
other members of the Bar, suitors, and Jurors attended the opening of the District Court at Bexar on the first Monday in September last and continued their labors during the first week at the end
of which they began to be somewhat interrupted by rumors that
some enemy was hovering about the place, using precautionary
measures for ascertaining the true character of the enemy
and from the fact of many previous courts having been broken
up by Indians and Mexicans the citizens of the place with the
strangers from the other parts were desirous of sustaining the supremacy of the laws and preventing the Court from being broken
up collected in order to repel the enemy unless they should prove
of such character as would induce them to retire to their homes
but before that fact could be ascertained and early on the
Morning of Sunday the 11th. in a dense fog Gen: Adrian Woll
entered at the head of a force said by himself to contain seventeen hundred men and being the advance of an invading army
and after meeting with resistance for a short time he sent to our
company requiring our surrender which took place upon the following terms towit. The persons of *all* concerned to be respected,
our lives secured, to be treated as prisoners of war, and our private
property not to be interrupted, which latter article was to include
our horses, upon which we were to the number of fifty-four immediately placed in close confinement we were during our stay at
Bexar supplied entirely by our own means or by the kindness of
a few families in the place and received nothing from our captors we were searched and even pencils pen knives and razors
were taken from our possession a few of which were afterwards returned our private papers were examined some of them pilfered
and clothing and valuables stolen.

On the 13th. Mr Callaghan merchant of Bexar was released On
the 14th. Messrs McClelland merchant and Menchaca, citizen were
released and on the 15th. John Johnson a youth was also discharged. We now numbered 52 of whom two Messrs Wilson J.
Riddle merchant of Bexar and Francis McKay of Bexar were
seized at their own houses and had not been taken in arms

with the others on the afternoon of this day we were marched
out under a strong guard for Mexico and were that evening again
searched and received orders for our conduct during our march
some few were allowed to ride but no respect was paid to
individual property and the undersigned was punished and ordered
to walk altho' he had a horse inventoried and then in company
rode by a soldier for refusing to sign his name *to* one of the many
documents drawn up for signature to be sent into Texas or left
behind us respecting our treatment and the undersigned avails
himself of the present occasion to protest against the validity
of any and all documents bearing his signature and obtained during his duress and now proclaims the same null and void except-
ing such as may by any future act be acknowledged by him.

On the 16th. our march was continued and until this evening
our captors had supplied us with nothing each prisoner was
now allowed one pint of coarse unbolted flour and one and a half
pounds of beef to be cooked by ourselves which rations continued
to be supplied to us daily during the journey. On the 19th Sept
John R. Cunningham Esquire Lawyer of Bexar was reported to
have died, two days previously he was sick and ordered into
the wagon which contained wounded soldiers and although we
urged the necessity of leaving with him a physician who was with
us or any one of the prisoners to attend him it was denied and
we saw him no more. Wĕ were detained at the Presidio Rio
Grande from the 23d to the 27th Sept and at San Fernando the
headquarters of the Northern Army under Genl: Ysidro Reyes
from the 28th Septr: to the 7th. October, On the 6th, Octr
the prisoners George Van Ness, Archd. Fitzgerald and Thomas
Hancock were put into the common prison and sentenced to death
(since which time their sentence has been commuted to ten years
imprisonment at San Juan de Uloa but the undersigned has no
knowledge of their present locality) On the morning of the 7th.
when about to leave ten prisoners survivors of Dawson's Fayette
county company were put with us and are in all respects treated
the same as the others, Our number was now 58 we were marched
by way of Monclova where we were kindly received and abundantly
supplied by the inhabitants to Saltillo where we arrived on the
23rd. October at this place we were confined closely until the 7th.

November during which time we petitioned for relief for the ten suffering prisoners of Fayette county who had been stripped by the soldiery of everything their money watches clothing blankets were all gone but the Governor turned a deaf ear to our petitions and naked and cold they would have sent us off but for the kindness of two Gentlemen of that place who supplied many wants Drs. J. D. Knight and Jas. Hewetson we were badly treated by the soldiery and abused and insulted if we asked for redress. some of the horses had been stolen also while here and the officers used no exertion to have them returned or replaced but laughed at the adroitness with which these thefts were committed. one of our number also who was sick was not allowed to remain at the place although he was not able to travel either on foot or horse without great suffering. we were glad to leave such an inhospitable region and arrived at San Luis Potosi on the 22nd. Nov. Here we were more kindly treated. some few blankets were furnished to the destitute and our quarters were comfortable. Simeon Glenn was here left being unable to travel any farther. his case is not a dangerous one and he was promised attention by all; On the 25th. we again continued our journey by way of Hidalgo, San Miguel de Allende, to Queretaro where we arrived on the first December. at this place Samuel G. Norvell was left dangerously sick On the 3rd we continued our march after having been robbed by the soldiery and pilfered by the officers to a considerable extent and arrived at Tula a town about 20 leagues from Mexico on the 6th. at this place orders were in waiting for us; in a few days we were received by a new officer and guard and informed that our destination was changed by the Supreme Government to the Castle of Perote and on the 11th. our march was resumed we had about this time frequent opportunities of writing to Mexico and embraced it by petitioning to the Govt. that we might be allowed to enter Mexico to set forth to the nation the nature and cause of our capture and not to be sent to a distant prison in a cold and uncharitable climate and that we might have communication with our friends through the foreigners of the city but all was denied us or at least unheeded and neglected and on the 13th. we were within five leagues of the city on the road to Perote by way of Puebla on the next evening when about 14 leagues from Mexico I escaped from prison and made my way to the city which I entered on the next morning from thence via Puebla Perote, Jalapa and Vera Cruz to New Orleans etc. On my passage through Perote I saw some of my companions in irons chained in pairs and was informed that they were set to work on the 2nd. January. they are not supplied with meat and are destitute of means of obtaining necessary articles for their comfort. they now number 55 a full list of whose names I beg leave to refer you annexed hereto as also those left elsewhere which together with the report of Chauncey Johnson commanding at Bexar of date at Puebla the 18th. December last and which is now filed in the Department of War and Marine[1] I beg leave most respectfully to refer you together with his Excellency for further information. And in case that any thing may be overlooked or neglected herein by me I can assure you that at all times it will afford me infinite pleasure to give the Department information as time and opportunity may occur hoping that you will not fail upon special matters to communicate with me by way of enquiry which will always be promptly answered to the best of my knowledge holding myself at all times individually responsible for whatever I communicate.

Accept assurances for yourself and His Excellency the President for the interest taken in my behalf while a prisoner of the respect and esteem with which I am

Your most obt. friend and sevt.

A. Neill

List of Prisoners[2] now in Perote Castle and elsewhere in Mexico.

1 Hon. A. Hutchinson, released 29 March 1843[3]
2 " Sam A. Maverick, released 29 March 1843[3]
3 " W. E. Jones, released 29 March 1843[3]
4 Mr. Chauncey Johnson, released 23 March 1844.

[1]This report has not been found.

[2]The numbering and arrangement of the names is Neill's. The statements concerning the release, escape or death of the prisoners have been added by the editor and unless credited to other sources are based on Green's *Journal of the Texian Expedition against Mier.*

[3]Hutchinson's Diary.

5   Mr. Geo. C. Hatch, escaped.
6   ” Ludo. Colquohoun, released 23 March 1844.
7   ” Wilson J. Riddle, released — March 1843[1]
8   S. Booker died in prison at Perote 21 March 1843.[2]
9   D. C. Ogden escaped from Perote 2 July 1843; recaptured; re-
      leased 23 March 1844.
10 John Trapnall died in prison at Perote.
11 J. C. Morgan, released 23 March 1844.
12 Jas. H. Brown, released 23 March 1844.
13 John Twohig escaped from Perote 2 July 1843; reached home.
14 Wm. J. O'Phelan, released — March 1843[1]
15 John Riddle, released — March 1843[1]
16 Francis McKay, released 23 March 1844.
17 Aug. Elley escaped from Perote 2 July 1843; recaptured; re-
      leased 23 March 1844.
18 Geo. P. Schaeffer, released 23 March 1844.
19 John Layman, released 23 March 1844.
20 Geo. Voss, released 23 March 1844.
21 David Morgan escaped.
22 Jas. L. Trueheart, released 23 March 1844.
23 Jas. W. Robinson, released — February (?) 1843[3]
24 H. A. Alsbury, released 23 March 1844.
25 John Smith, released 23 March 1844.
26 Nath: Harbert, released 23 March 1844.
17 Willm. Bugg, released 23 March 1844.
28 Jos. A. Crews died in prison at Perote about 1 February 1844.[4]
29 French S. Gray died in prison at Perote.
30 C. W. Peterson, released 23 March 1844.
31 John Lee, released 23 March 1844.
32 Marcus L. B. Rapier, released 23 March 1844.
33 Truman B. Beck escaped from Perote 2 July 1843; recap-
      tured; released 23 March 1844.
34 J. F. Leslie, released 23 March 1844.
35 S. L. Noble, released 23 March 1844.

[1]*Telegraph and Texas Register*, 3 May 1843.
[2]Hutchinson's Diary.
[3]*The Morning Star*, 1 April 1843.
[4]THE QUARTERLY, II, 234.

36 J. T. Davis escaped from Perote 2 July 1843; recaptured; released 23 March 1844.

37 R. S. Neighbors, released 23 March 1844.

38 John Perry, released 23 March 1844.

39 Riley Jackson died in prison at Perote 1 April 1843.[1]

40 Jno. Dalrymple escaped from Perote 2 July 1843; reached home.

41 Isaac Allen escaped from Perote 2 July 1843; recaptured; released 23 March 1844.

42 John Forrester escaped from Perote 2 July 1843; reached home.

43 Saml. Stone escaped from Perote 2 July 1843; recaptured; released 23 March 1844.

44 John Young escaped from Perote 2 July 1843; recaptured; released 23 March 1844.

45 Edwd. Brown, released 23 March 1844.

of those taken at Bexar on the 11th. Sept/42

and

1. John Bradley, released 22 September 1843.[2]

2 James Shaw, released 23 March 1844.

3 Ed. Manton, released 23 March 1844.

4 Wm. Coltrin

5 Wm. Trimble died in prison at Perote.

6 David E. Kornegay escaped from Perote 2 July 1843; reached home.

7 Richd. Barkley escaped from Perote 2 July 1843; reached home.

8 Nat: W. Faison, released 23 March 1844.

9 Joel Robinson, released 23 March 1844.

10 Allen H. Morrell, released 23 March 1844.

survivors of Dason's company.

all of the above are at Perote

1 Simeon Glenn, sick at San Luis Potosi[3]

---

[1]"Richard Jackson, one of the prisoners captured at Bexar last autumn, died at Perote on the first of April last." (*Telegraph and Texas Register,* 10 May 1843.)

[2]Stapp, 113.

[3]Simeon Glenn was released 23 March 1844.

2   Saml. G. Norvell, do. at Queretaro[1]
3   John R. Cunningham died 19th. Sep:
    and
4   Geo. Van Ness[2] 5   Arch Fitzgerald[3]
6   and Tho. Hancock[4]—left at San Fernando
7   and Andrew Neill *escaped*[5]

III.   JONES'S NARRATIVE.[6]

Washington 1 Feby 1844

Dear Sir,

In compliance with your request, I give you below, a hasty sketch of the circumstances attending the capture and imprisonment of a number of the citizens of Texas, at San Antonio de Bexar in Sept. 1842

During the session of the District Court of Bexar county, for September 1842, a rumor reached the place that a Mexican army of from 1500 to 3000 men was on its way to attack the place. The rumor was sufficiently authenticated to induce the belief that a force of some character was advancing, but the impression was pretty general that it was only a party of marauders and not reg-

[1]"Mr. S. G. Norvell, one of the prisoners captured at Bexar by Gen. Woll, came over on the New York, having been liberated through the intervention of Col. Carasco." (*Telegraph and Texas Register*, 8 March 1843.)

[2]Geo. Van Ness was released — April 1844. (Stapp, 123.)

[3]Fitzgerald died of wounds received at Salado, 11 February 1843.

[4]Thos. Hancock escaped from Perote 2 July 1843; recaptured; released 23 March 1844.

[5]These seven names do not appear in Hutchinson's list. The names of the five Dawson prisoners given below are not included either in Hutchinson's or Neill's list.
Milvern Harrell, a youth, released 23 March 1844.
John Higgerson, killed at Salado, 11 February 1843.
McReady, or McCrady, drowned in the Rio Grande river, November, 1842.
Pattison, drowned in the Rio Grande river, November, 1842.
Norman Woods, died in prison at Perote.
Higgerson's name appears in Green (pp. 141, 177) only. Milvern Harrell mentions the names of McReady, Pattison and Woods. (*Dallas News*, June 16, 1907.)

[6]This is an unsigned letter found in the Lamar Papers, which were purchased by Governor Campbell, July 20, 1909, under an act of the Thirty-first Legislature, and deposited in the State Library. The letter is endorsed on the back: "From Wm. E. Jones respecting his captivity," and was evidently written at the request of General Lamar with a view of incorporating the information in his projected history of Texas.

ular troops, who were endeavoring to create the impression that their force was much stronger than it really was, for the purpose of better enabling them to take the place without resistance and plunder it with impunity. Col. Hays with five other well mounted men went out to make discoveries, and taking the public roads saw nothing and did not return to San Antonio until too late to enter it. Three Mexicans were also despatched, who promised to ascertain the character of the approaching force if to be found. they found the camp of Gen. Woll at a short distance from San Antonio; were made prisoners and not permitted to return to us. The whole day of 10th September was thus passed and neither spies nor Mexicans returning strengthened the general belief that the rumor was either a hoax or the character of the force advancing misrepresented.

At day light on the morning of 11th Sept. we were aroused from our slumbers by the firing of a piece of cannon almost in the edge of the town, succeeded immediately by the sound of martial music and the tramp of a body of men. A dense fog obscured them from actual observation until after they had advanced into the public square, when they were immediately fired upon by our party, who amounted to about fifty in number—the fire was soon returned by the Mexicans with volleys of musketry and rapid discharges from a six and a four pounder. This lasted a few minutes when the fog disappearing discovered to us that we were surrounded on all sides by bodies of regular troops. We were then called upon to surrender by order of Genl. Woll—the firing ceased on both sides and after a parley in which the most ample pledges were given for our good treatment etc etc we surrendered prisoners of war, and were immediately put into prison with a strong guard over us.

General Woll had cut off all communication between the Rio Grande and Bexar, and taking a circuitous route thro' the wilderness at the foot of the Mountains had in this manner secretly advanced upon the place and was actually within three leagues of it before any suspicion was even entertained that such an expedition was contemplated. His force was 1000 regulars and about 600 Presidial troops.

We were detained prisoners five days in San Antonio, and then

ordered to march under a guard of 150 or 160 men for the Rio
Grande. Some of us by special favor permitted to ride—others
from inability to walk were also allowed horses if they could
get them. In 8 days we reached the Rio Grande, a bold, rapid
river two hundred and fifty or three hundred yards wide, which
was crossed in two canoes. The day was pretty much spent in
getting over and we spent the night on the opposite bank. Here
we learned the death of John R. Cunningham who had been
compelled to leave Bexar sick with congestive fever and had been
left behind on the third day in one of the carts which conveyed.
the Mexicans wounded in our fight, who numbered about thirty.
Cunningham died from want of attention and were there not so
many stains upon the Mexican character for other and more enor-
mous atrocities, it would be recorded and remembered to their
eternal disgrace as a nation.

We had been promised by General Woll that on our arrival at
the Rio Grande, we would be released by his Superior Genl. Reyes.
We found ourselves deceived and after a detention of seven days
at San Fernando were ordered to march for the City of Mexico.
Our escort consisted of about 80 men, all mounted, who rode on
each side of us while we occupied the road. Our journeys were
long or short each day to suit the country thro' which we traveled,
and some days we were marched from daylight until near night,
making 13 and 14 leagues. The country thro' which we travelled
from San Fernando to Monclova was generally poor, broken, sometimes mountainous. Here and there rich bodies of land susceptible of irrigation by streams from the mountains and producing
corn etc very abundantly—no timber except musquit and chaperal
thickets. From Monclova to Saltillo the character of the country
was very similar, except the first two days travel which was thro'
a wretched barren country in which no body lived and none could
live, being destitute of water.

Saltillo the capital of Coahuila is a city of 18 or 20,000 inhabitants, built after the Spanish style and here we were detained for
16 days closely housed up and never permitted to leave the Cuartel.
From Saltillo to Matahuala we passed thro' a poor and almost
unpopulated country. from Matahuala to San Luis Potosi the

country is more thickly populated and in many places there are handsome estates.

San Luis Potosi is a handsome city of 40,000 inhabitants. We were paraded through every public street in it as a show, followed by an immense crowd of people chiefly of the lower classes. We remained here two days and were visited by the Governor and several persons of distinction in that country, besides many foreigners.

From San Luis to the City of Mexico is 300 miles. the road passes many splendid estates the entire grounds of some of which are enclosed by stone walls beautifully constructed. One enclosure was said to contain 36 square miles. On arriving within twenty leagues of the City we were detained a week in a miserable prison at a place called Tula, where we were informed that our destination was not the City of Mexico, but the Castle of Perote, and that we would not be permitted to pass through the city although we should go in sight of it.

On the 22 Dec. we arrived at the Castle of Perote. a very strong fortress at the foot of the extinct Volcano called "Confra de Perote." The Castle is on the Table Lands, just at the point at which the descent to the Gulf commences—its elevation 7500 feet —it was built in 1773—mounts 96 pieces of cannon and covers 26 acres inside of the outer pickets. The main building within the mote covers ten acres or near it. Well manned I should say that this fortress would resist a very powerful force.

The first four days after our arrival we were allowed to go about the castle. On the fifth we were chained in pairs—and on the eighth or tenth day were put to work, packing sand stone lime etc into the castle. Our food consisted of poor beef, one day in three; beans, potatoes, rice and bread—badly cooked—the rations of these articles were always small, not being sufficient for a hearty man. At night we were locked up—in the morning the doors were opened—at nine o'clock paraded and counted—put to work ·immediately afterwards—the same after dinner etc.

On the 22 March Judge Hutchinson Mr. Maverick and myself were ordered to the City of Mexico under guard, our chains having been knocked off before we left the castle. We were permitted to ride by paying the hire of horses; we paid also *our own expenses* although we were still prisoners. This journey gave us many opportunities of witnessing the complete and perfect dominion of the military over the civil authorities. On our arrival at the City of Mexico we were first paraded for a quarter of an hour ragged and dirty, in front of the Palace—then escorted into it and finally sent to prison. We were however released soon after and took lodgings at the same house at which Genl. Thompson boarded—to whom we were indebted for our liberty entirely—it having been granted as a personal favor to him. Mr. Maverick and myself were acquainted with him in the U. S.

We remained three days in the City at perfect liberty—endeavoring to see everything to be seen in that remarkable place, in that short time. Our passage to Vera Cruz and thence to Pensacola etc it is unnecessary to speak of in a sketch like this.

I should have been glad had the opportunity been such as to permit the attempt, to have given you such information as I obtained in relation the affairs of Mexico—Her Government—her military organization—the church—the peon or slave system—the probable plans of Santa Anna—their views in relation to Texas; the causes of the continuance of the war—the causes of the treatment we received etc etc but it is useless to make the attempt here. Many incidents and details of our journey would be interesting.

The prisoners taken at San Antonio consisted of the Judge of the District—the District attorney, clerk—all the members of the bar except one—together with citizens of Bexar and the adjacent counties. The names have all been published several times.

NOTES AND FRAGMENTS.

GOVERNOR BELL'S RECORD—A CORRECTION.—The following extracts from letters of recent date will serve to correct certain statements concerning Governor P. H. Bell which were published in THE QUARTERLY some years ago.[1]

Z. T. FULMORE.

RALEIGH, N. C., *November 30, 1909.*

HON. Z. T. FULMORE, *Austin, Texas.*

MY DEAR SIR: . . . I knew him [Governor Bell] from the year 1867, until he died and . . . I was his legal adviser for many years. He lived in the past almost entirely. His heart was always with his adopted State, Texas . . . He often told me how he left home and came down to Petersburg, from which place he went to join the patriot army of Texas. . . . He married Ella Eaton Dickens, a daughter of William Eaton, a wealthy planter, who lived in the Roanoke River section in Warren County, N. C., and the widow of Benjamin Dickens. Mr. Eaton was a gentleman of large property in lands and negroes, but there was no distribution of his property until his death in 1869. . . . I never heard him [Governor Bell] allude to the war between the States, and therefore I always thought he was not a secessionist. He took no part in that war and lived through the four years in retirement on the plantation of Mrs. Bell in Granville County, N. C. . . . No greater error could be made in reference to that period of his life than the statement that he acquired through his wife a large number of slaves and that he enlisted, equipped, and commanded a regiment of troops in the Confederate service. . . .

Yours very Respectfully.
WALTER A. MONTGOMERY,[2]
Raleigh, N. C."

LITTLETON COLLEGE
OFFICE OF THE PRESIDENT
J. M. RHODES, LITTLETON, N. C.

January 14, 1910.

MR. Z. T. FULMORE, *Austin, Texas.*

MY DEAR SIR: I trust you will excuse my delay in replying to your favor of November 13th. I saw much of ex-Governor Bell,

[1] See Vol. III, p. 51.
[2] Judge Montgomery was for some years associate justice of the supreme court of North Carolina.—Z. T. F.

both while he was living in Warrenton and since his removal to Littleton. . . . Replying to your inquiries, I beg to say that Governor Bell was born in Culpepper County, Virginia, near Fredericksburg; and that, so far as I have been able to learn, he was educated in the schools of his county. It is not known by me that he went to college. He had no profession prior to going to Texas. He did not raise and equip at his own expense a regiment for the Confederate War. He was offered the place of colonel of a regiment by President Davis, but declined, sharing the feeling of many in Warren County of small faith in the Confederacy. He rendered no conspicuous service after his marriage. . . . He and his wife sleep in the same grave in our cemetery, which is very much neglected, and is in serious need of attention. . . . I saw him often . . . for several years before his death and admired him greatly. . . .

Yours very truly,

J. M. RHODES.

LITTLETON COLLEGE
OFFICE OF THE PRESIDENT.
J. M. RHODES, LITTLETON, N. C.

January 22, 1910.

MR. Z. T. FULMORE, *Att'y at Law, Austin, Texas:*

. . I have just sent one of my stenographers over to the cemetery to copy the inscription on Governor Bell's tomb, which I herewith enclose. The grave is in the Littleton cemetery, inside the corporation of the town, located immediately on the Seaboard Air Line Railroad, opposite a portion of the College campus. The grave is about one hundred yards from the railroad. Governor and Mrs. Bell are both buried in the same grave, over which there is a hollow brick wall, or a wall about eight inches thick and about three feet high. On top of this lies a marble slab, long enough and wide enough to cover both graves. On the slab is the inscription, a copy of which I enclose. . . .

Yours very truly,

J. M. RHODES.

The inscription above mentioned is as follows:

Peter H. Bell.
Ex-Governor of Texas.
Died March 8, 1898.
Age 90 years.

Died July 16, 1897.
Ella Rives Bell
Wife of
Ex-Governor Bell
In her Sixty-second Year.

'Rock of ages, cleft for me,'
'Let me hide myself in thee.'

'And that thou bidst me come to thee.'
'Oh Lamb of God, I come.'

'From my mother, from my boyhood,
Truth, Justice, Mercy.'

BOOK NOTICES.

In the series of Columbia University *Studies in History, Economics, and Public Law,* there has recently appeared, under the title "Reconstruction in Texas," (No. 95 of the series) the first systematic treatment of this subject that has been given to the public. The work referred to is by Charles W. Ramsdell, sometime university fellow in Columbia University, instructor in history, University of Texas, and fellow and recently corresponding secretary and treasurer of the Texas State Historical Association. It is a monograph of 324 pages octavo, beginning with a brief review of Secession, the history of Texas during the Civil War, and the conditions under which the Reconstruction *régime* was inaugurated, and covering in detail the whole history of Presidential and Congressional Reconstruction down to 1873. The value of the work is much enhanced by a well-organized table of contents, a bibliography, and an index.

An arrangement has been made whereby the members of the Association can procure this number of the *Studies* at two dollars per copy bound, plus sixteen cents for postage. The publishers' price is two dollars and a half for unbound, and three dollars for hound copies. Orders should be sent to Mr. Charles W. Ramsdell, University Station, Austin, Texas.

A review of the monograph will appear in a subsequent number of THE QUARTERLY.

———

Leona Vicario, Heroina Insurgente. Por Genaro Garcia. Mexico: Museo Nacional de Arqueologia, Historia y Etnologia. 1910. pp. 210.

Leona Vicario was the heroine of the Mexican war of independence. Gently born and wealthy, she cast her lot with Hidalgo's insurgents and performed useful service in secretly providing supplies for them and transmitting their correspondence. She was discovered, tried, and imprisoned, but escaped and fled to the camps of the patriots. Following them in their campaigns for several years, she did the work of a modern Red Cross nurse. During this period she married Andres Quintana Roos, a prominent revolutionist. With him she was pardoned by the Spanish government in 1819, but she and Roos remained Liberals at heart and after independence from Spain was accomplished they again got into trouble through their opposition to the tyrannical administration. of President Bustamante. Leona's influence in recruiting powerful insurgents and her material services during the revolution were deeply appreciated by her countrymen, and the legislature of Coahuila and Texas honored her in 1827 by changing the name of the capital, Saltillo, to Leona Vicario. She died in 1842. In following the life of his heroine Señor Garcia gives a rapid, but useful sketch of the revolution. The present volume is one of an edition of three hundred copies for private distribution, and is beautifully printed and illustrated.   E. C. B.

AFFAIRS OF THE ASSOCIATION.

The fourteenth annual meeting of the Association was held at the University March 2, 1910. The program consisted of two papers, one by Mr. E. W. Winkler and the other by Judge Z. T. Fulmore. Mr. Winkler's paper, which appears at length in this number of THE QUARTERLY, was entitled "The Journal of a Bexar Prisoner"; Judge Fulmore's article was entitled "Geography and History in the Two Hundred and Forty-five County Names of Texas." In it he explained the origin of many of the county names, and briefly sketched the history of a few of the men for whom counties have been named. This paper was made up of extracts from a book of the same title which Judge Fulmore will publish in the near future.

In the business meeting, which folowed the public exercises, the following officers were elected:

Judge A. W. Terrell, president.

Hon. Beauregard Bryan, first vice-president.

Mr. R. L. Batts, second vice-president.

Dr. M. J. Bliem, third vice-president.

Mr. Luther W. Clark, fourth vice-president.

Mr. J. L. Worley, corresponding secretary and treasurer.

President S. P. Brooks and Mr. E. C. Barker, members of the Council from the Fellows.

Twenty new members were added to the Association. Mr. C. T. Neu was elected a Fellow.

Gifts and Exchanges for the Year Ending March 2, 1910.

AMERICAN ANTIQUARIAN SOCIETY.—Worcester, Mass.—Proceedings of the Society, as issued.

AMERICAN SOCIETY FOR INTERNATIONAL CONCILIATION.—International Conciliation.

AMERICAN CATHOLIC HISTORICAL SOCIETY, Philadelphia, Pa.—Records, as issued.

AMERICAN CATHOLIC HISTORICAL RESEARCHES, Philadelphia, Pa. —This magazine, as issued.

AMERICAN ECONOMIC ASSOCIATION, Baltimore, Md.—Economic Bulletin, as issued.

BANKER'S MAGAZINE, New York.—Reprint, "The Truth about Mexico."

BOLETIN DE LA REAL ACADEMIA DE HISTORIA, Madrid.—This Bulletin, as issued, 1909.

BUFFALO HISTORICAL SOCIETY, Buffalo,. N. Y.—Canal Enlargement in New York State, Bulletin.

BUREAU OF AMERICAN ETHNOLOGY, Washington, D. C.—Bulletins 47, 48, 49.

BULLETIN OF BIBLIOGRAPHY, Boston, Mass.—This Bulletin, as issued.

CAMBRIDGE HISTORICAL SOCIETY, Cambridge, Mass.—Publications, as issued.

CHICAGO HISTORICAL SOCIETY, Chiago, Ill.—Annual Report, 1909; A study of the Hudson Bay Company.

COLLEGE OF INDUSTRIAL ARTS, Denton Texas.—Bulletin.

COLORADO COLLEGE, Colorado Springs, Colo.—Publications of the College, as issued.

COLUMBIA UNIVERSITY, New York.—Political Science Quarterly, as Issued.

ESSEX INSTITUTE, Salem,· Mass.—Historical Collections, as issued.

FRAGMENTS OF LOUISIANA JURISPRUDENCE.—A speech by W. O. Hart, of New Orleans, La.

FIFTY-FIRST SESSION OF THE (PRESBYTERIAN) SYNOD OF TEXAS.

GENARO GARCIA, Mexico, D. F.—Leona Vicario, Heroina Insurgente. Documentos para la Historia de México.

GRAFTON MAGAZINE OF HISTORY AND GENEALOGY, New York.—January and March, 1910.

HARVARD UNIVERSITY, Cambridge, Mass.—The Quarterly Journal of Economics, as issued.

HISTŌRICAL DEPARTMENT OF IOWA, Des Moines, Iowa.—Annals of Iowa, as issued.

HISTORICAL AND PHILOSOPHICAL SOCIETY OF OHIO, Cincinnati, Ohio.—Quarterly Publication, as issued.

HISTORICAL SOCIETY OF SOUTHREN CALIFORNIA, Los Angeles, Cal.—Annual Publication.

HISTORICAL SOCIETY OF PENNSYLVANIA, Philadelphia, Pa.— Pennsylvania Magazine of History and Biography, as issued.

HUIZINGA, GEO. FORD.—What the Dutch Have Done in the West of the United States.

ILLINOIS STATE HISTORICAL SOCIETY, Springfield, Ill.—Journal, as issued.

INTERNAL REVENUE SERVICE.—Bulletins, as issued.

IOWA JOURNAL OF HISTORY AND POLITICS, Iowa City, Iowa.—This journal, as issued.

JACKSON, GEO., Dallas, Texas.—Sixty Years in Texas.

JOURNAL OF HISTORY, Lamoni, Iowa.—This journal, as issued.

JOHNS HOPKINS UNIVERSITY, Baltimore, Md.—Studies in Historical and Political Science; England and the French Revolution.

KENTUCKY STATE HISTORICAL SOCIETY, Louisville, Ky.—Register, as issued.

LIBRARY OF CONGRESS, Washington, D. C.—Publications, as issued; Annual Report.

MCMILLAN CO., Lancaster, Pa.—The American Historical Review, as issued.

MISSISSIPPI HISTORICAL SOCIETY, Oxford, Miss.—Publications, as issued

MONTANA HISTORICAL AND MISCELLANEOUS LIBRARY, Helena, Mont.—State Publications, as issued.

MISSOURI HISTORICAL SOCIETY.—The Evolution of the State Universal from an American Standpoint; Missouri Historical Review, as issued.

MUSEO NACIONAL DE ARQUEOLOGIA, Mexico, D. F.—Anales de Arqueologia, Historia y Ethnologia, as issued.

MUSEO NACIONAL, Mexico, D. F.—Boletin, as issued.

NATIONAL AMERICANA SOCIETY, New York.—Americana, as issued.

NORTH CAROLINA HISTORICAL SOCIETY, Chapel Hill, N. C.— James Sprunt Historical Publications, as issued.

NEW ENGLAND HISTORICAL AND GENEALOGICAL REGISTER, Boston, Mass.—Vol. LXIV.

NEW JERSEY HISTORICAL SOCIETY, Newark, N. J.—Proceedings, as issued.

NEW YORK PUBLIC LIBRARY, New York.—Bulletin, as issued.

New York State Education Department, Albany, N. Y.—Calendar of the Sir William Johson Manuscripts, 1909.

Ohio Archaeological and Historical Society, Columbus, Ohio. —Ohio Archaelogical and Historical Quarterly.

Oklahoma Historical Society, Oklahoma City, Okla.—Historia; Publications of the Oklahoma Historical Society.

"Old Northwest" Genealogical Society, Columbus, Ohio.— The "Old Northwest" Genealogical Quarterly, as issued.

Oregon Historical Society, Portland, Ore.—Quarterly, as issued.

Our Dumb Animals, Boston, Mass.—This magazine, as issued.

Out West, Los Angeles, Cal.—This magazine, as issued.

Pennsylvania Magazine of History and Biography, Philadelphia, Pa.—This magazine, as issued.

Royal Historical Society, London.—Transactions, 1909.

Science, New York.—Vol. XXX, No. 762.

Sewanee Review, The, Sewanee, Tenn.—This Quarterly, as issued.

Smithsonian Institution, Washington, D. C.—Catalogues of the Exhibits at the Alaska-Yukon-Pacific Exposition.

South Atlantic Quarterly, The; Durham, N. C.—This Quarterly, as issued.

South Carolina Historical Society, Charleston, S. C.—South Carolina Historical and Genealogical Magazine, as issued.

Southern Educational Review, Chattanooga, Tenn.—This magazine, as issued.

Southern Workman, The; Hampton, Va.—This magazine, as issued.

Southwestern Farmer, The; Houston, Texas.—This weekly, as issued.

Stechert, G. E., and Co., Brooklyn, N. Y.—Putnam Anniversary Volume.

Straley, W., Nelson, Neb.—Archaic Gleanings.

Texas Magazine, The; Houston, Texas.—Vol. 1, No. 1.

Texas Methodist Historical Quarterly, Georgetown, Texas.— Volume I.

Texas School Journal, Dallas, Texas.—This magazine, as issued.

Texas Stockman and Farmer, San Antonio, Texas.—This magazine, as issued.

UNIVERSITY PRESS, Berkeley, Cal.—Publications of the University of California.

UNIVERSITY PRESS, BURNET WOODS, Cincinnati, Ohio.—University of Cincinnati Record, as issued.

UNIVERSITY OF COLORADO, Boulder, Colo.—Publications of the University, as issued; Studies.

UTAH GENEALOGICAL AND HISTORICAL SOCIETY, Salt Lake City, Utah.—Genealogical and Historical Magazine, January, 1910.

VERMONT HISTORICAL SOCIETY, Burlington, Vt.—Proceedings, 1908, 1909.

VIRGINIA HISTORICAL SOCIETY, Richmond, Va.—The Virginia Magazine of History and Biography, as issued.

WILLIAM AND MARY COLLEGE, Williamsburg, Va.—Quarterly of the College, as issued.

WISCONSIN HISTORICAL SOCIETY, Madison, Wis.—Wisconsin Historical Collections, Vols. IX, X (Reprints); Proceedings, 1909.

YALE UNIVERSITY, New Haven, Conn.—Bulletin, 1909-10.

TREASURER'S REPORT, MARCH 1, 1909, TO MARCH 1, 1910.

Receipts.

Membership dues..........................$ 46 00		
Current dues............................ 709 65		
Back dues............................... 487 80		
Life membership......................... 30 00		
Sale of QUARTERLY....................... 55 27		
Interest 142 20		
Acounts collected....................... 7 05		
Donation 3 00		
Sale of binding......................... 7 50		
	$1,488 47	
Balance on hand, last report.............	3,021 63	
	$4,510 10	

Expenditures.

Printing QUARTERLY.....................$686 14		
Reprinting QUARTERLY................... 351 72		
Clerical expenses....................... 128 10		
Postage 82 37		
Binding 35 00		
Stationery 49 60		
Miscellaneous expense................... 79 42		
	$1,412 35	
Balance on hand........................	3,097 75	

NOTE.—In printing the statement of expenditures for 1908-1909 (Vol. XII, p. 328) three errors were made:

In Special Expense read $71.02 for $65.52.

In Stationery read $9.95 for $59.95.

In Balance on Hand read $3,021.63 for $2,977.13.

H. Y. BENEDICT.

The above statements are derived from the books of the Treasurer of the Texas State Historical Association which I have examined and found to be correct.

H. Y. BENEDICT.

February 28, 1910.

Inventory of Unbound Reprints on Hand November 24, 1909.

Volume I, Number 1.................................... 256
Volume I, Number 3.................................... 248
Volume I, Number 4.................................... 256
Volume II, Number 1................................... 283

Received Reprints April 2, 1910.

Volume III, Number 1................................. 304

INDEX OF VOLUME XIII.

Affairs of the Association, 330.

African slave trade in Texas, 231.

Allen, Isaac, 87.

Allen, J. M., Mayor of Galveston, 113.

Allen, Martin, 142.

Anderson, T. P., 86.

Archer, Branch T., commissioner to the United States, 167.

Archer, the, 13, 119, 120.

Atkins, Thomas, 112.

Austin, John, 78, 171.

Austin, S. F., A characterization of, 60; loyalty to Mexico, 158, 163, 283; commissioner to the United States, 167; on the boundary of Texas, 174; address at Louisville, 181; appeal to President Jackson for aid, 185; complains of lack of support from Texan government, 187; Secretary of State of Texas, 221; attitude toward the independence of Texas, 173, 257-284; attitude toward the Fredonian Rebellion, 257, 258; toward Guerrero's emancipation decree, 259; toward the law of April 6, 1830, 259; arrest at Saltillo, 264; in the convention of 1832, 261; in the convention of 1833, 263; in Mexico as agent of Texas, 263; letters from prison, 265-67; denounced by Anthony Butler, 268; correspondence with H. Meigs, 269; letter to Mrs. Holley, 271; elected to committee of vigilance and correspondence in San Felipe, 274; efforts to prepare Texas for war, 275-76; explains his attitude to McKinney, 276; advises the declaration of November 7, 278; urges declaration of independence, 282-84; condemned by McKinney for attitude toward independence, 283; by Royall, 283.

Austin, Stephen F., and the Independen ence of Texas, by Eugene C. Bark 257-284.

Austin, the, delivered to the gover ment, 11; history of, 86, 90, 94, 10 107, 114, 119, 120.

Baker, Mosely, 147.

Barker, Eugene C., *James H. C. Mill and Edward Gritten,* 145-153; *Steph F. Austin and the Independence Texas,* 257-284; 330.

Barrett, D. C., 278.

Barrington, William, 88.

Barrow, John E., 126.

Batts, R. L., 330.

Baudin, Admiral Charles, visits Galve ton, 6.

Beason's settlement in 1828, 64.

Bell, Governor P. H., a correction by T. Fulmore, 325-327.

Bexar and Dawson Prisoners, The, e ited by E. W. Winkler, 292-324; li of 312-313, 317-320.

Black, John, 307.

Bliem, M. J., 330.

Bloodgood, —, 136.

Book notices, 328-329.

Bowie, James, 285.

Boyle, Andrew A., *Reminiscences of t Texas Revolution,* 285-291.

Bradburn, J. D., 260.

Brashear, William C., 114, 119.

Brooks, John Sowers, 289.

Brooks, S. P., 330.

Brown, James, 112.

Bryan, Andrew Jackson, 112.

Bryan, William, 102, 177, 291, 330.

Burleson, Edward, 129.

Burnet, David G., 38, 192.

Burnet, Thomas, 112.

Bustillo, Domingo, 294.

Butler, Anthony, 209; denounces Austin, 268.

Calder, Mrs. Loretta, daughter of M. B. Lamar, 82.

Caldwell, "Old Paint," 293, 297.

Calecik, Alexandro, urges imprisonment of Austin, 267.

Carbajal, J. M., 150.

Carson, Samuel, 196.

Catlett, Fairfax, secretary of legation to United States, 225.

Charleston, the, name changed to *Zavala,* 7.

Chavez, Ignacio, 294.

Childress, George C., agent to United States, 195.

Clark, J., captain of the *Archer,* 19.

Clark, Luther W., 330.

Clopper, A. M., 44; losses during Texas Revolution, 135; not in the battle of San Jacinto, 136.

Clopper, Edward, death of, 136.

Clopper, J. C., forms Texas Trading Association, 44; *Journal and Book of Memoranda for 1828,* 44-80.

Clopper, Nicholas, 44, 128.

Clopper Correspondence, 1834-1838, The, 128-144.

Coleto, battle of, 287.

Collinsworth, James, commissioner to United States, 201; opinion of Jackson's attitude toward Texas, 207.

Colorado, the, 10.

"Comanche," a scout, 285.

Commissioners to the United States, the first, 163; loans in New Orleans, 175; design flag for Texas, 177; difficulties at Washington, 183; loan in New York, 186; return to Texas, 187; Report of work, 189.

Commissioners to the United States, the second, the work of, 191-201.

Commissioners to the United States, the third, the work of, 201-208.

Congress of the United States, its attitude toward the recognition of Texas, in 1836, 212-220.

Convention of 1832 in Texas, 261.

Convention of 1833 in Texas, 263.

Cooke, William G., 105.

Cos, Martin P. de, surrender of San tonio, 129.

Cousins, Hon. R. B., 83.

Cox, C. C., midshipman in the navy Texas, 28, 81.

Cox, Mrs. Nellie Stedman, death of,

Culp, F. R., 96.

Cummings, Cyrus, 86, 124.

Crisp, D. H., commander of the S Bernard, 94.

Crittenden, Lieutenant George, 13, 3

Crockett, David, 285.

Cunningham, John R., 315, 322.

Davis, George, 112.

Dawson Prisoners, the, 292-324; list names, 312-313, 317-320.

Dawson, Frederick, lends money for p chase of naval vessels, 8.

Dearborn, W. H., 85.

Declaration of November 7, 1835, 1£ 278.

Desha, Isaac B., 64.

DeWitt, Green, description of, 67.

Dickens, Ella Eaton, wife of Govern P. H. Bell, 325.

Dienst, Alex, *The Navy of the Republ of Texas,* 1-43, 85-127.

Edwards, B. W., trouble with the poli ical chief, 258, 259.

Edwards, Hayden, the Fredonian Reb lion, 258-259.

Este, Edward, 131.

Fannin, James W., surrender to Urre 288.

Fitzgerald, A., 315.

Fisher, George, collector of the port Galveston, 260.

Flag of Texas, 177.

Flores, Salvador, 294.

Forsyth, Captain Cyrus, 154.

Forsyth, Hamilton, 154.

Forsyth, Joseph, 154.

Forsyth, Thomas Scott, 154.

Forsyths, The, in Texas, 154.

Fuller, Charles, lieutenant on the *San Antonio*, 85.

Fuller, George F., midshipman in the navy of Texas, 14.

Fulmore, Z. T., *Governor Bell's Record*, 325-327.

Garay, Francisco, 289, 291.

García, Genaro, 328.

Garrison, Profesor George P., 83.

Gaines, General E. P., occupies Nacogdoches, 211.

Georgia Battalion, 286.

Gifts to the Association, 330-334.

Goliad Massacre, 289, 296.

Gray, A. G., lieutenant in the navy of Texas, 34, 86, 124.

Grayson, Peter W., 3, 201, 206.

Gregg, Darius, 44, 142.

Gritten, Edward, 145; his services to Texas, 149-153; Ugartechea's opinion of, 150; Austin's opinion of, 152; Gail Borden's opinion of, 153.

Guerrero, President, issues emancipation proclamation, 259.

Gutierrez, J., letter concerning a plot to keep Austin in prison in Mexico, 267.

Hall, Edward, 177.

Hamilton, M. C., acting secretary of war and marine, 95.

Hamilton, Robert, agent to United States, 195.

Hancock, Thomas, 315.

Harrell, Milvern, Reminiscences of, 292.

Harris, William P., 137.

Harrisburg, description of in 1828, 52.

Hays, Jack, 294.

Hewitson, Dr. James, 305, 316.

Hill, G. W., secretary of war and marine, 88.

Hinton, A. C., commander of naval station at Galveston, 5; commission withdrawn, 15; reinstated, 16.

Historical commission of Texas, 82.

Hogan, Terence, 112.

Holford, James, advances money for purchase of the *Charleston*, 7.

Holley, Mrs. M. A., letter from Aust 271-273.

Hopes, T., 132.

Houston, President Sam, refuses to s port the navy, 93, 96, 100; conditic ally recalls Commodore Moore to G veston, 96, 100; proclaims Moore mutineer, 110; letter from S. F. A tin advising declaration of indepei ence, 282.

Houston, beginnings of the town of, 1 140.

Hudgins, James, 87.

Humphries, P. W., 124.

Hunt, Memucan, minister to Unit States, 225.

Hurd, N., purser in navy of Texas, 99, 124.

Hutchinson, Judge Anderson, sketch 294; journal of, 294-313.

Iiams, John, 129.

Ingham, The, 177.

Invincible, The, 131.

Jack, Miss Elizabeth B., 132.

Jack, William, secretary of state, 202.

Jackson, President, attitude toward ne trality, 210; correspondence w Santa Anna, 227, 230, 247; attitu toward recognition of Texas, 235-2 241-252.

Johnson, Chauncey, 294, 317.

Johnson, John, 316.

Johnson, F. W., 129, 147.

Jones, William E., 292, 298; Narrati of the Bexar and Dawson Prisone 320-324.

Keenan, Edward, 88.

King, Captain, 286.

Knight, Dr. J. D., 303, 316.

Lamar, President M. B., refuses to 1 tire the navy, 16-18; alliance wi Yucatán, 30; 38-39, 292.

Lamar Papers, purchased by the Thirt first Legislature, 81.

Land, price of in 1836, 138.

Lansing, J. P., 86.

Lewis, A. Irvine, lieutenant in the navy of Texas, 35, 124, 126.

Littlefield, Major G. W., 83.

Long, Mrs. Jane, description of in 1828, ·59·

Looscan, Mrs. Adele B., 81.

Lothrop, J. T. K., commander in navy of Texas, 86; dismissed, 114, 127.

Louisville address of S. F. Austin, 181.

Lyndsay, Captain, 129.

Mabry, James L., midshipman in navy of Texas 23-25.

Mays, Hon. Richard, 83.

McComb, Col., death of, 141.

McDuffie, Governor of South Carolina, on recognition of Texan independence, ·217·

McHay, Francis, 314.

McKinney, Thomas F., 276, 283.

Meigs, Henry, 171; correspondence with S. F. Austin, 269.

Mexia, J. A., interest in Texas land, 267; offers aid to Texas, 279.

Miller, James H. C., 145; efforts to prevent the Texas Revolution, 145-149.

Miller, James H. C., and Edward Gritten, by Eugene C. Barker, 145-153.

Miracle, Julian, promises help from Mexican Liberals, 279.

Moore, Edwin Ward, sketch of, 13; voyage to Sisal, 33; saves crew and cargo of the *Sylph*, 35; recalled from Yucatán by President Houston and disobeys, 37; uses own funds to equip vessels, 91; conditionally ordered to Galveston, 96, 100; treaty with Yucatán, 9, 92, 99, 101; proclaimed a mutineer, 110; discharged from the service, 114; vindicated, 115, 117-118; paid by Texas, 127.

Morgan, James, 102, 105, 130, 138.

Morfit, Henry M., report on Texas, 159, 220, 239.

Navy of the Republic of Texas, The, by Alex Dienst, 1-43, 85-127.

Navy, the second of Texas, its purcha 13; vessels composing it, 13; Co gress orders retirement of, and Pr ident Lamar refuses, 16-18; officers at time of annexation, 121-123, 124.

Neill, A., narrative of the Bexar a Dawson prisoners, 313-317.

Neu, C. T., 330.

Norris, John, 112.

Notes and Fragments, 81, 154, 325.

Norvell, Samuel G., 317.

Officers of the Texas navy, 19, 125.

Oliver, Captain Robert, death of, 96.

Oliver, William, 124.

Oswald, Seymour, 86.

Owings, Thomas D., 177.

Patrick, Dr. George M., 44, 130.

Parez, Antonio, 294.

Peraza, Martin F., governor of Yucatá 101.

Perry, Captain Daniel, 136.

Phillips, R. D., 301.

Pierpont, W. J. D., 126.

Potomac, The, history of, 4-5.

Prices in 1836, 137.

Progress, The, capture of by the Tex navy, 35, 36.

Ramsdell, C. W., 328.

Rather, Ethel Zivley, *Recognition of t Republic of Texas by the Unit States,* 155-256.

Reminiscences of the Texas Revolutic by Andrew A. Boyle, 285-291.

Revolution, the Texas, conditions prece ing, 128; losses during, 135; *Re niscences* of, by Andrew A. Boyle, 28 291.

Riddle, Wilson J., 314.

Roark, Jack, 136.

Roberts, Samuel A., secretary of sta 30.

Robinson, James W., 160.

Robinson, Joseph C., 292.

Royall, R. R., opinion of S. F. Austi 283.

"Runaway Scrape," 142.

San Antonio, The, 10; mutiny on board, 85; movements of, 85, 87, 90, 97, 99, 129.

San Bernard, The, 10; movements of, 87, 90, 94, 97, 119, 120.

San Felipe, description of in 1828, 59.

San Jacinto, The, 10, 26.

Santa Anna, asks intervention of President Jackson, 226, 227; visits Jackson, 230.

Seeger, William, lieutenant in navy of Texas, 34, 43, 126.

Shackelford, Jack, 286.

Shepherd, Frederick, 87.

Shepherd, James L., 309.

Shepherd, Joseph D., 87.

Shepherd, William M., acting secretary of the navy, 2.

Simpson, William, 87.

Smith, Henry, quarrel with the General Council, 157, 167; secretary of the treasury, 221.

Smith, J. W., 147, 291.

Smythe, H. M., 113.

Snow, C. B., 114, 115, 124.

Stephens, John F., 124.

Tobasco, the capture of, 28.

Taylor, T. A., commander of the *San Bernard,* 26.

Terrell, A. W., 330.

Terrell, Mrs. J. C., 83.

Texas Library and Historical Commission, 82.

Texas Revolution, conditions preceding, 128; losses during, 135, 142; sympathy for in the United States, 171.

Texas Trading Association, 47.

Tennison, William A., midshipman in navy of Texas, 5, 114, 119, 124, 126.

Tod, John G., 9, 13, 122.

Tories on the Trinity River, 136.

Travis, William B., his opinion of S. F. Austin, 276.

Treasurer's Report, 335.

Ugartechea, Domingo de, 147.

United States, sympathy in for Texas during the Revolution, 171.

Van Buren, Martin, his influence Jackson and the Texas Question, 24

Van Ness, George, 315.

Vicario, Leona, reviewed, 328.

Vidal, General Luis, 297.

Ward, Colonel, 286, 289.

Wells, F. T., purser in Texas navy, 9

Westover, Captain, 285.

Wharton, John A., report in favor of i dependence, 160.

Wharton, William H., opinion of t declaration of November 7, 159, 16 commissioner to the United State 167; remarks on the boundary Texas, 174; minister to the Unit States, 222-224; efforts to secure re ognition of Texas, 234-253, 261.

Wharton, The, 11, 91, 94, 99, 105, 10 114, 119, 120.

Wheelwright, George, captain of t *Wharton,* 19.

White, George R., 96.

Whiting, Dr., 136.

Wilber, T. C., 86.

Williams, H. H., Texan consul at Bal more, 12.

Williams, John, 88, 136.

Williams, S. M., agent to purchase nav 3, 9, 147.

Williamson, R. M., 147.

Williamson, W. S., lieutenant on t *Brazos,* 5.

Willson, W., 132.

Winkler, E. W., 82, 83; edits *The Bex and Dawson Prisoners,* 292-324.

Woll, General Adrian, 293; captures Sa Antonio, 295; claimed to have co vinced Santa Anna of impropriety Goliad massacre, 296.

Worley, John L., 330.

Yates, A. J., 177, 183.

Yucatán, cruise of the Texan fleet to i 1840, 18-29; alliance with Texas, 2 43.

Zavala, Lorenzo de, 147.

Zavala, The, 7, 93, 120.

Lightning Source UK Ltd.
Milton Keynes UK
UKHW012224110219
337137UK00006B/1286/P